Sho Beat
MANGA from the HEART

OTOMEN

STORY AND ART BY
AYA KANNO

VAMPIRE KNIGHT

STORY AND ART BY
MATSURI HINO

Natsume's BOOK of FRIENDS

STORY AND ART BY
YUKI MIDORIKAWA

Want to see more of what you're looking for?

Let your voice be heard!

hojobeat.com/mangasurvey

Help us give you more manga from the heart!

www.viz.com

Shojo Beat

OTOMEN

Story & Art by
Aya Kanno

Volume
SIX

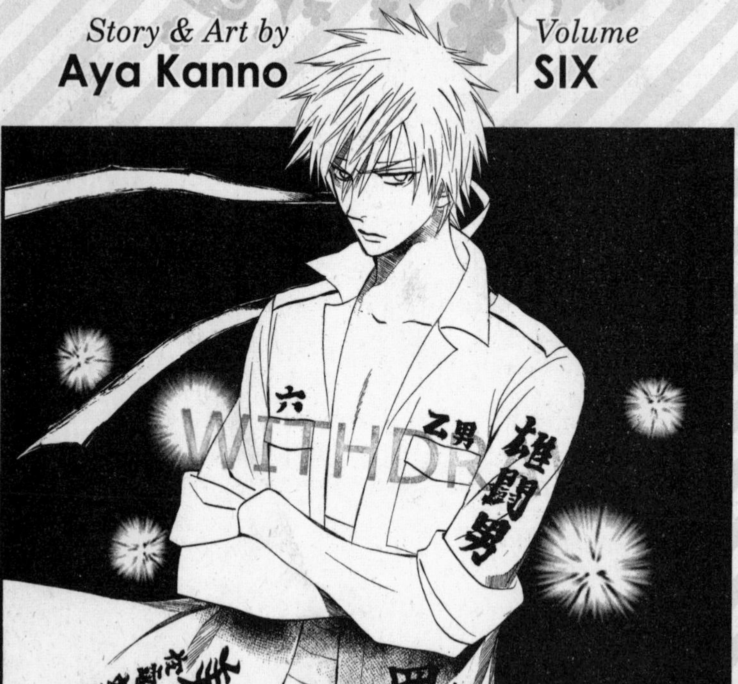
六
乙男
雄闘男
銀百合制覇
斗鬼滅鬼上等

OTOMEN CHARACTERS & STORY

What is an OTOMEN?

O•to•men *[OH-toe-men]*

1) A young man with girlish interests and thoughts.

2) A young man who has talent for cooking, needlework and general housework.

3) A manly young man with a girlish heart.

Asuka Masamune

The captain of Ginyuri Academy High School's kendo team. He is handsome, studious and (to the casual observer) the perfect high school student. But he is actually an *otomen*, a man with a girlish heart. He loves cute things ♥, and he has a natural talent for cooking, needlework and general housekeeping. He's even a big fan of the shojo manga *Love Chick*.

STORY

Asuka Masamune, the kendo captain, is actually an *otomen* (a girlish guy)— a man who likes cute things, housework and shojo manga. When he was young, his father left home to become a woman. His mother was traumatized, and ever since then, he has kept his girlish interests a secret. However, things change when he meets Juta, a guy who is using Asuka as the basis for the female character in the shojo manga he is writing (←top secret). Asuka also starts having feelings for a tomboy girl who is good at martial arts. Because of this, he's slowly reverting to his true *otomen* self!

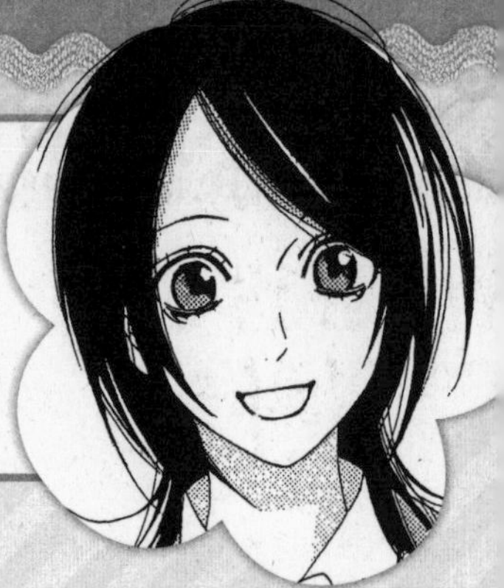

Ryo Miyakozuka

Asuka's classmate for whom he has feelings. She has studied martial arts under her father ever since she was little, and she is very good at it. On the other hand, her housekeeping skills are disastrous. She's a very eccentric beauty.

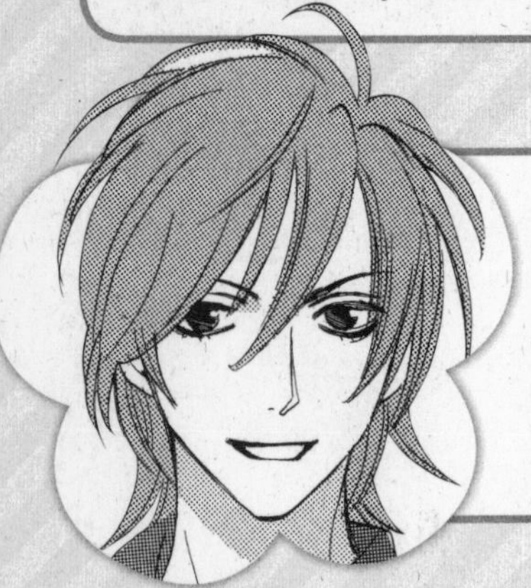

Juta Tachibana

Asuka's classmate. He's flirtatious, but he's actually the popular shojo manga artist Jewel Sachihana. He is using Asuka and Ryo as character concepts in his manga *Love Chick*, which is being published in the shojo magazine *Hana to Mame*. His personal life is a mystery!

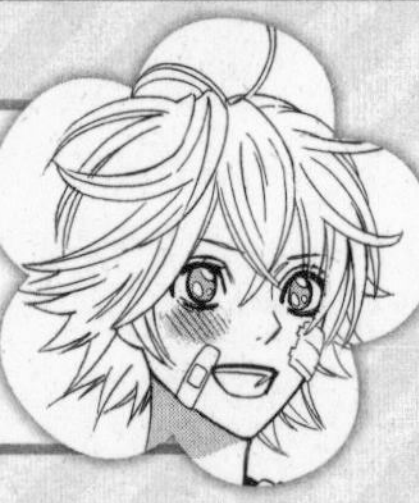

Yamato Ariake

Underclassman at Asuka's school. He looks like a girl, but he admires manliness and has long, delusional fantasies about being manly…

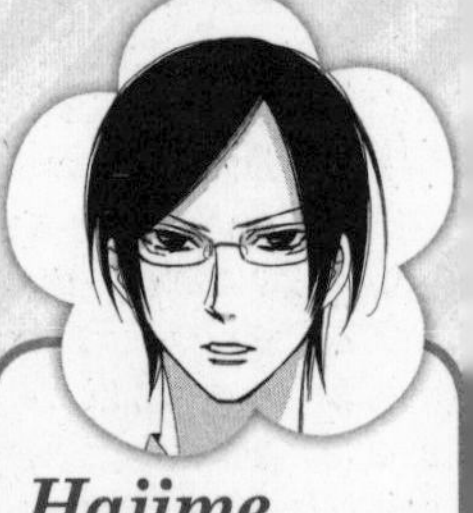

Hajime Tonomine

The captain of Kinbara High School's kendo team, he sees Asuka as his lifelong rival. He is the strong and silent type but is actually an *otomen* who is good with makeup. A *Tsun-sama*.

("Tsun-sama" © Juta Tachibana.)

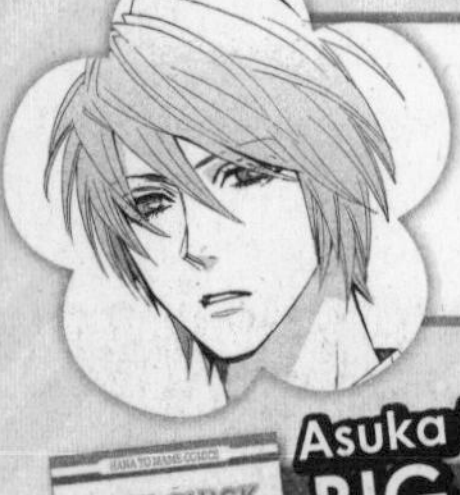

Kitora Kurokawa

Asuka's classmate. He is obsessed with the beauty of flowers. He is an *otomen* who refers to himself as the Flower Evangelist.

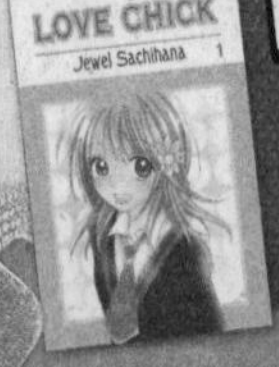
HANA TO MAME COMICS
LOVE CHICK
Jewel Sachihana 1

Asuka is also a BIG FAN!

Hana to Mame Comics

LOVE CHICK by Jewel Sachihana

(Now serialized in *Hana to Mame*)

The very popular shojo comic that Juta writes (under the pen name Jewel Sachihana).

OTOMEN

volume 6
CONTENTS

OTOMEN
Vol. 6
Shojo Beat Edition

Story and Art by | **AYA KANNO**

Translation & Adaptation | **JN Productions**
Touch-up Art & Lettering | **Mark McMurray**
Design | **Fawn Lau**
Editor | **Amy Yu**

VP, Production | **Alvin Lu**
VP, Sales & Product Marketing | **Gonzalo Ferreyra**
VP, Creative | **Linda Espinosa**
Publisher | **Hyoe Narita**

Otomen by Aya Kanno © Aya Kanno 2008
All rights reserved. First published in Japan in 2008 by HAKUSENSHA, Inc., Tokyo.
English language translation rights arranged with HAKUSENSHA, Inc., Tokyo.

The rights of the author(s) of the work(s) in this publication to be so identified
have been asserted in accordance with the Copyright, Designs and Patents Act 1988.
A CIP catalogue record for this book is available from the British Library.

Printed in the U.S.A.

Published by VIZ Media, LLC
P.O. Box 77010
San Francisco, CA 94107

10 9 8 7 6 5 4 3 2 1
First printing, May 2010

PARENTAL ADVISORY
OTOMEN is rated T for Teen and is recommended
for ages 13 and up. This volume contains
suggestive themes.
ratings.viz.com

www.viz.com

www.shojobeat.com

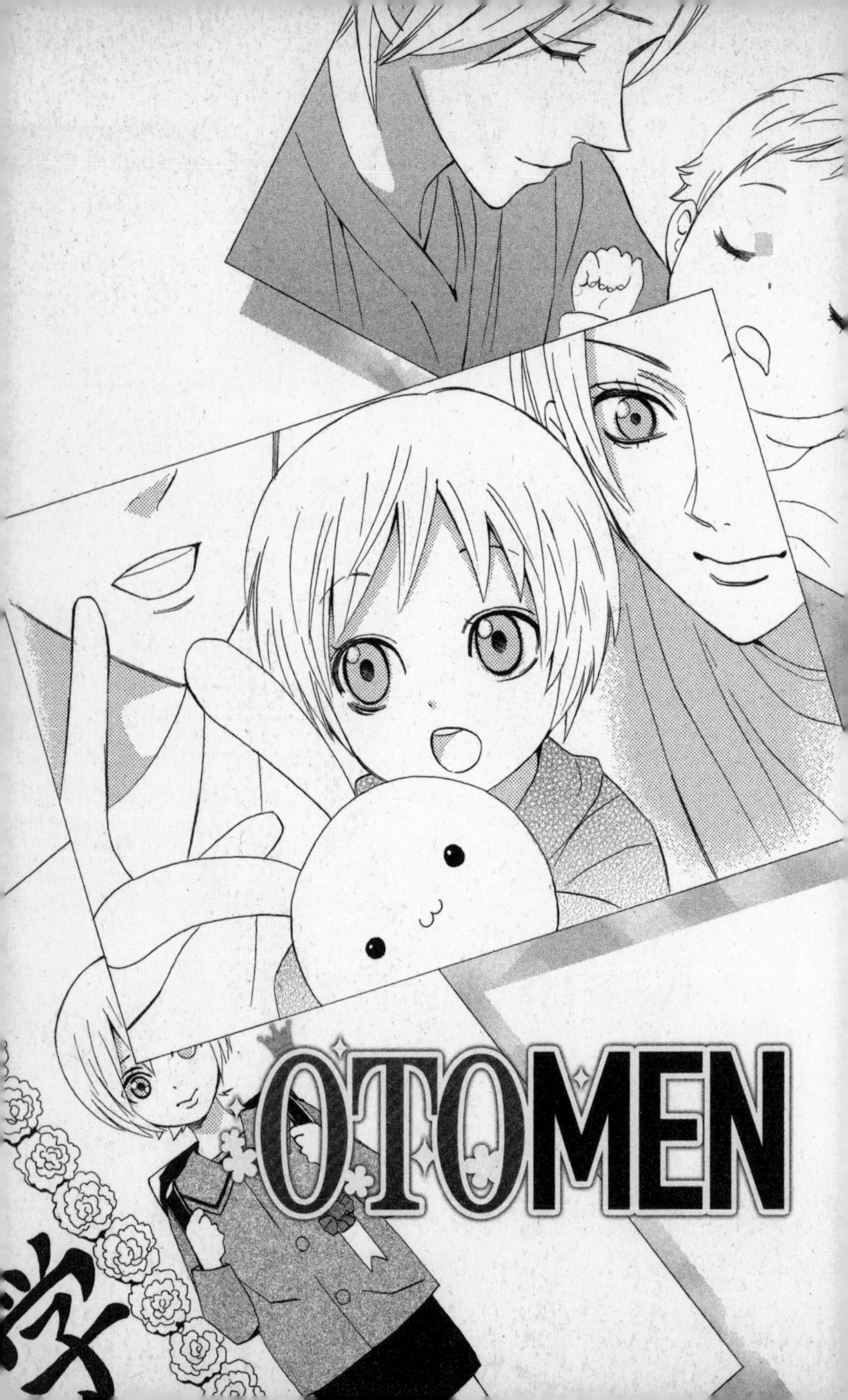
OTOMEN

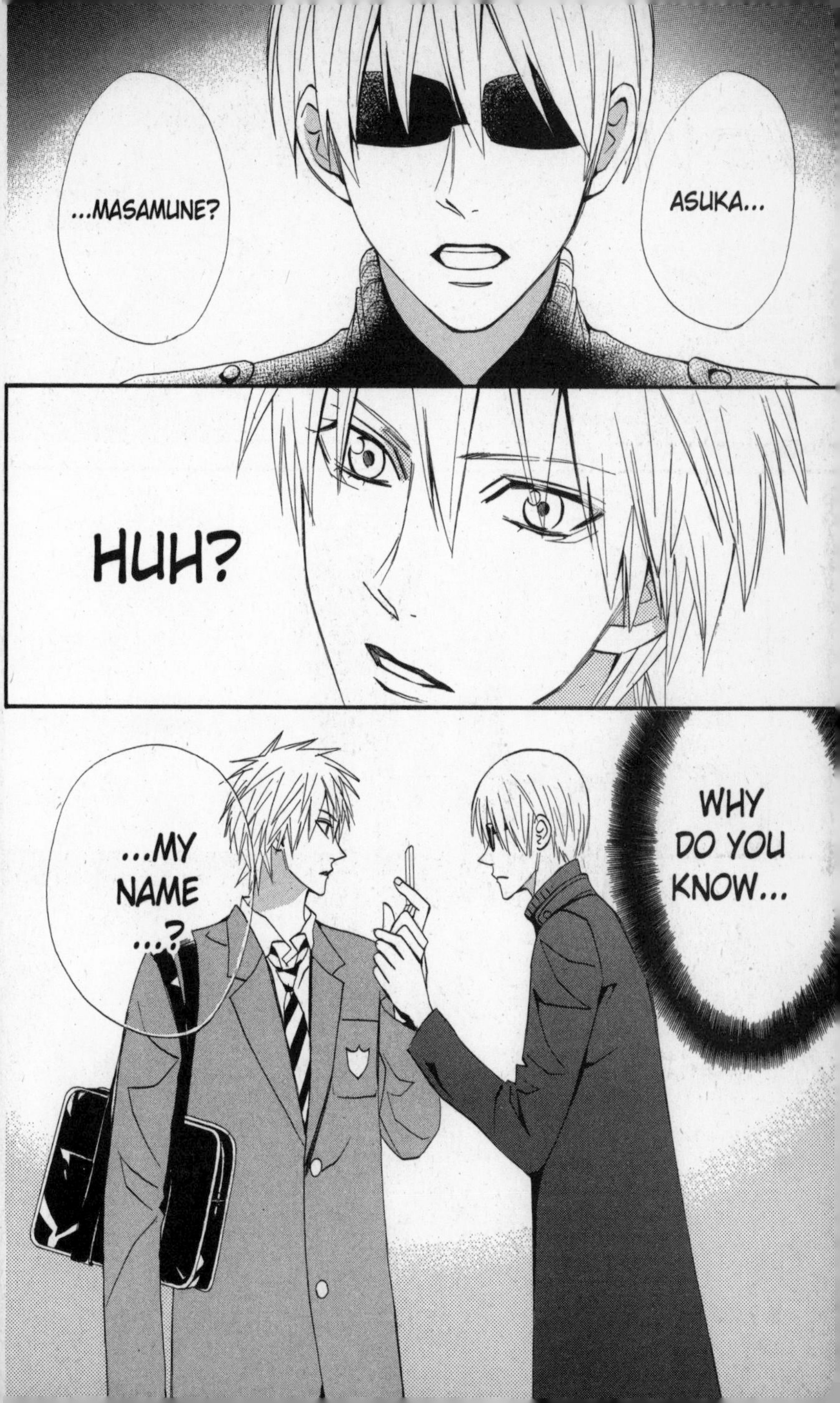
ASUKA...
...MASAMUNE?
HUH?
WHY DO YOU KNOW...
...MY NAME ...?

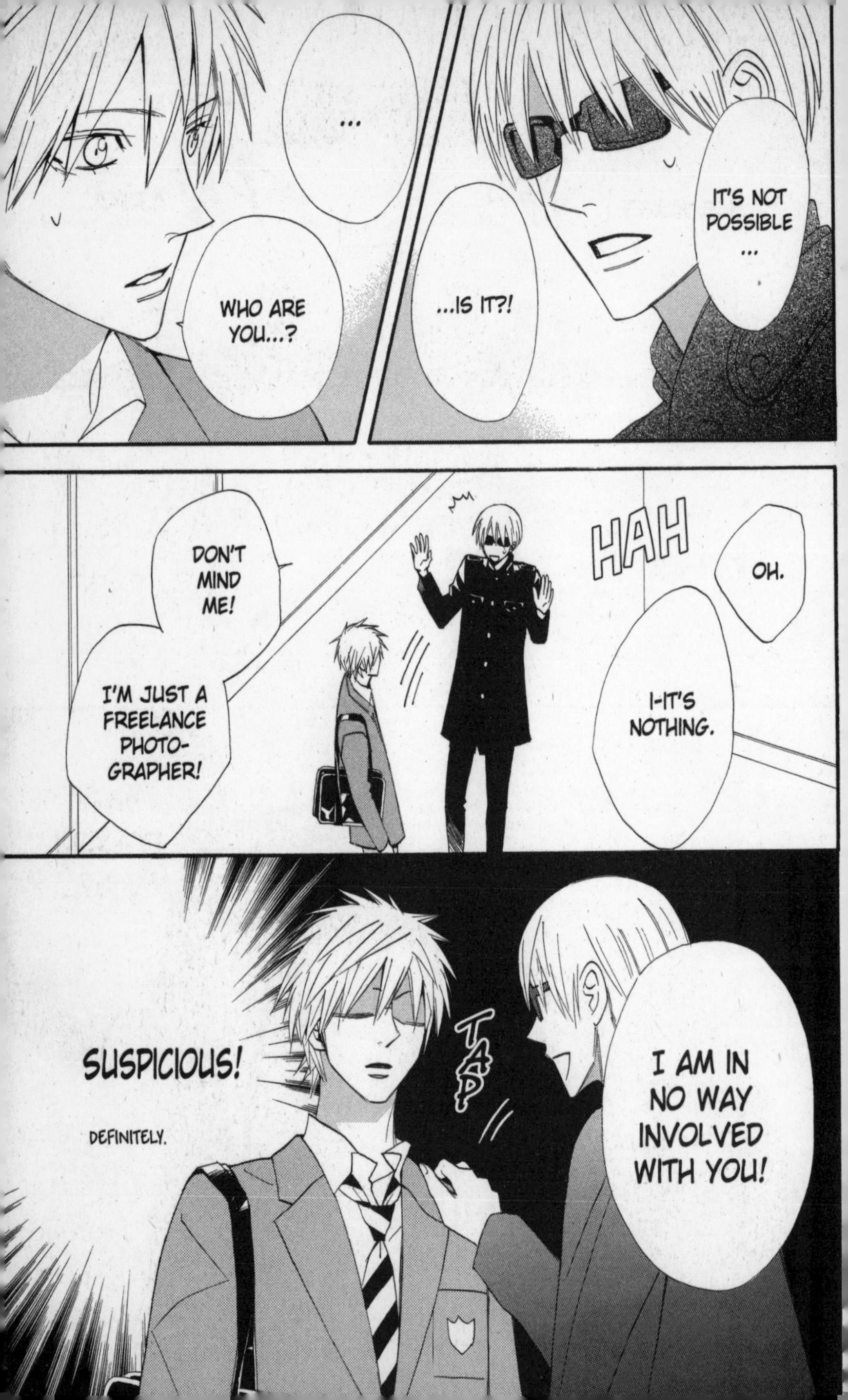
IT'S NOT POSSIBLE ...
...IS IT?!
...
WHO ARE YOU...?
OH.
HAH
I-IT'S NOTHING.
DON'T MIND ME!
I'M JUST A FREELANCE PHOTO-GRAPHER!
I AM IN NO WAY INVOLVED WITH YOU!
TAP
SUSPICIOUS!
DEFINITELY.

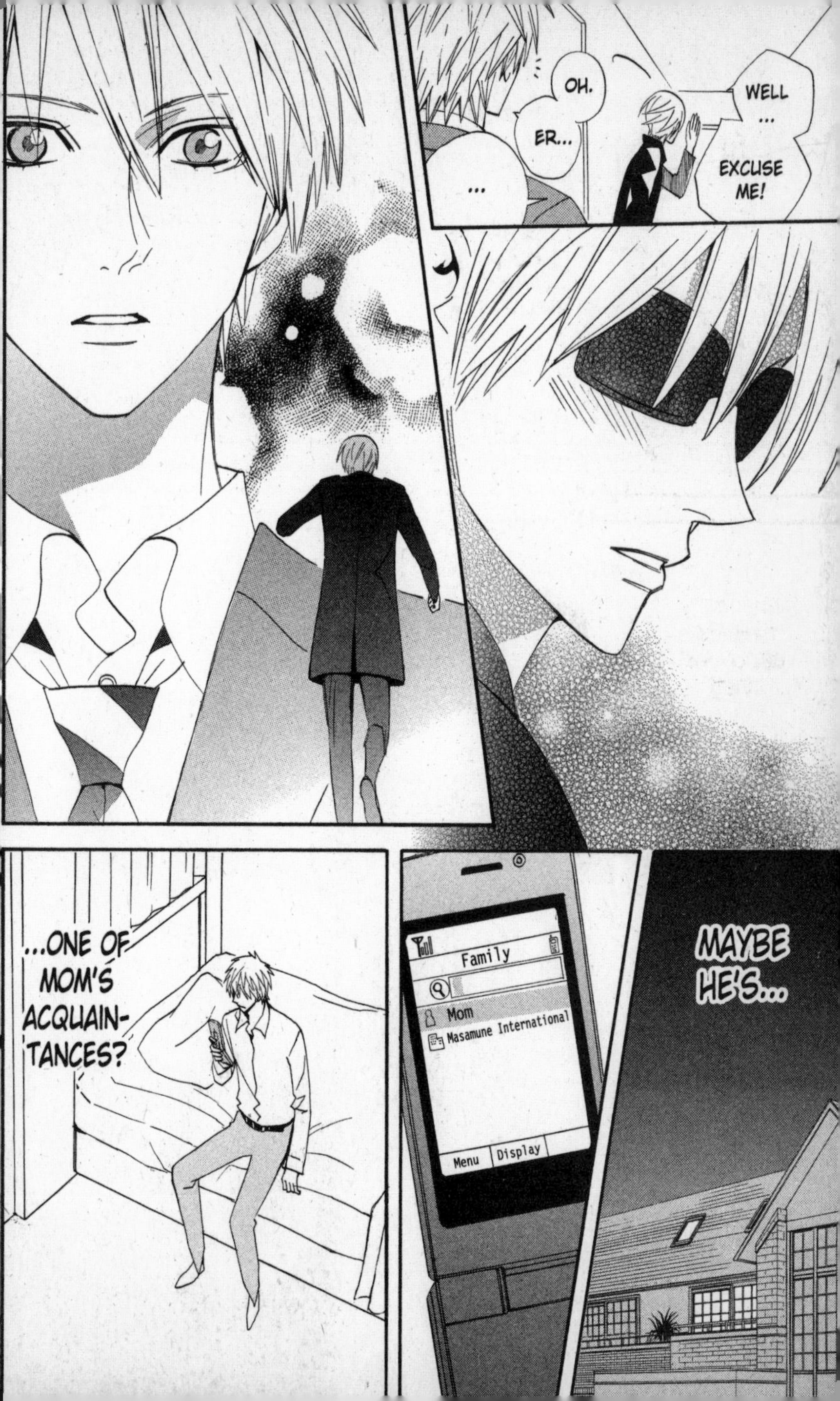
WELL ... EXCUSE ME!
OH.
ER...
...
MAYBE HE'S...
Family
Mom
Masamune International
Menu
Display
...ONE OF MOM'S ACQUAIN-TANCES?

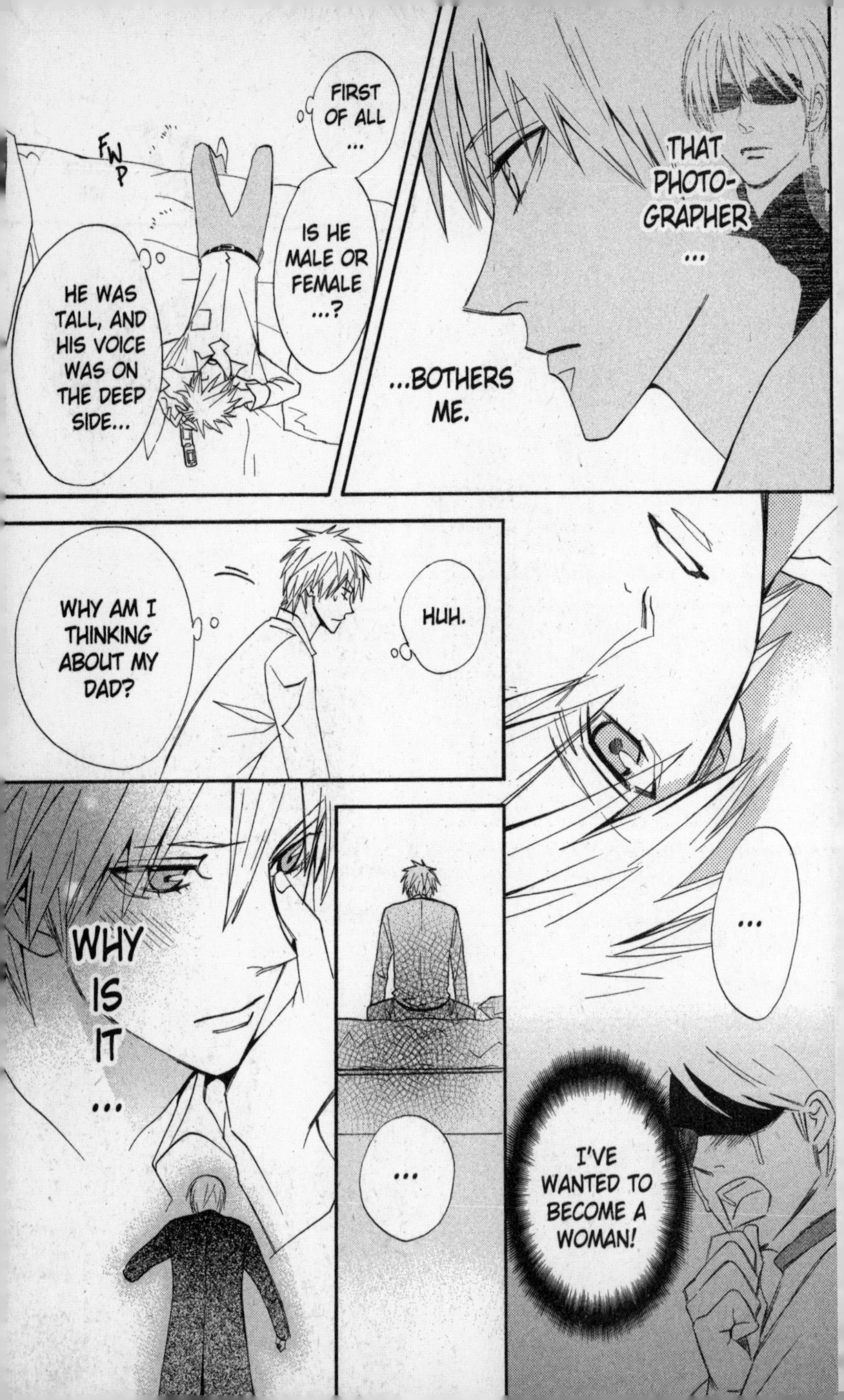
THAT PHOTO-GRAPHER ...
...BOTHERS ME.
FIRST OF ALL ...
IS HE MALE OR FEMALE ...?
FWP
HE WAS TALL, AND HIS VOICE WAS ON THE DEEP SIDE...
...
I'VE WANTED TO BECOME A WOMAN!
HUH.
WHY AM I THINKING ABOUT MY DAD?
...
WHY IS IT ...

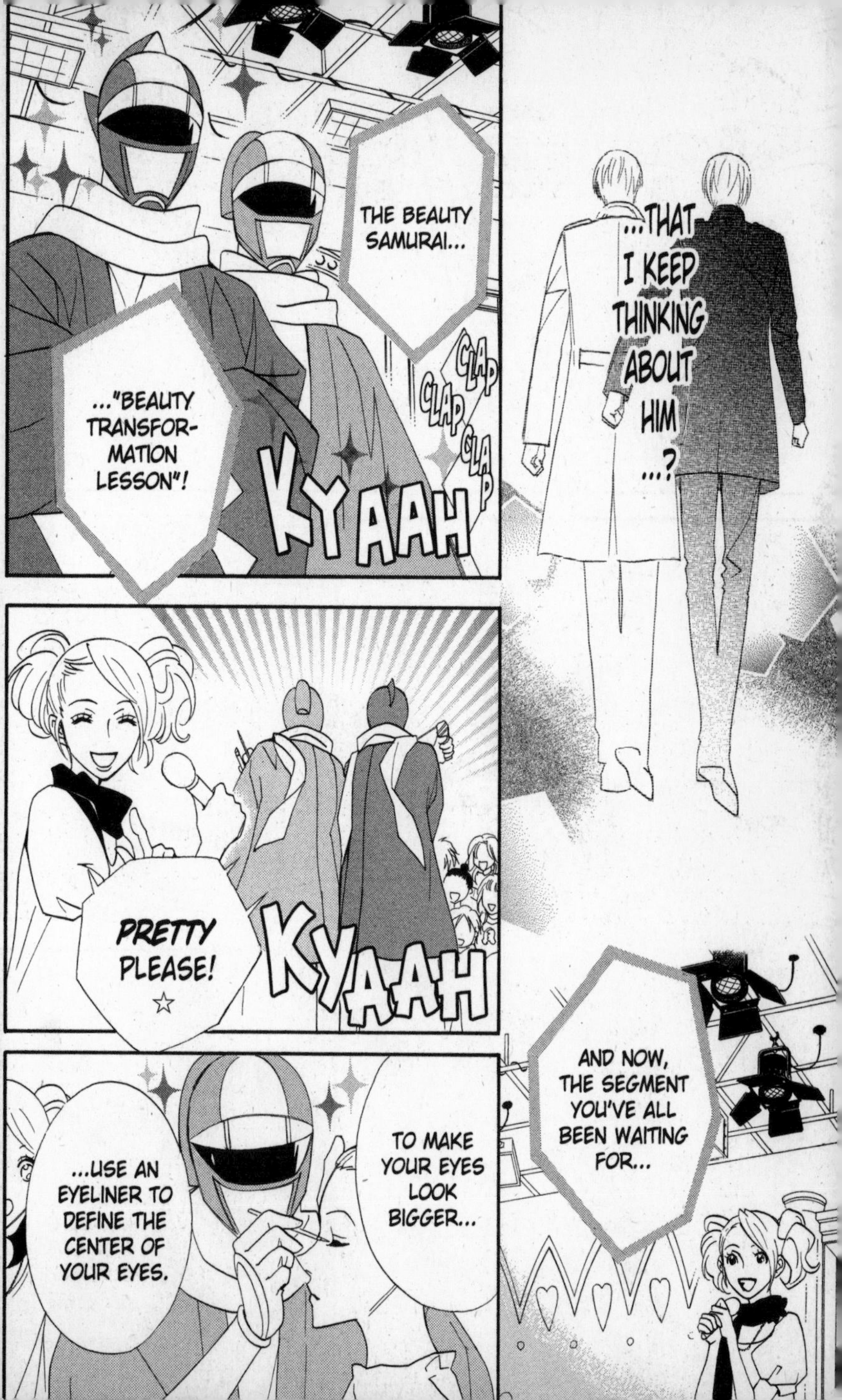
...THAT I KEEP THINKING ABOUT HIM ...?
AND NOW, THE SEGMENT YOU'VE ALL BEEN WAITING FOR...
THE BEAUTY SAMURAI...
..."BEAUTY TRANSFORMATION LESSON"!
CLAP CLAP CLAP
KYAAH
PRETTY PLEASE! ☆
KYAAH
TO MAKE YOUR EYES LOOK BIGGER...
...USE AN EYELINER TO DEFINE THE CENTER OF YOUR EYES.

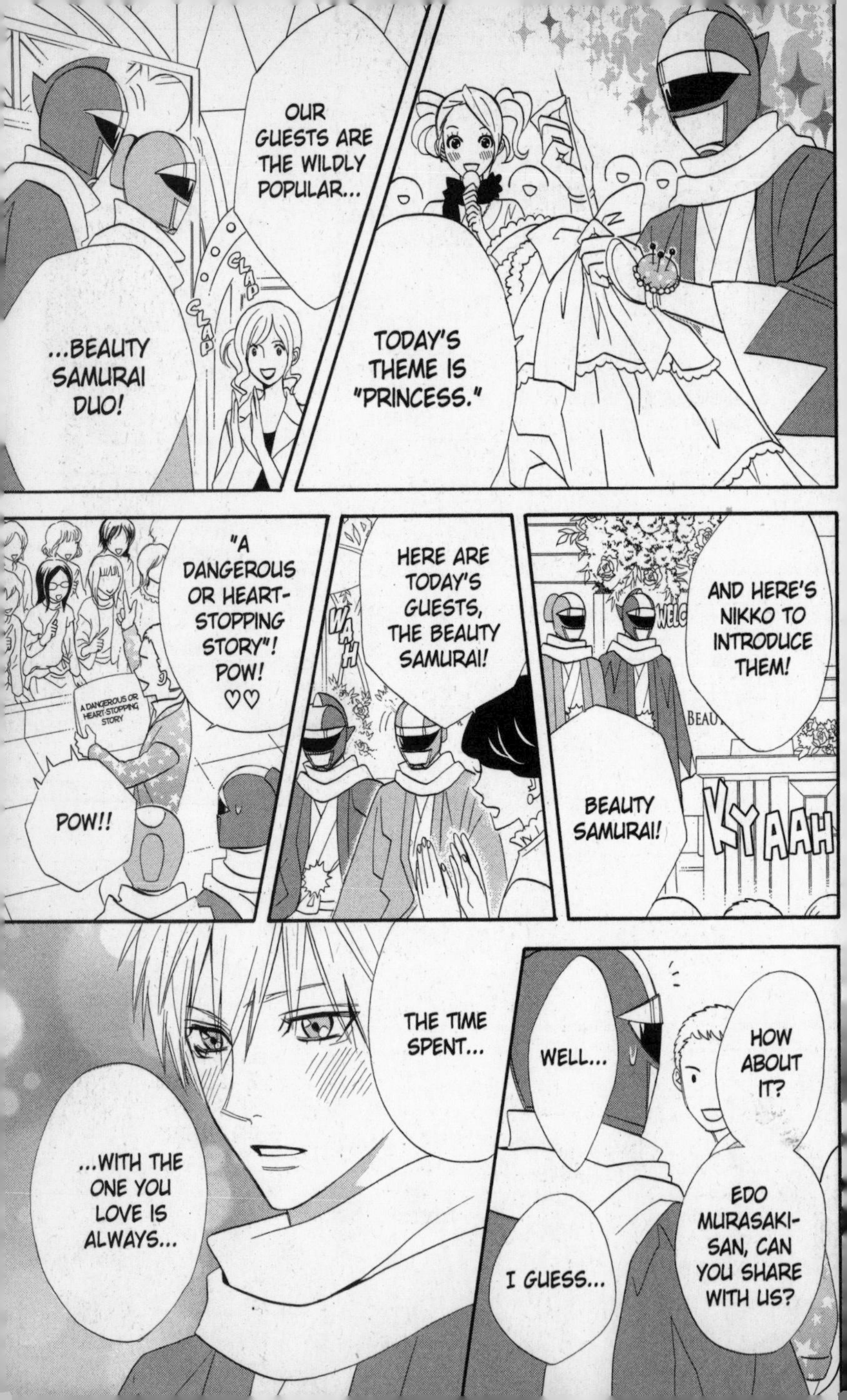
TODAY'S THEME IS "PRINCESS."
OUR GUESTS ARE THE WILDLY POPULAR...
CLAP
CLAP
...BEAUTY SAMURAI DUO!
AND HERE'S NIKKO TO INTRODUCE THEM!
BEAUTY SAMURAI!
KYAAH
HERE ARE TODAY'S GUESTS, THE BEAUTY SAMURAI!
WAAH
"A DANGEROUS OR HEART-STOPPING STORY"! POW! ♡♡
A DANGEROUS OR HEART-STOPPING STORY
POW!!
HOW ABOUT IT?
EDO MURASAKI-SAN, CAN YOU SHARE WITH US?
WELL...
I GUESS...
THE TIME SPENT...
...WITH THE ONE YOU LOVE IS ALWAYS...

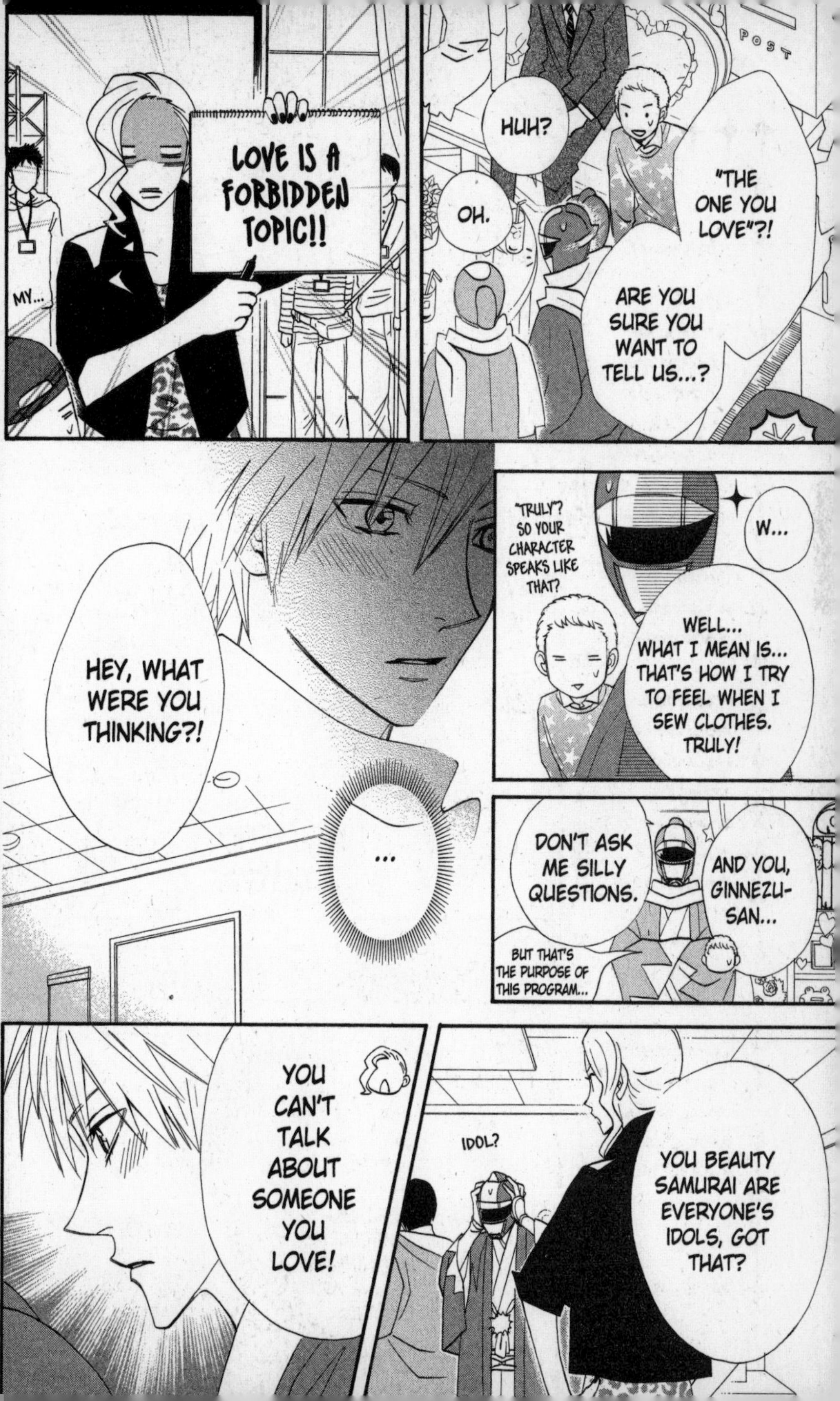
"THE ONE YOU LOVE"?!
HUH?
OH.
ARE YOU SURE YOU WANT TO TELL US...?
LOVE IS A FORBIDDEN TOPIC!!
MY...
W...
WELL... WHAT I MEAN IS... THAT'S HOW I TRY TO FEEL WHEN I SEW CLOTHES. TRULY!
"TRULY"? SO YOUR CHARACTER SPEAKS LIKE THAT?
AND YOU, GINNEZU-SAN...
DON'T ASK ME SILLY QUESTIONS.
BUT THAT'S THE PURPOSE OF THIS PROGRAM...
HEY, WHAT WERE YOU THINKING?!
...
YOU BEAUTY SAMURAI ARE EVERYONE'S IDOLS, GOT THAT?
IDOL?
YOU CAN'T TALK ABOUT SOMEONE YOU LOVE!

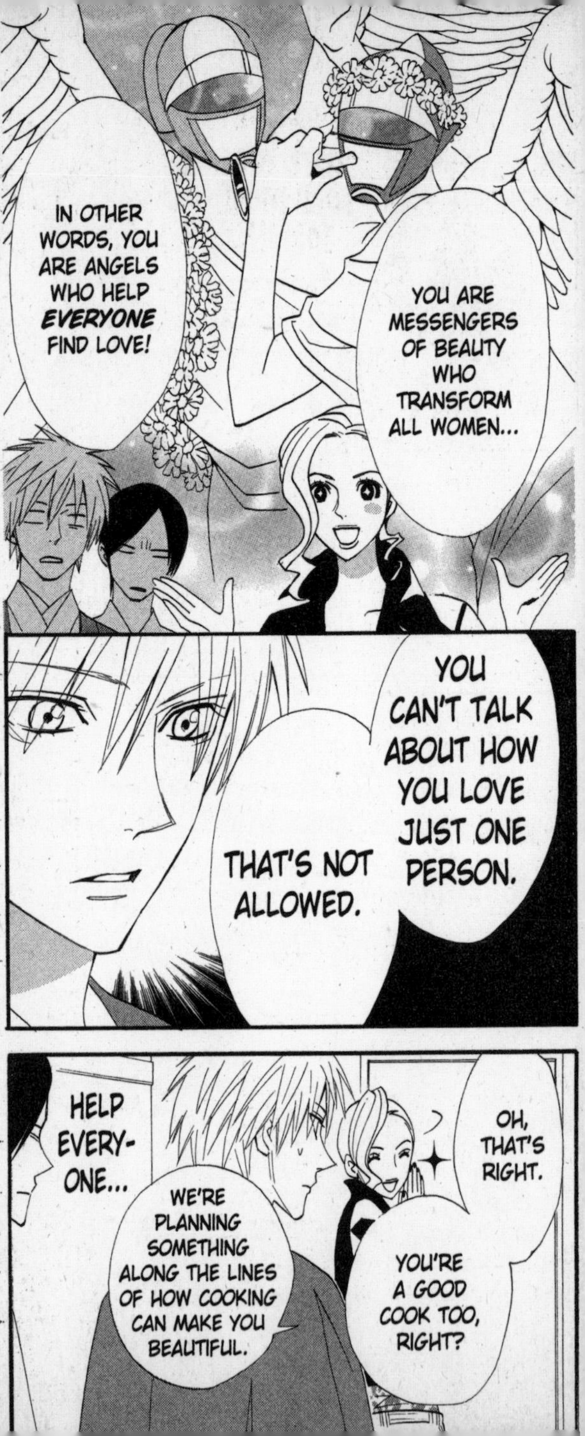
YOU ARE MESSENGERS OF BEAUTY WHO TRANSFORM ALL WOMEN...
IN OTHER WORDS, YOU ARE ANGELS WHO HELP ***EVERYONE*** FIND LOVE!
YOU CAN'T TALK ABOUT HOW YOU LOVE JUST ONE PERSON.
THAT'S NOT ALLOWED.
OH, THAT'S RIGHT.
YOU'RE A GOOD COOK TOO, RIGHT?
HELP EVERY-ONE...
WE'RE PLANNING SOMETHING ALONG THE LINES OF HOW COOKING CAN MAKE YOU BEAUTIFUL.

It's volume 6.

Hello.
I'm so glad we could meet again. The cover art is a pinup of Asuka for a change. Actually, I had planned to draw Yamato, but I diverged. The color illustration for the fourth chapter of this volume was supposed to be Yamato at first too, but I ended up drawing five characters (which energized me). Yamato is always getting the short end of the stick. I like him though.

I'm sorry this volume is sort of complicated. The plot is all over the place, isn't it?

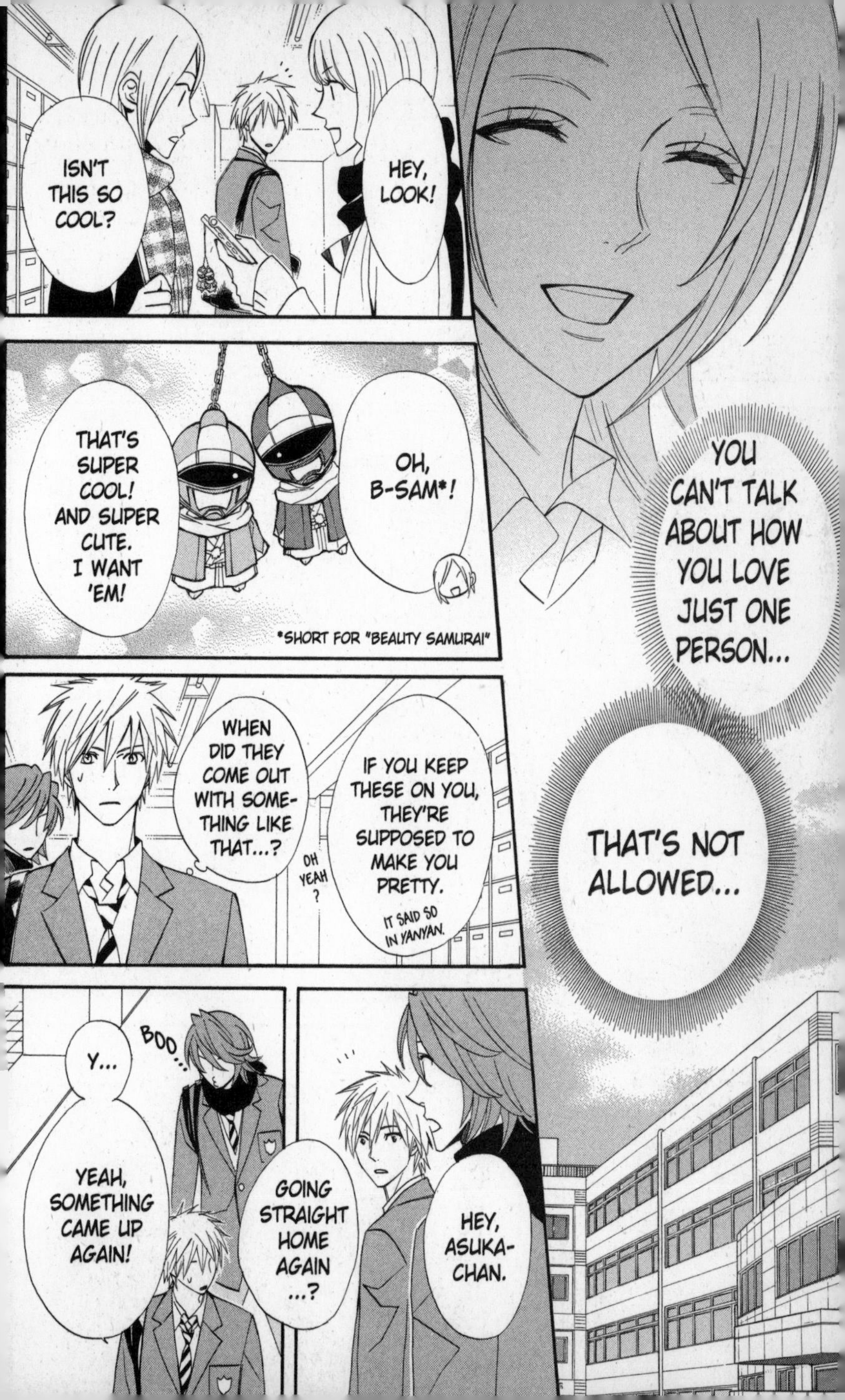
YOU CAN'T TALK ABOUT HOW YOU LOVE JUST ONE PERSON...
THAT'S NOT ALLOWED...
HEY, LOOK!
ISN'T THIS SO COOL?
OH, B-SAM*!
THAT'S SUPER COOL! AND SUPER CUTE. I WANT 'EM!
*SHORT FOR "BEAUTY SAMURAI"
IF YOU KEEP THESE ON YOU, THEY'RE SUPPOSED TO MAKE YOU PRETTY.
IT SAID SO IN YANYAN.
OH YEAH?
WHEN DID THEY COME OUT WITH SOMETHING LIKE THAT...?
HEY, ASUKA-CHAN.
GOING STRAIGHT HOME AGAIN...?
BOO...
Y...
YEAH, SOMETHING CAME UP AGAIN!

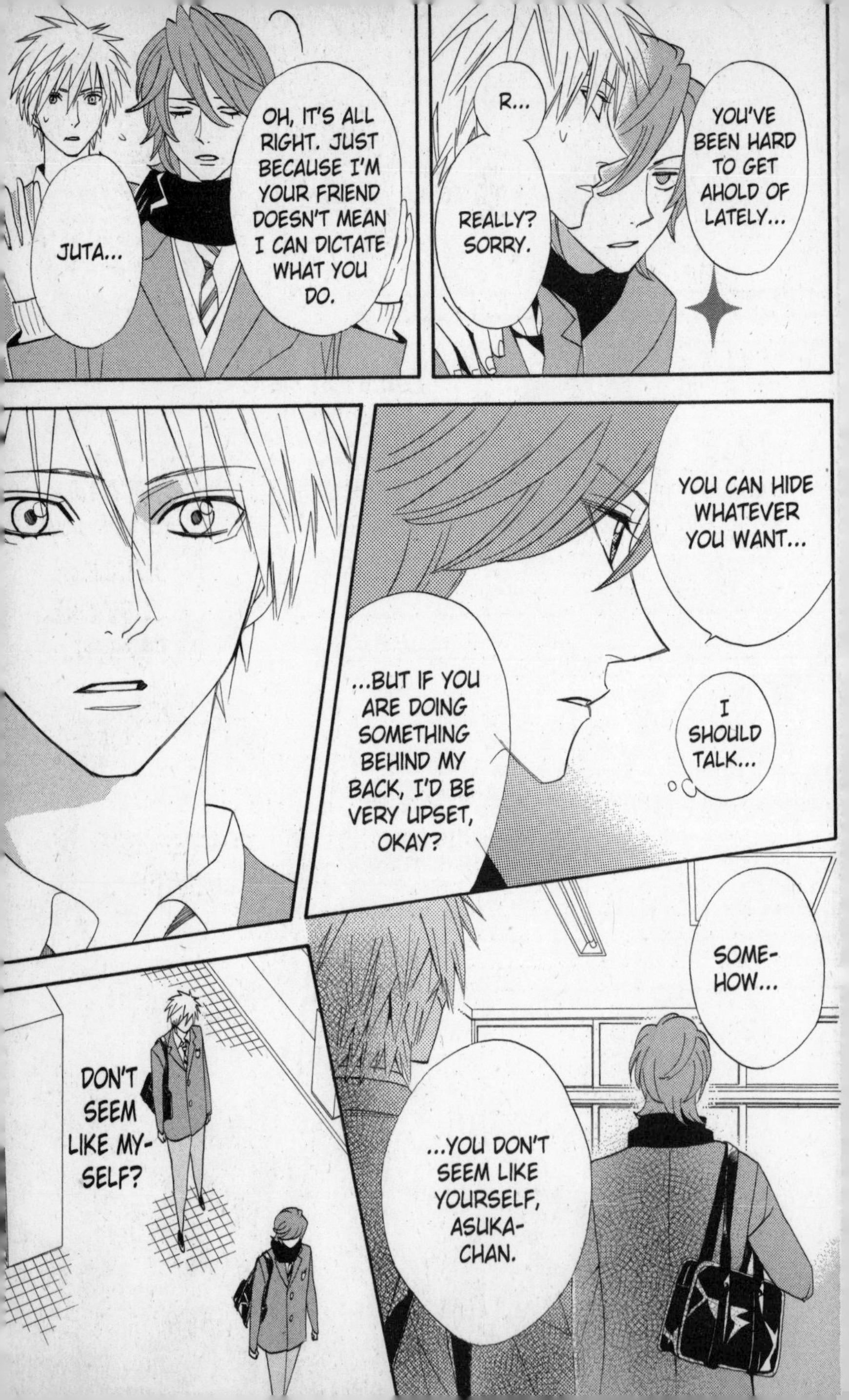
YOU'VE BEEN HARD TO GET AHOLD OF LATELY...
R...
REALLY? SORRY.
OH, IT'S ALL RIGHT. JUST BECAUSE I'M YOUR FRIEND DOESN'T MEAN I CAN DICTATE WHAT YOU DO.
JUTA...
YOU CAN HIDE WHATEVER YOU WANT...
...BUT IF YOU ARE DOING SOMETHING BEHIND MY BACK, I'D BE VERY UPSET, OKAY?
I SHOULD TALK...
SOME-HOW...
...YOU DON'T SEEM LIKE YOURSELF, ASUKA-CHAN.
DON'T SEEM LIKE MY-SELF?

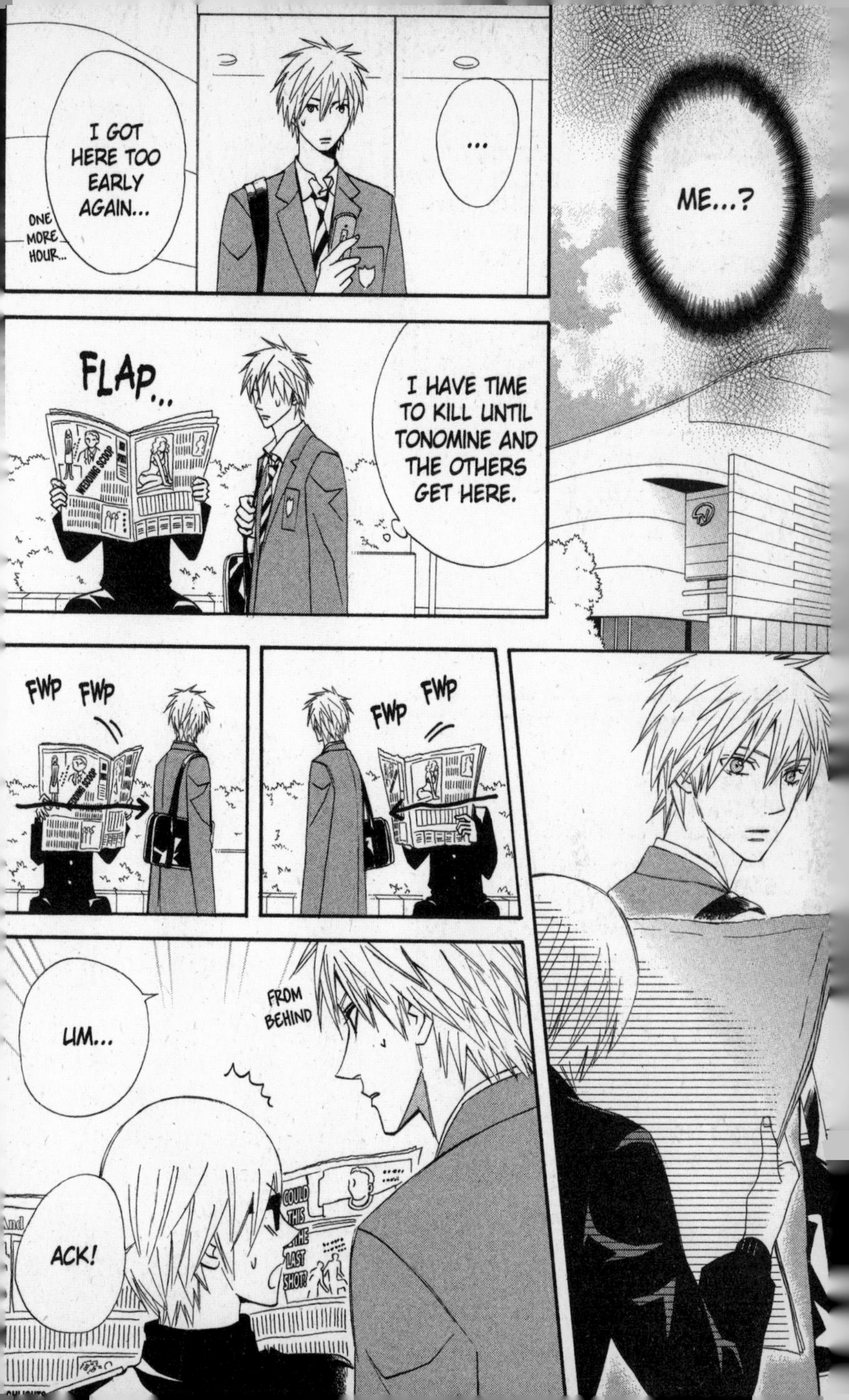
ME...?
...
I GOT HERE TOO EARLY AGAIN...
ONE MORE HOUR...
I HAVE TIME TO KILL UNTIL TONOMINE AND THE OTHERS GET HERE.
FLAP...
WEDDING SCOOP
FWP FWP
FWP FWP
WEDDING SCOOP
FROM BEHIND
UM...
COULD THIS BE THE LAST SHOT?
ACK!

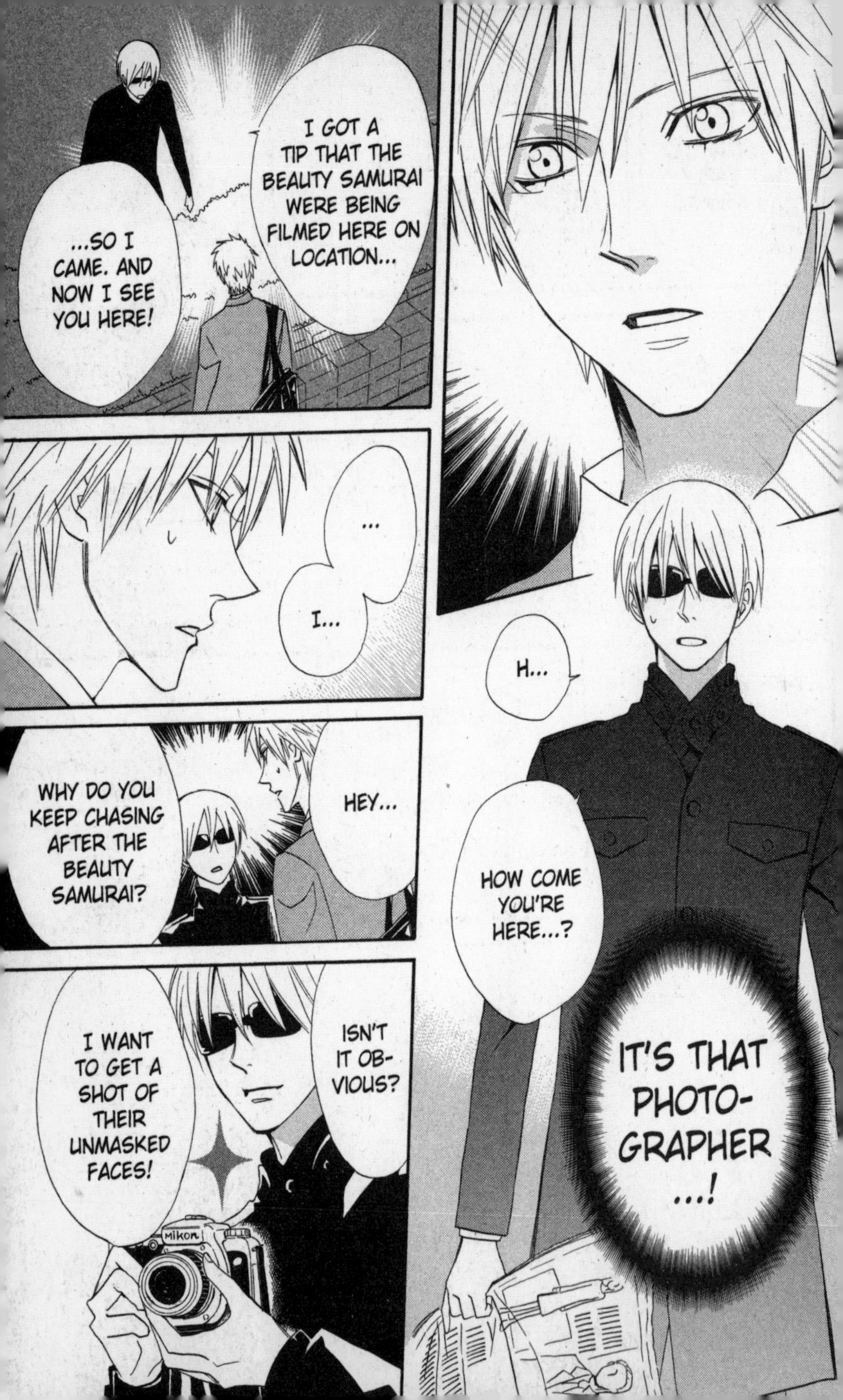
H...
HOW COME YOU'RE HERE...?
IT'S THAT PHOTO-GRAPHER ...!
I GOT A TIP THAT THE BEAUTY SAMURAI WERE BEING FILMED HERE ON LOCATION...
...SO I CAME. AND NOW I SEE YOU HERE!
...
I...
HEY...
WHY DO YOU KEEP CHASING AFTER THE BEAUTY SAMURAI?
ISN'T IT OB-VIOUS?
I WANT TO GET A SHOT OF THEIR UNMASKED FACES!

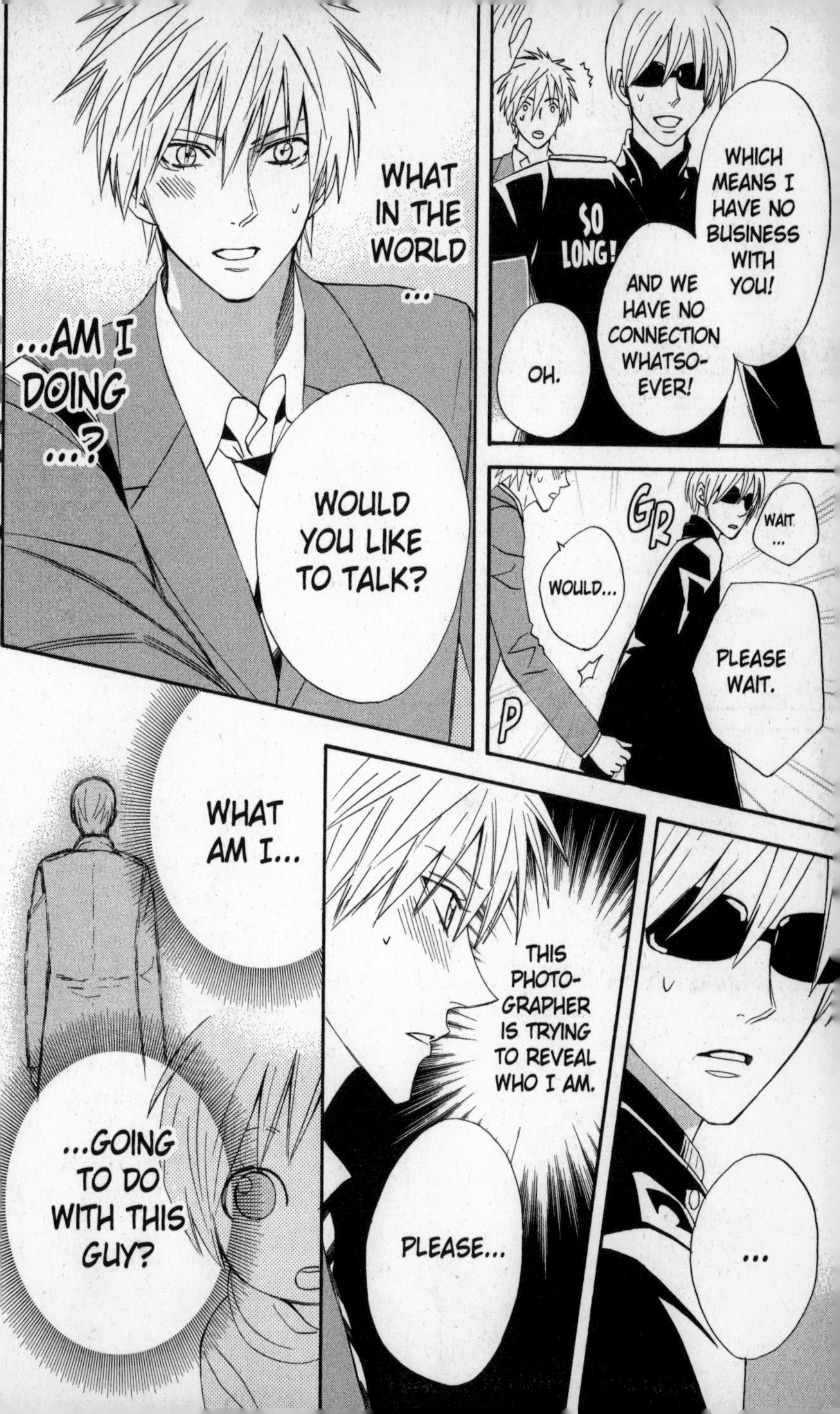
WHICH MEANS I HAVE NO BUSINESS WITH YOU!
SO LONG!
AND WE HAVE NO CONNECTION WHATSO-EVER!
OH.
WAIT...
GR
PLEASE WAIT.
WOULD...
P
WHAT IN THE WORLD...
...AM I DOING...?
WOULD YOU LIKE TO TALK?
...
THIS PHOTO-GRAPHER IS TRYING TO REVEAL WHO I AM.
PLEASE...
WHAT AM I...
...GOING TO DO WITH THIS GUY?

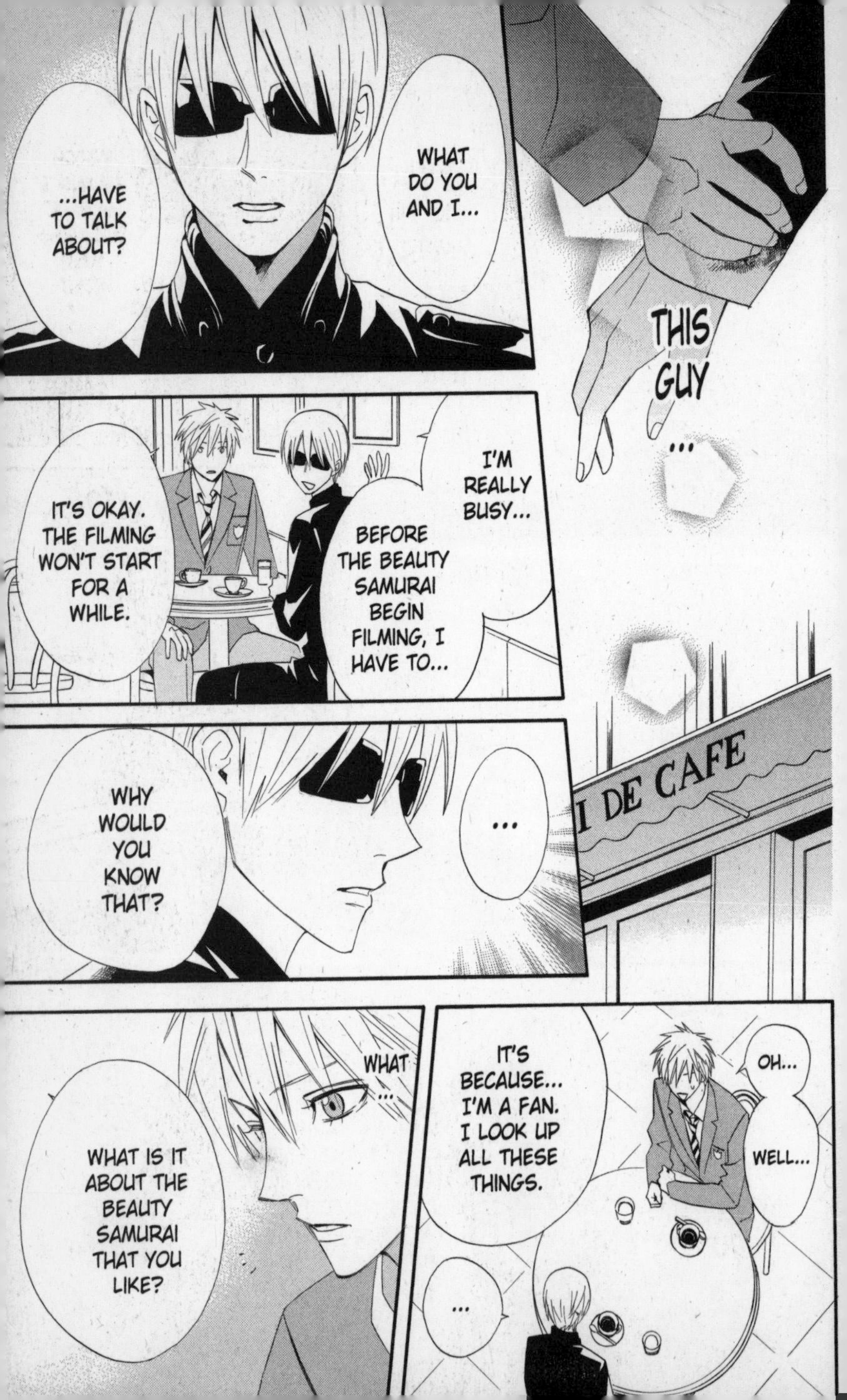
THIS GUY ...
I DE CAFE
WHAT DO YOU AND I...
...HAVE TO TALK ABOUT?
I'M REALLY BUSY...
BEFORE THE BEAUTY SAMURAI BEGIN FILMING, I HAVE TO...
IT'S OKAY. THE FILMING WON'T START FOR A WHILE.
...
WHY WOULD YOU KNOW THAT?
OH...
WELL...
IT'S BECAUSE... I'M A FAN. I LOOK UP ALL THESE THINGS.
...
WHAT ...
WHAT IS IT ABOUT THE BEAUTY SAMURAI THAT YOU LIKE?

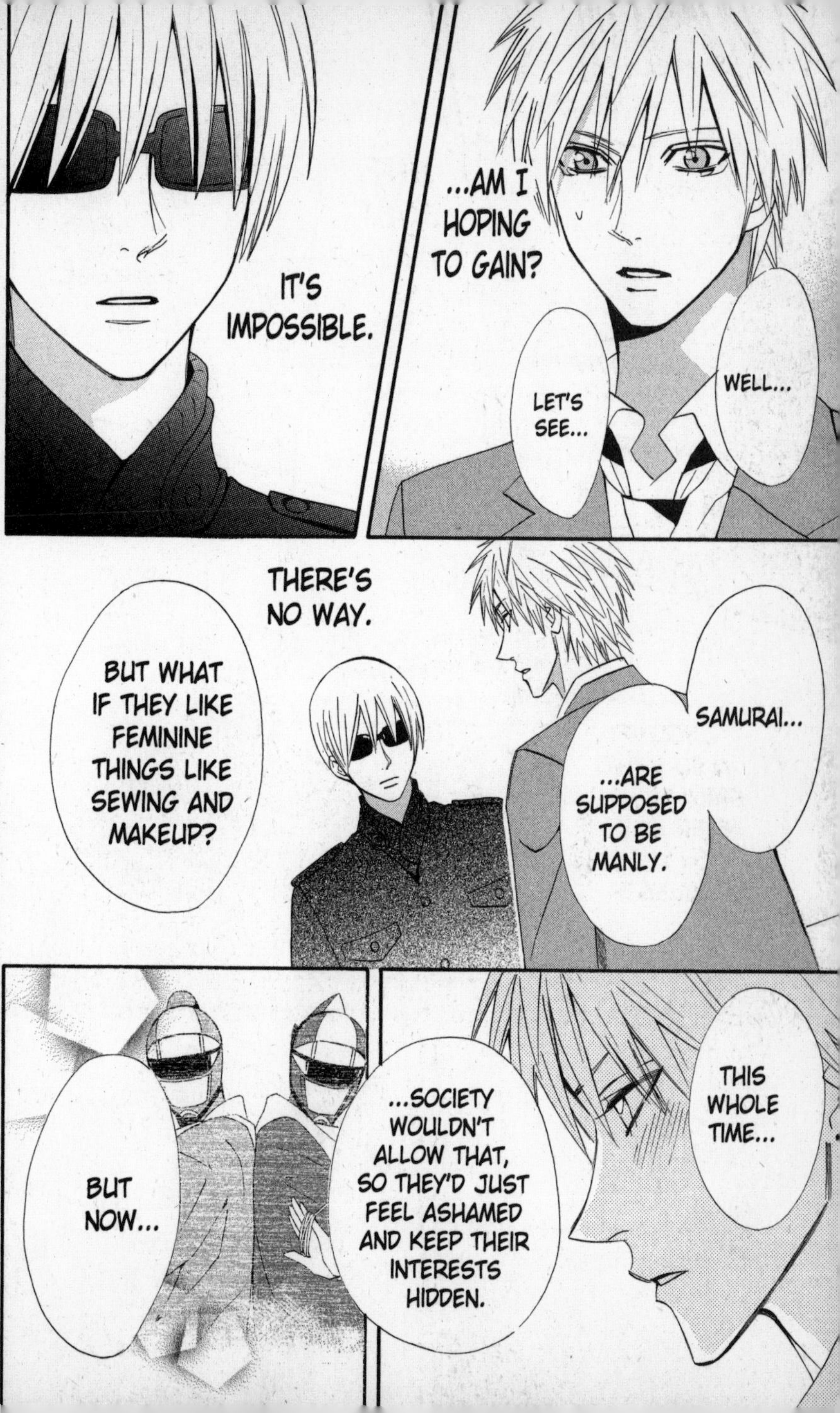
...AM I HOPING TO GAIN?
WELL...
LET'S SEE...
IT'S IMPOSSIBLE.
SAMURAI...
...ARE SUPPOSED TO BE MANLY.
THERE'S NO WAY.
BUT WHAT IF THEY LIKE FEMININE THINGS LIKE SEWING AND MAKEUP?
THIS WHOLE TIME...
...SOCIETY WOULDN'T ALLOW THAT, SO THEY'D JUST FEEL ASHAMED AND KEEP THEIR INTERESTS HIDDEN.
BUT NOW...

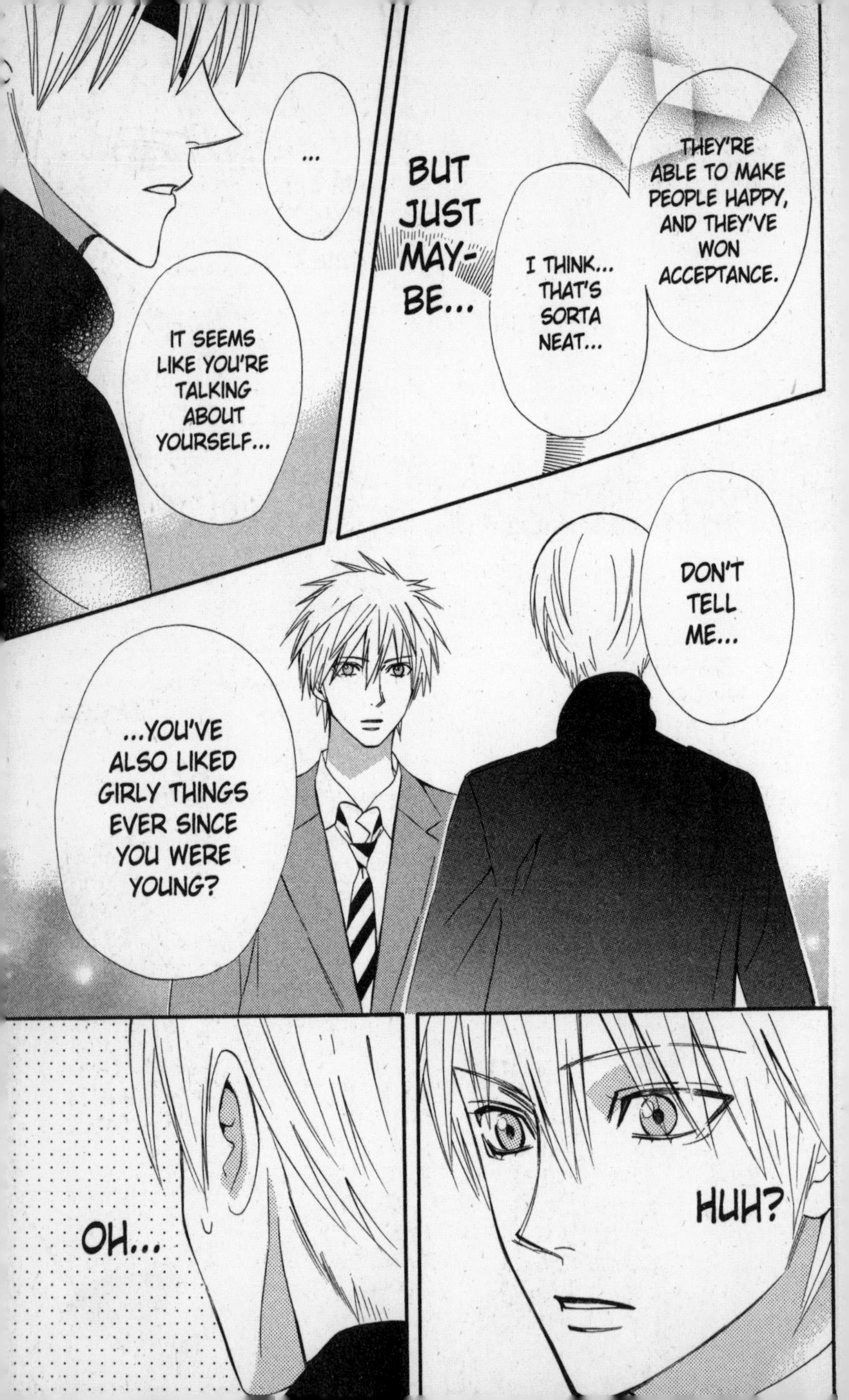
THEY'RE ABLE TO MAKE PEOPLE HAPPY, AND THEY'VE WON ACCEPTANCE.
I THINK... THAT'S SORTA NEAT...
BUT JUST MAY-BE...
...
IT SEEMS LIKE YOU'RE TALKING ABOUT YOURSELF...
DON'T TELL ME...
...YOU'VE ALSO LIKED GIRLY THINGS EVER SINCE YOU WERE YOUNG?
HUH?
OH...

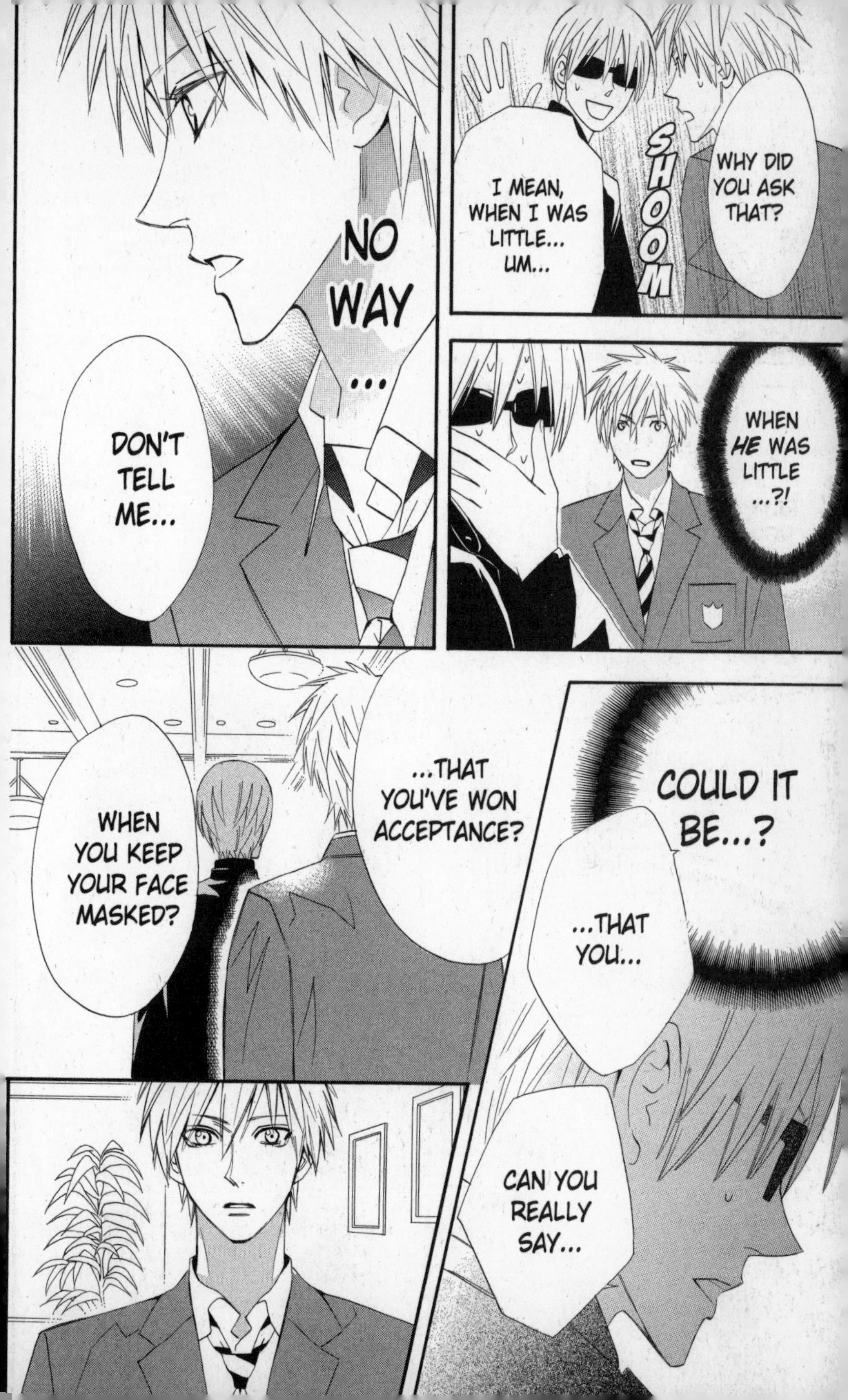
WHY DID YOU ASK THAT?
SHOOM
I MEAN, WHEN I WAS LITTLE... UM...
WHEN *HE* WAS LITTLE ...?!
NO WAY ...
DON'T TELL ME...
COULD IT BE...?
...THAT YOU...
CAN YOU REALLY SAY...
...THAT YOU'VE WON ACCEPTANCE?
WHEN YOU KEEP YOUR FACE MASKED?

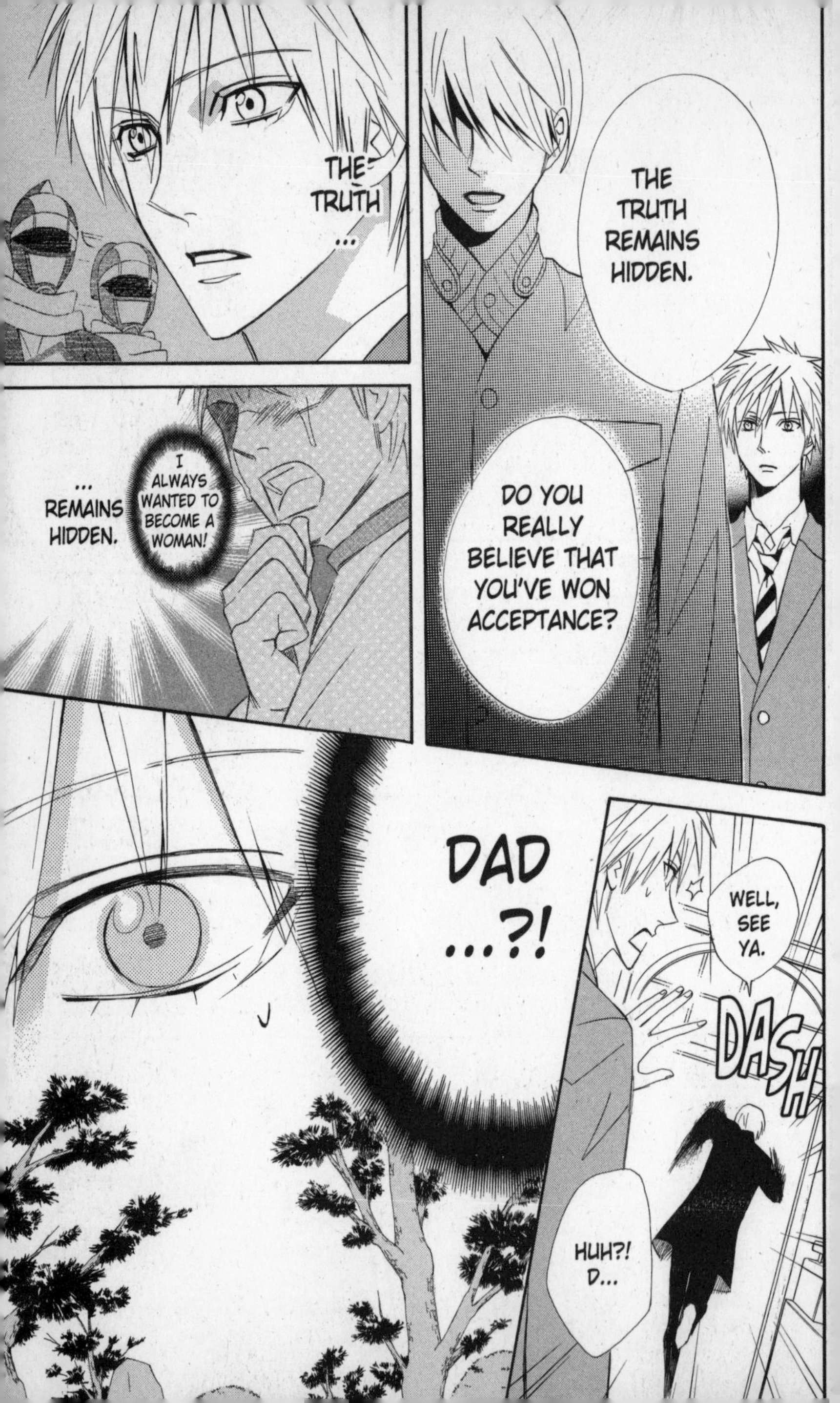
THE TRUTH REMAINS HIDDEN.
DO YOU REALLY BELIEVE THAT YOU'VE WON ACCEPTANCE?
THE TRUTH ...
I ALWAYS WANTED TO BECOME A WOMAN!
... REMAINS HIDDEN.
WELL, SEE YA.
DASH
HUH?! D...
DAD ...?!

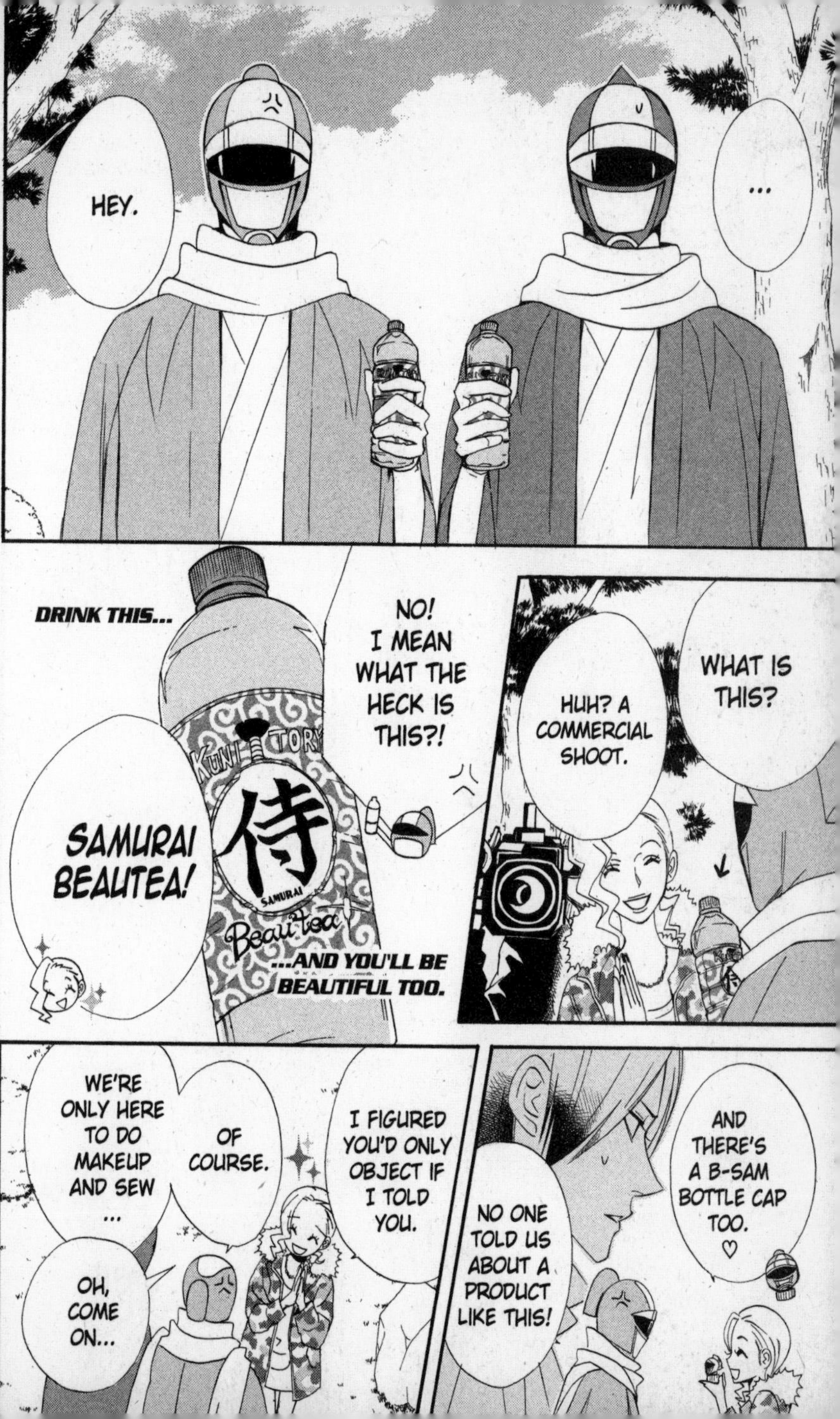
...
HEY.
WHAT IS THIS?
HUH? A COMMERCIAL SHOOT.
NO! I MEAN WHAT THE HECK IS THIS?!
DRINK THIS...
KUNI TORY
侍
SAMURAI
Beau tea
SAMURAI BEAUTEA!
...AND YOU'LL BE BEAUTIFUL TOO.
AND THERE'S A B-SAM BOTTLE CAP TOO. ♡
NO ONE TOLD US ABOUT A PRODUCT LIKE THIS!
I FIGURED YOU'D ONLY OBJECT IF I TOLD YOU.
OF COURSE.
WE'RE ONLY HERE TO DO MAKEUP AND SEW ...
OH, COME ON...

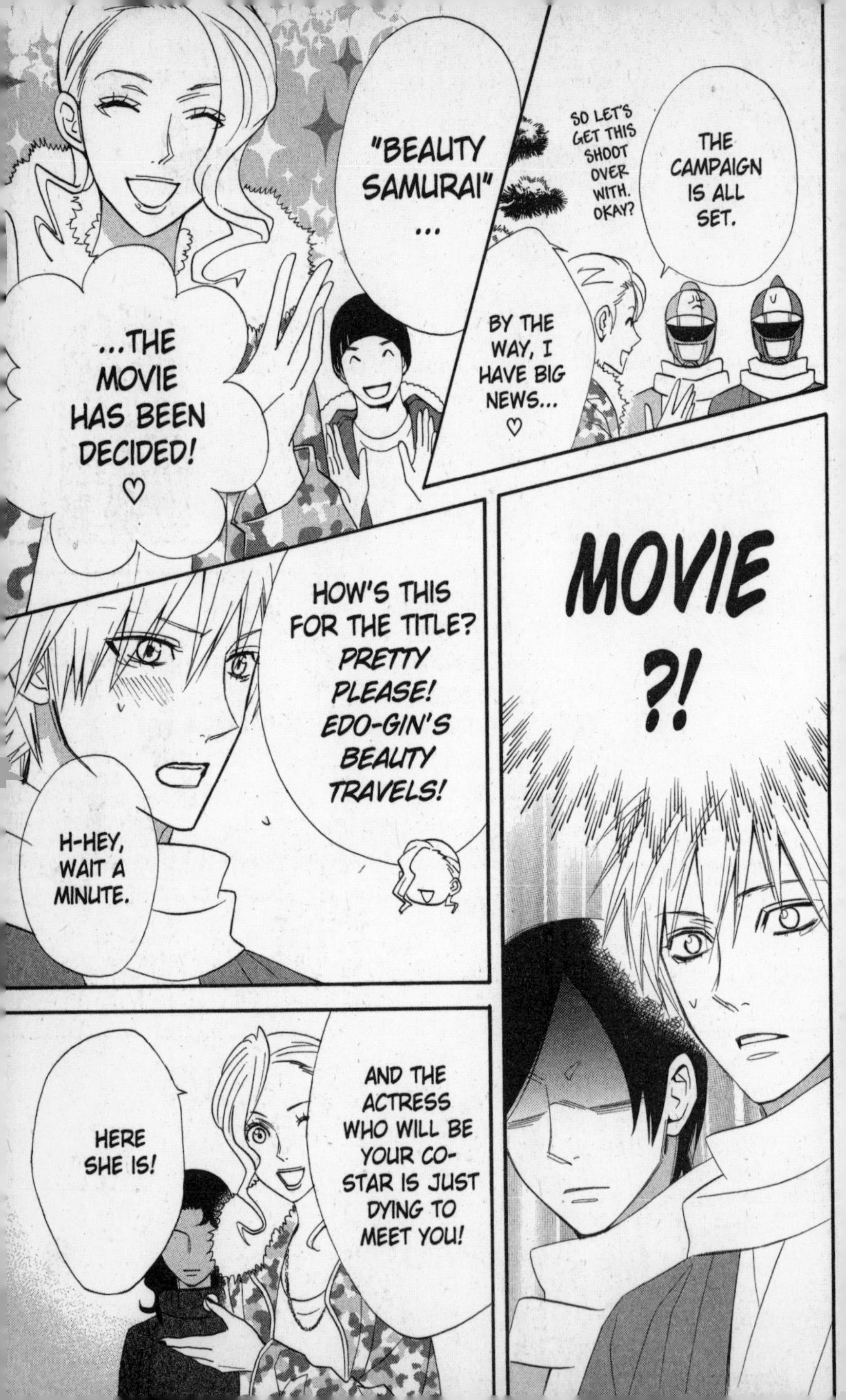
THE CAMPAIGN IS ALL SET.
SO LET'S GET THIS SHOOT OVER WITH. OKAY?
BY THE WAY, I HAVE BIG NEWS... ♡
"BEAUTY SAMURAI" ...
...THE MOVIE HAS BEEN DECIDED! ♡
MOVIE ?!
HOW'S THIS FOR THE TITLE? *PRETTY PLEASE! EDO-GIN'S BEAUTY TRAVELS!*
H-HEY, WAIT A MINUTE.
AND THE ACTRESS WHO WILL BE YOUR CO-STAR IS JUST DYING TO MEET YOU!
HERE SHE IS!

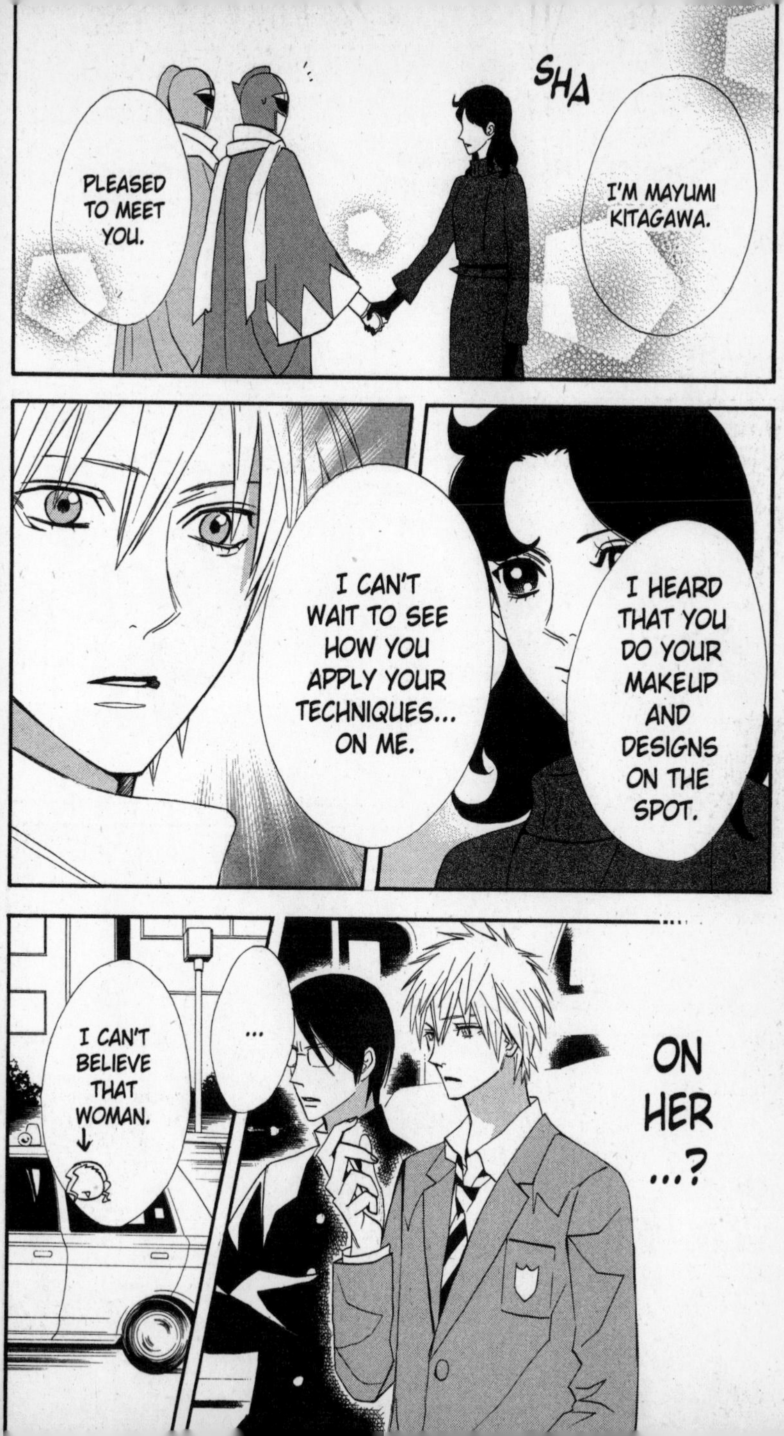
SHA
I'M MAYUMI KITAGAWA.
PLEASED TO MEET YOU.
I HEARD THAT YOU DO YOUR MAKEUP AND DESIGNS ON THE SPOT.
I CAN'T WAIT TO SEE HOW YOU APPLY YOUR TECHNIQUES... ON ME.
ON HER ...?
...
I CAN'T BELIEVE THAT WOMAN.

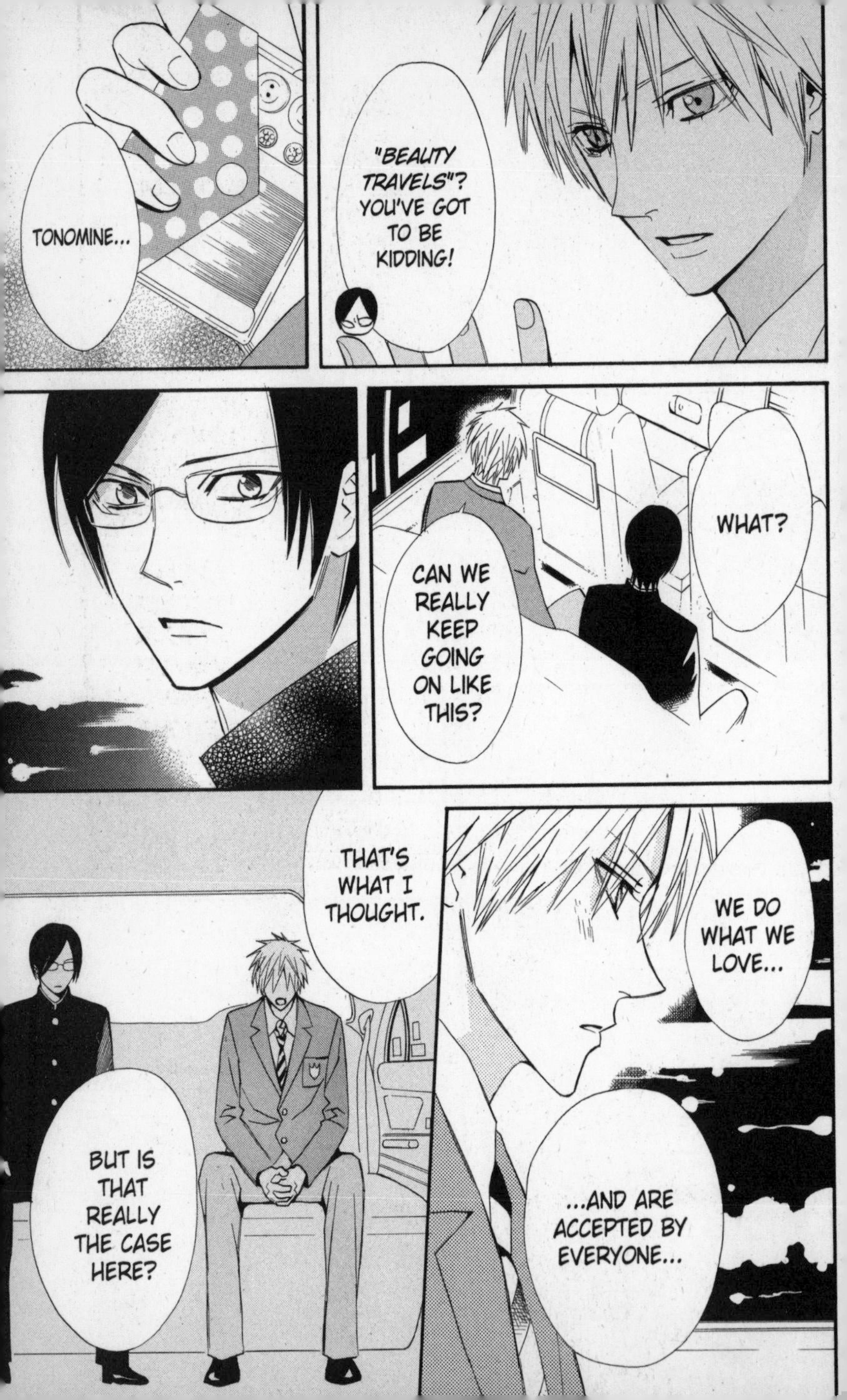
"BEAUTY TRAVELS"? YOU'VE GOT TO BE KIDDING!
TONOMINE...
WHAT?
CAN WE REALLY KEEP GOING ON LIKE THIS?
WE DO WHAT WE LOVE...
...AND ARE ACCEPTED BY EVERYONE...
THAT'S WHAT I THOUGHT.
BUT IS THAT REALLY THE CASE HERE?

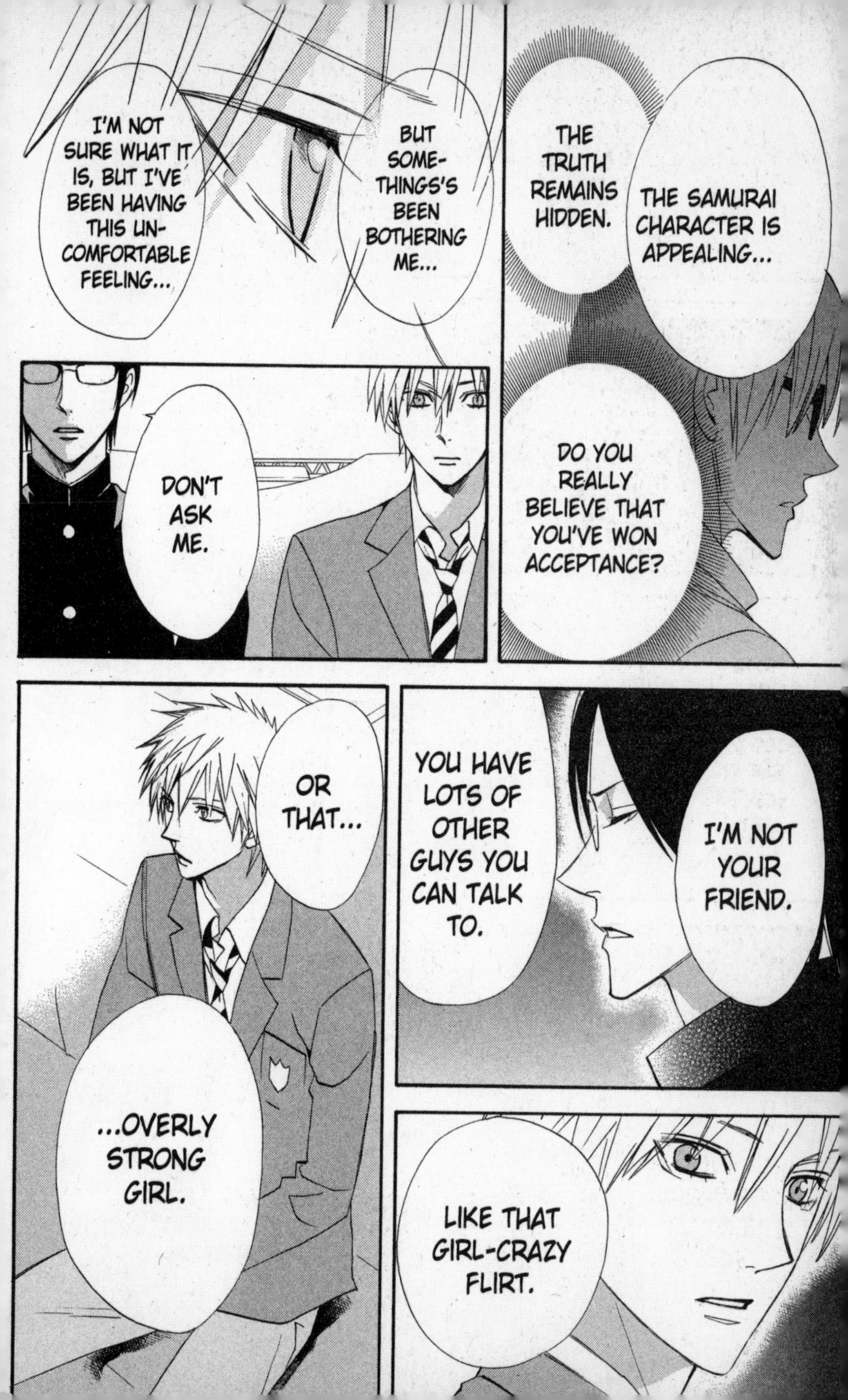
THE SAMURAI CHARACTER IS APPEALING...
THE TRUTH REMAINS HIDDEN.
DO YOU REALLY BELIEVE THAT YOU'VE WON ACCEPTANCE?
BUT SOME-THINGS'S BEEN BOTHERING ME...
I'M NOT SURE WHAT IT IS, BUT I'VE BEEN HAVING THIS UN-COMFORTABLE FEELING...
DON'T ASK ME.
I'M NOT YOUR FRIEND.
YOU HAVE LOTS OF OTHER GUYS YOU CAN TALK TO.
LIKE THAT GIRL-CRAZY FLIRT.
OR THAT...
...OVERLY STRONG GIRL.

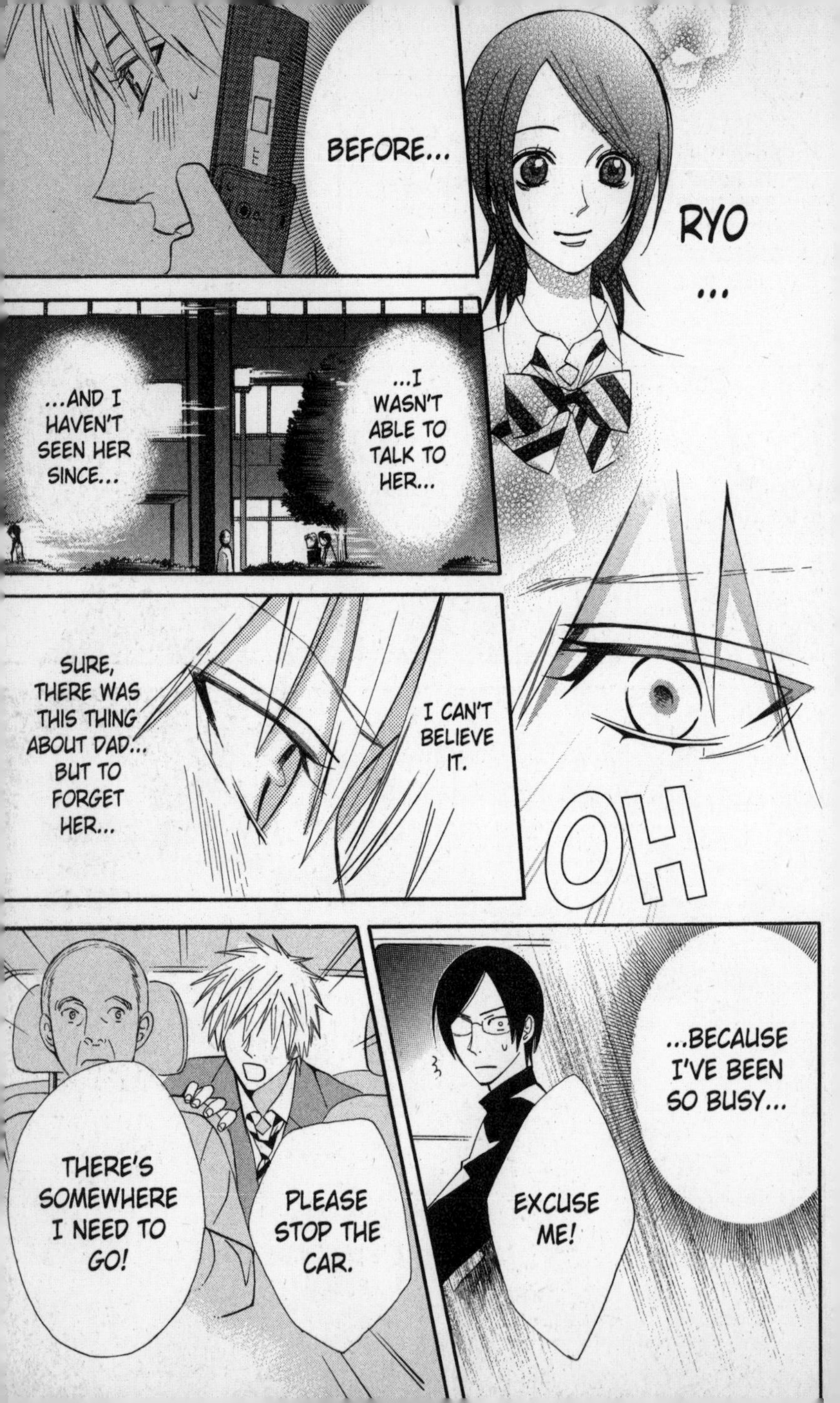
RYO ...
BEFORE...
...I WASN'T ABLE TO TALK TO HER...
...AND I HAVEN'T SEEN HER SINCE...
OH
I CAN'T BELIEVE IT.
SURE, THERE WAS THIS THING ABOUT DAD... BUT TO FORGET HER...
...BECAUSE I'VE BEEN SO BUSY...
EXCUSE ME!
PLEASE STOP THE CAR.
THERE'S SOMEWHERE I NEED TO GO!

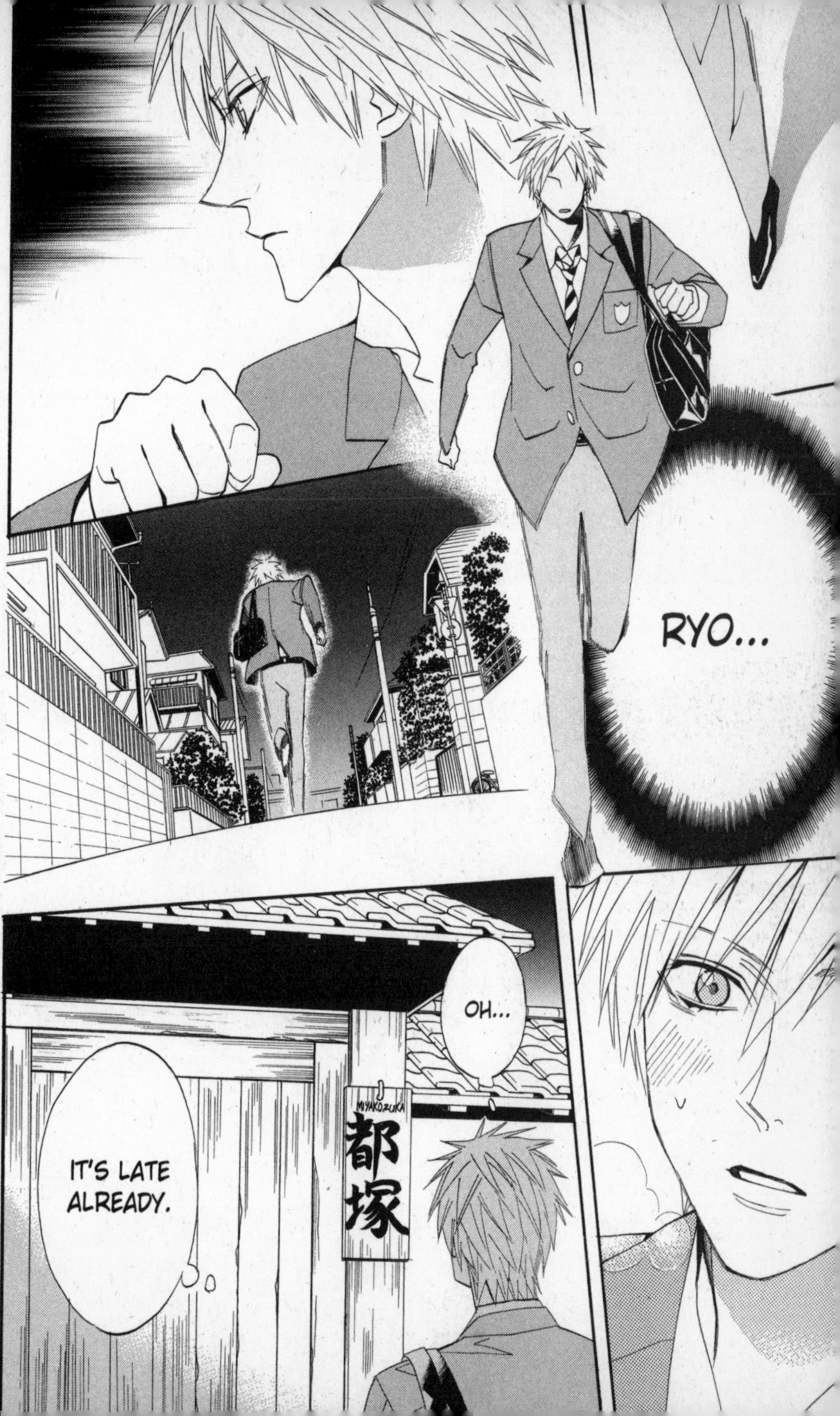
RYO...
OH...
IT'S LATE ALREADY.
MIYAKOZUKA
都塚

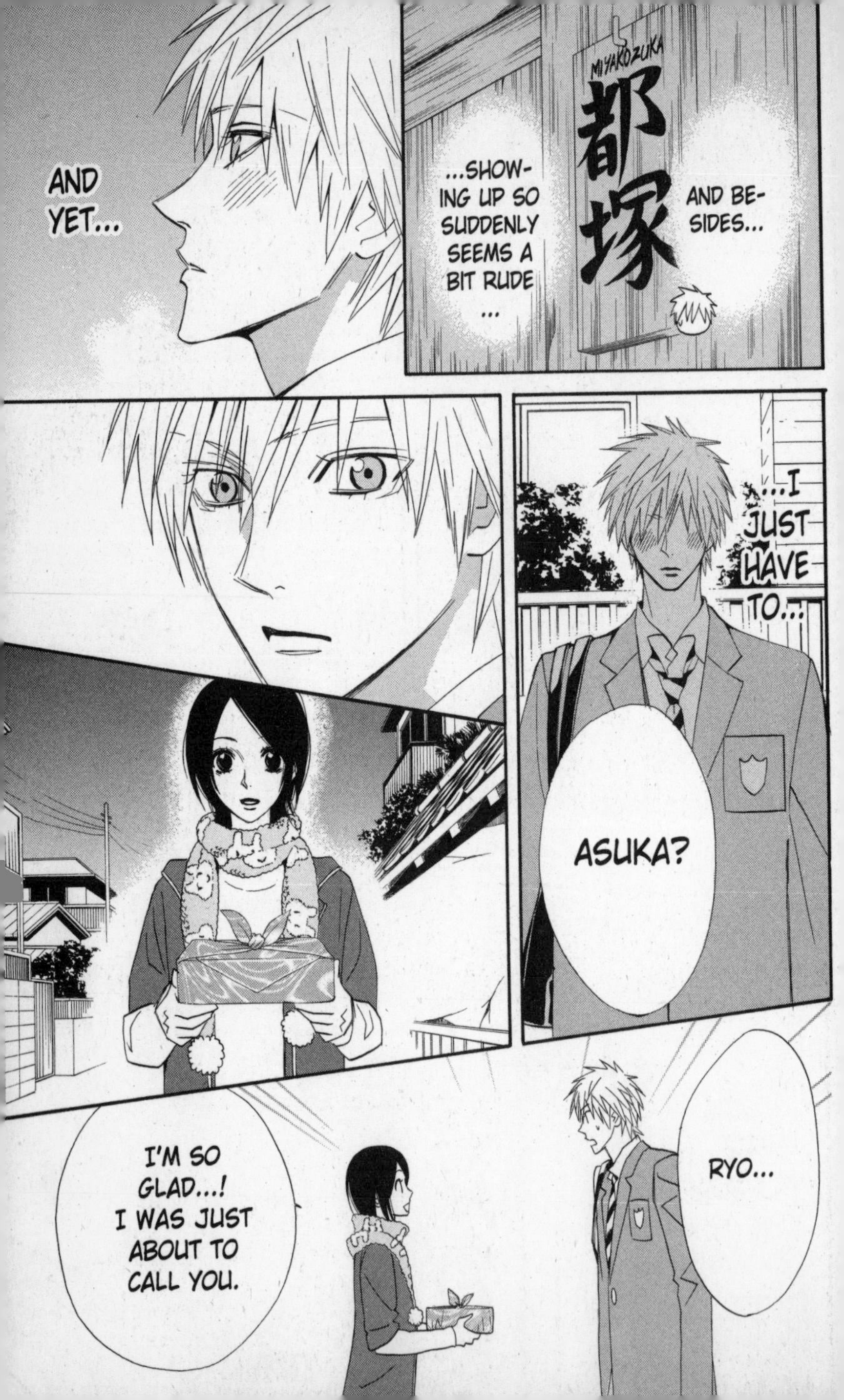
MIYAKOZUKA
都塚
AND BE-SIDES...
...SHOW-ING UP SO SUDDENLY SEEMS A BIT RUDE ...
AND YET...
...I JUST HAVE TO...
ASUKA?
RYO...
I'M SO GLAD...! I WAS JUST ABOUT TO CALL YOU.

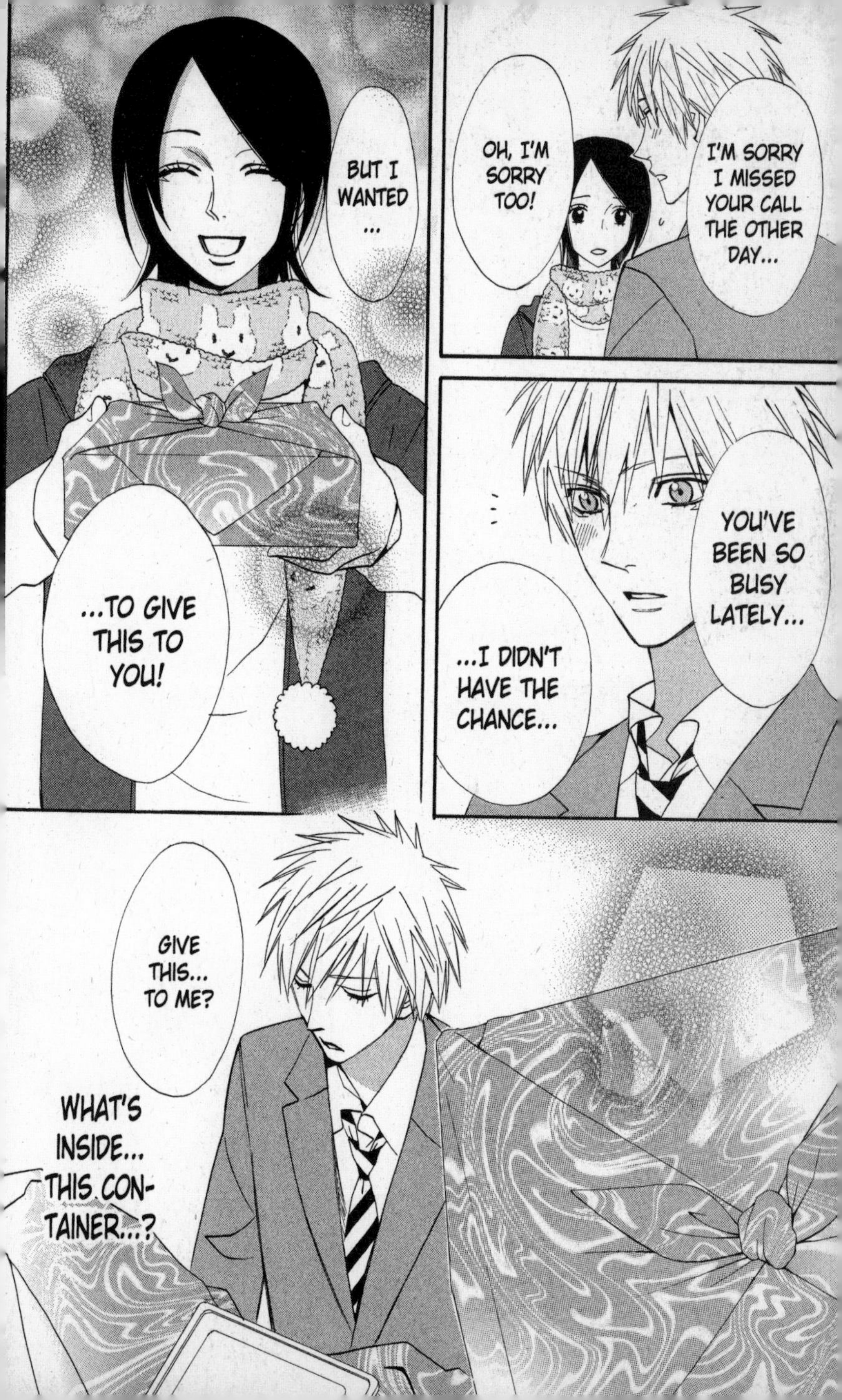
I'M SORRY I MISSED YOUR CALL THE OTHER DAY...
OH, I'M SORRY TOO!
YOU'VE BEEN SO BUSY LATELY...
...I DIDN'T HAVE THE CHANCE...
BUT I WANTED ...
...TO GIVE THIS TO YOU!
GIVE THIS... TO ME?
WHAT'S INSIDE... THIS CON-TAINER...?

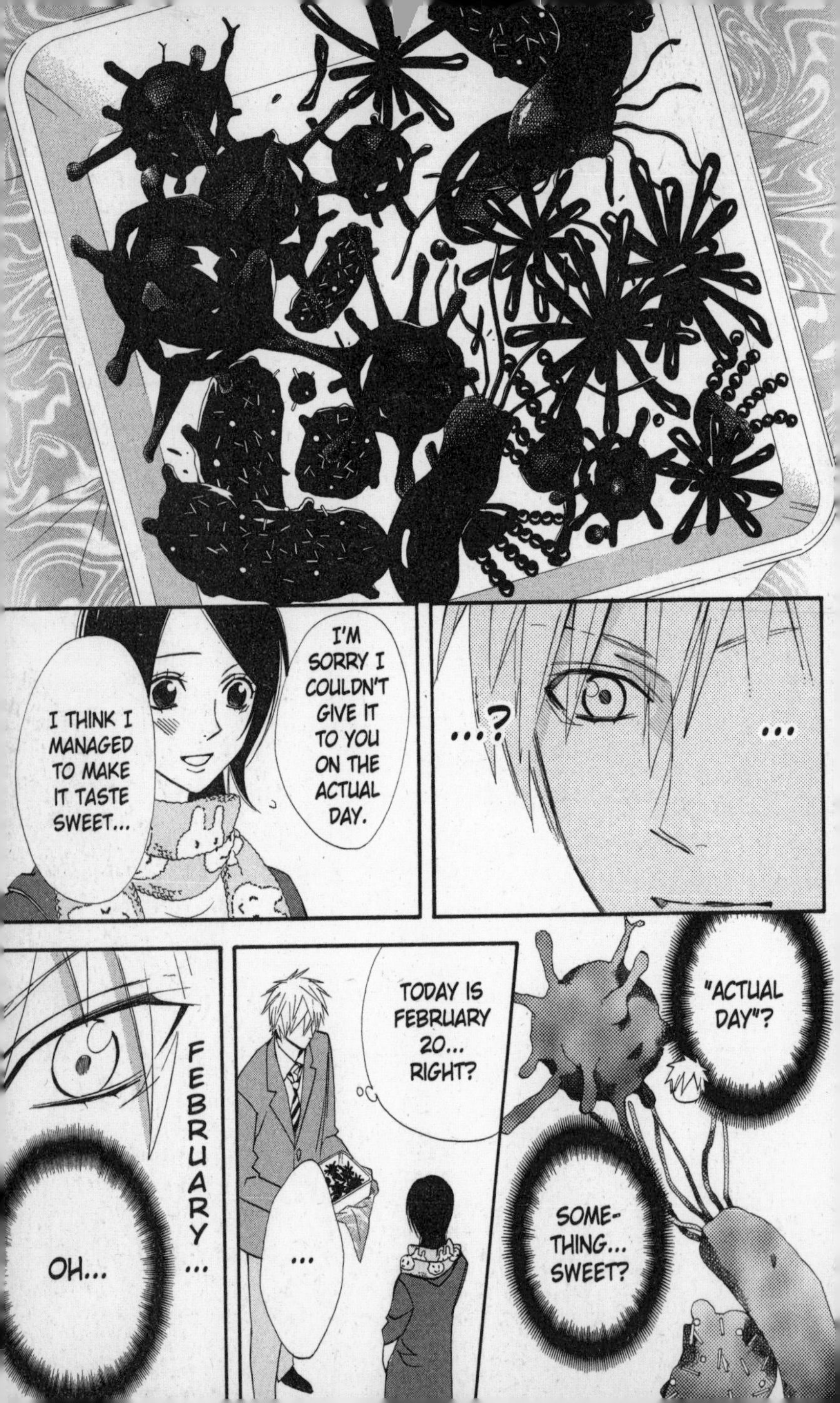
...
...?
I'M SORRY I COULDN'T GIVE IT TO YOU ON THE ACTUAL DAY.
I THINK I MANAGED TO MAKE IT TASTE SWEET...
"ACTUAL DAY"?
SOME-THING... SWEET?
TODAY IS FEBRUARY 20... RIGHT?
...
FEBRUARY...
OH...

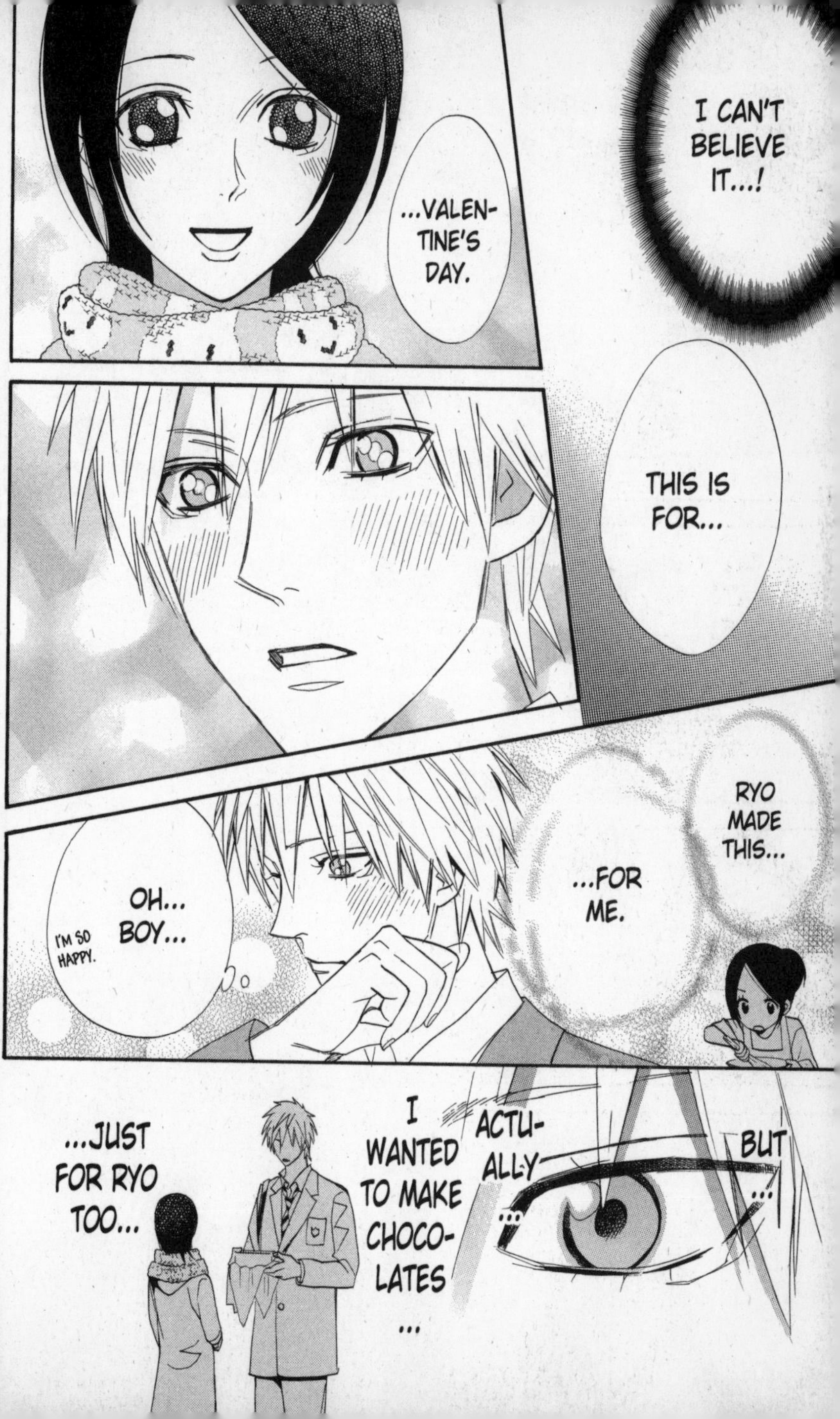
I CAN'T BELIEVE IT...!
...VALEN-TINE'S DAY.
THIS IS FOR...
RYO MADE THIS...
...FOR ME.
OH... BOY...
I'M SO HAPPY.
BUT...
ACTU-ALLY...
I WANTED TO MAKE CHOCO-LATES...
...JUST FOR RYO TOO...

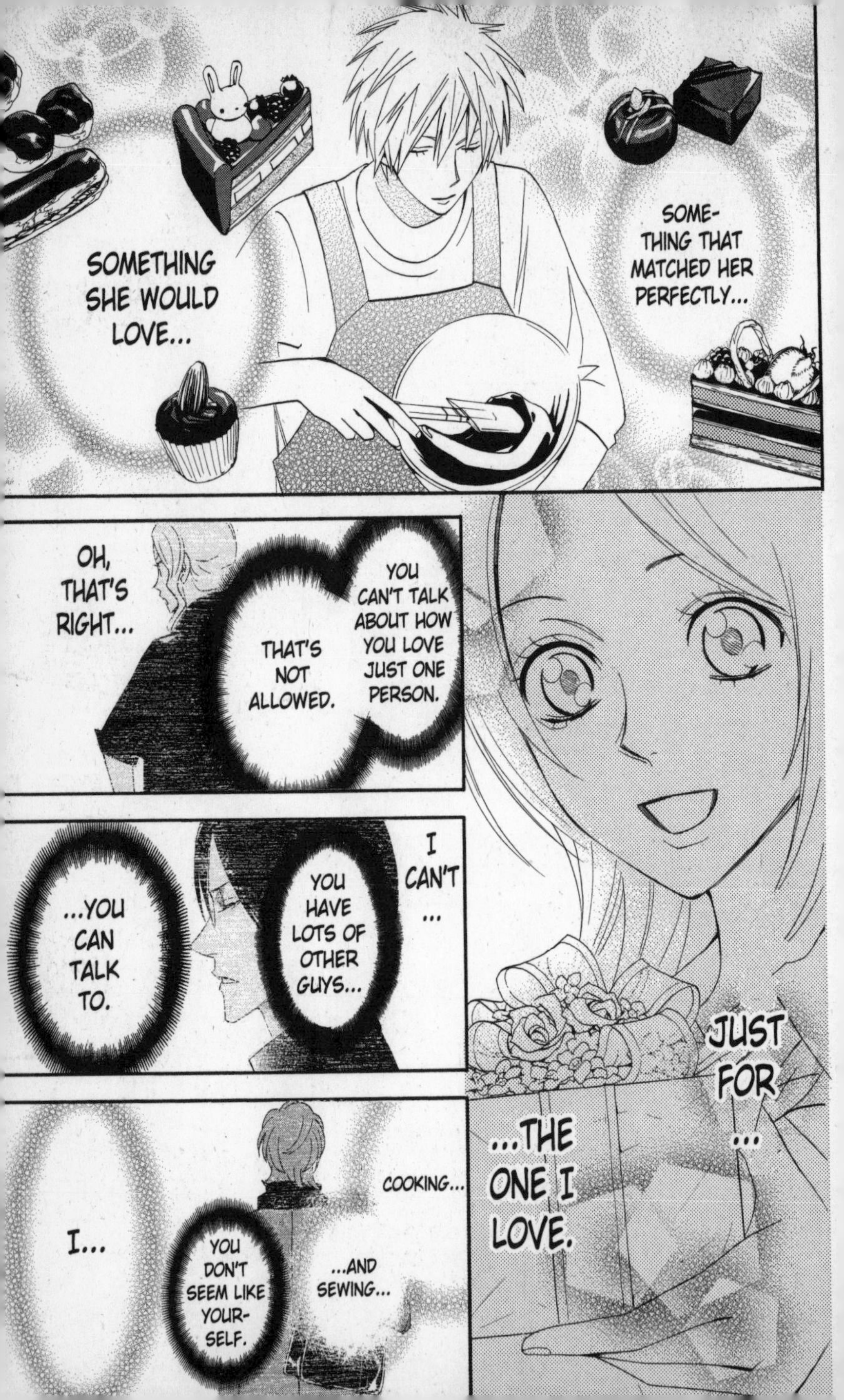
SOME-THING THAT MATCHED HER PERFECTLY...
SOMETHING SHE WOULD LOVE...
JUST FOR ...
...THE ONE I LOVE.
YOU CAN'T TALK ABOUT HOW YOU LOVE JUST ONE PERSON.
THAT'S NOT ALLOWED.
OH, THAT'S RIGHT...
I CAN'T ...
YOU HAVE LOTS OF OTHER GUYS...
...YOU CAN TALK TO.
COOKING...
...AND SEWING...
YOU DON'T SEEM LIKE YOUR-SELF.
I...

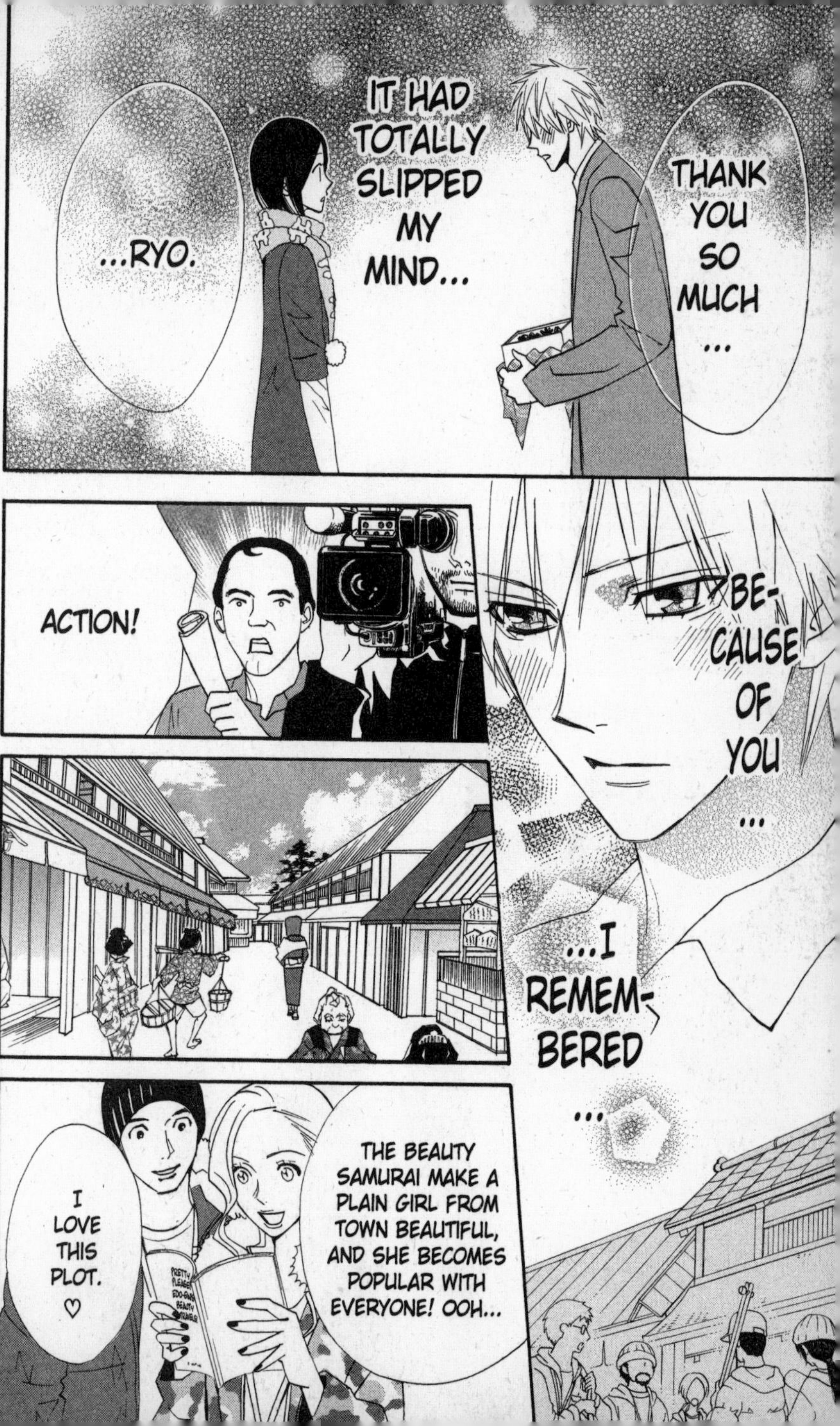
THANK YOU SO MUCH...
IT HAD TOTALLY SLIPPED MY MIND...
...RYO.
BECAUSE OF YOU...
...I REMEMBERED...
ACTION!
THE BEAUTY SAMURAI MAKE A PLAIN GIRL FROM TOWN BEAUTIFUL, AND SHE BECOMES POPULAR WITH EVERYONE! OOH...
I LOVE THIS PLOT. ♡

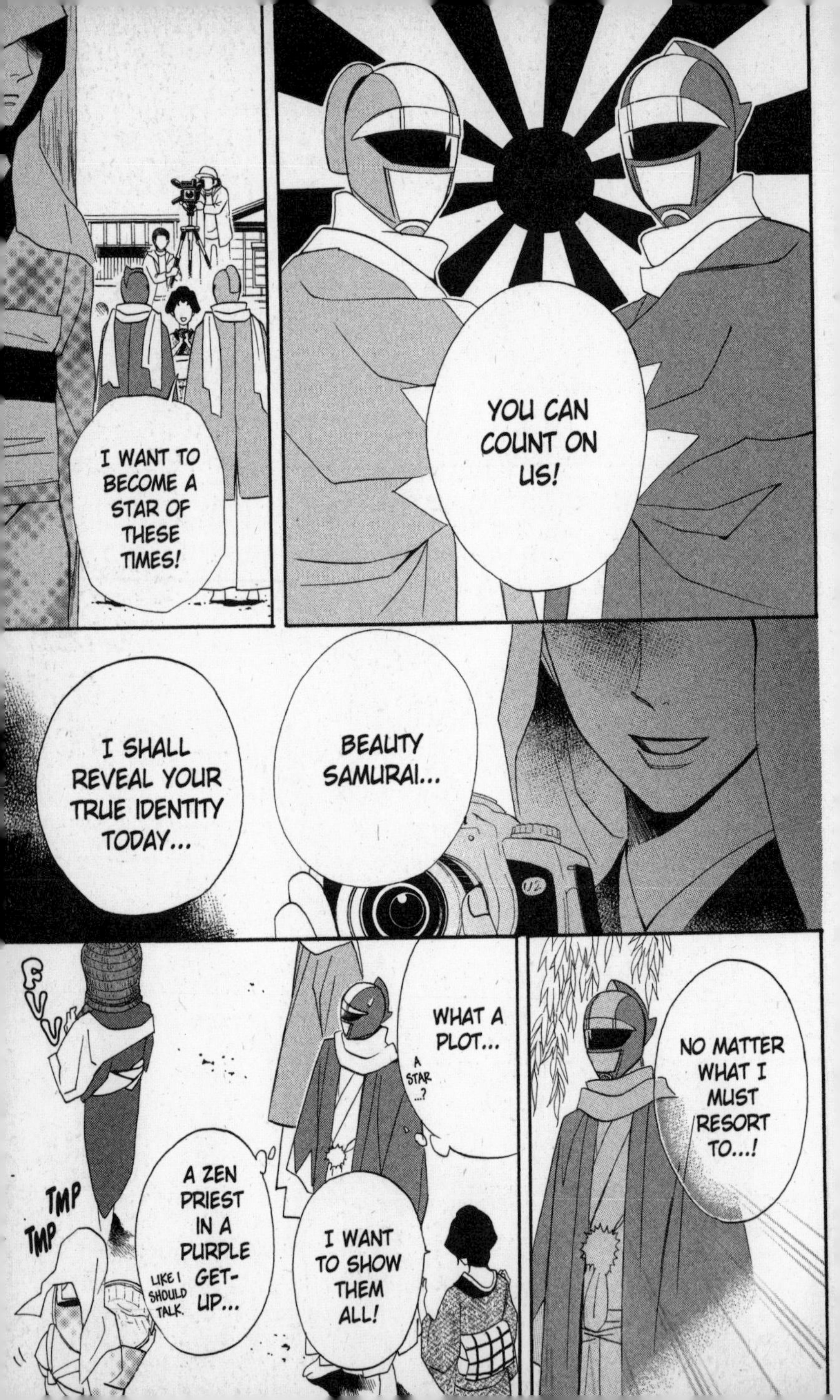
YOU CAN COUNT ON US!
I WANT TO BECOME A STAR OF THESE TIMES!
BEAUTY SAMURAI...
I SHALL REVEAL YOUR TRUE IDENTITY TODAY...
NO MATTER WHAT I MUST RESORT TO...!
WHAT A PLOT...
A STAR ...?
I WANT TO SHOW THEM ALL!
FVV
A ZEN PRIEST IN A PURPLE GET-UP...
LIKE I SHOULD TALK.
TMP TMP

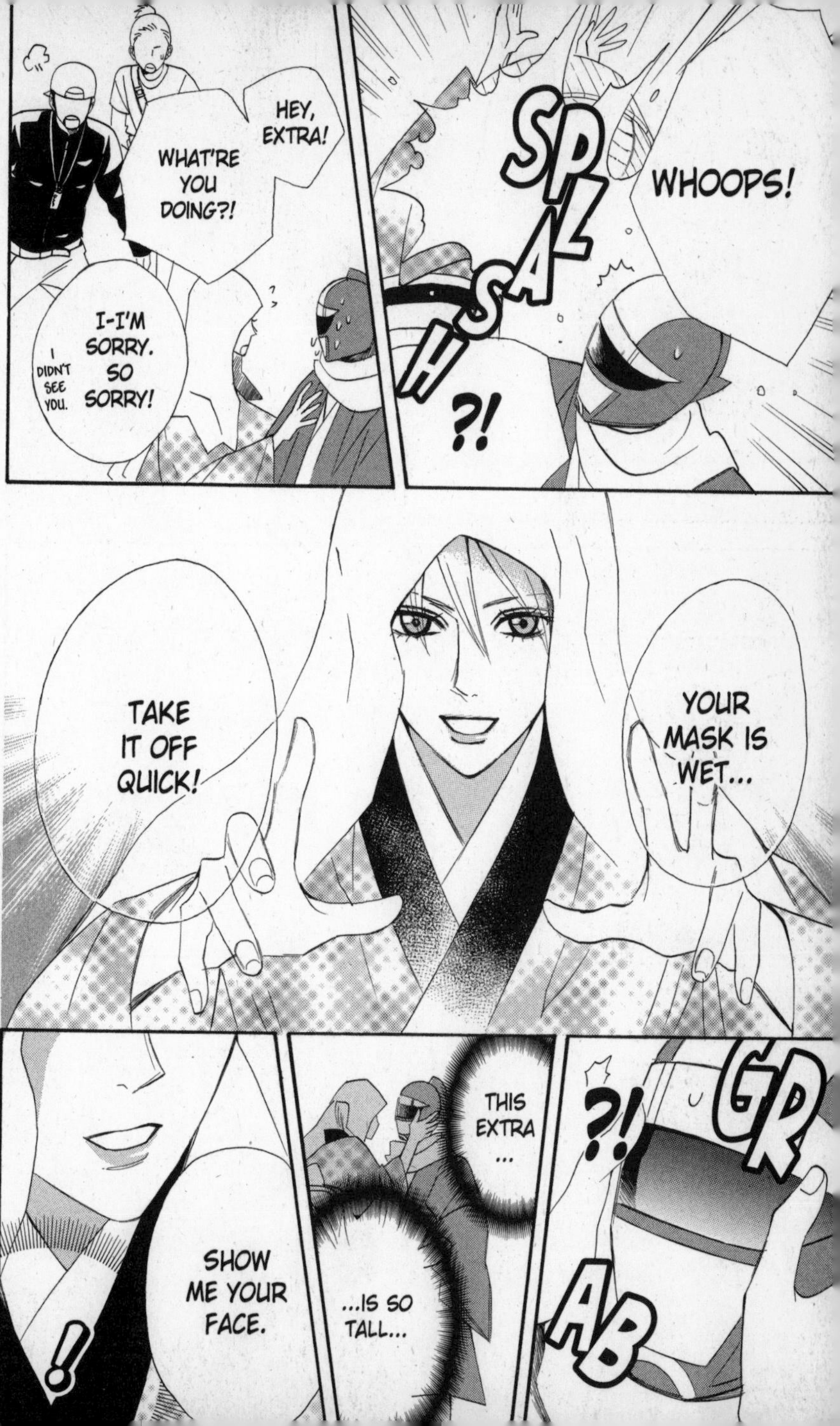
WHOOPS!
SPLASH
?!
HEY, EXTRA!
WHAT'RE YOU DOING?!
I-I'M SORRY. SO SORRY!
I DIDN'T SEE YOU.
YOUR MASK IS WET...
TAKE IT OFF QUICK!
GRAB
?!
THIS EXTRA ...
...IS SO TALL...
SHOW ME YOUR FACE.
!

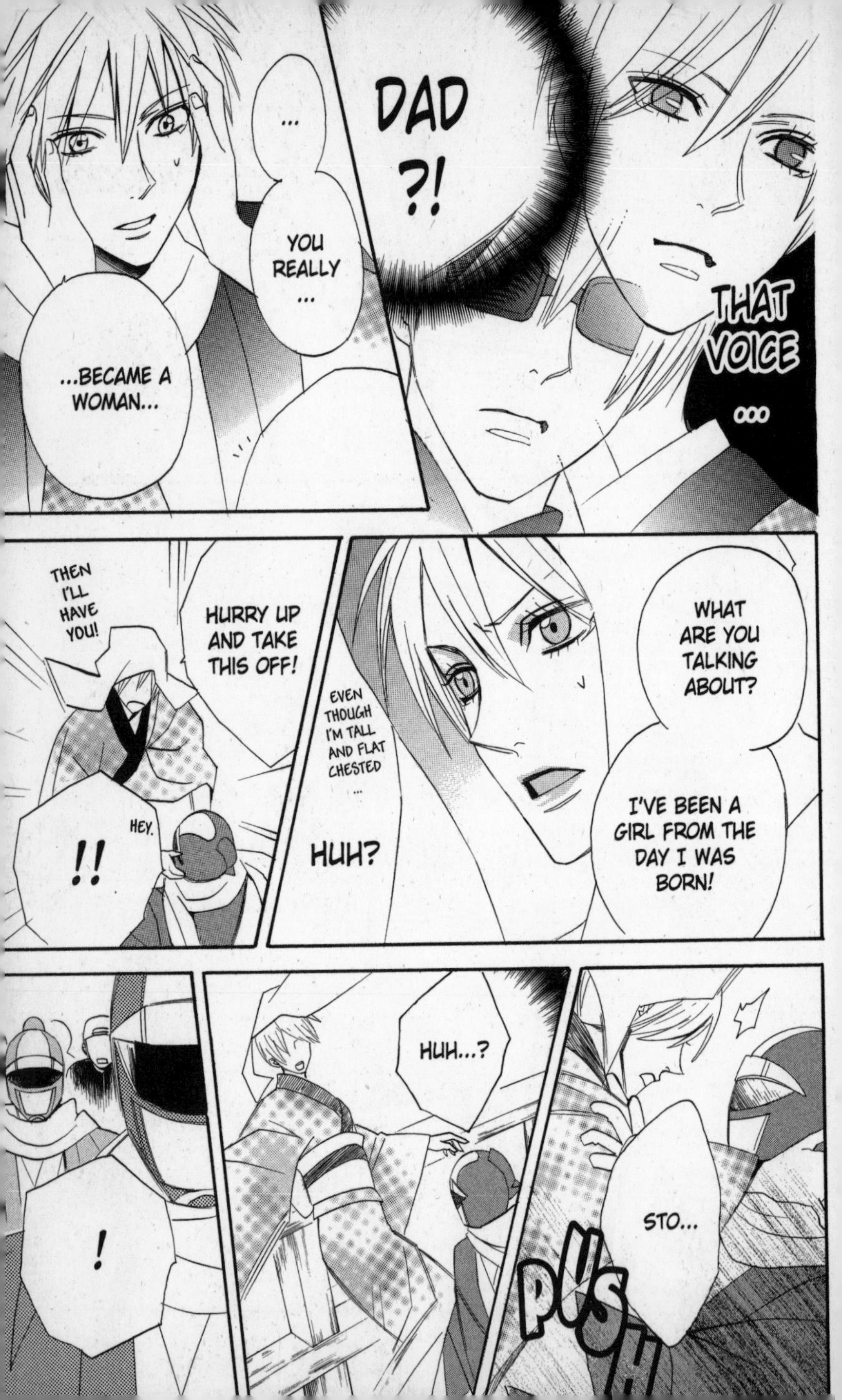
THAT VOICE ...
DAD ?!
...
YOU REALLY ...
...BECAME A WOMAN...
WHAT ARE YOU TALKING ABOUT?
I'VE BEEN A GIRL FROM THE DAY I WAS BORN!
HUH?
EVEN THOUGH I'M TALL AND FLAT CHESTED ...
HURRY UP AND TAKE THIS OFF!
THEN I'LL HAVE YOU!
HEY.
!!
STO...
PUSH
HUH...?
!

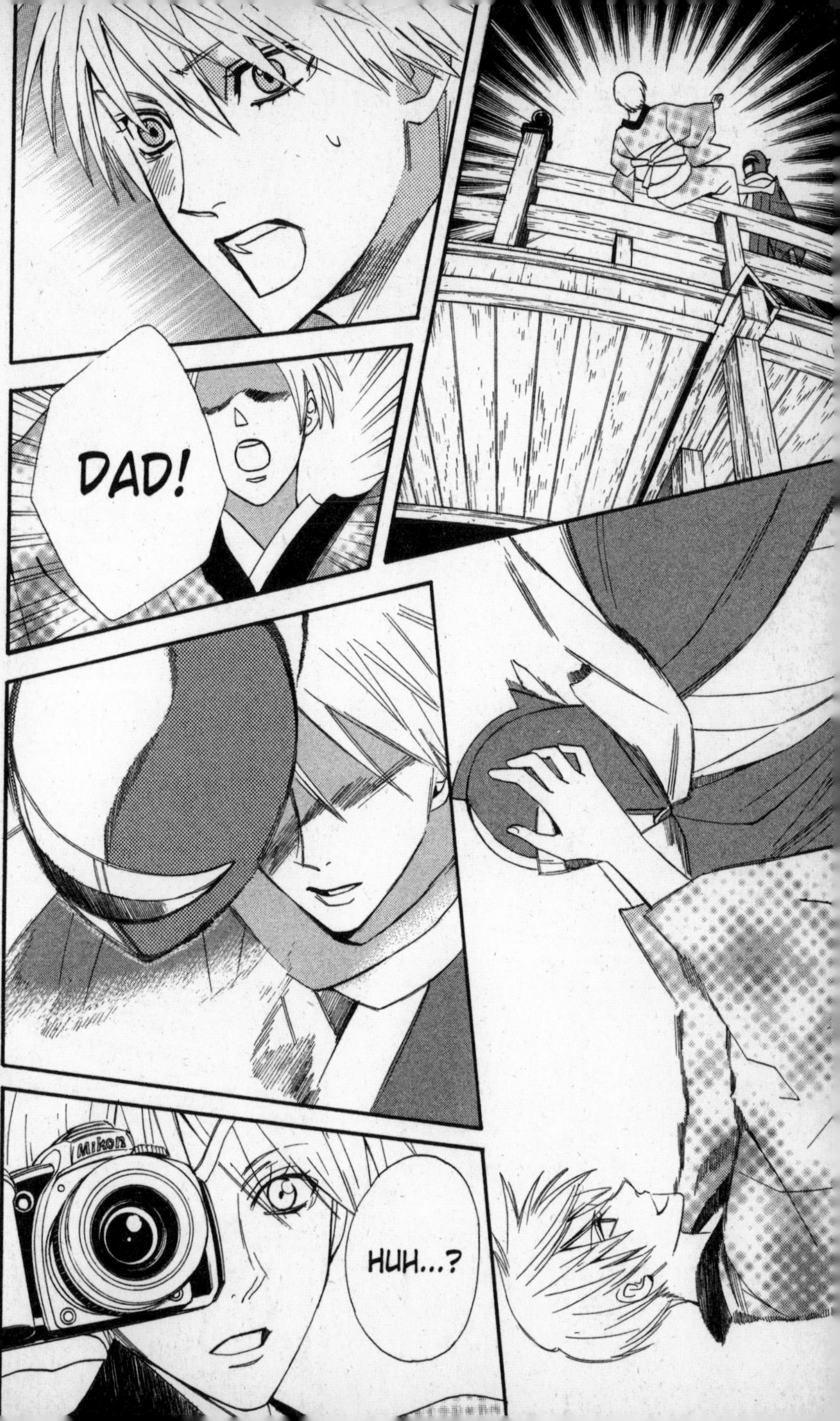
DAD!
HUH...?

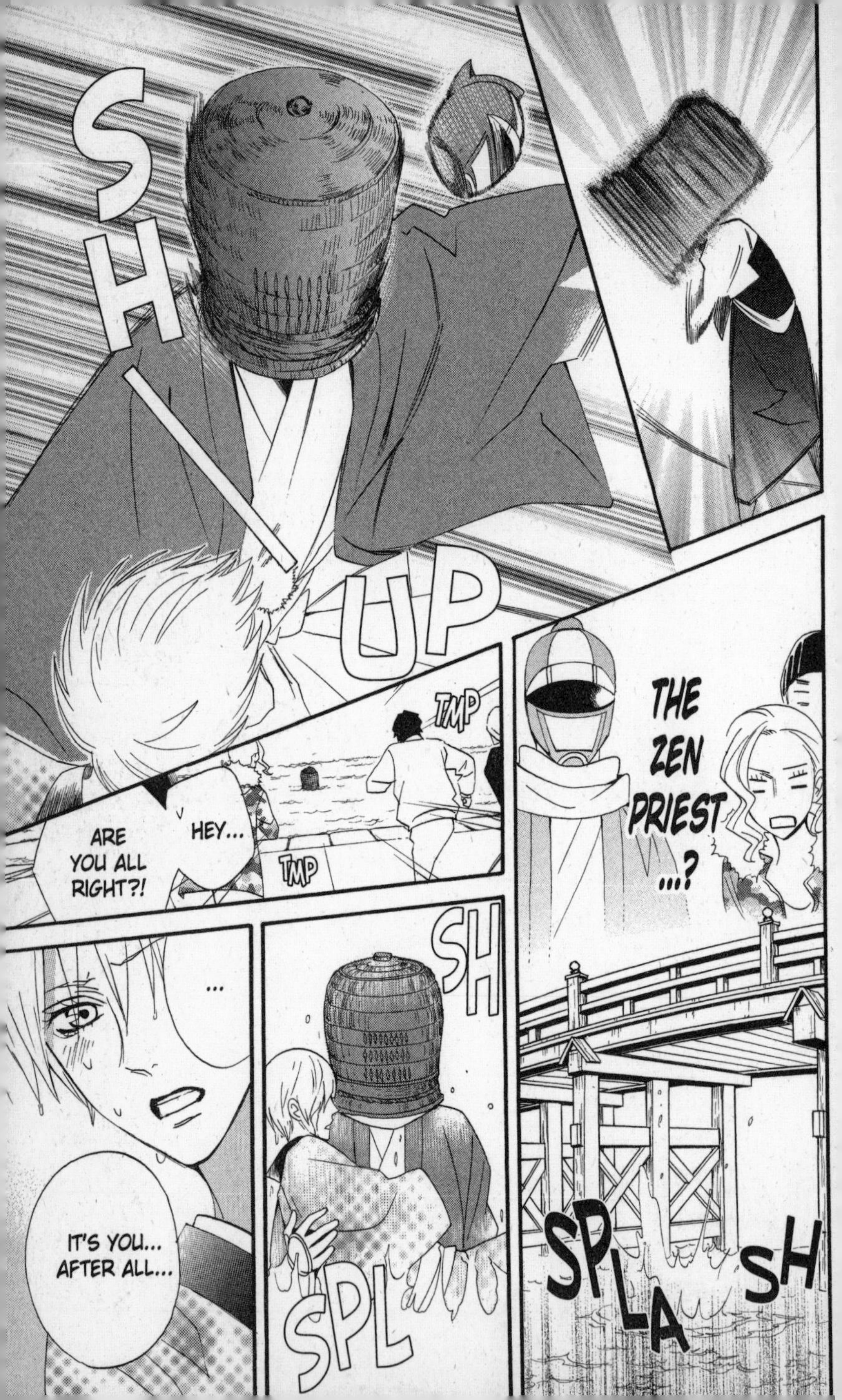
SH
UP
THE ZEN PRIEST ...?
TMP
HEY...
ARE YOU ALL RIGHT?!
TMP
SPLASH
SH
SPL
...
IT'S YOU... AFTER ALL...

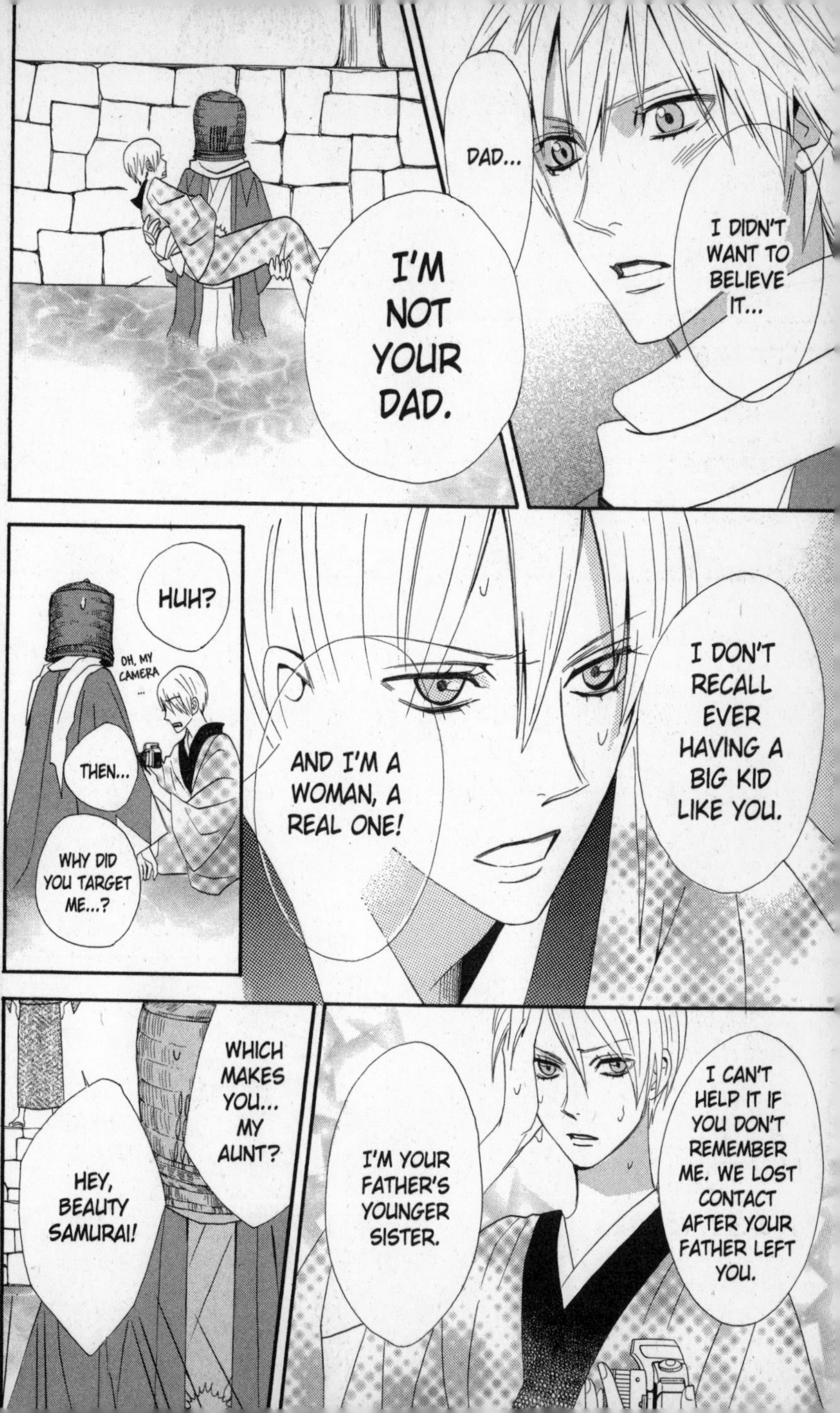
I DIDN'T WANT TO BELIEVE IT...
DAD...
I'M NOT YOUR DAD.
I DON'T RECALL EVER HAVING A BIG KID LIKE YOU.
AND I'M A WOMAN, A REAL ONE!
HUH?
OH, MY CAMERA ...
THEN...
WHY DID YOU TARGET ME...?
I CAN'T HELP IT IF YOU DON'T REMEMBER ME. WE LOST CONTACT AFTER YOUR FATHER LEFT YOU.
I'M YOUR FATHER'S YOUNGER SISTER.
WHICH MAKES YOU... MY AUNT?
HEY, BEAUTY SAMURAI!

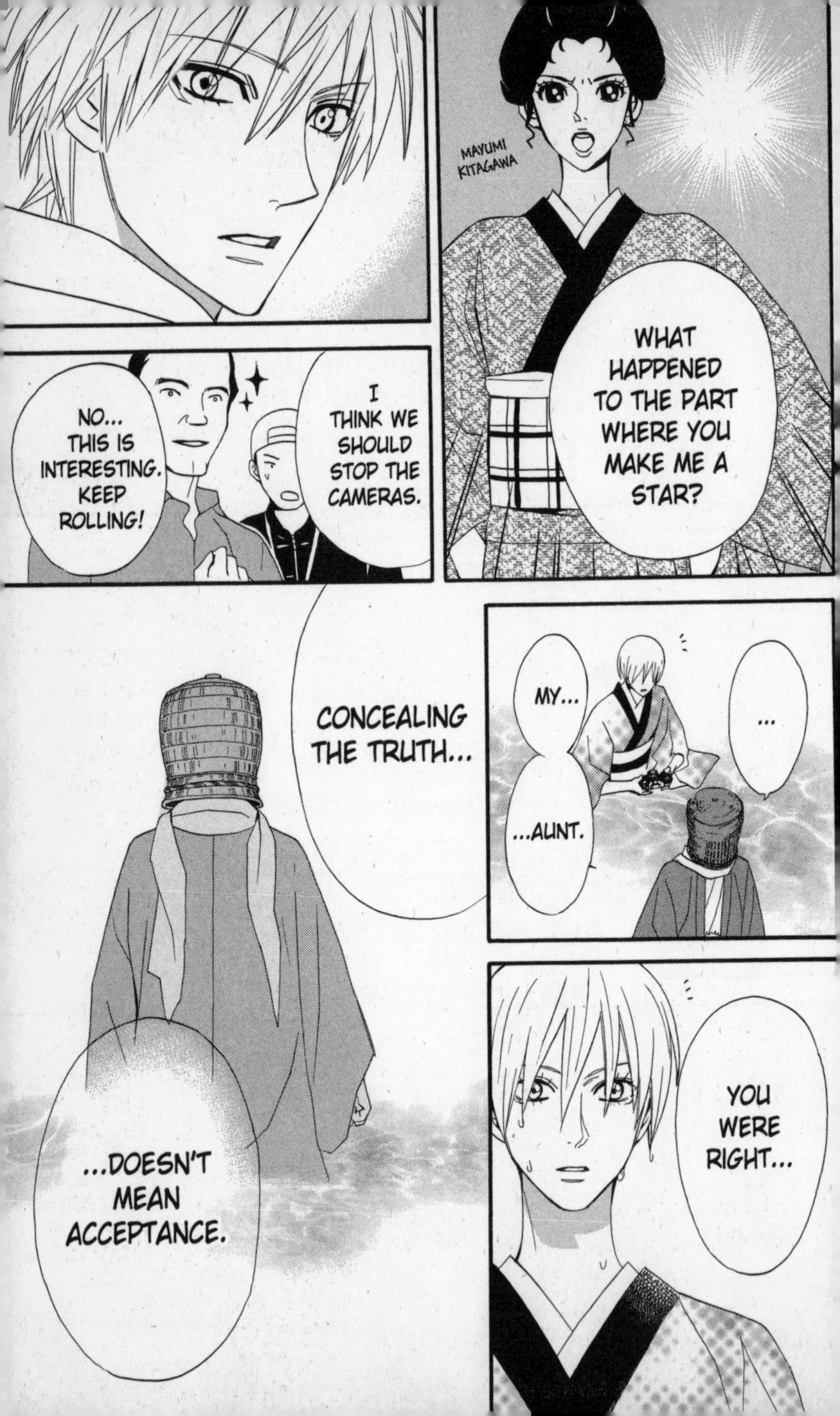
MAYUMI KITAGAWA
WHAT HAPPENED TO THE PART WHERE YOU MAKE ME A STAR?
I THINK WE SHOULD STOP THE CAMERAS.
NO... THIS IS INTERESTING. KEEP ROLLING!
...
MY...
...AUNT.
YOU WERE RIGHT...
CONCEALING THE TRUTH...
...DOESN'T MEAN ACCEPTANCE.

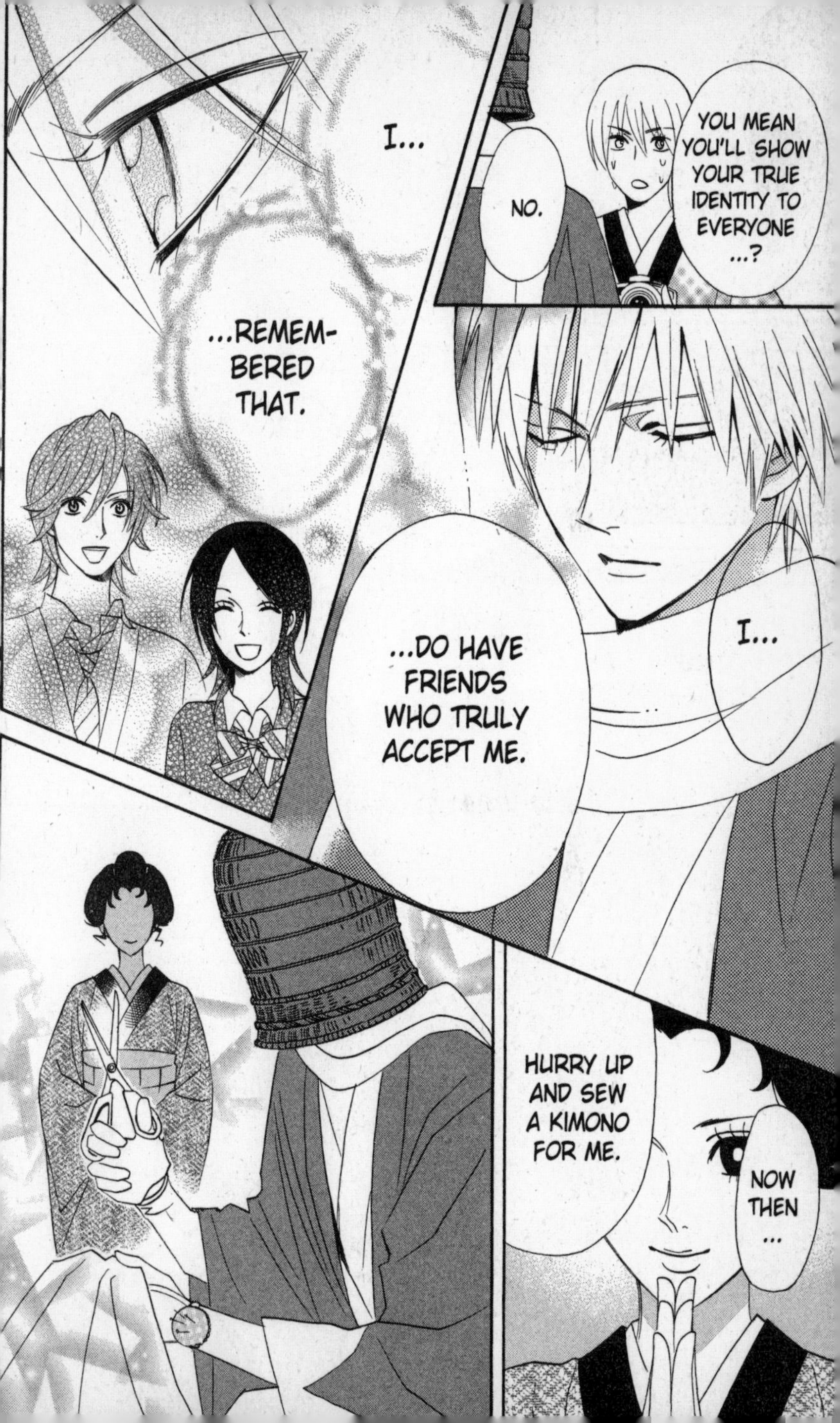

YOU MEAN YOU'LL SHOW YOUR TRUE IDENTITY TO EVERYONE ...?
NO.
I...
...DO HAVE FRIENDS WHO TRULY ACCEPT ME.
I...
...REMEM-BERED THAT.
NOW THEN ...
HURRY UP AND SEW A KIMONO FOR ME.

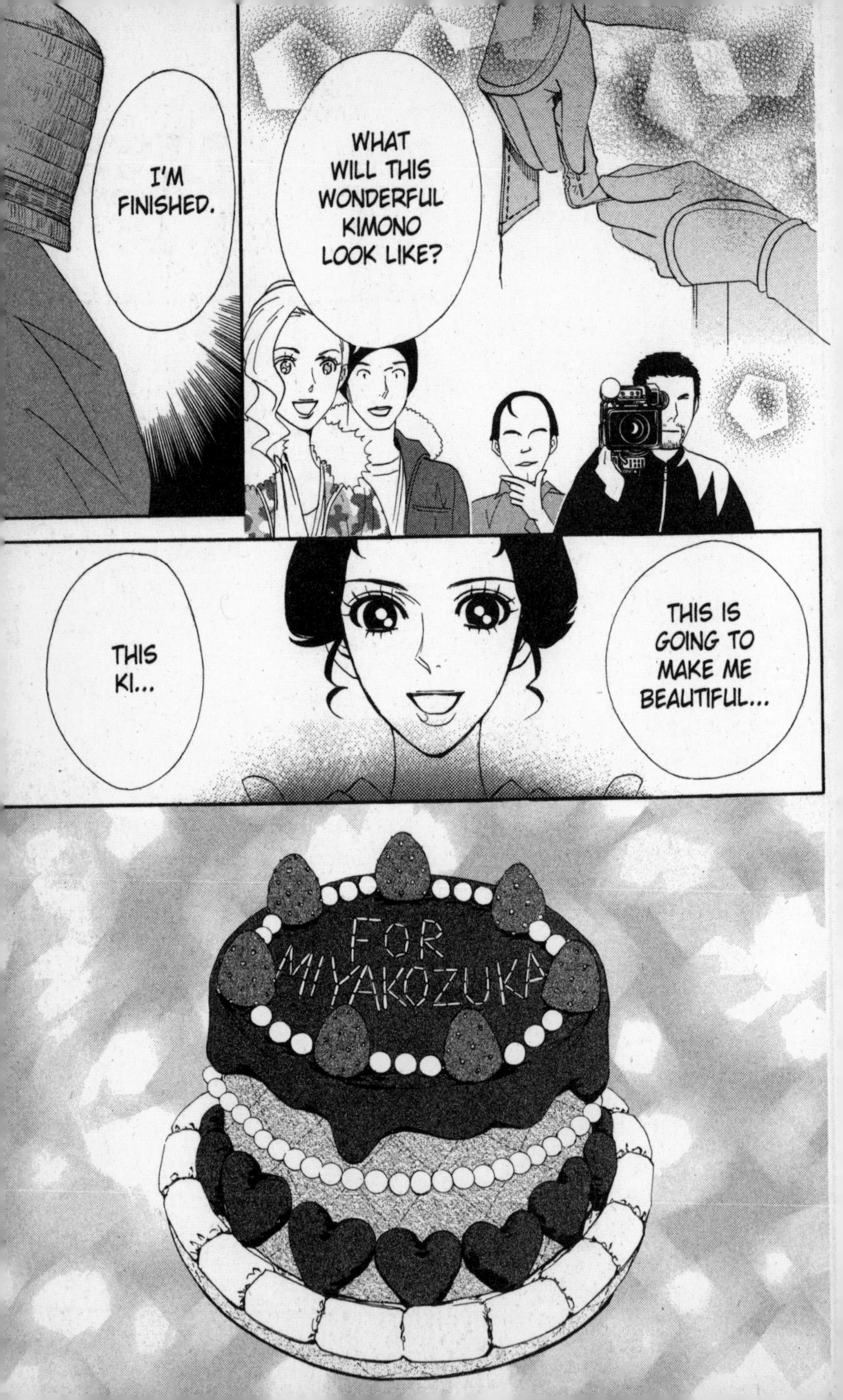
WHAT WILL THIS WONDERFUL KIMONO LOOK LIKE?
I'M FINISHED.
THIS IS GOING TO MAKE ME BEAUTIFUL...
THIS KI...
FOR MIYAKOZUKA

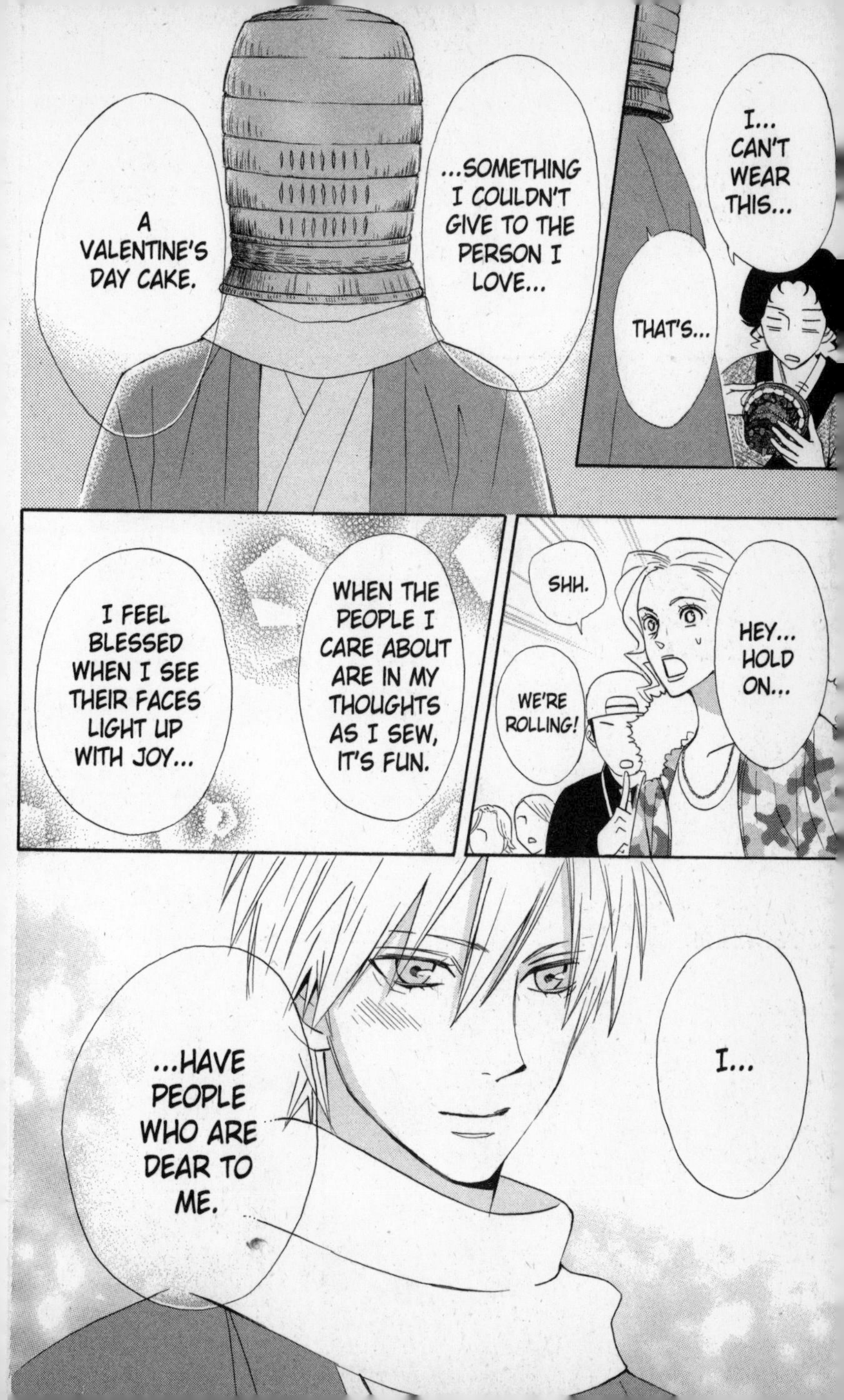
I... CAN'T WEAR THIS...
THAT'S...
...SOMETHING I COULDN'T GIVE TO THE PERSON I LOVE...
A VALENTINE'S DAY CAKE.
HEY... HOLD ON...
SHH.
WE'RE ROLLING!
WHEN THE PEOPLE I CARE ABOUT ARE IN MY THOUGHTS AS I SEW, IT'S FUN.
I FEEL BLESSED WHEN I SEE THEIR FACES LIGHT UP WITH JOY...
I...
...HAVE PEOPLE WHO ARE DEAR TO ME.

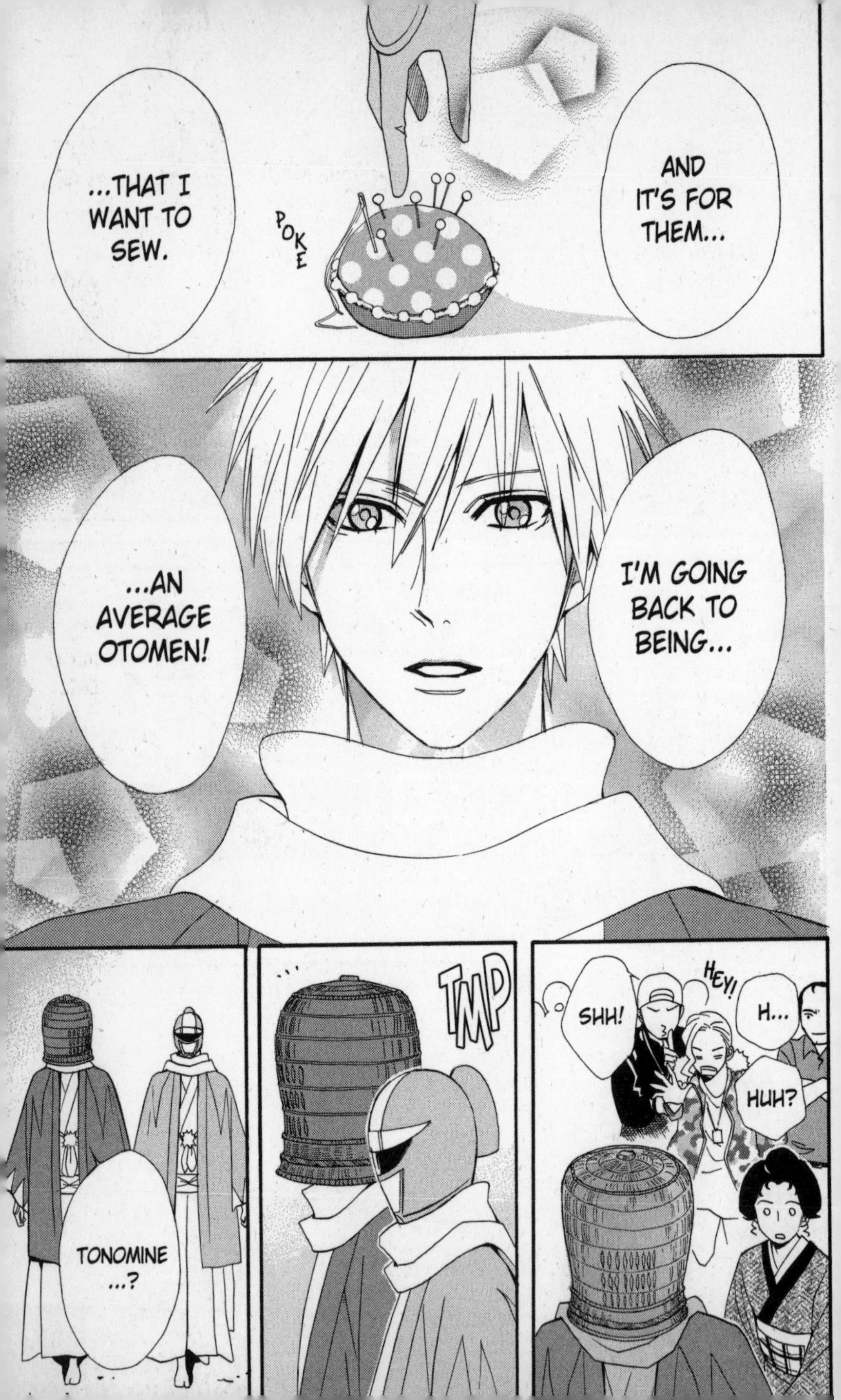
AND IT'S FOR THEM...
POKE
...THAT I WANT TO SEW.
I'M GOING BACK TO BEING...
...AN AVERAGE OTOMEN!
H...
HEY!
SHH!
HUH?
TMP
TONOMINE ...?

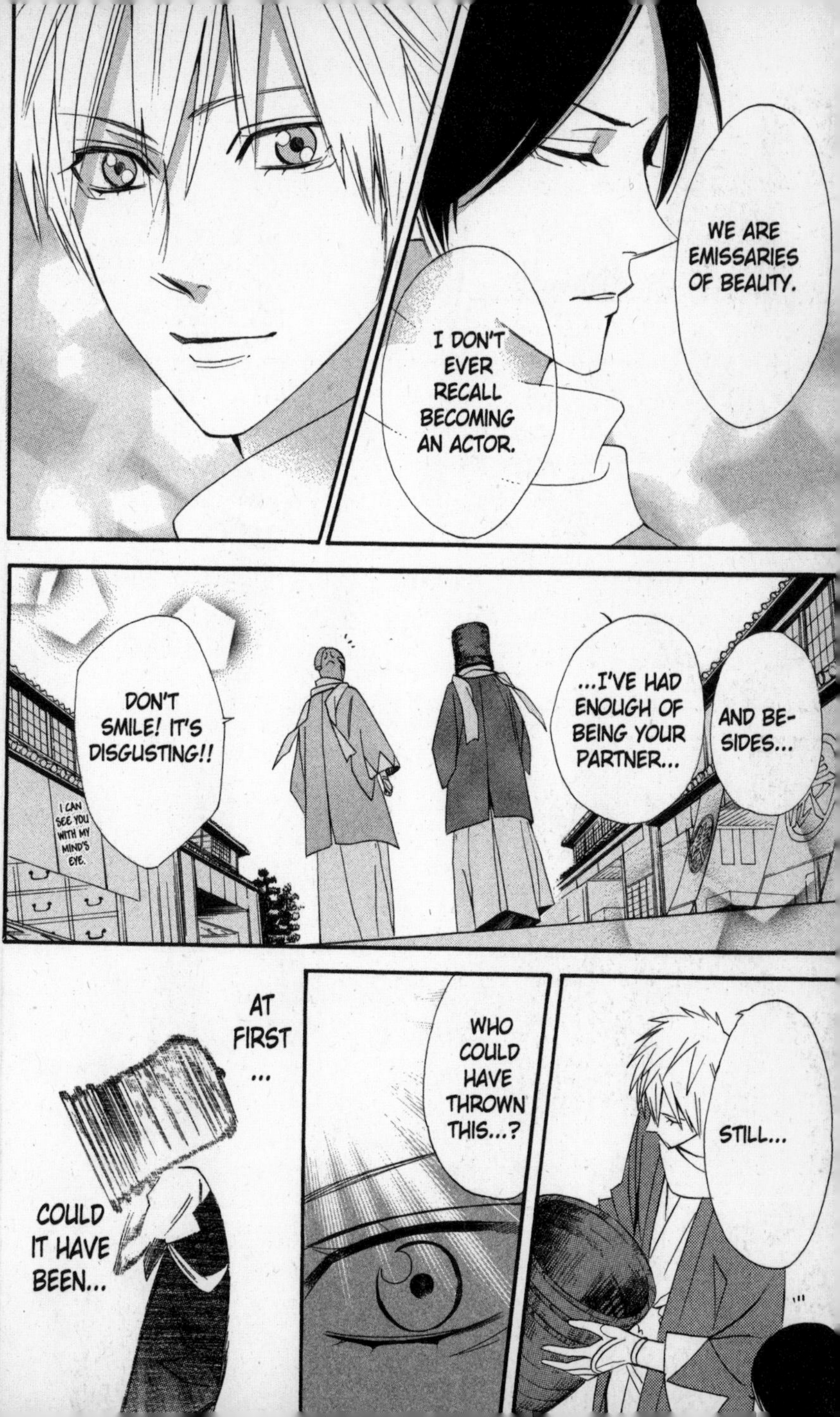
WE ARE EMISSARIES OF BEAUTY.
I DON'T EVER RECALL BECOMING AN ACTOR.
AND BE-SIDES...
...I'VE HAD ENOUGH OF BEING YOUR PARTNER...
DON'T SMILE! IT'S DISGUSTING!!
I CAN SEE YOU WITH MY MIND'S EYE.
STILL...
...
WHO COULD HAVE THROWN THIS...?
AT FIRST...
COULD IT HAVE BEEN...

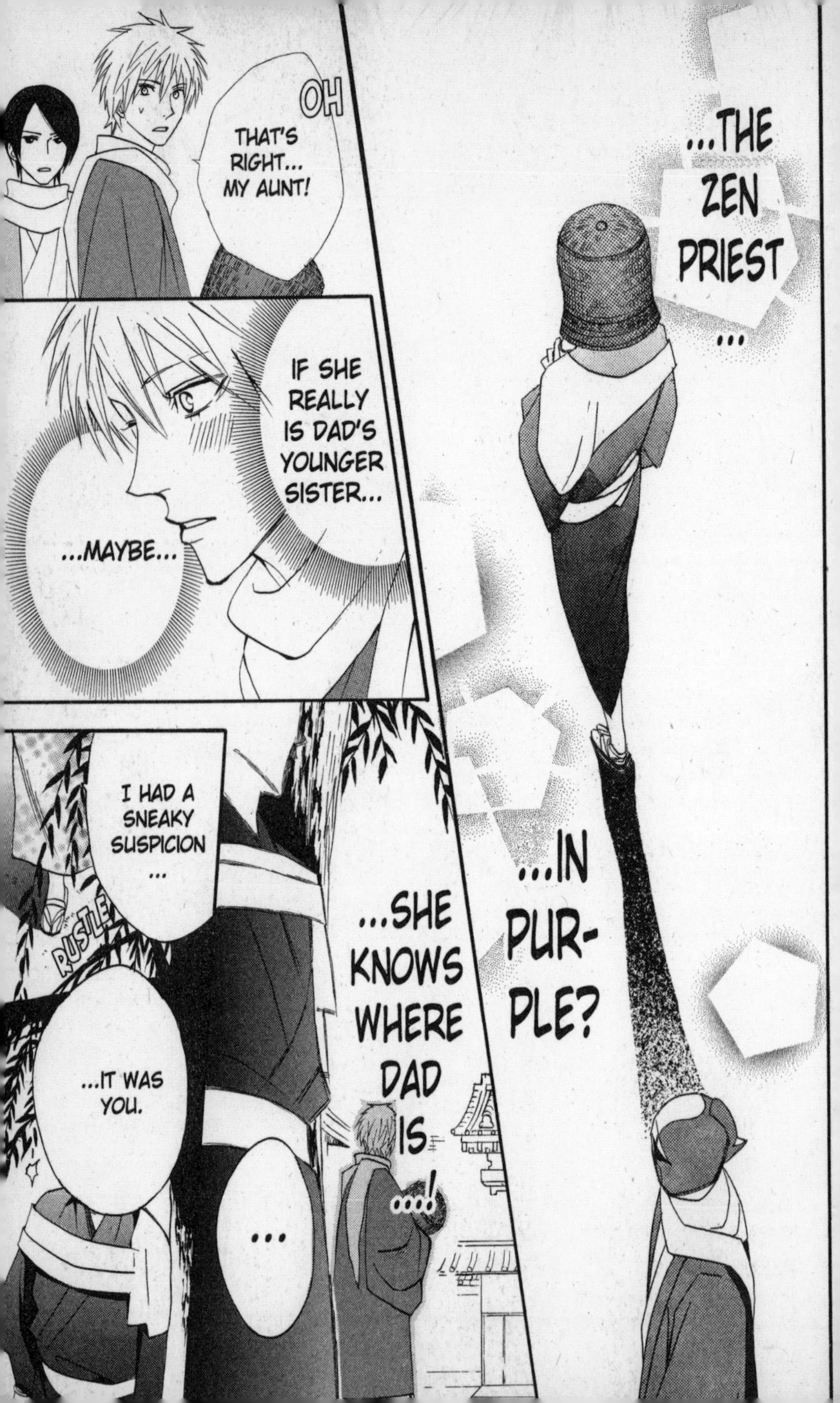
...THE ZEN PRIEST ...
...IN PUR-PLE?
OH
THAT'S RIGHT... MY AUNT!
IF SHE REALLY IS DAD'S YOUNGER SISTER...
...MAYBE...
...SHE KNOWS WHERE DAD IS...!
I HAD A SNEAKY SUSPICION ...
RUSTLE
...IT WAS YOU.
...

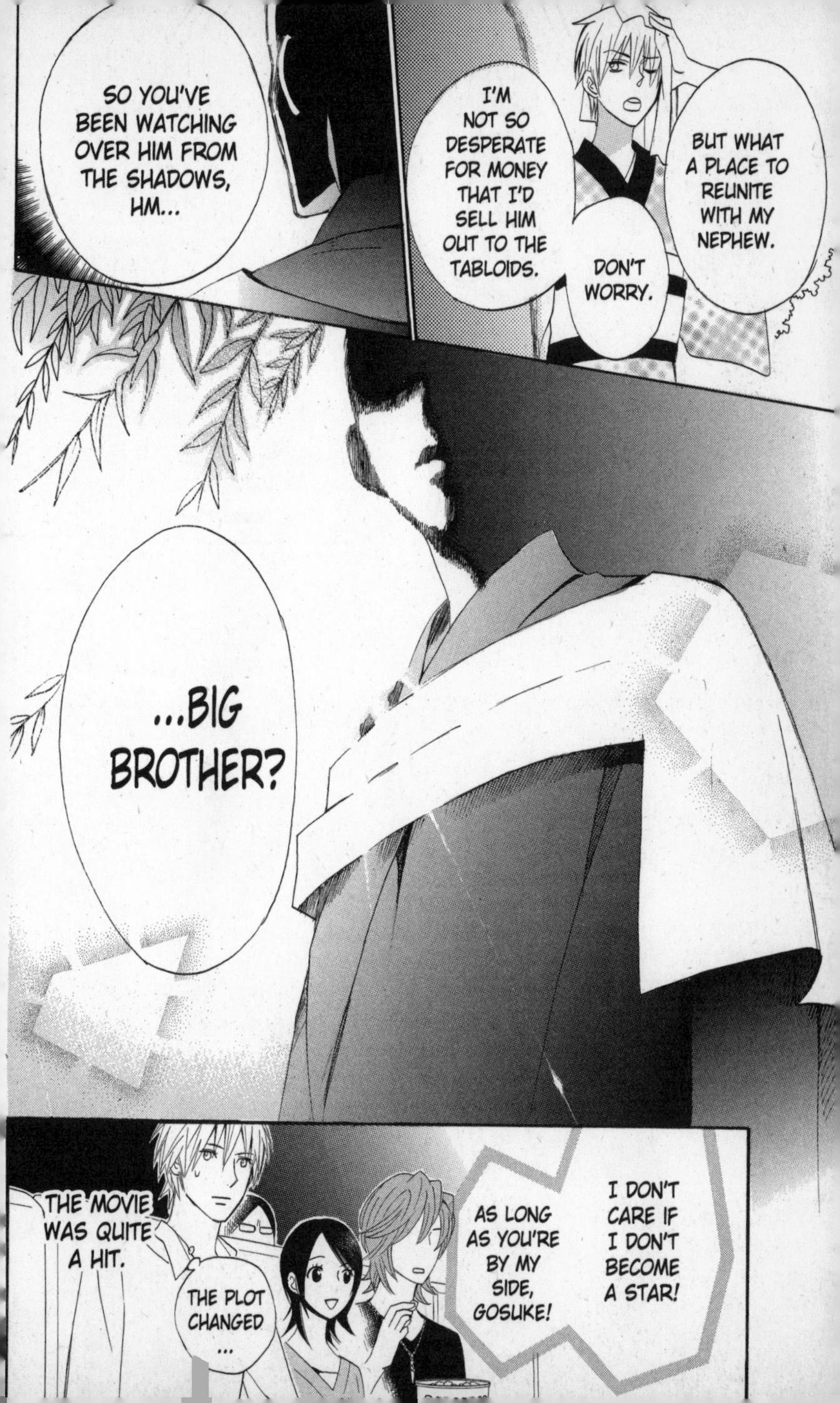
BUT WHAT A PLACE TO REUNITE WITH MY NEPHEW.
DON'T WORRY.
I'M NOT SO DESPERATE FOR MONEY THAT I'D SELL HIM OUT TO THE TABLOIDS.
SO YOU'VE BEEN WATCHING OVER HIM FROM THE SHADOWS, HM...
...BIG BROTHER?
I DON'T CARE IF I DON'T BECOME A STAR!
AS LONG AS YOU'RE BY MY SIDE, GOSUKE!
THE MOVIE WAS QUITE A HIT.
THE PLOT CHANGED ...

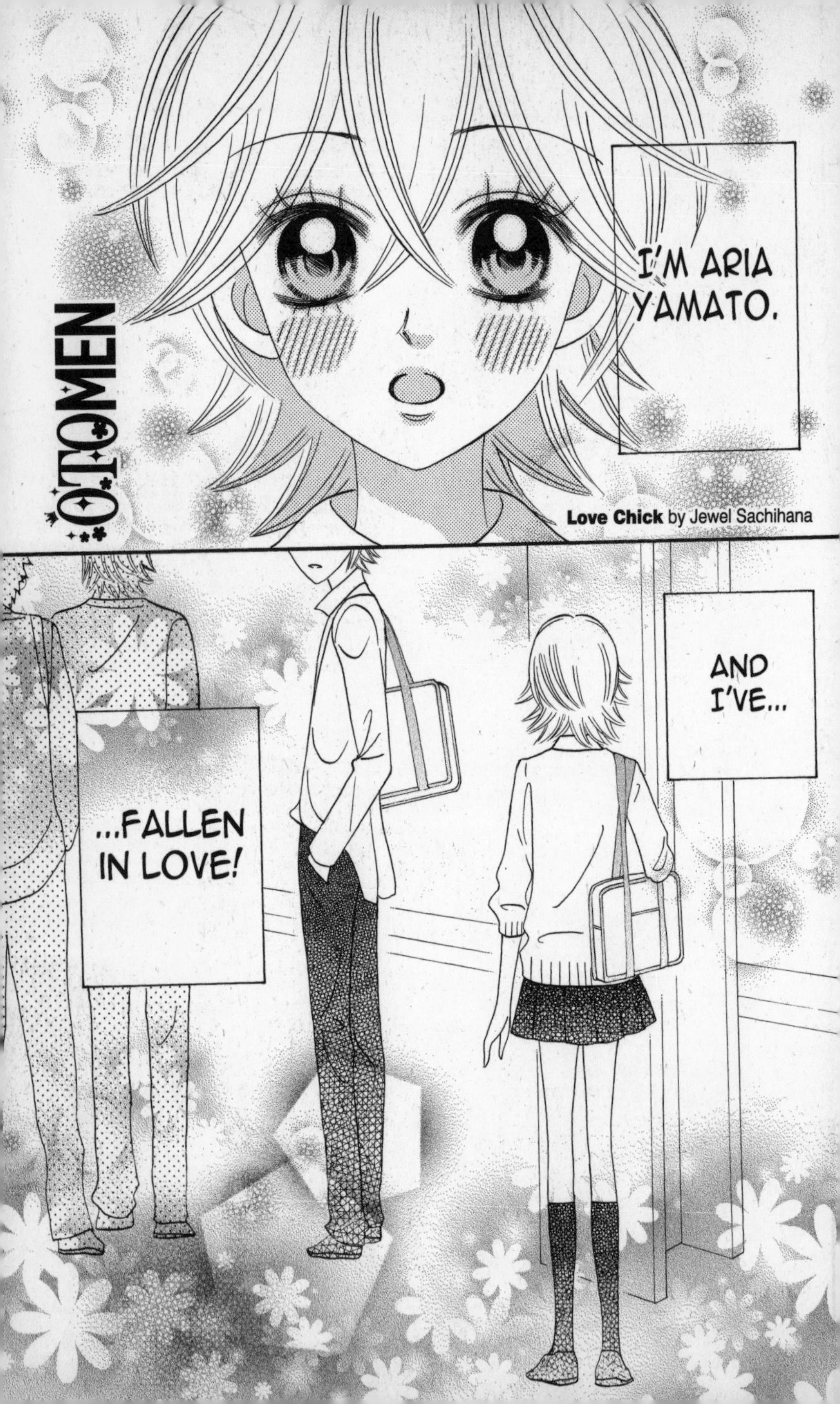
I'M ARIA YAMATO.
OTOMEN
Love Chick by Jewel Sachihana
AND I'VE...
...FALLEN IN LOVE!

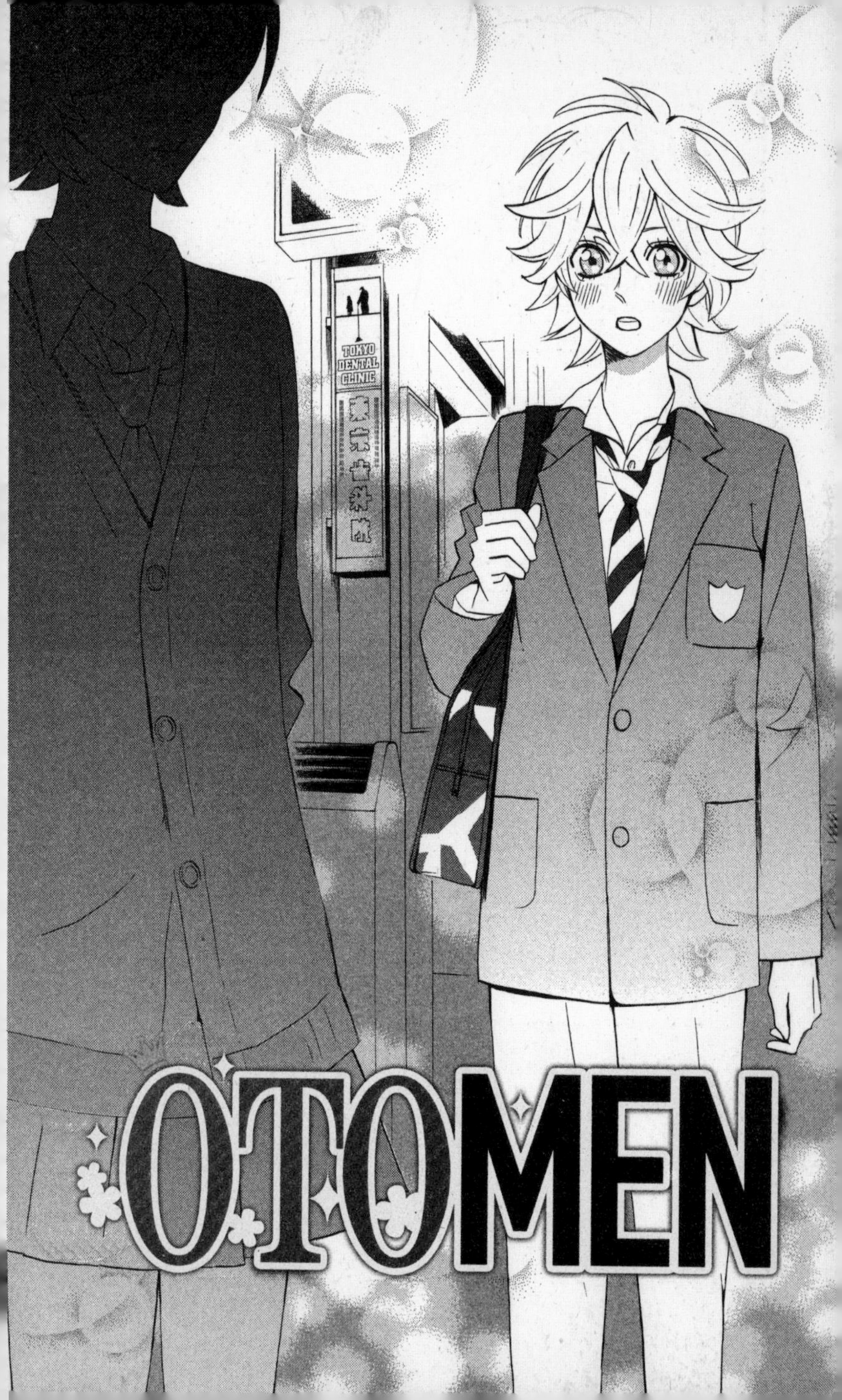
TOKYO DENTAL CLINIC
OTOMEN

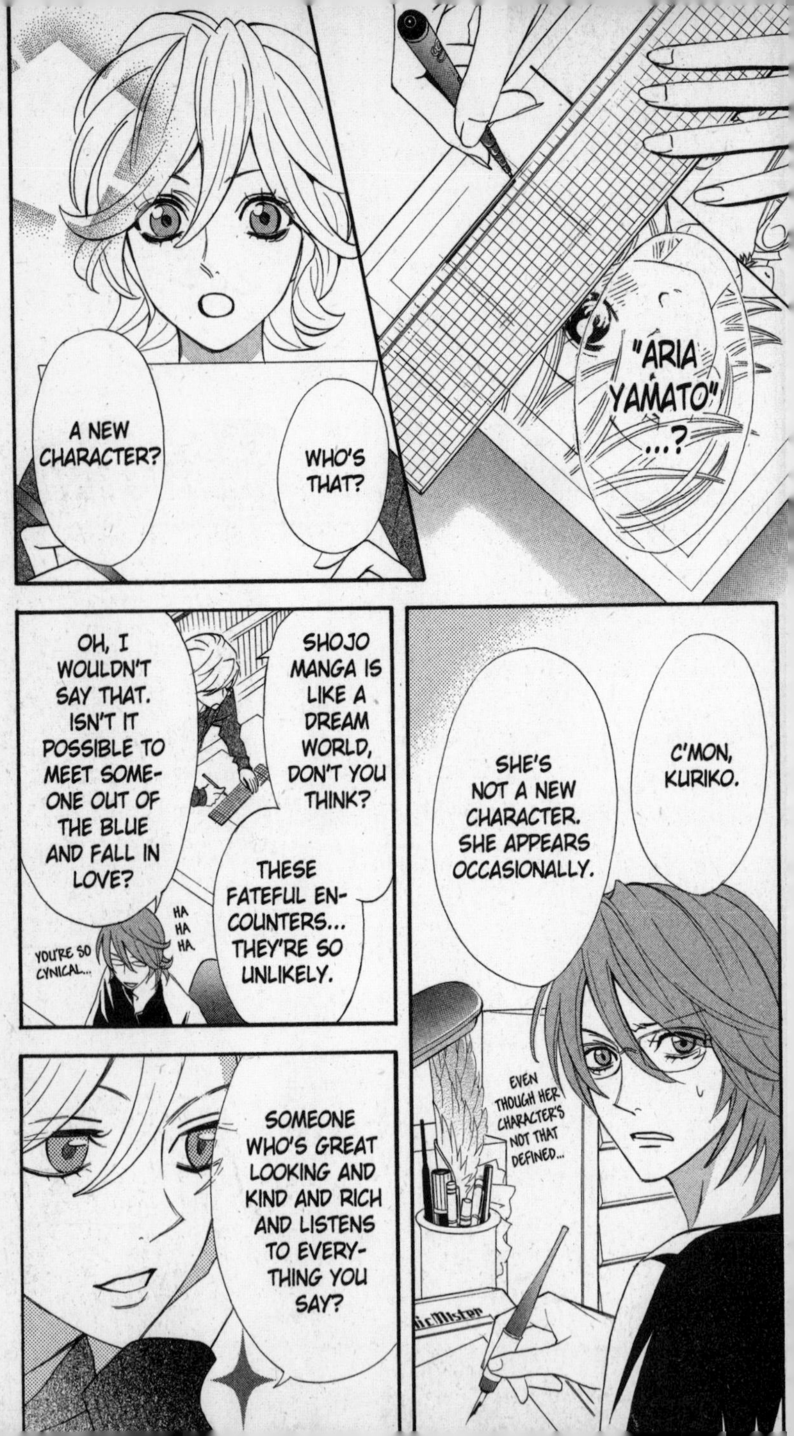
"ARIA YAMATO" ...?
WHO'S THAT?
A NEW CHARACTER?
C'MON, KURIKO.
SHE'S NOT A NEW CHARACTER. SHE APPEARS OCCASIONALLY.
EVEN THOUGH HER CHARACTER'S NOT THAT DEFINED...
SHOJO MANGA IS LIKE A DREAM WORLD, DON'T YOU THINK?
OH, I WOULDN'T SAY THAT. ISN'T IT POSSIBLE TO MEET SOME-ONE OUT OF THE BLUE AND FALL IN LOVE?
THESE FATEFUL EN-COUNTERS... THEY'RE SO UNLIKELY.
HA HA HA.
YOU'RE SO CYNICAL...
SOMEONE WHO'S GREAT LOOKING AND KIND AND RICH AND LISTENS TO EVERY-THING YOU SAY?

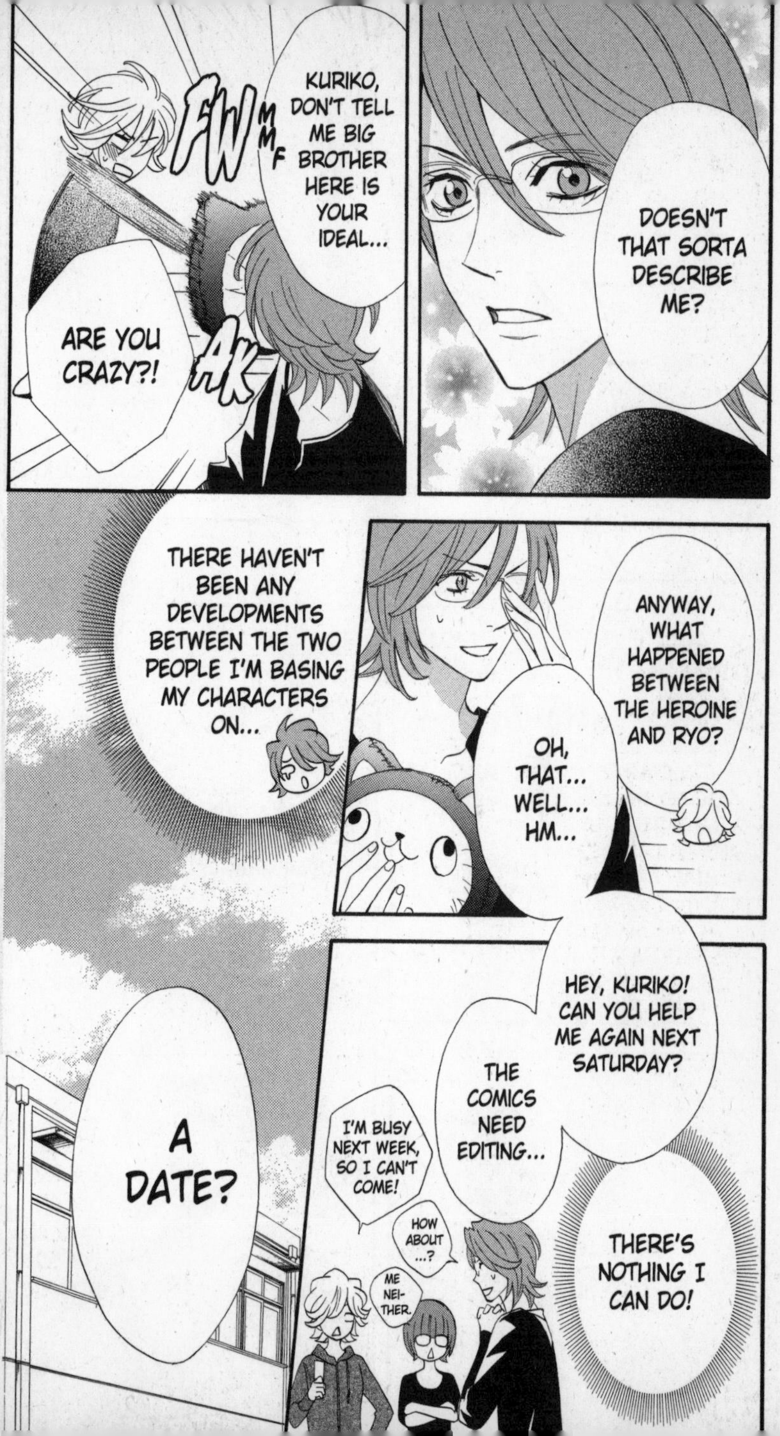
DOESN'T THAT SORTA DESCRIBE ME?
KURIKO, DON'T TELL ME BIG BROTHER HERE IS YOUR IDEAL...
FWMMF
ARE YOU CRAZY?!
AK
ANYWAY, WHAT HAPPENED BETWEEN THE HEROINE AND RYO?
OH, THAT... WELL... HM...
HEY, KURIKO! CAN YOU HELP ME AGAIN NEXT SATURDAY?
THE COMICS NEED EDITING...
THERE'S NOTHING I CAN DO!
HOW ABOUT ...?
I'M BUSY NEXT WEEK, SO I CAN'T COME!
ME NEITHER.
THERE HAVEN'T BEEN ANY DEVELOPMENTS BETWEEN THE TWO PEOPLE I'M BASING MY CHARACTERS ON...
A DATE?

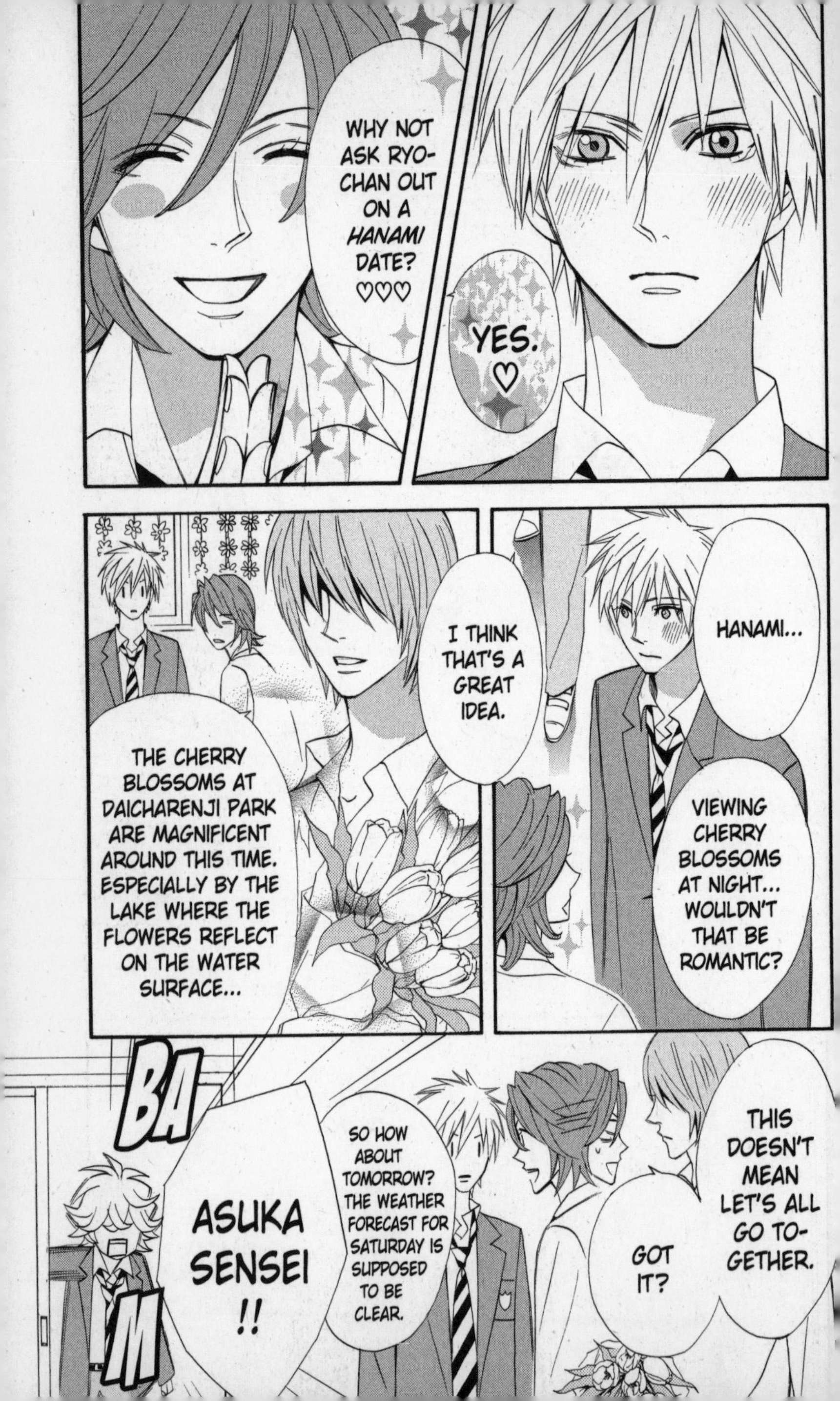
YES. ♡
WHY NOT ASK RYO-CHAN OUT ON A *HANAMI* DATE? ♡♡♡
HANAMI...
VIEWING CHERRY BLOSSOMS AT NIGHT... WOULDN'T THAT BE ROMANTIC?
I THINK THAT'S A GREAT IDEA.
THE CHERRY BLOSSOMS AT DAICHARENJI PARK ARE MAGNIFICENT AROUND THIS TIME. ESPECIALLY BY THE LAKE WHERE THE FLOWERS REFLECT ON THE WATER SURFACE...
THIS DOESN'T MEAN LET'S ALL GO TO-GETHER.
GOT IT?
SO HOW ABOUT TOMORROW? THE WEATHER FORECAST FOR SATURDAY IS SUPPOSED TO BE CLEAR.
ASUKA SENSEI !!
BAM

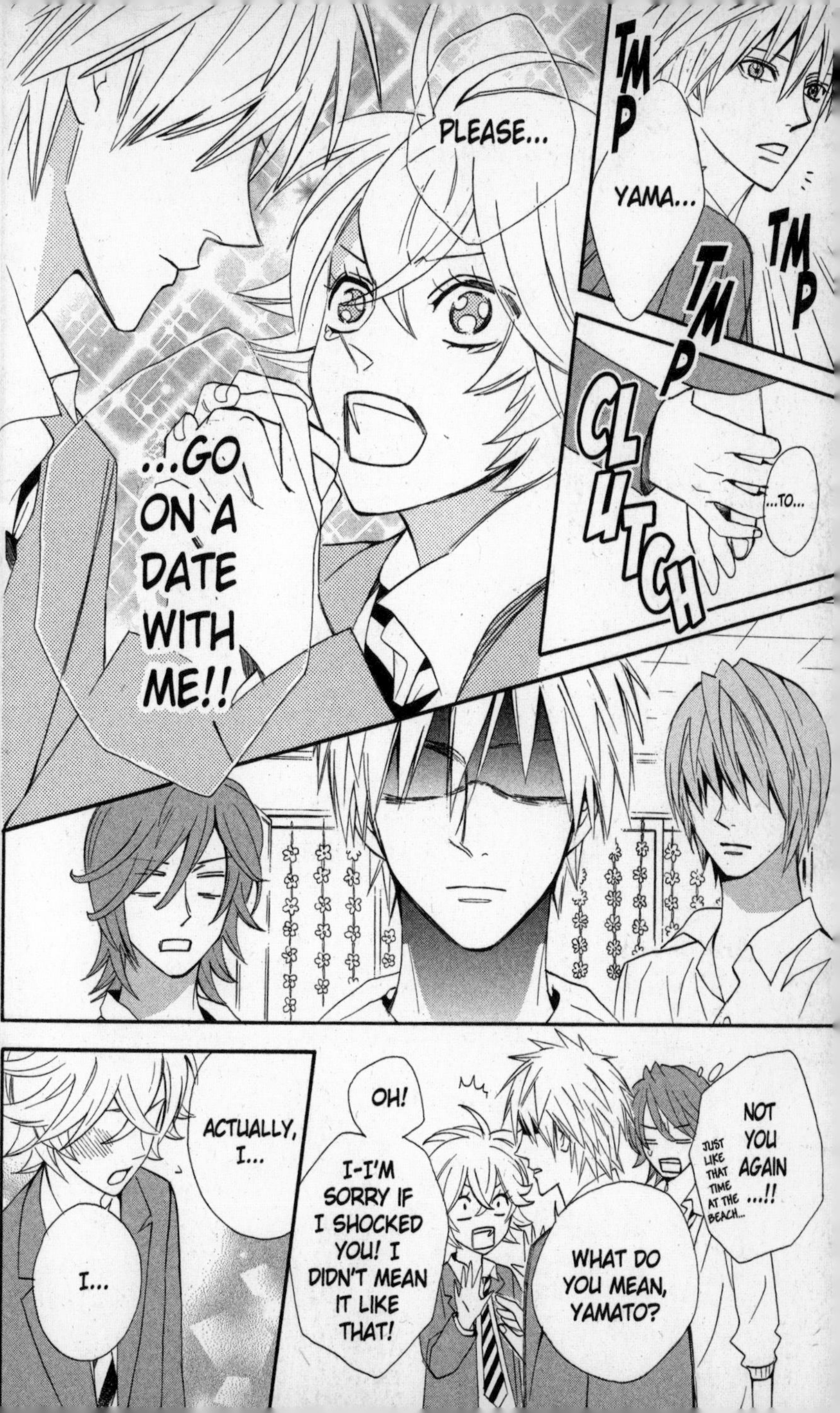
TMP
YAMA...
TMP
TMP
CLUTCH
...TO...
PLEASE...
...GO ON A DATE WITH ME!!
NOT YOU AGAIN ...!!
JUST LIKE THAT TIME AT THE BEACH...
WHAT DO YOU MEAN, YAMATO?
OH!
I-I'M SORRY IF I SHOCKED YOU! I DIDN'T MEAN IT LIKE THAT!
ACTUALLY, I...
I...

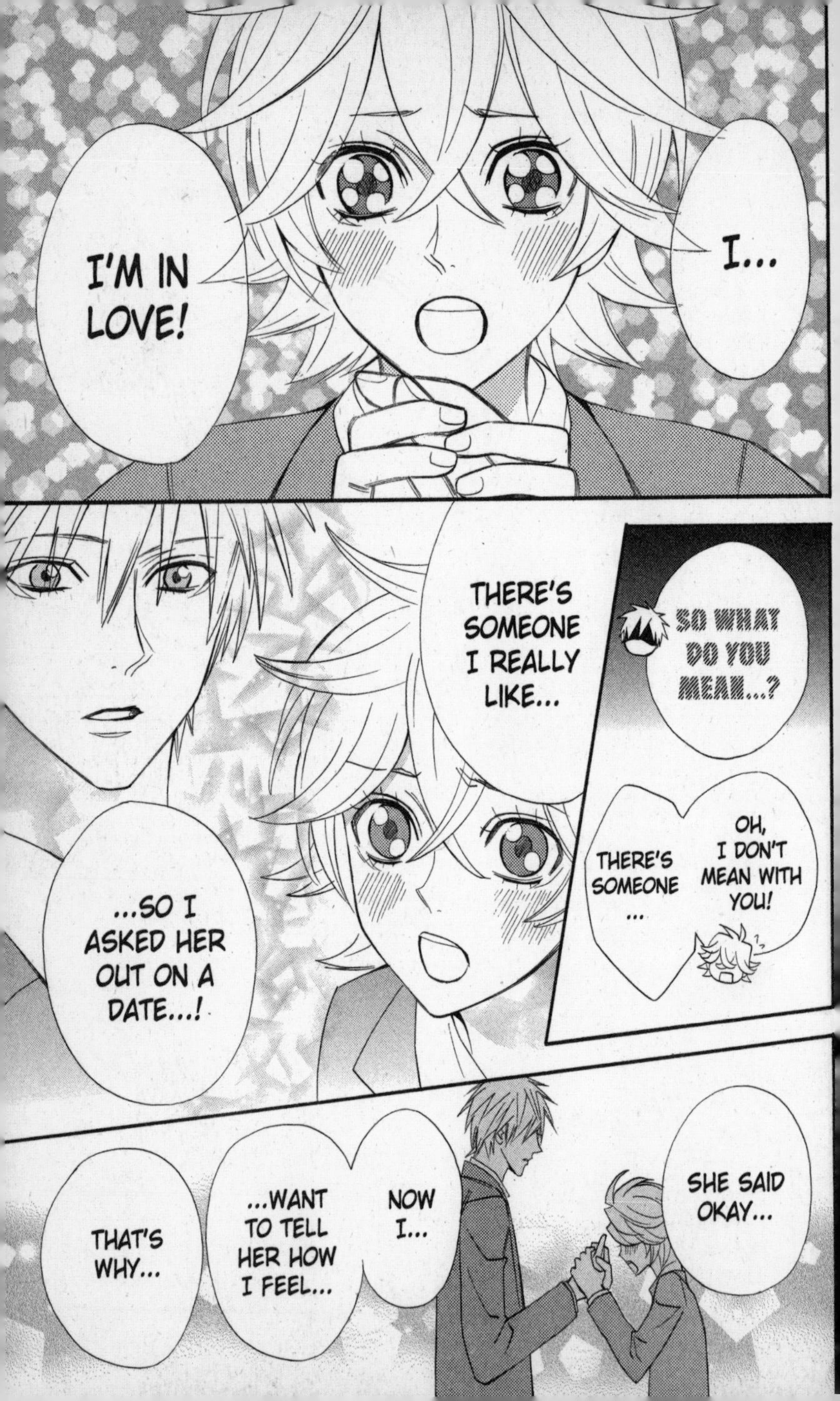
I...
I'M IN LOVE!
SO WHAT DO YOU MEAN...?
OH, I DON'T MEAN WITH YOU!
THERE'S SOMEONE ...
THERE'S SOMEONE I REALLY LIKE...
...SO I ASKED HER OUT ON A DATE...!
SHE SAID OKAY...
NOW I...
...WANT TO TELL HER HOW I FEEL...
THAT'S WHY...

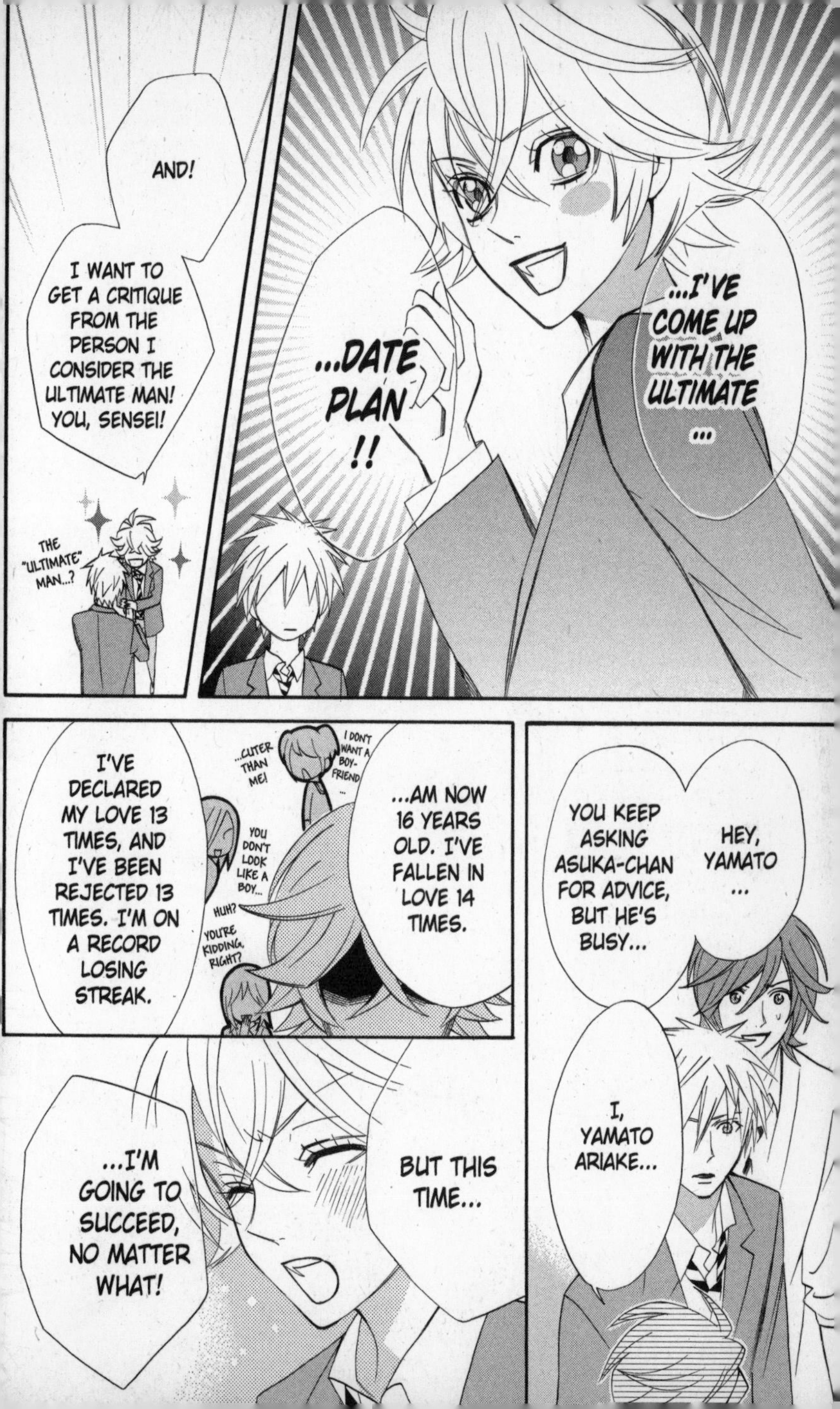

...I'VE COME UP WITH THE ULTIMATE ...
...DATE PLAN !!
AND!
I WANT TO GET A CRITIQUE FROM THE PERSON I CONSIDER THE ULTIMATE MAN! YOU, SENSEI!
THE "ULTIMATE" MAN...?
HEY, YAMATO ...
YOU KEEP ASKING ASUKA-CHAN FOR ADVICE, BUT HE'S BUSY...
I, YAMATO ARIAKE...
...AM NOW 16 YEARS OLD. I'VE FALLEN IN LOVE 14 TIMES.
I DON'T WANT A BOY-FRIEND ...
...CUTER THAN ME!
YOU DON'T LOOK LIKE A BOY...
HUH?
YOU'RE KIDDING, RIGHT?
I'VE DECLARED MY LOVE 13 TIMES, AND I'VE BEEN REJECTED 13 TIMES. I'M ON A RECORD LOSING STREAK.
BUT THIS TIME...
...I'M GOING TO SUCCEED, NO MATTER WHAT!

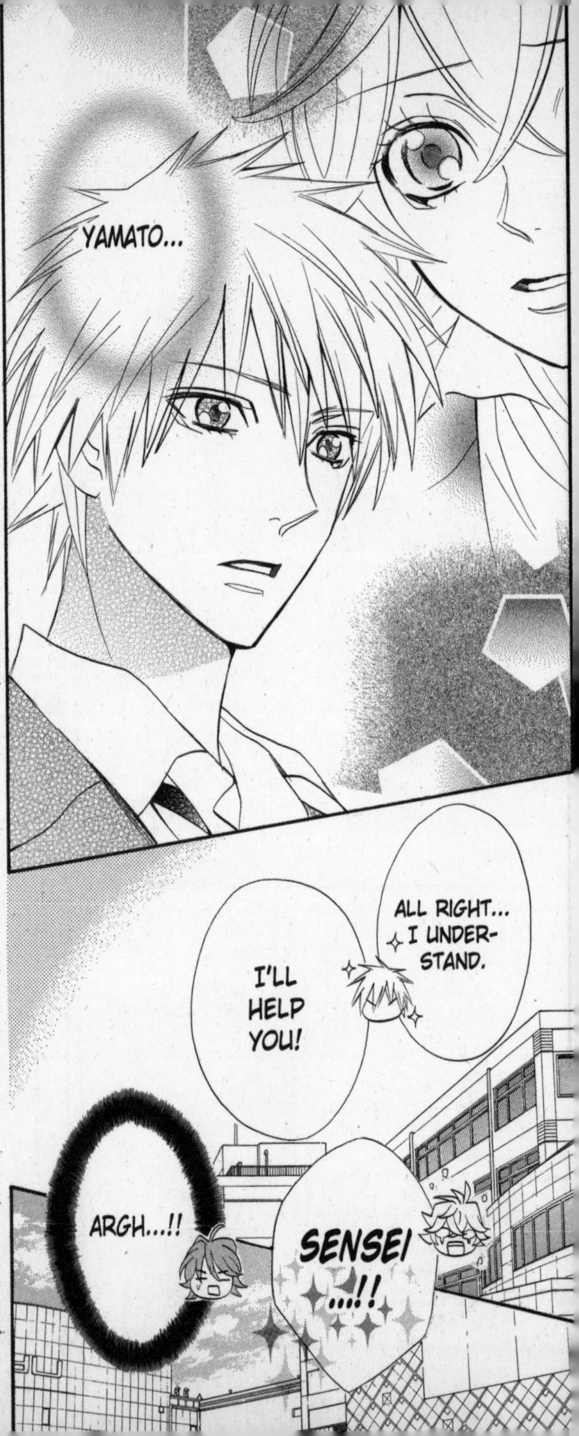
YAMATO...
ALL RIGHT... I UNDER-STAND.
I'LL HELP YOU!
SENSEI ...!!
ARGH...!!

There's a magazine called *M★n's Kn★ck★e* that I love.
By the way, I didn't notice it when I was drawing, but Yamato and Kuriko look so much alike.
The hairstyle, the face—they're almost like twins...
I realized it for the first time when my assistant pointed it out to me. I draw them separately, so I didn't realize how much their looks overlap.
Anyway, they got matched up. And I'll have to live with that.

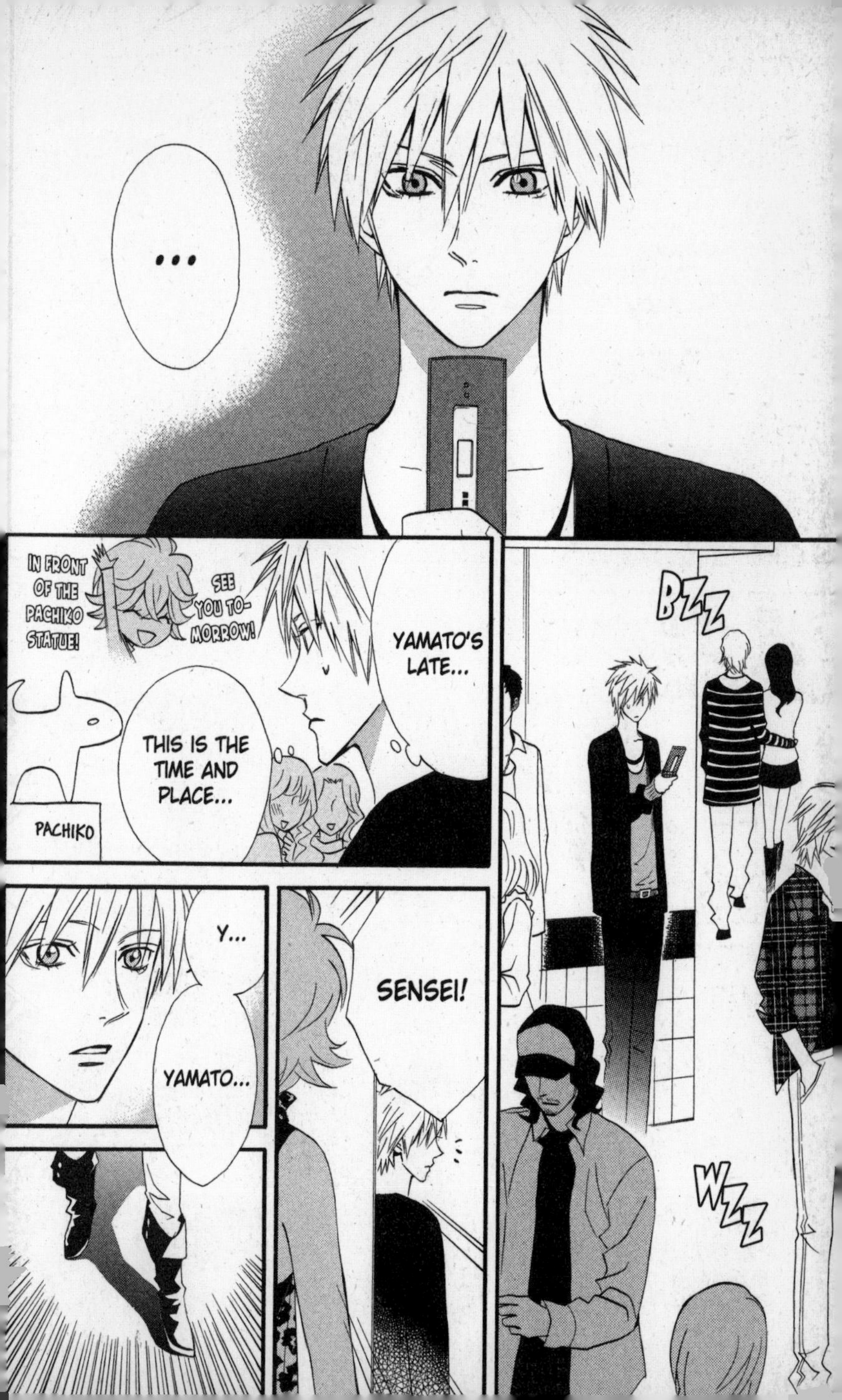
...
BZZ
WZZ
YAMATO'S LATE...
SEE YOU TO-MORROW!
IN FRONT OF THE PACHIKO STATUE!
THIS IS THE TIME AND PLACE...
PACHIKO
SENSEI!
Y...
YAMATO...

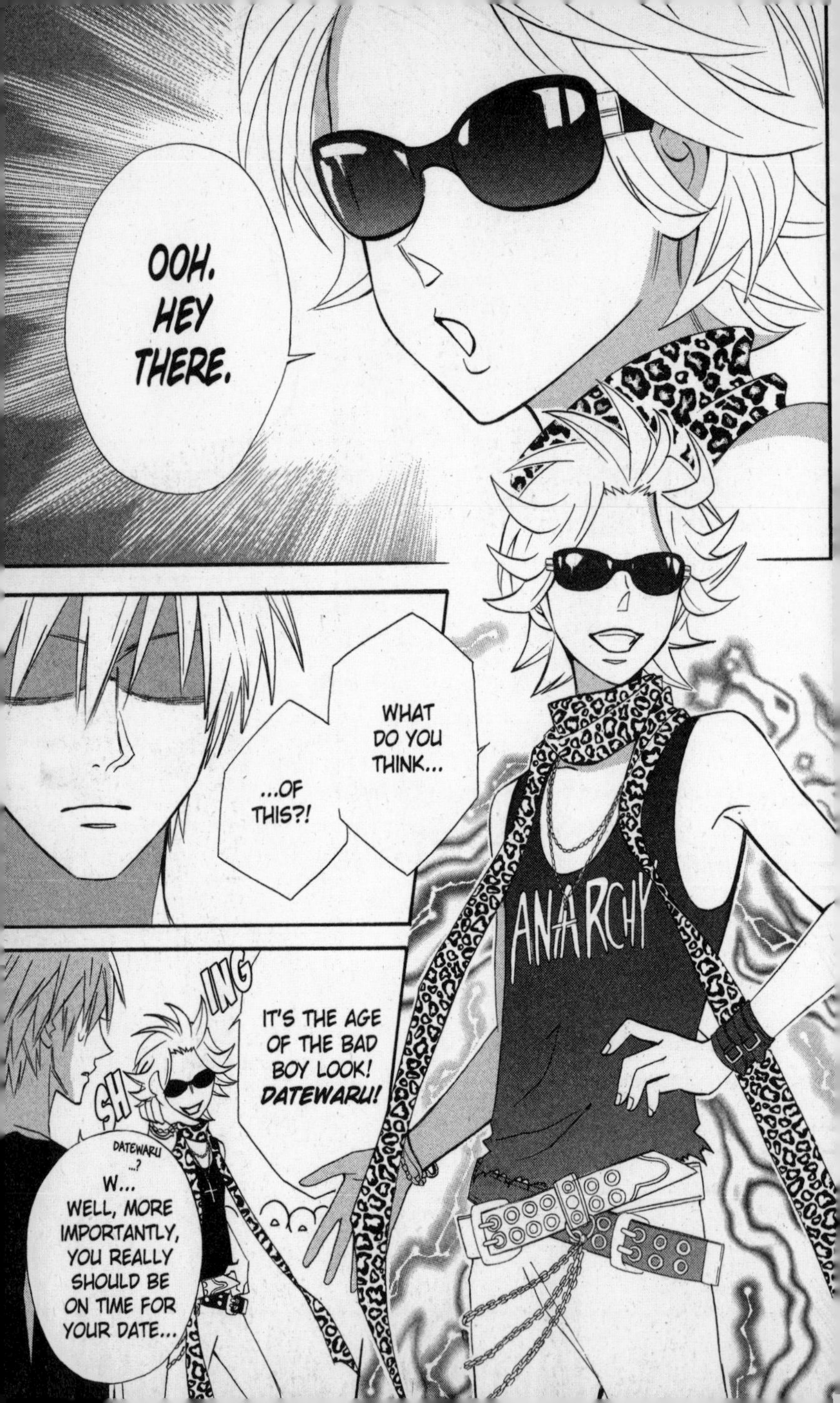

OOH. HEY THERE.
WHAT DO YOU THINK...
...OF THIS?!
IT'S THE AGE OF THE BAD BOY LOOK! **DATEWARU!**
SHING
DATEWARU ...?
W... WELL, MORE IMPORTANTLY, YOU REALLY SHOULD BE ON TIME FOR YOUR DATE...

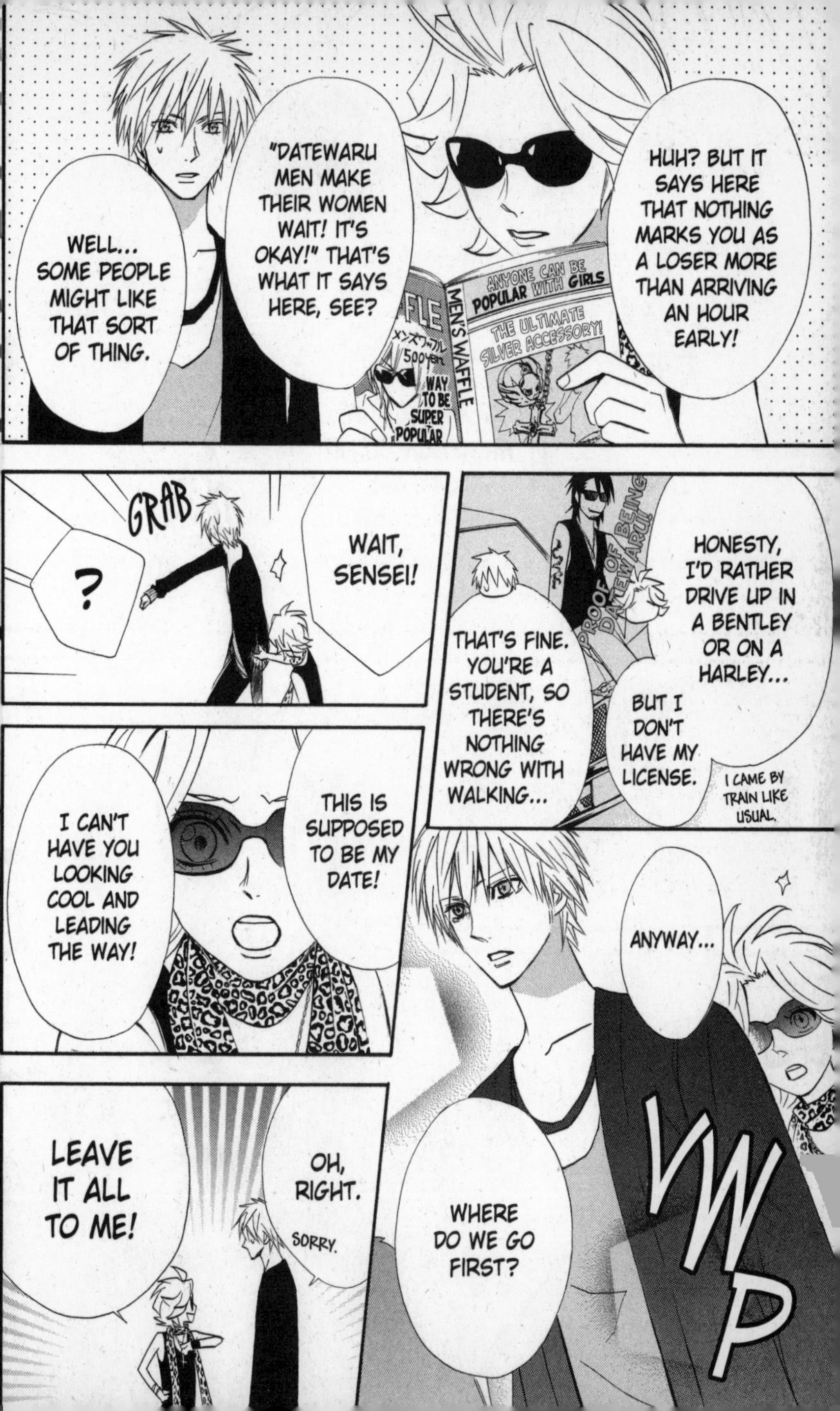
HUH? BUT IT SAYS HERE THAT NOTHING MARKS YOU AS A LOSER MORE THAN ARRIVING AN HOUR EARLY!
ANYONE CAN BE POPULAR WITH GIRLS
THE ULTIMATE SILVER ACCESSORY!
MEN'S WAFFLE
メンズワッフル 500yen
WAY TO BE SUPER POPULAR
"DATEWARU MEN MAKE THEIR WOMEN WAIT! IT'S OKAY!" THAT'S WHAT IT SAYS HERE, SEE?
WELL... SOME PEOPLE MIGHT LIKE THAT SORT OF THING.
HONESTY, I'D RATHER DRIVE UP IN A BENTLEY OR ON A HARLEY...
PROOF OF BEING DATEWARU!
BUT I DON'T HAVE MY LICENSE.
I CAME BY TRAIN LIKE USUAL.
THAT'S FINE. YOU'RE A STUDENT, SO THERE'S NOTHING WRONG WITH WALKING...
WAIT, SENSEI!
GRAB
?
THIS IS SUPPOSED TO BE MY DATE!
I CAN'T HAVE YOU LOOKING COOL AND LEADING THE WAY!
ANYWAY...
WHERE DO WE GO FIRST?
VWP
OH, RIGHT.
SORRY.
LEAVE IT ALL TO ME!

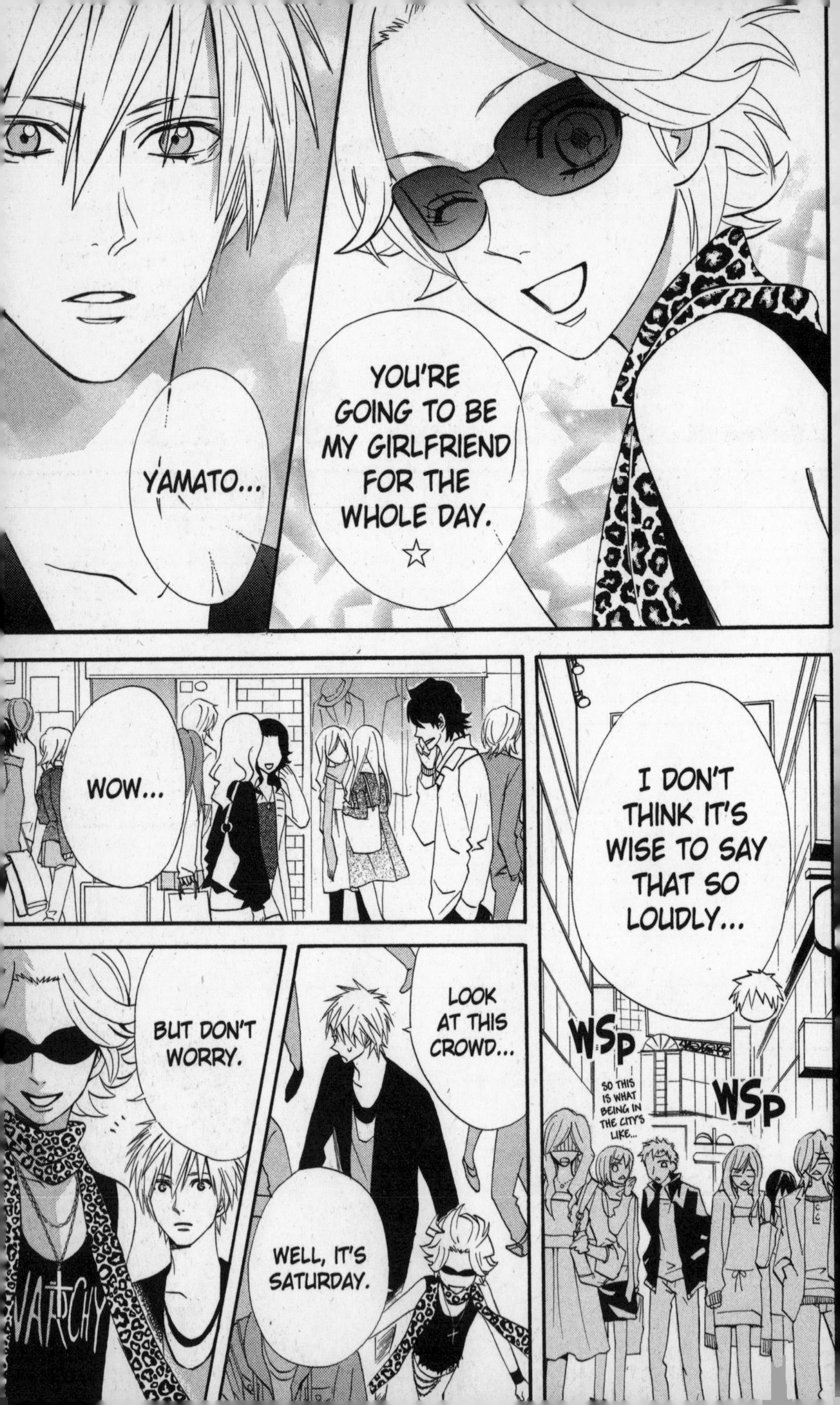
YOU'RE GOING TO BE MY GIRLFRIEND FOR THE WHOLE DAY. ☆
YAMATO...
I DON'T THINK IT'S WISE TO SAY THAT SO LOUDLY...
WSP
SO THIS IS WHAT BEING IN THE CITY'S LIKE...
WSP
WOW...
LOOK AT THIS CROWD...
WELL, IT'S SATURDAY.
BUT DON'T WORRY.

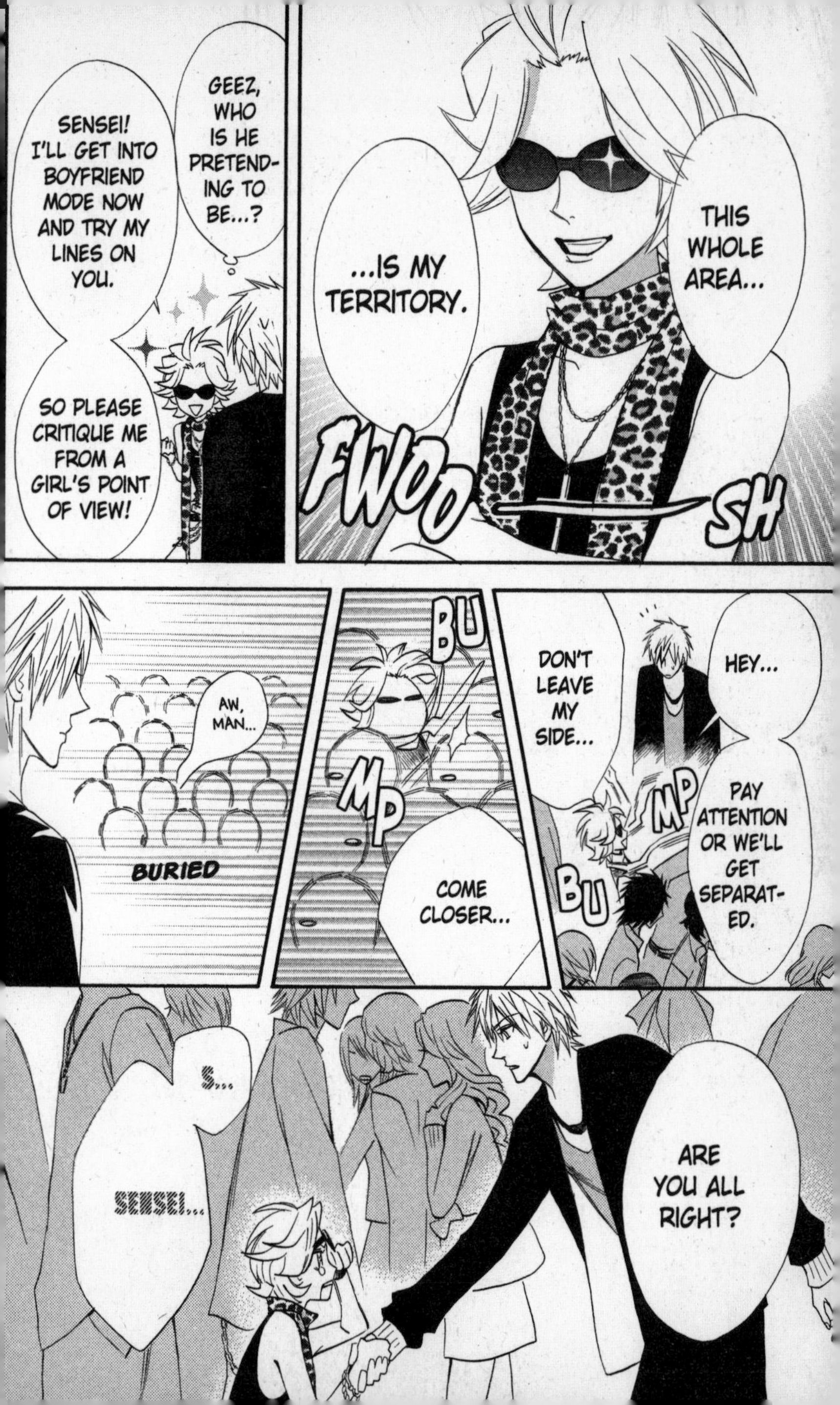
THIS WHOLE AREA...
...IS MY TERRITORY.
FWOOSH
GEEZ, WHO IS HE PRETENDING TO BE...?
SENSEI! I'LL GET INTO BOYFRIEND MODE NOW AND TRY MY LINES ON YOU.
SO PLEASE CRITIQUE ME FROM A GIRL'S POINT OF VIEW!
HEY...
PAY ATTENTION OR WE'LL GET SEPARATED.
DON'T LEAVE MY SIDE...
BUMP
BUMP
COME CLOSER...
AW, MAN...
BURIED
ARE YOU ALL RIGHT?
S...
SENSEI...

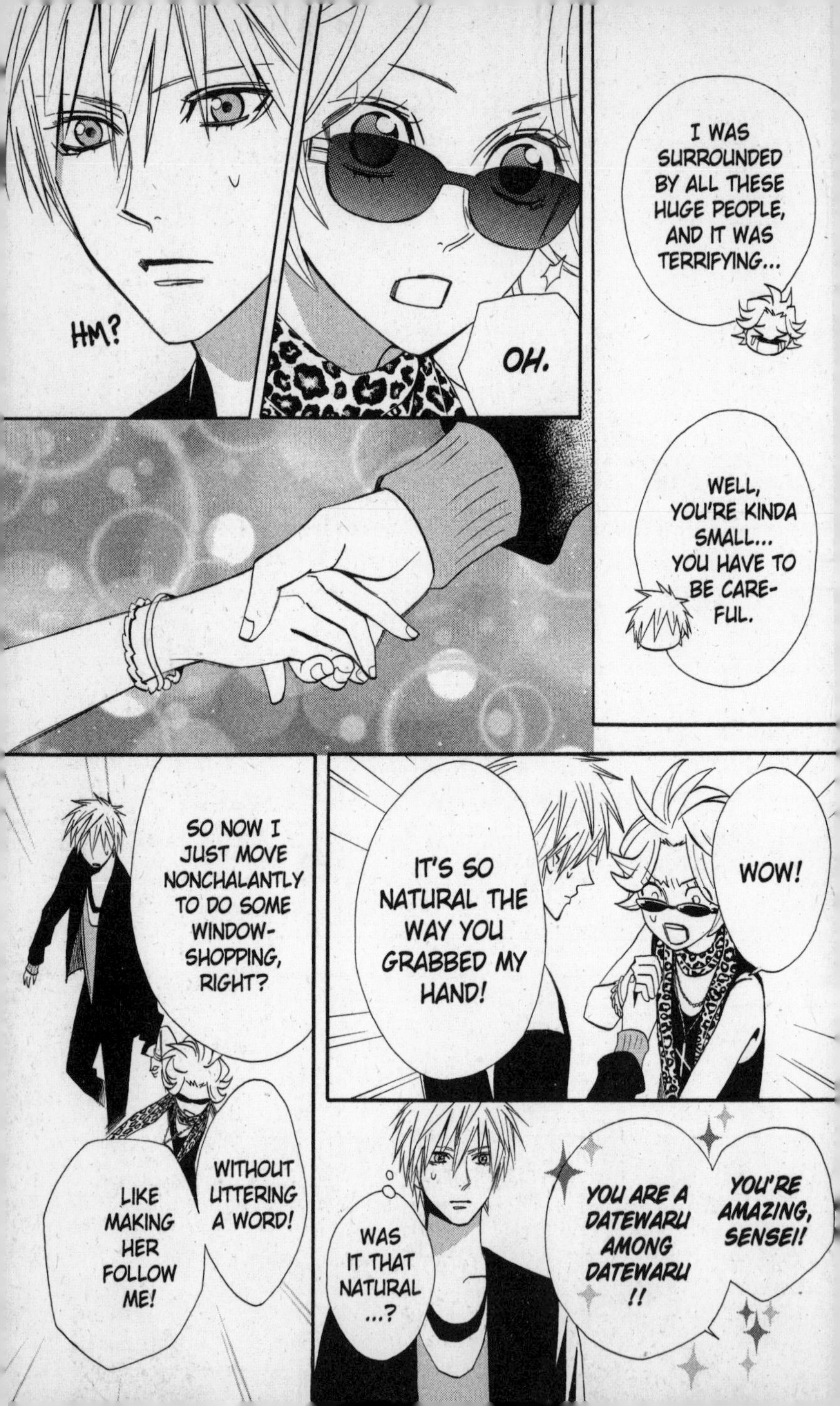
I WAS SURROUNDED BY ALL THESE HUGE PEOPLE, AND IT WAS TERRIFYING...
WELL, YOU'RE KINDA SMALL... YOU HAVE TO BE CARE-FUL.
OH.
HM?
WOW!
IT'S SO NATURAL THE WAY YOU GRABBED MY HAND!
YOU'RE AMAZING, SENSEI!
YOU ARE A DATEWARU AMONG DATEWARU!!
WAS IT THAT NATURAL...?
SO NOW I JUST MOVE NONCHALANTLY TO DO SOME WINDOW-SHOPPING, RIGHT?
WITHOUT UTTERING A WORD!
LIKE MAKING HER FOLLOW ME!

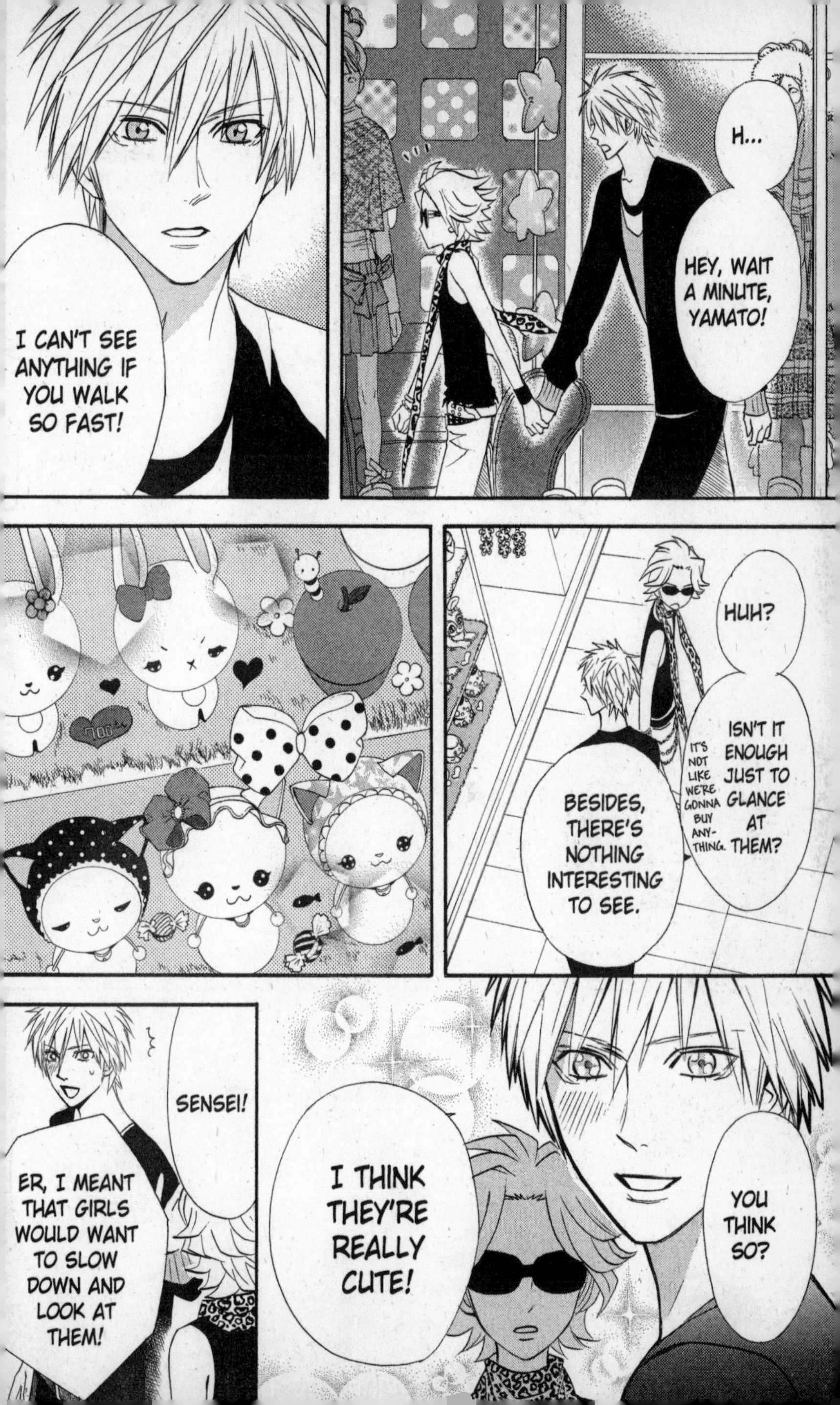
H...
HEY, WAIT A MINUTE, YAMATO!
I CAN'T SEE ANYTHING IF YOU WALK SO FAST!
HUH?
ISN'T IT ENOUGH JUST TO GLANCE AT THEM?
IT'S NOT LIKE WE'RE GONNA BUY ANY-THING.
BESIDES, THERE'S NOTHING INTERESTING TO SEE.
YOU THINK SO?
I THINK THEY'RE REALLY CUTE!
SENSEI!
ER, I MEANT THAT GIRLS WOULD WANT TO SLOW DOWN AND LOOK AT THEM!

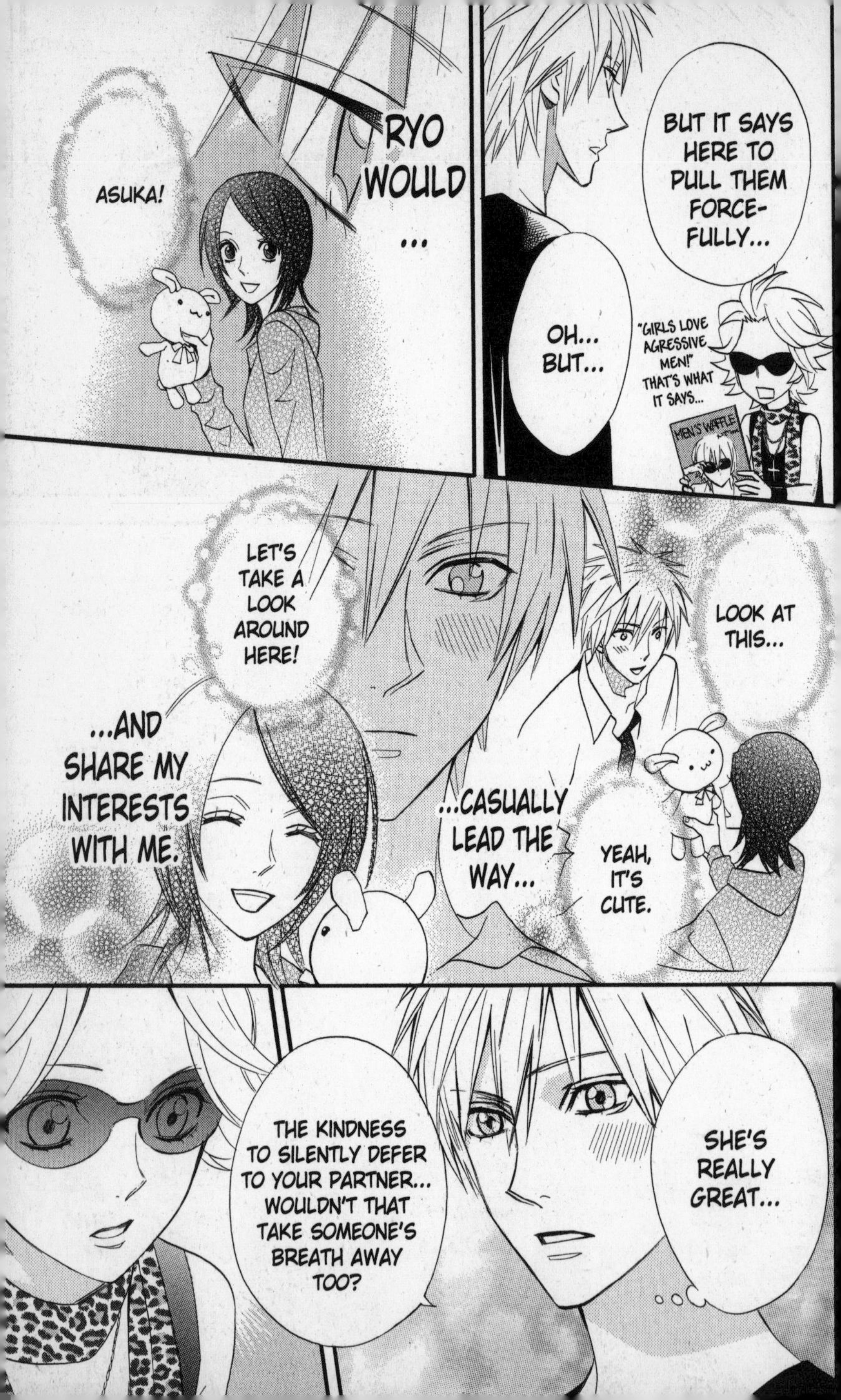
BUT IT SAYS HERE TO PULL THEM FORCE-FULLY...
"GIRLS LOVE AGRESSIVE MEN!" THAT'S WHAT IT SAYS...
MEN'S WAFFLE
OH... BUT...
RYO WOULD ...
ASUKA!
LOOK AT THIS...
LET'S TAKE A LOOK AROUND HERE!
YEAH, IT'S CUTE.
...CASUALLY LEAD THE WAY...
...AND SHARE MY INTERESTS WITH ME.
SHE'S REALLY GREAT...
THE KINDNESS TO SILENTLY DEFER TO YOUR PARTNER... WOULDN'T THAT TAKE SOMEONE'S BREATH AWAY TOO?

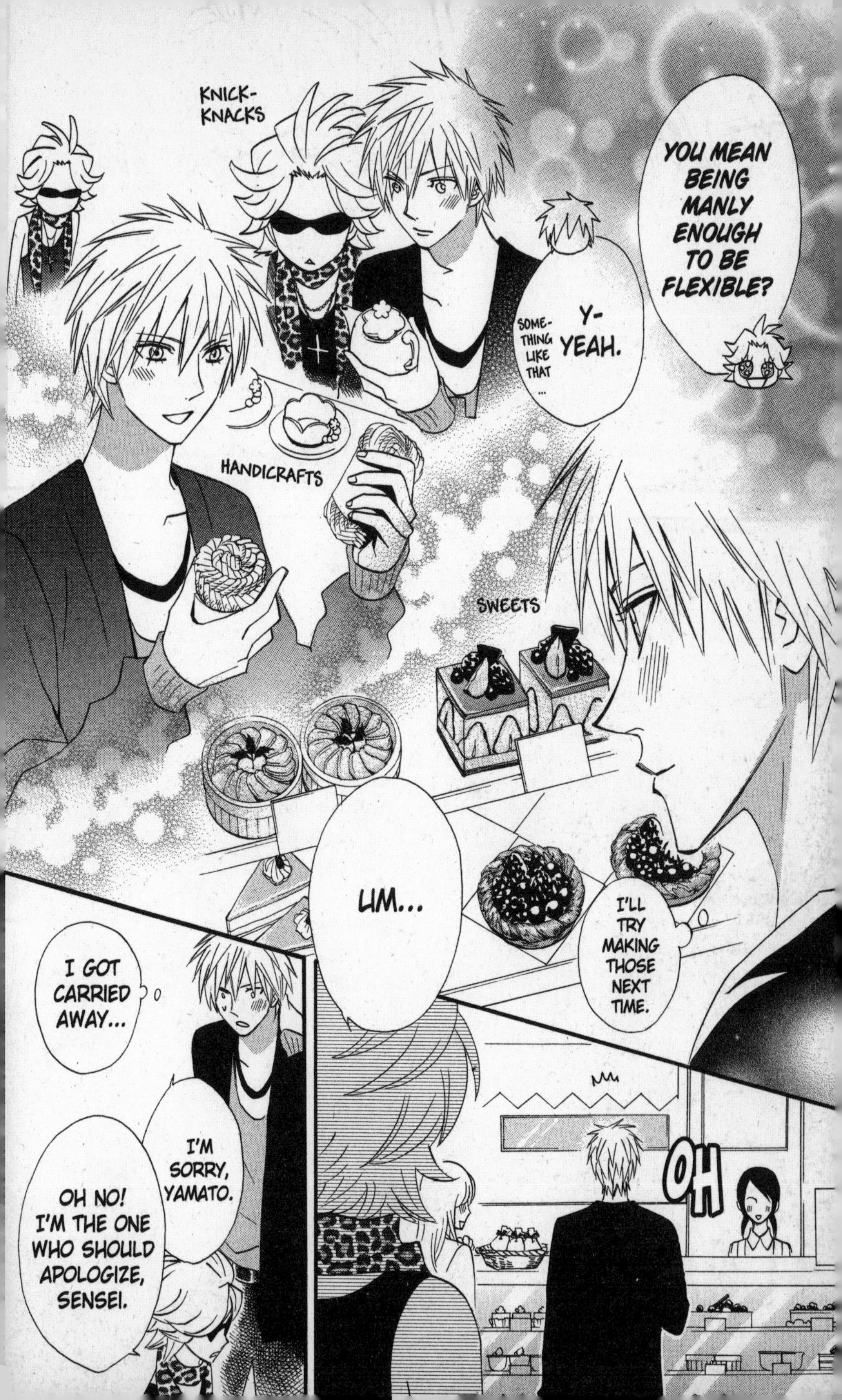
YOU MEAN BEING MANLY ENOUGH TO BE FLEXIBLE?
Y-YEAH.
SOMETHING LIKE THAT ...
KNICK-KNACKS
HANDICRAFTS
SWEETS
I'LL TRY MAKING THOSE NEXT TIME.
UM...
OH
I GOT CARRIED AWAY...
I'M SORRY, YAMATO.
OH NO! I'M THE ONE WHO SHOULD APOLOGIZE, SENSEI.

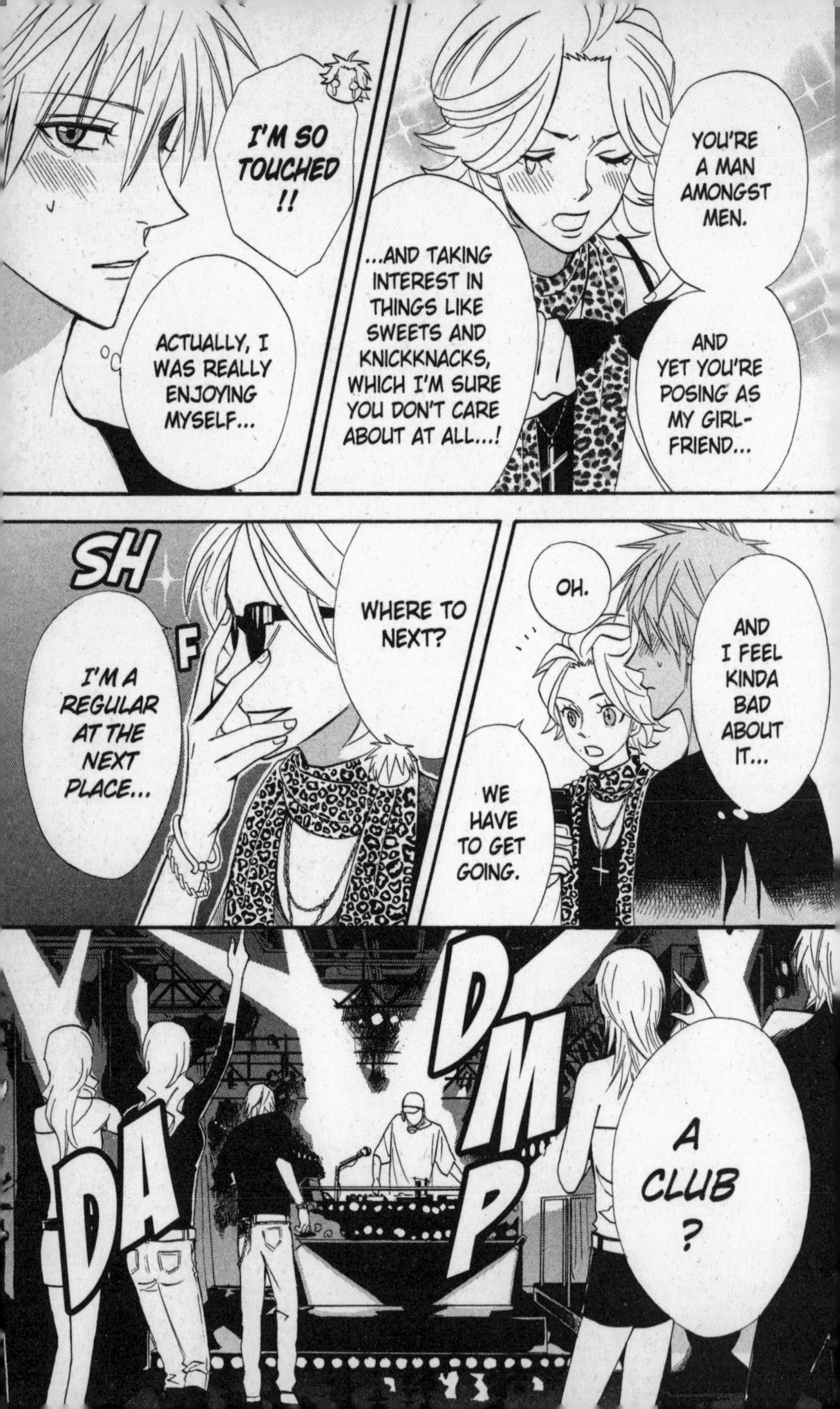
YOU'RE A MAN AMONGST MEN.
AND YET YOU'RE POSING AS MY GIRL-FRIEND...
...AND TAKING INTEREST IN THINGS LIKE SWEETS AND KNICKKNACKS, WHICH I'M SURE YOU DON'T CARE ABOUT AT ALL...!
I'M SO TOUCHED !!
ACTUALLY, I WAS REALLY ENJOYING MYSELF...
OH.
AND I FEEL KINDA BAD ABOUT IT...
WE HAVE TO GET GOING.
WHERE TO NEXT?
SH
F
I'M A REGULAR AT THE NEXT PLACE...
A CLUB ?
DMP
DA

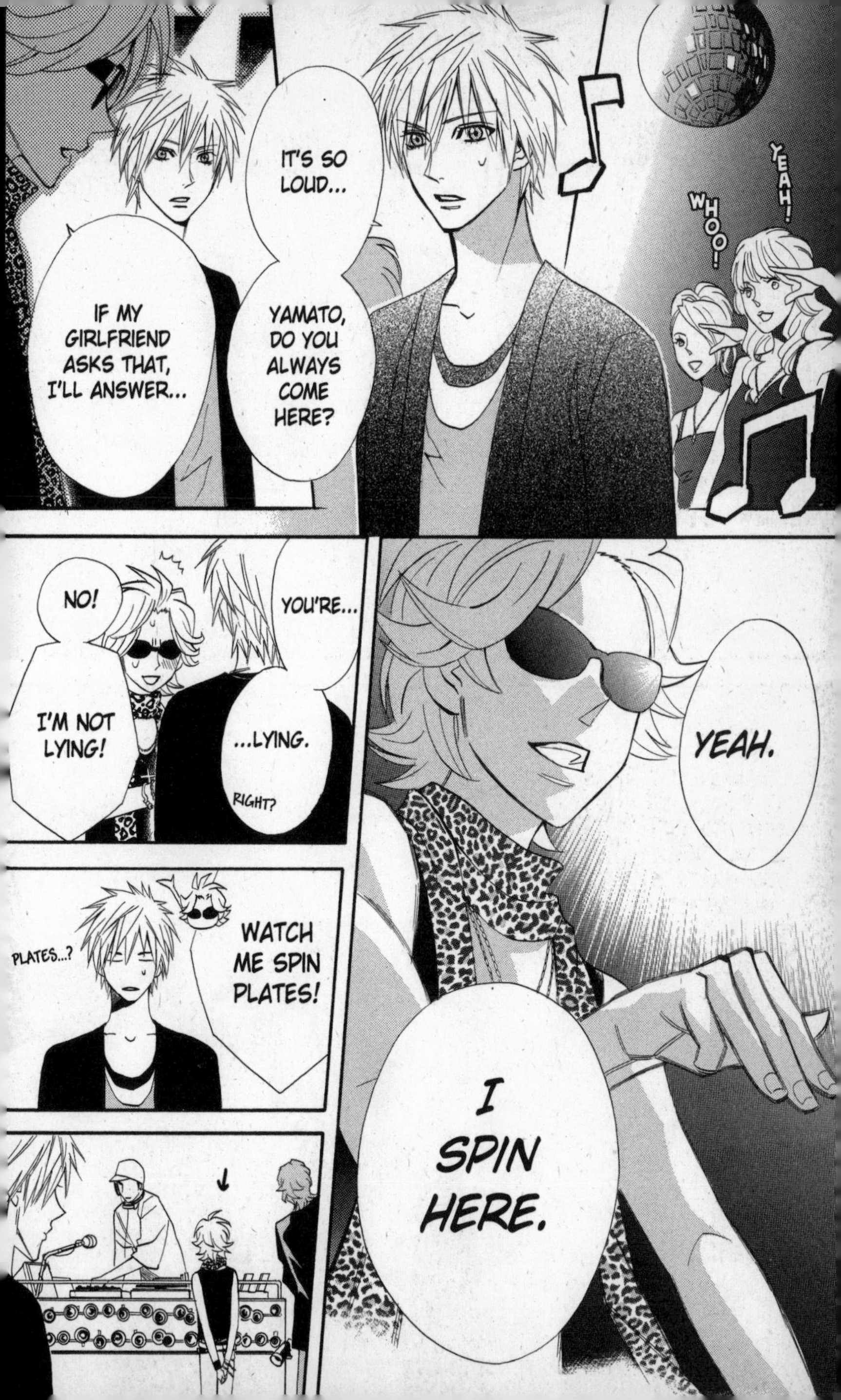
YEAH!
WHOO!
IT'S SO LOUD...
YAMATO, DO YOU ALWAYS COME HERE?
IF MY GIRLFRIEND ASKS THAT, I'LL ANSWER...
YEAH.
I SPIN HERE.
YOU'RE...
...LYING.
RIGHT?
NO!
I'M NOT LYING!
WATCH ME SPIN PLATES!
PLATES...?

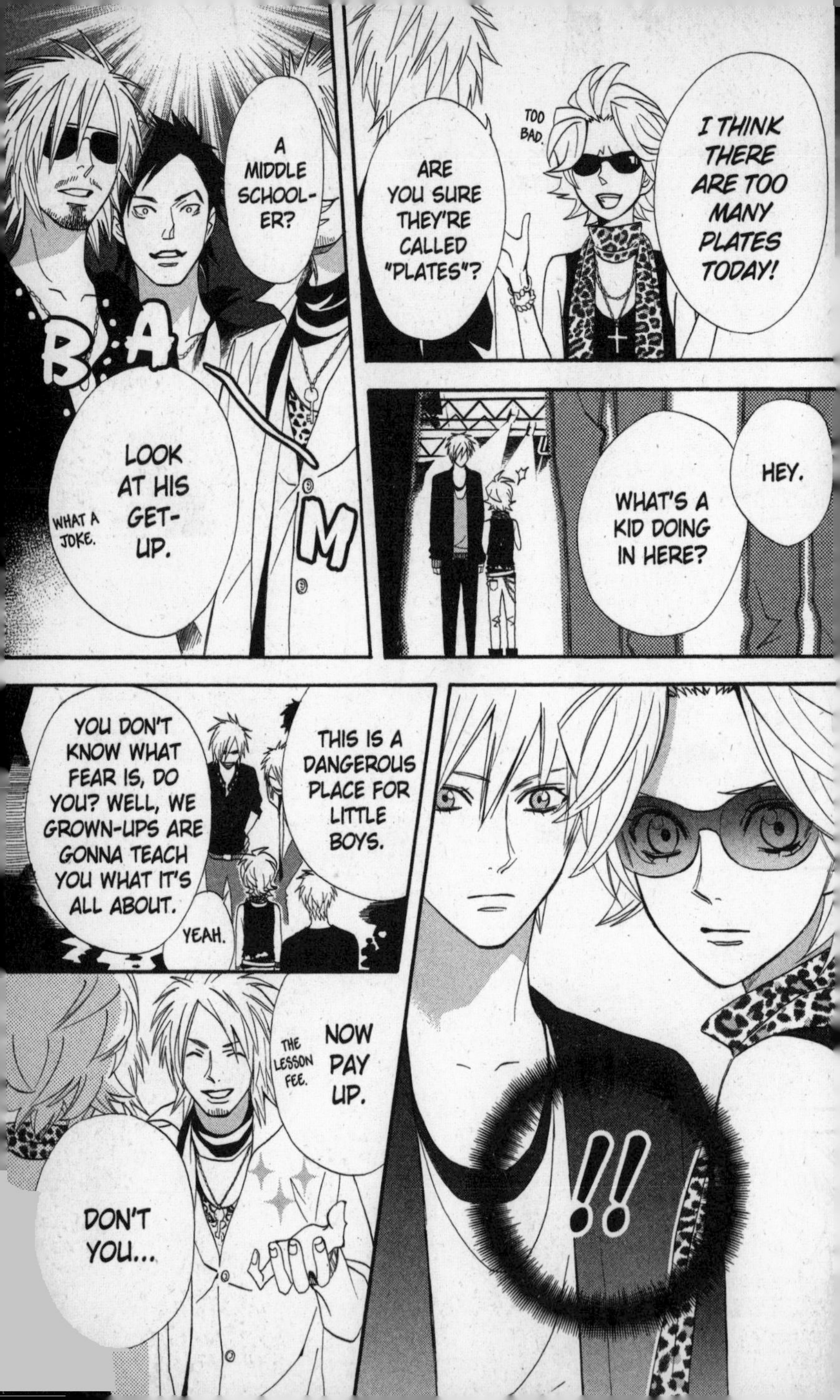

I THINK THERE ARE TOO MANY PLATES TODAY!
TOO BAD.
ARE YOU SURE THEY'RE CALLED "PLATES"?
HEY.
WHAT'S A KID DOING IN HERE?
A MIDDLE SCHOOL-ER?
BAM
LOOK AT HIS GET-UP.
WHAT A JOKE.
!!
THIS IS A DANGEROUS PLACE FOR LITTLE BOYS.
YOU DON'T KNOW WHAT FEAR IS, DO YOU? WELL, WE GROWN-UPS ARE GONNA TEACH YOU WHAT IT'S ALL ABOUT.
YEAH.
NOW PAY UP.
THE LESSON FEE.
DON'T YOU...

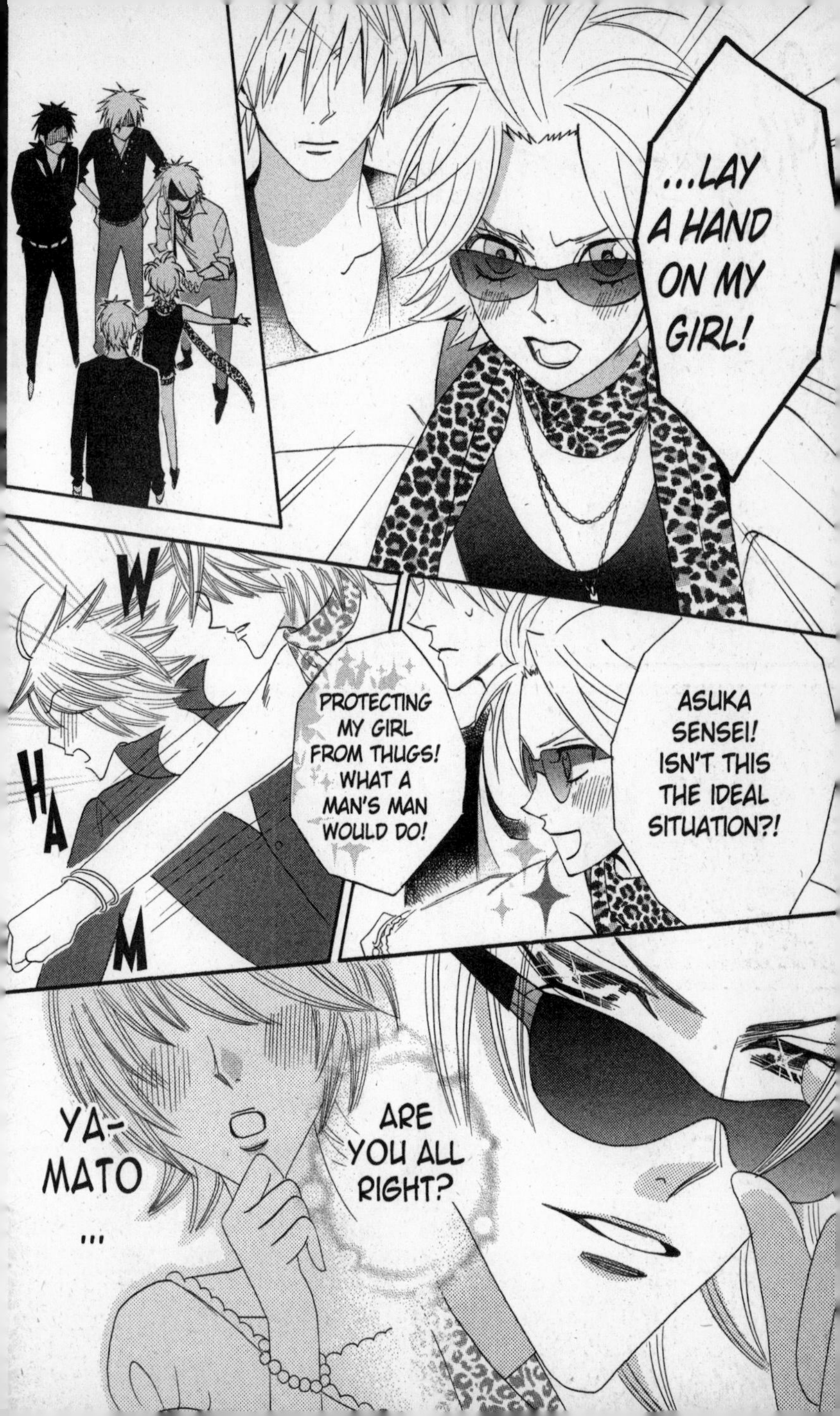
...LAY A HAND ON MY GIRL!
ASUKA SENSEI! ISN'T THIS THE IDEAL SITUATION?!
PROTECTING MY GIRL FROM THUGS! WHAT A MAN'S MAN WOULD DO!
WHAM
ARE YOU ALL RIGHT?
YA-MATO ...

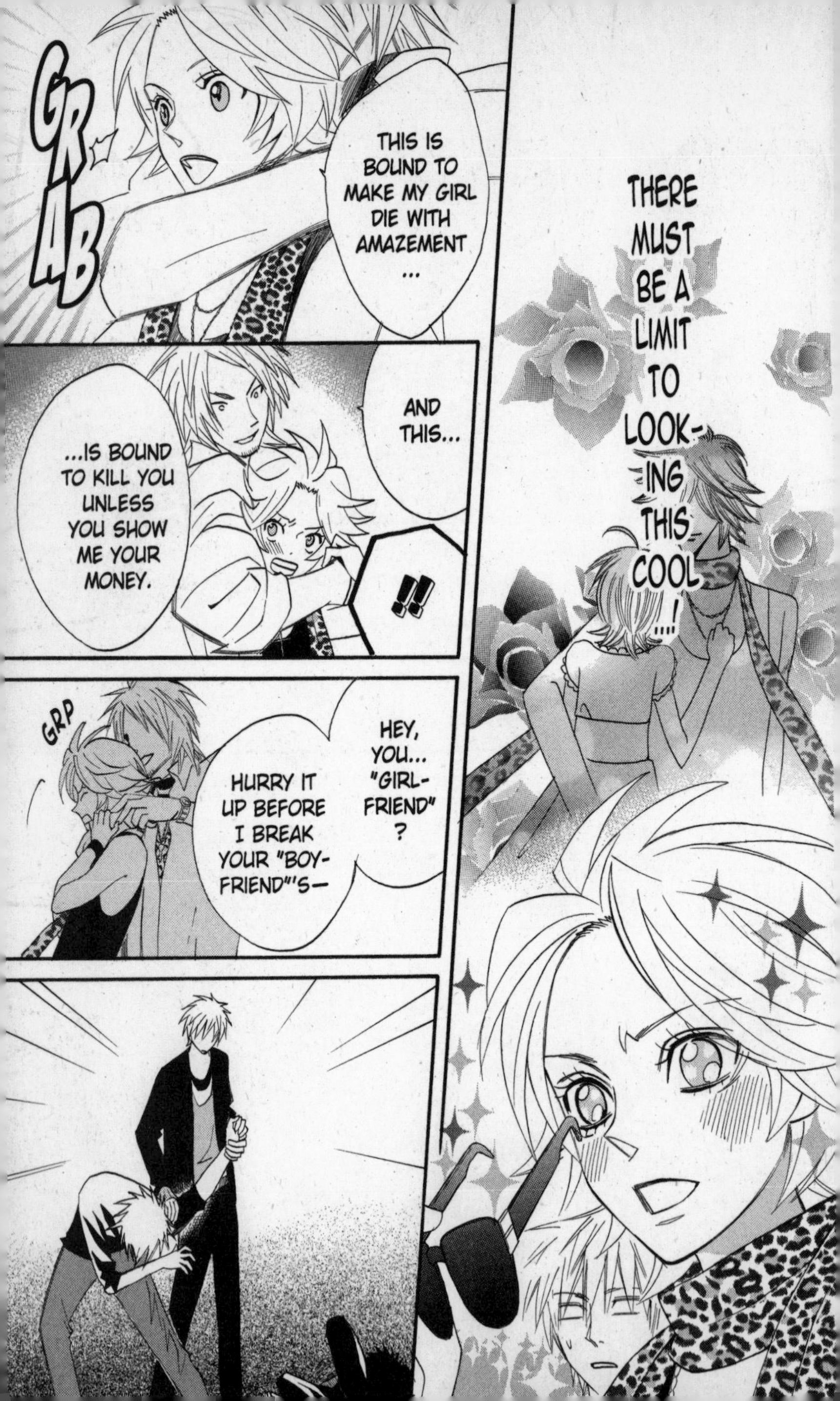
THERE MUST BE A LIMIT TO LOOK-ING THIS COOL...!
GRAB
THIS IS BOUND TO MAKE MY GIRL DIE WITH AMAZEMENT...
AND THIS...
...IS BOUND TO KILL YOU UNLESS YOU SHOW ME YOUR MONEY.
!!
HEY, YOU... "GIRL-FRIEND"?
HURRY IT UP BEFORE I BREAK YOUR "BOY-FRIEND"'S—
GRP

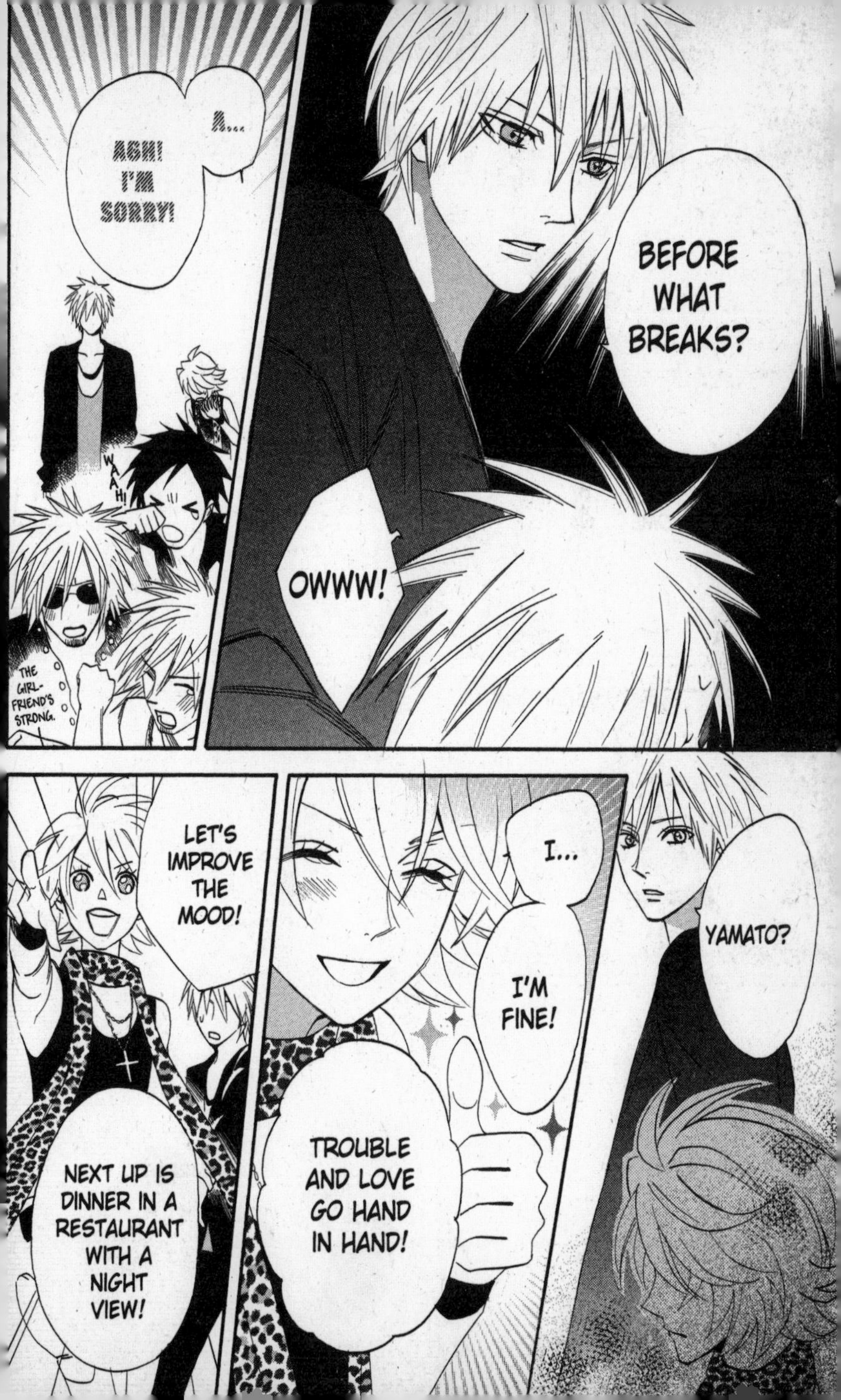
BEFORE WHAT BREAKS?
OWWW!
A...
AGH! I'M SORRY!
WAAAH!
THE GIRLFRIEND'S STRONG.
YAMATO?
I...
I'M FINE!
TROUBLE AND LOVE GO HAND IN HAND!
LET'S IMPROVE THE MOOD!
NEXT UP IS DINNER IN A RESTAURANT WITH A NIGHT VIEW!

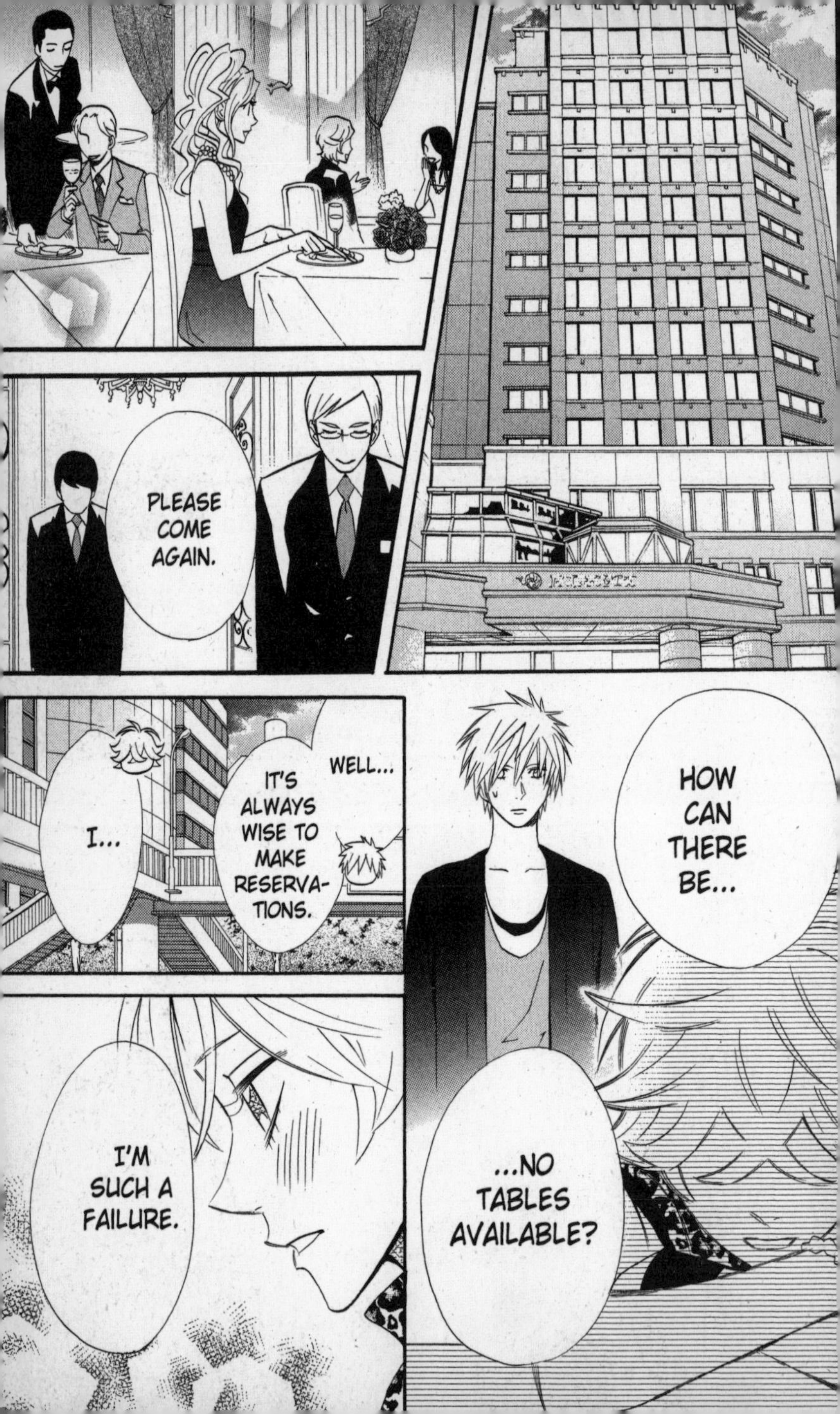
PLEASE COME AGAIN.
HOW CAN THERE BE...
...NO TABLES AVAILABLE?
WELL...
IT'S ALWAYS WISE TO MAKE RESERVATIONS.
I...
I'M SUCH A FAILURE.

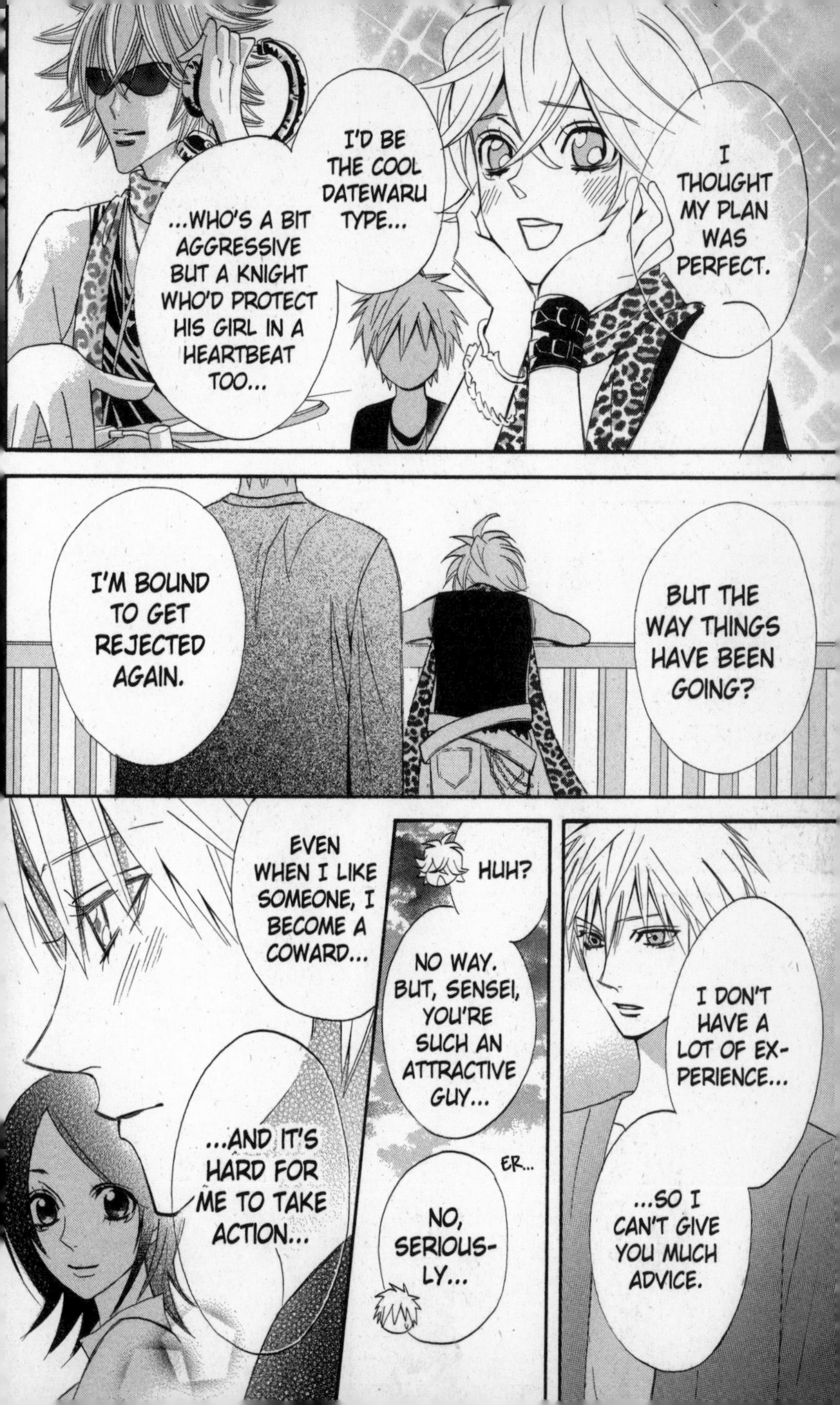
I THOUGHT MY PLAN WAS PERFECT.
I'D BE THE COOL DATEWARU TYPE...
...WHO'S A BIT AGGRESSIVE BUT A KNIGHT WHO'D PROTECT HIS GIRL IN A HEARTBEAT TOO...
BUT THE WAY THINGS HAVE BEEN GOING?
I'M BOUND TO GET REJECTED AGAIN.
I DON'T HAVE A LOT OF EX-PERIENCE...
...SO I CAN'T GIVE YOU MUCH ADVICE.
HUH?
NO WAY. BUT, SENSEI, YOU'RE SUCH AN ATTRACTIVE GUY...
ER...
NO, SERIOUS-LY...
EVEN WHEN I LIKE SOMEONE, I BECOME A COWARD...
...AND IT'S HARD FOR ME TO TAKE ACTION...

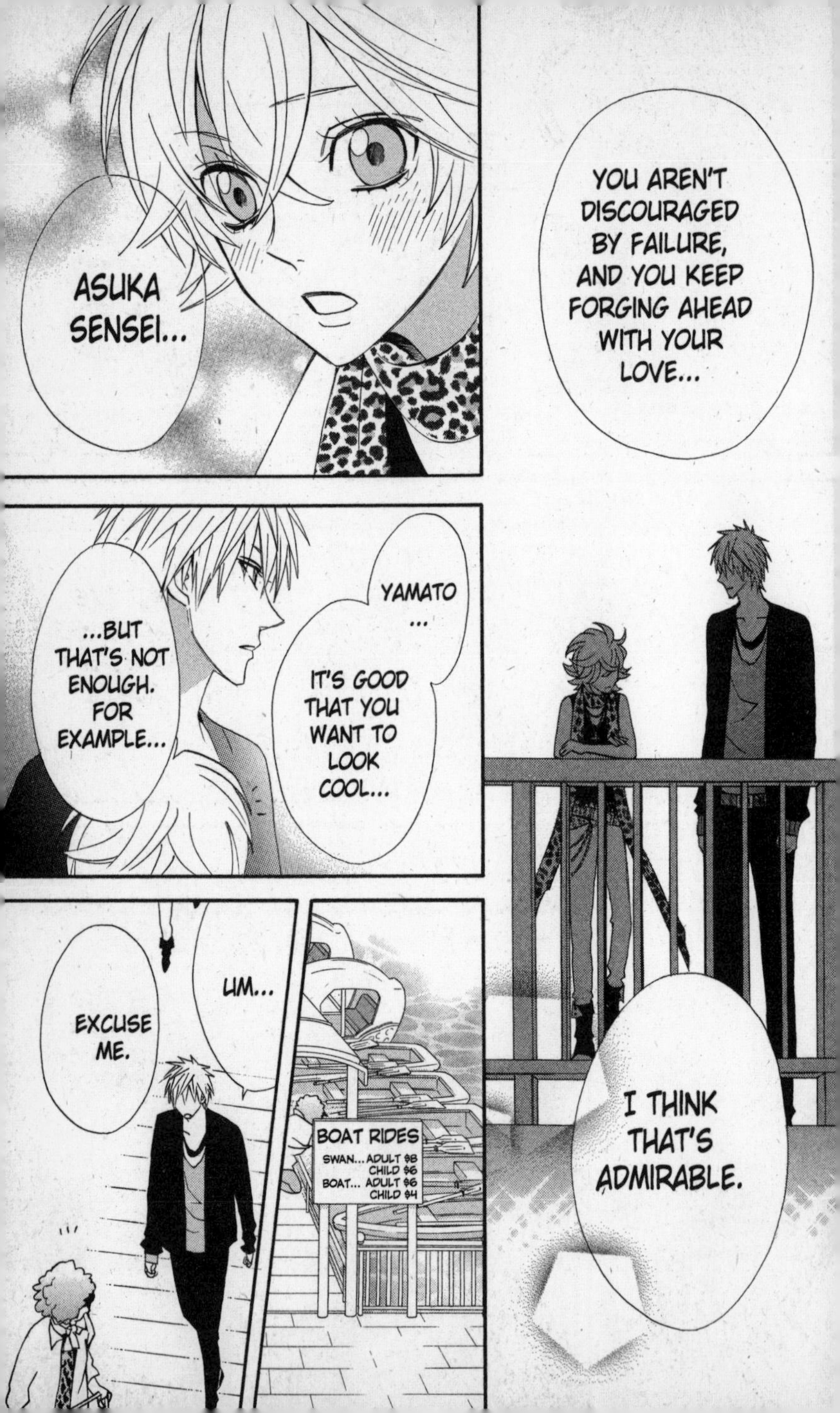
YOU AREN'T DISCOURAGED BY FAILURE, AND YOU KEEP FORGING AHEAD WITH YOUR LOVE...
I THINK THAT'S ADMIRABLE.
ASUKA SENSEI...
YAMATO...
IT'S GOOD THAT YOU WANT TO LOOK COOL...
...BUT THAT'S NOT ENOUGH. FOR EXAMPLE...
BOAT RIDES
SWAN... ADULT $8 CHILD $6
BOAT... ADULT $6 CHILD $4
UM...
EXCUSE ME.

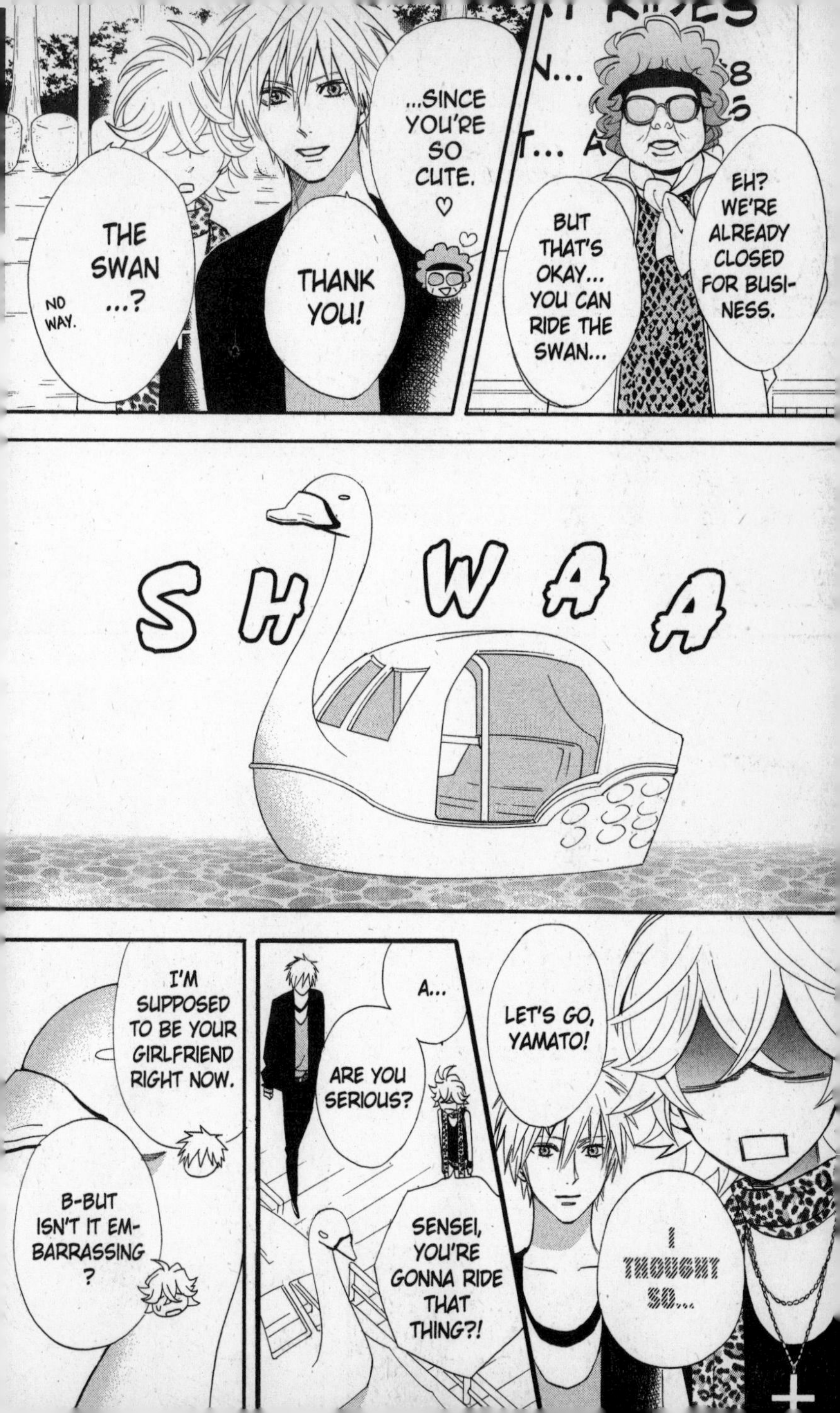
EH? WE'RE ALREADY CLOSED FOR BUSI-NESS.
BUT THAT'S OKAY... YOU CAN RIDE THE SWAN...
...SINCE YOU'RE SO CUTE. ♡
THANK YOU!
THE SWAN ...?
NO WAY.
SHWAA
LET'S GO, YAMATO!
A...
ARE YOU SERIOUS?
I THOUGHT SO...
SENSEI, YOU'RE GONNA RIDE THAT THING?!
I'M SUPPOSED TO BE YOUR GIRLFRIEND RIGHT NOW.
B-BUT ISN'T IT EM-BARRASSING ?

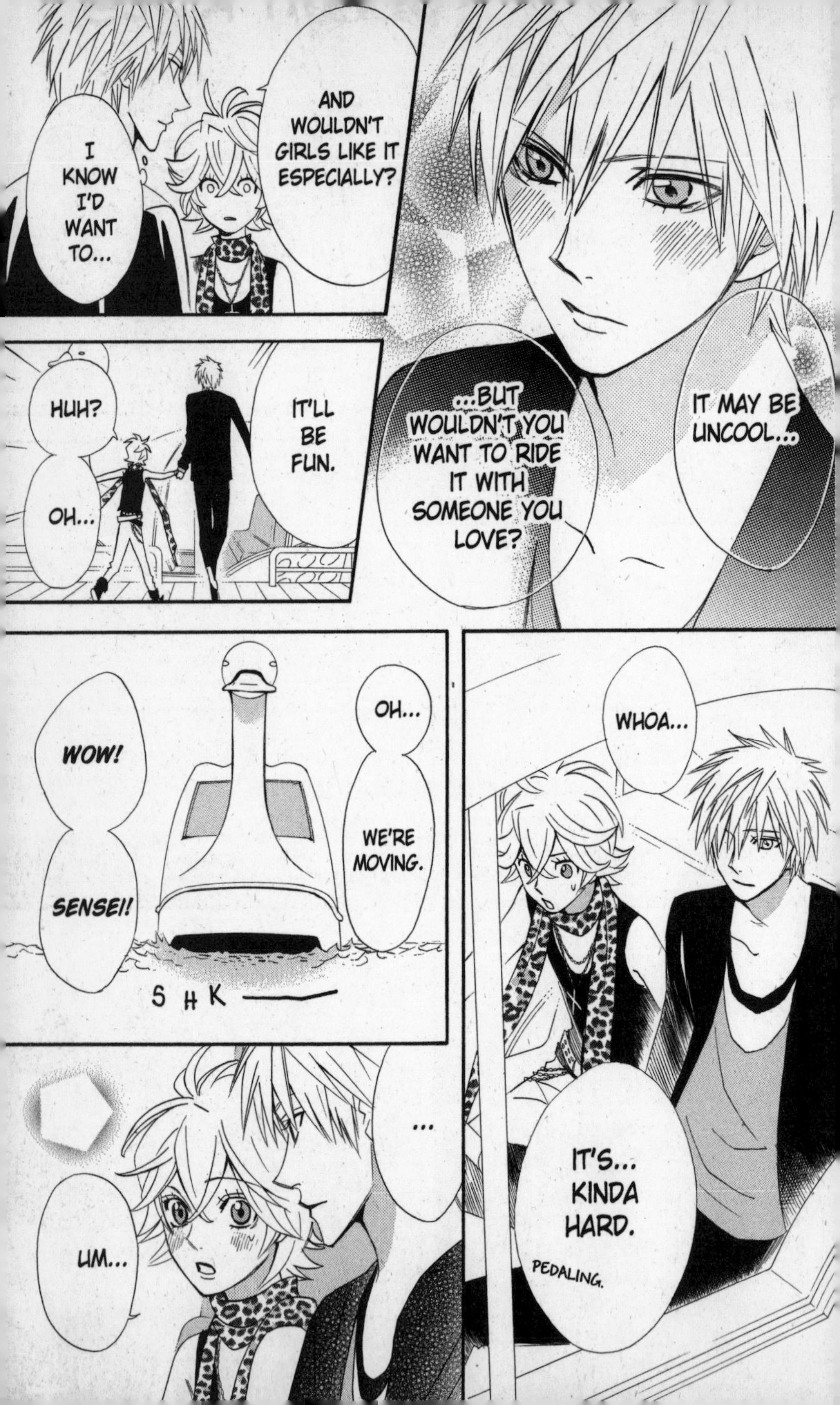
IT MAY BE UNCOOL...
...BUT WOULDN'T YOU WANT TO RIDE IT WITH SOMEONE YOU LOVE?
AND WOULDN'T GIRLS LIKE IT ESPECIALLY?
I KNOW I'D WANT TO...
IT'LL BE FUN.
HUH?
OH...
WHOA...
IT'S... KINDA HARD.
PEDALING.
OH...
WE'RE MOVING.
WOW!
SENSEI!
SHK
...
UM...

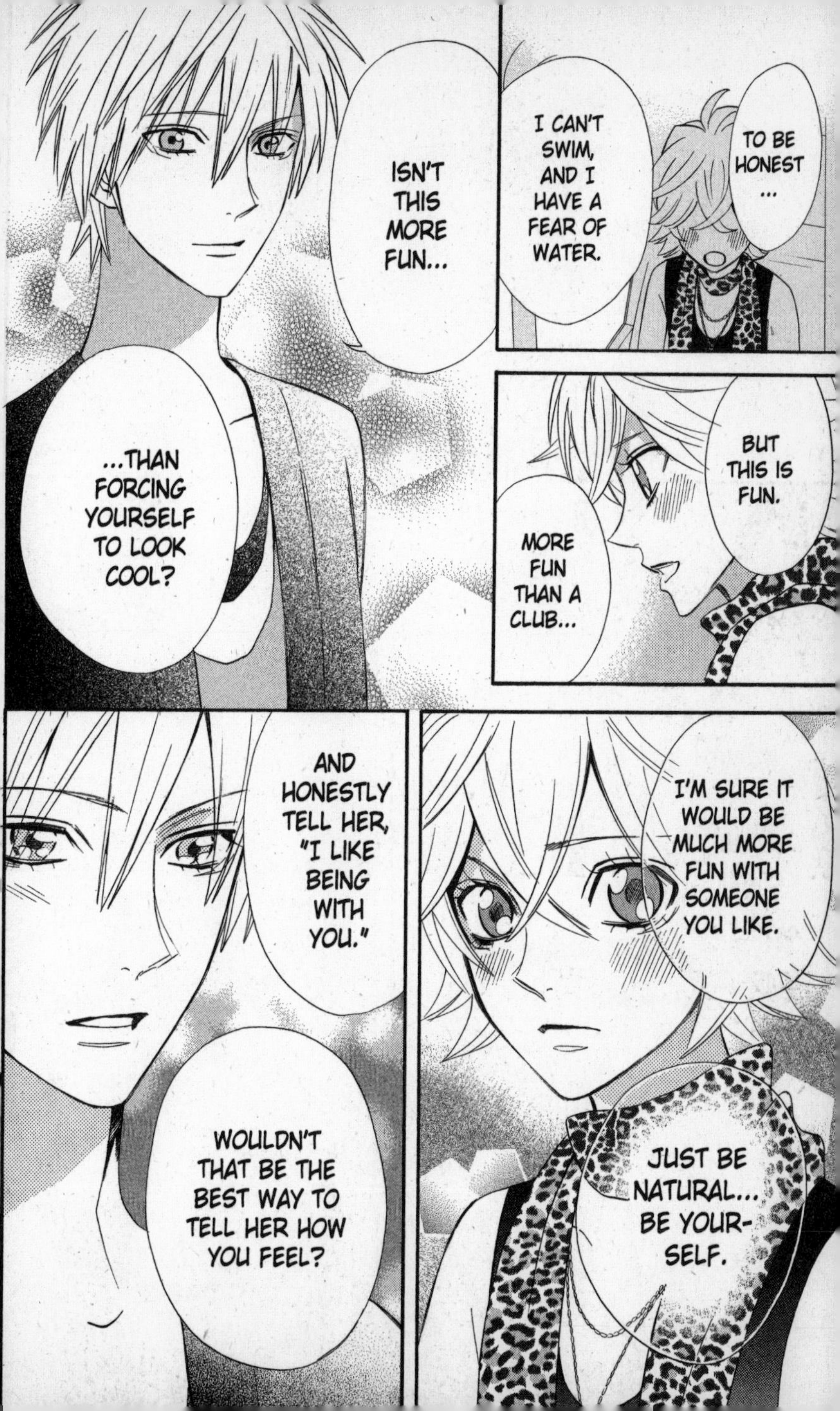
TO BE HONEST...
I CAN'T SWIM, AND I HAVE A FEAR OF WATER.
BUT THIS IS FUN.
MORE FUN THAN A CLUB...
ISN'T THIS MORE FUN...
...THAN FORCING YOURSELF TO LOOK COOL?
I'M SURE IT WOULD BE MUCH MORE FUN WITH SOMEONE YOU LIKE.
JUST BE NATURAL... BE YOUR-SELF.
AND HONESTLY TELL HER, "I LIKE BEING WITH YOU."
WOULDN'T THAT BE THE BEST WAY TO TELL HER HOW YOU FEEL?

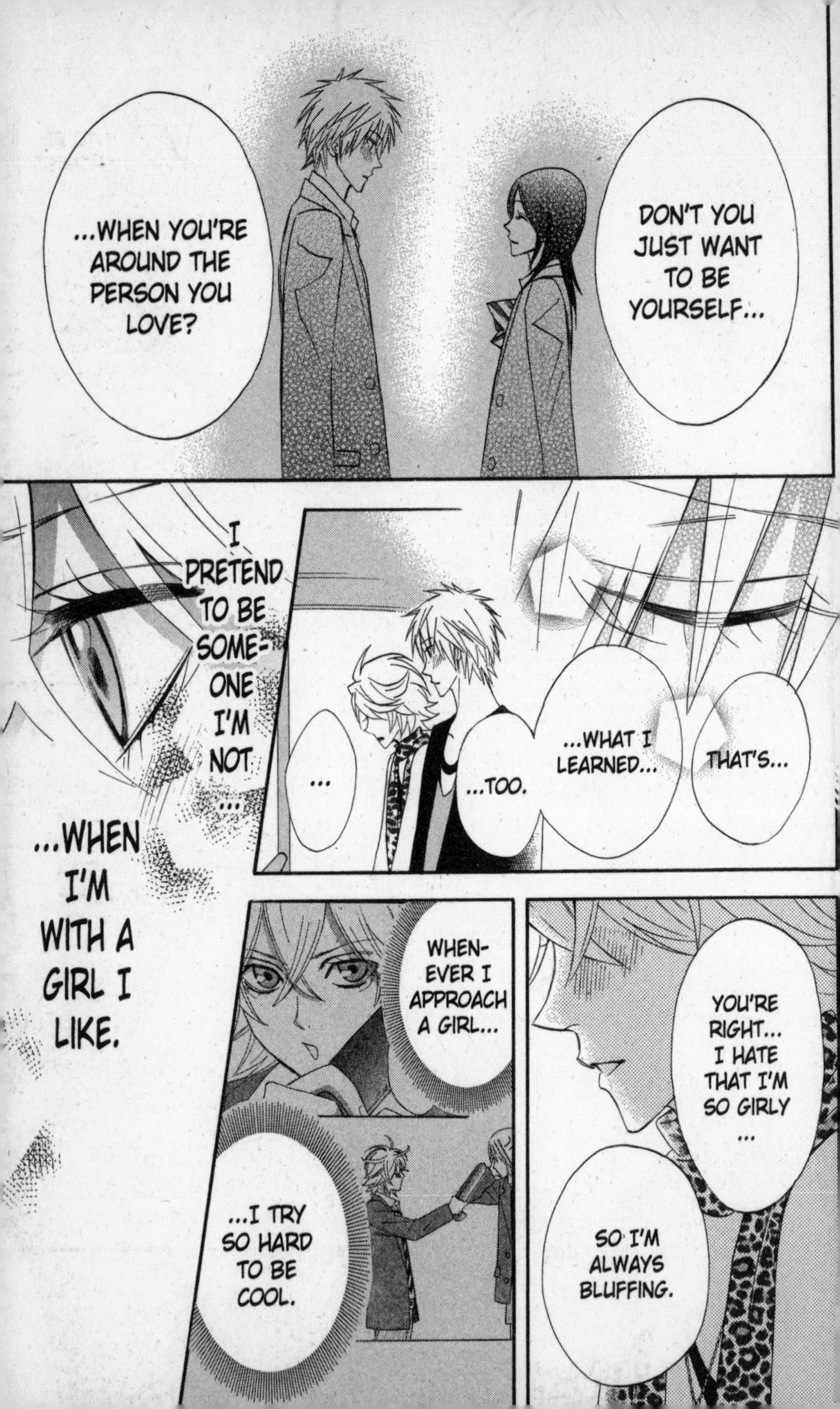

DON'T YOU JUST WANT TO BE YOURSELF...
...WHEN YOU'RE AROUND THE PERSON YOU LOVE?
THAT'S...
...WHAT I LEARNED...
...TOO.
...
YOU'RE RIGHT... I HATE THAT I'M SO GIRLY...
SO I'M ALWAYS BLUFFING.
WHEN-EVER I APPROACH A GIRL...
...I TRY SO HARD TO BE COOL.
I PRETEND TO BE SOME-ONE I'M NOT...
...WHEN I'M WITH A GIRL I LIKE.

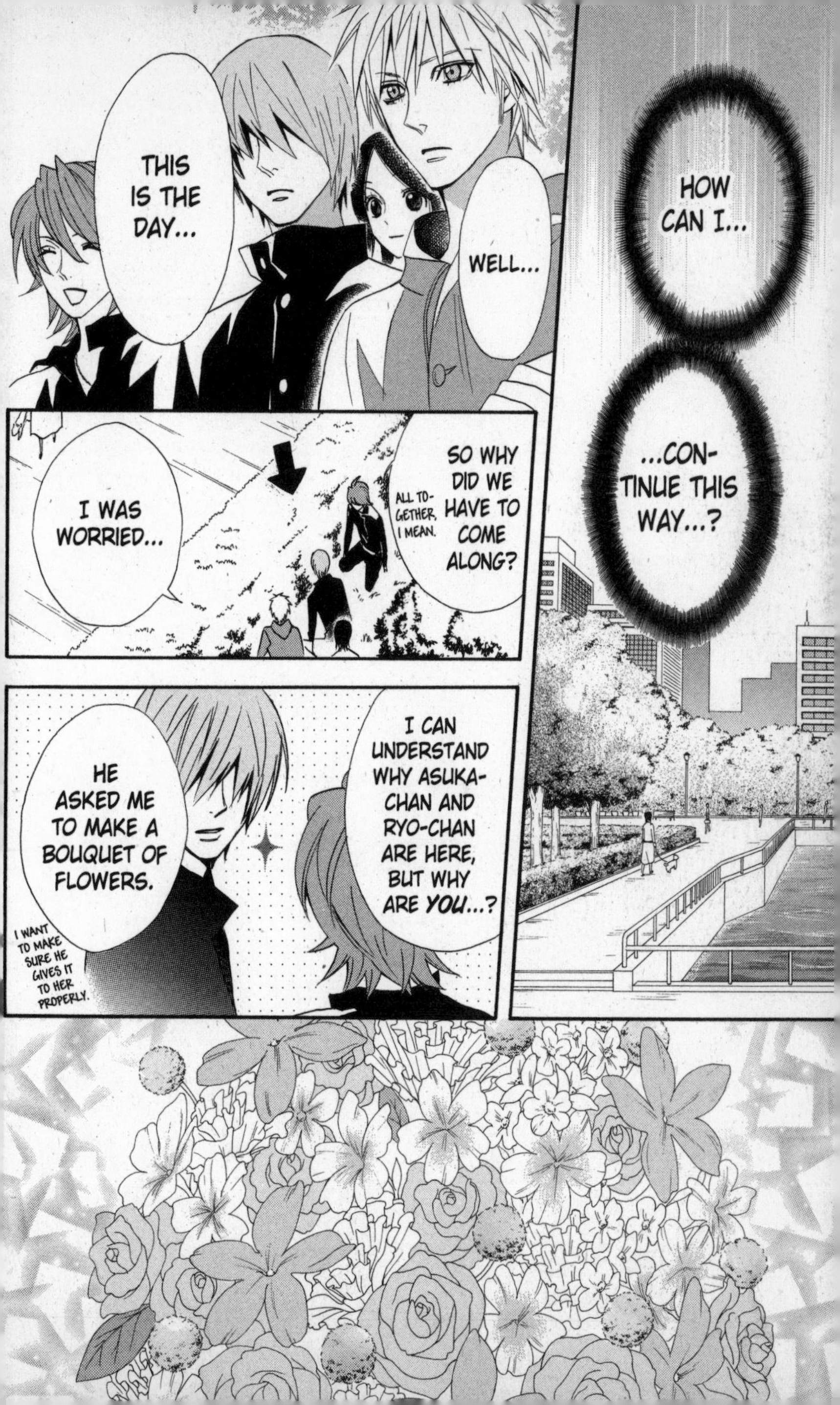
HOW CAN I...
...CON-TINUE THIS WAY...?
WELL...
THIS IS THE DAY...
SO WHY DID WE HAVE TO COME ALONG?
ALL TO-GETHER, I MEAN.
I WAS WORRIED...
I CAN UNDERSTAND WHY ASUKA-CHAN AND RYO-CHAN ARE HERE, BUT WHY ARE *YOU*...?
HE ASKED ME TO MAKE A BOUQUET OF FLOWERS.
I WANT TO MAKE SURE HE GIVES IT TO HER PROPERLY.

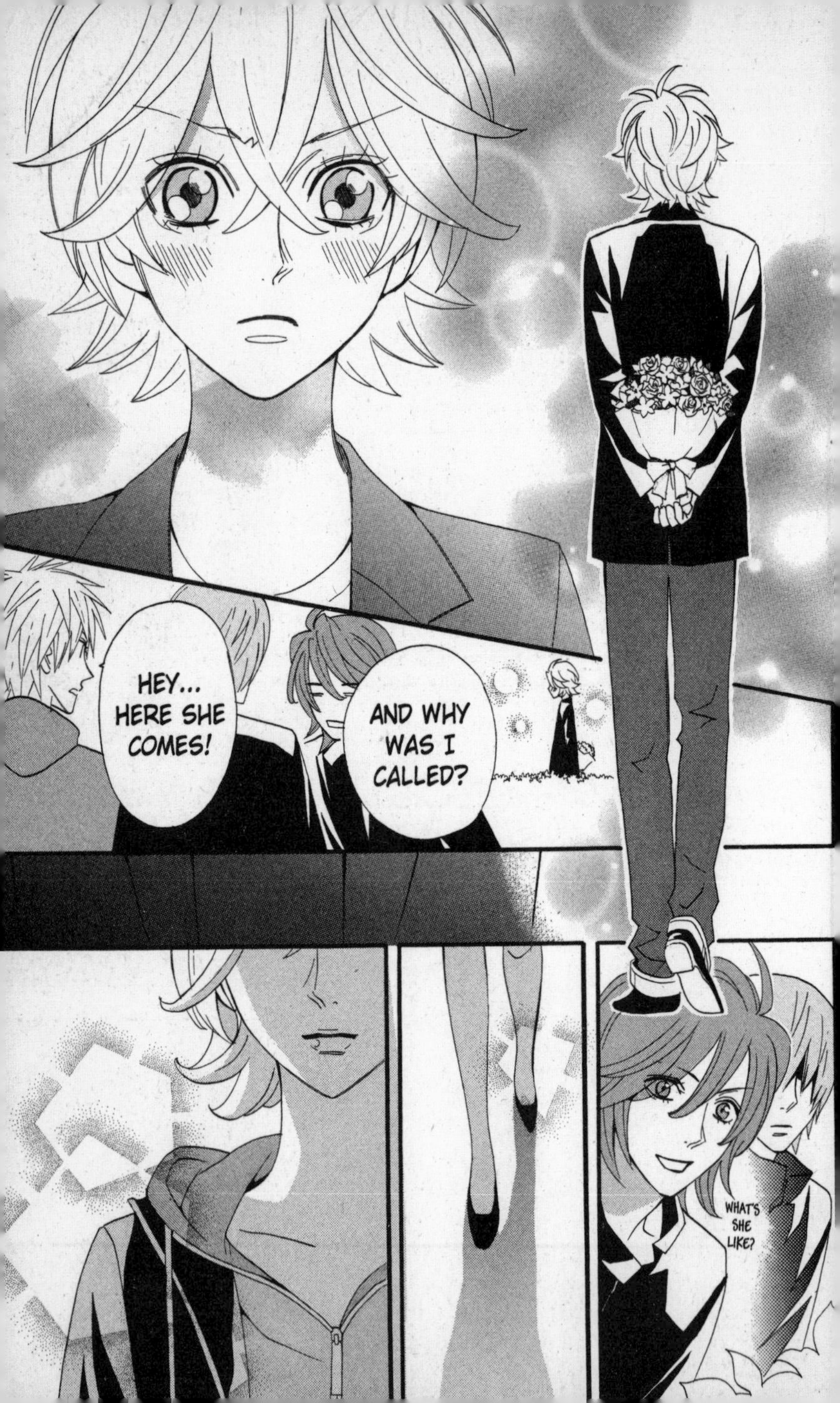
AND WHY WAS I CALLED?
HEY... HERE SHE COMES!
WHAT'S SHE LIKE?

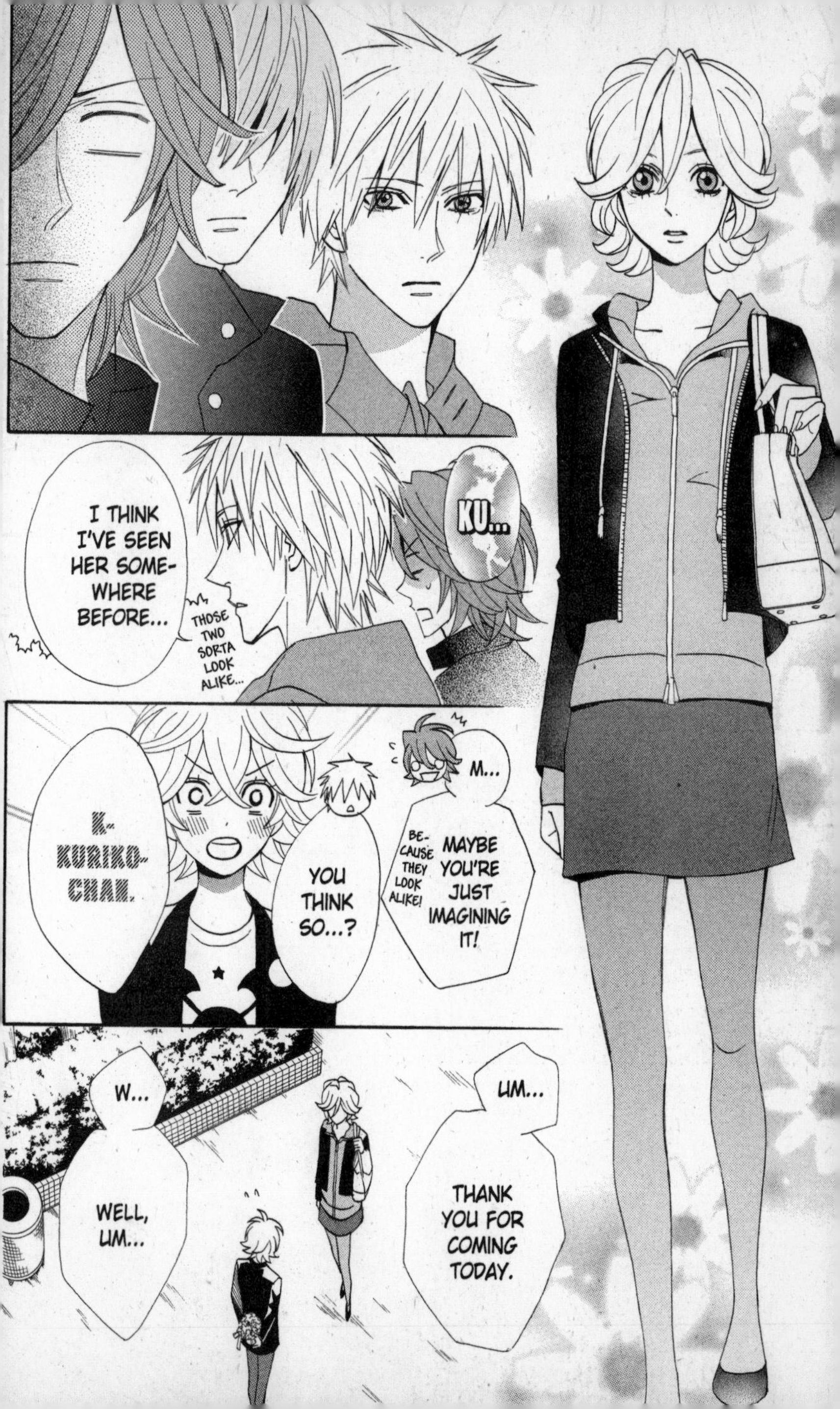
KU...
I THINK I'VE SEEN HER SOME-WHERE BEFORE...
THOSE TWO SORTA LOOK ALIKE...
M...
MAYBE YOU'RE JUST IMAGINING IT!
BE-CAUSE THEY LOOK ALIKE!
YOU THINK SO...?
K-KURIKO-CHAN.
UM...
THANK YOU FOR COMING TODAY.
W...
WELL, UM...

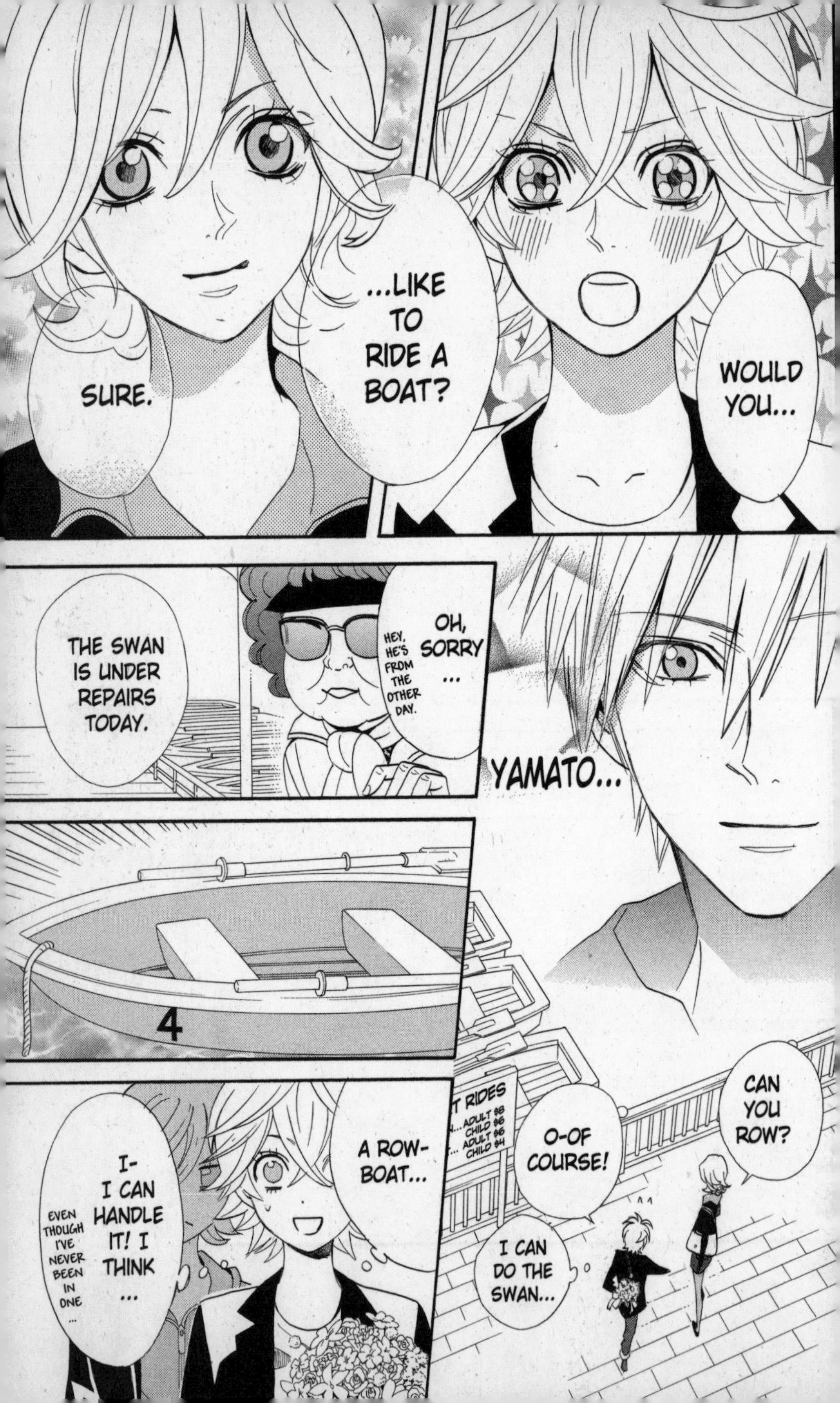
WOULD YOU...
...LIKE TO RIDE A BOAT?
SURE.
YAMATO...
OH, SORRY ...
HEY, HE'S FROM THE OTHER DAY.
THE SWAN IS UNDER REPAIRS TODAY.
4
CAN YOU ROW?
T RIDES
ADULT $8
CHILD $6
ADULT $6
CHILD $4
O-OF COURSE!
I CAN DO THE SWAN...
A ROW-BOAT...
I- I CAN HANDLE IT! I THINK ...
EVEN THOUGH I'VE NEVER BEEN IN ONE ...

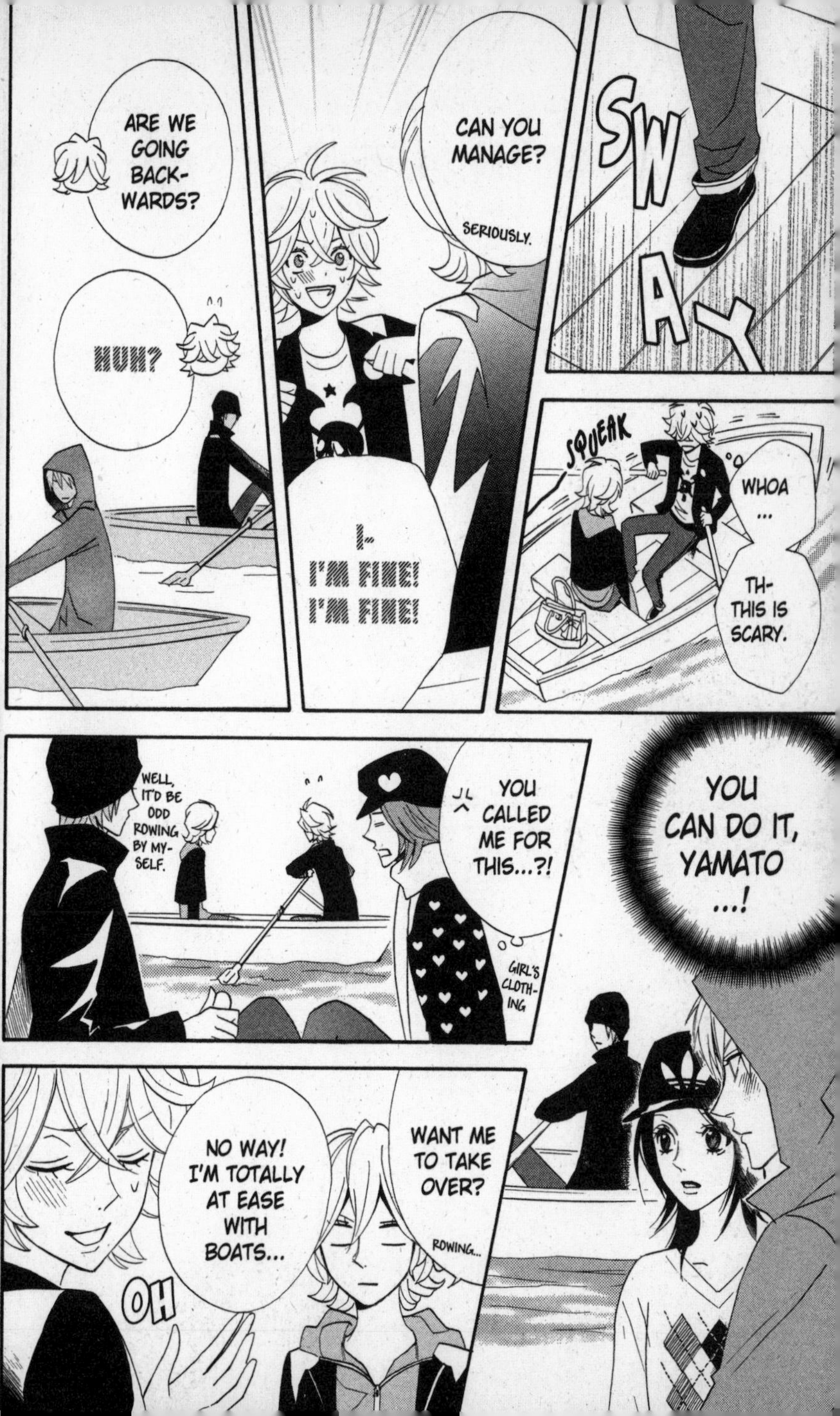
SWAY
SQUEAK
WHOA ...
TH- THIS IS SCARY.
CAN YOU MANAGE?
SERIOUSLY.
I- I'M FINE! I'M FINE!
ARE WE GOING BACK- WARDS?
HUH?
YOU CAN DO IT, YAMATO ...!
YOU CALLED ME FOR THIS...?!
GIRL'S CLOTH- ING
WELL, IT'D BE ODD ROWING BY MY- SELF.
WANT ME TO TAKE OVER?
ROWING...
NO WAY! I'M TOTALLY AT EASE WITH BOATS...
OH

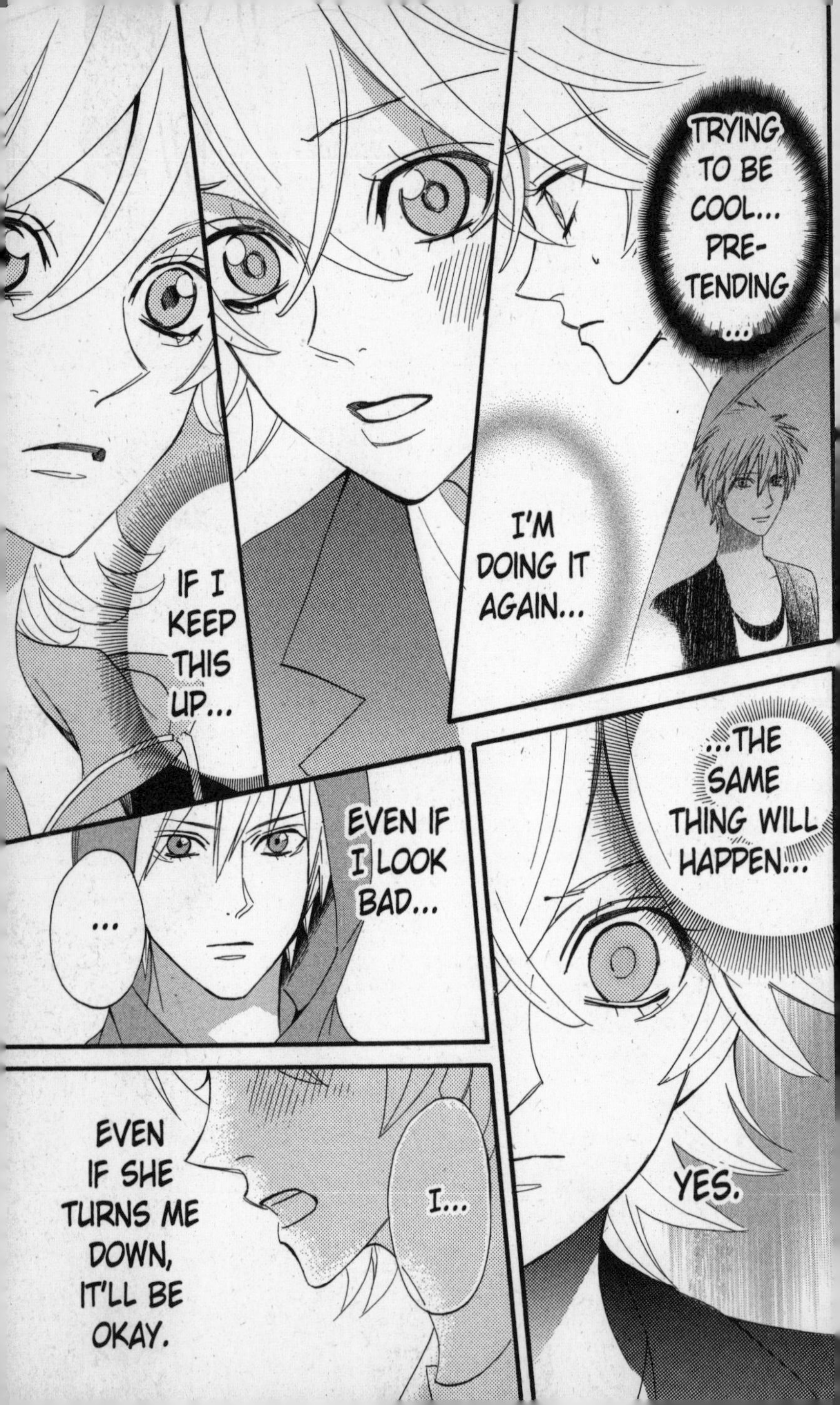
TRYING TO BE COOL... PRE-TENDING...
I'M DOING IT AGAIN...
IF I KEEP THIS UP...
...THE SAME THING WILL HAPPEN...
YES.
EVEN IF I LOOK BAD...
...
EVEN IF SHE TURNS ME DOWN, IT'LL BE OKAY.
I...

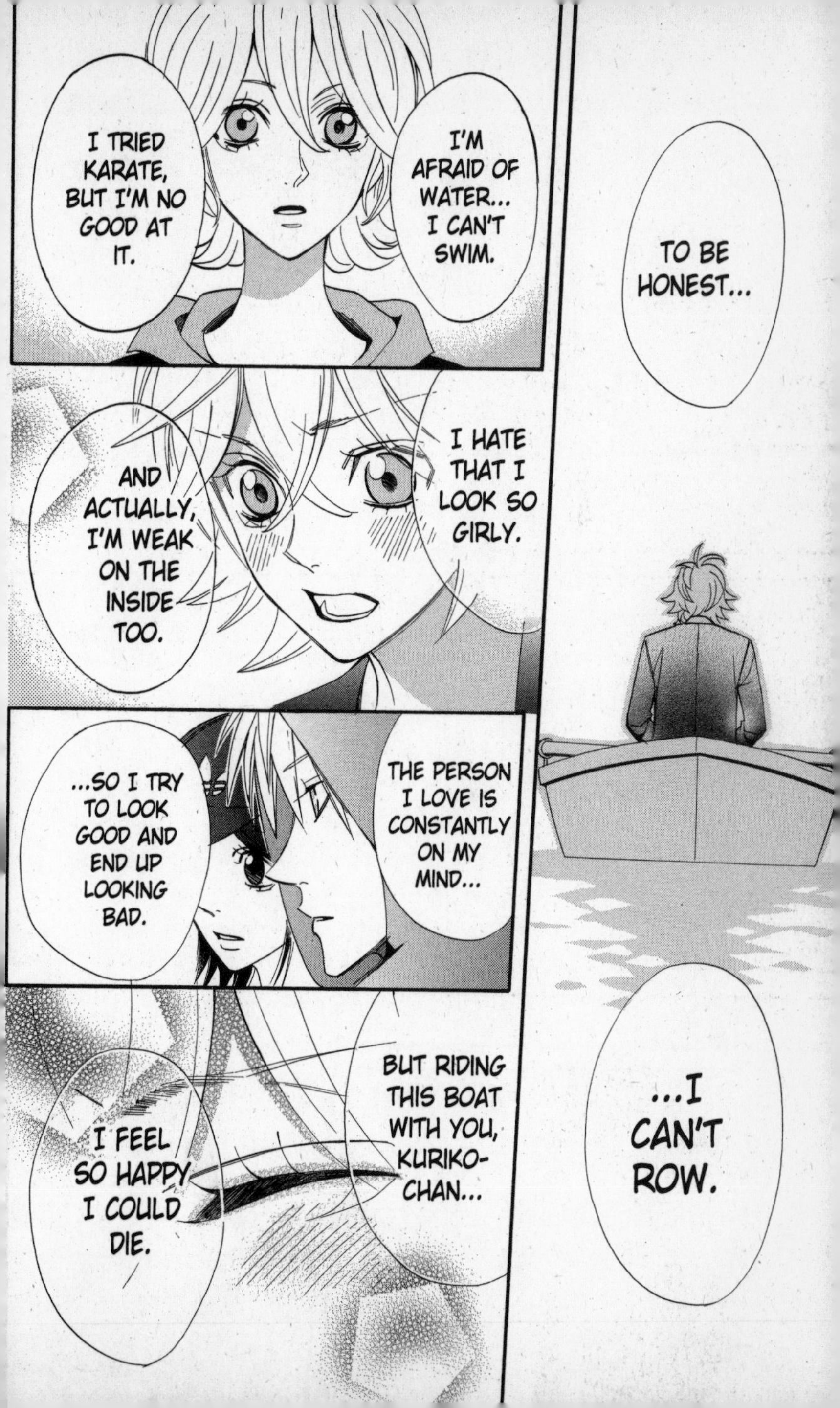
TO BE HONEST...
...I CAN'T ROW.
I'M AFRAID OF WATER... I CAN'T SWIM.
I TRIED KARATE, BUT I'M NO GOOD AT IT.
I HATE THAT I LOOK SO GIRLY.
AND ACTUALLY, I'M WEAK ON THE INSIDE TOO.
THE PERSON I LOVE IS CONSTANTLY ON MY MIND...
...SO I TRY TO LOOK GOOD AND END UP LOOKING BAD.
BUT RIDING THIS BOAT WITH YOU, KURIKO-CHAN...
I FEEL SO HAPPY I COULD DIE.

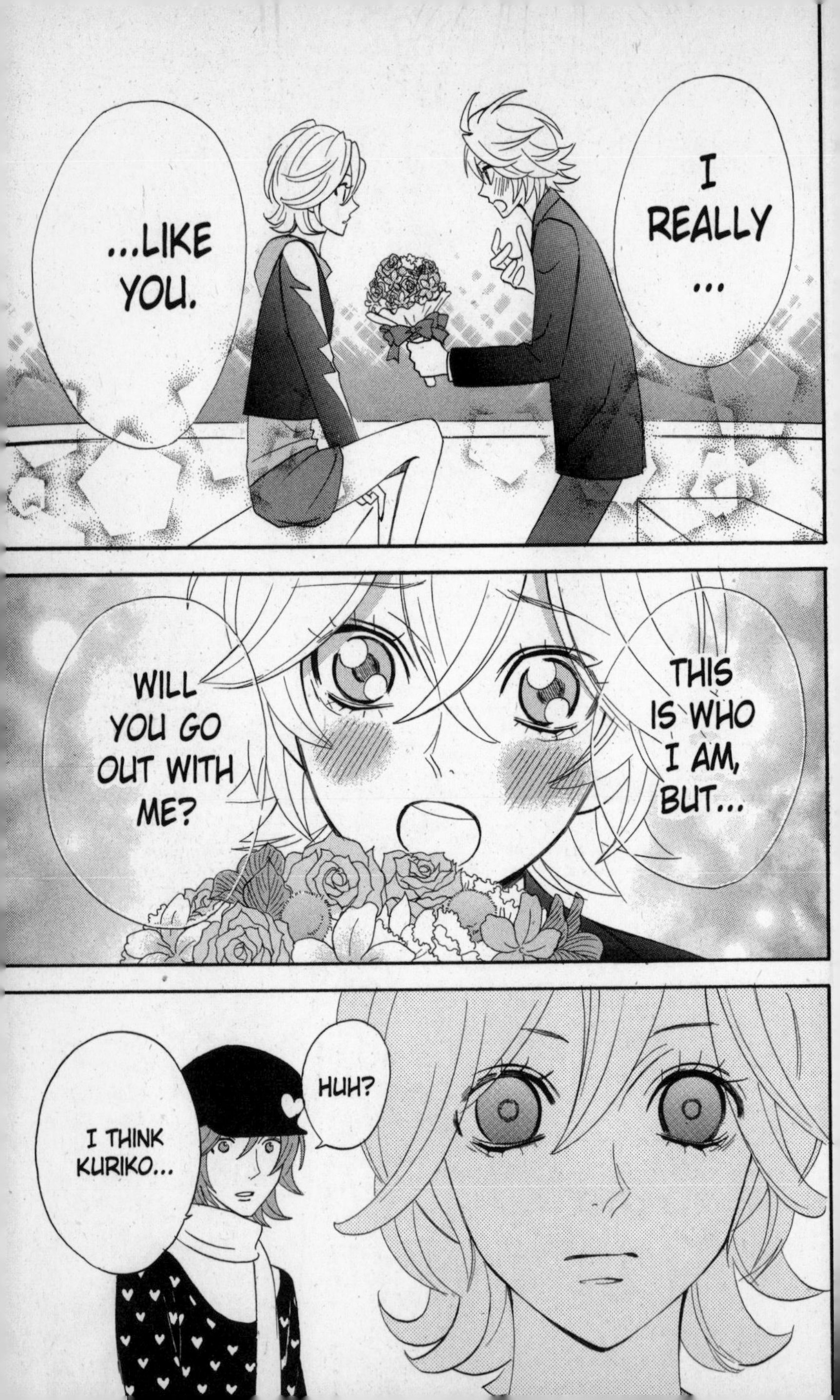
I REALLY ...
...LIKE YOU.
THIS IS WHO I AM, BUT...
WILL YOU GO OUT WITH ME?
HUH?
I THINK KURIKO...

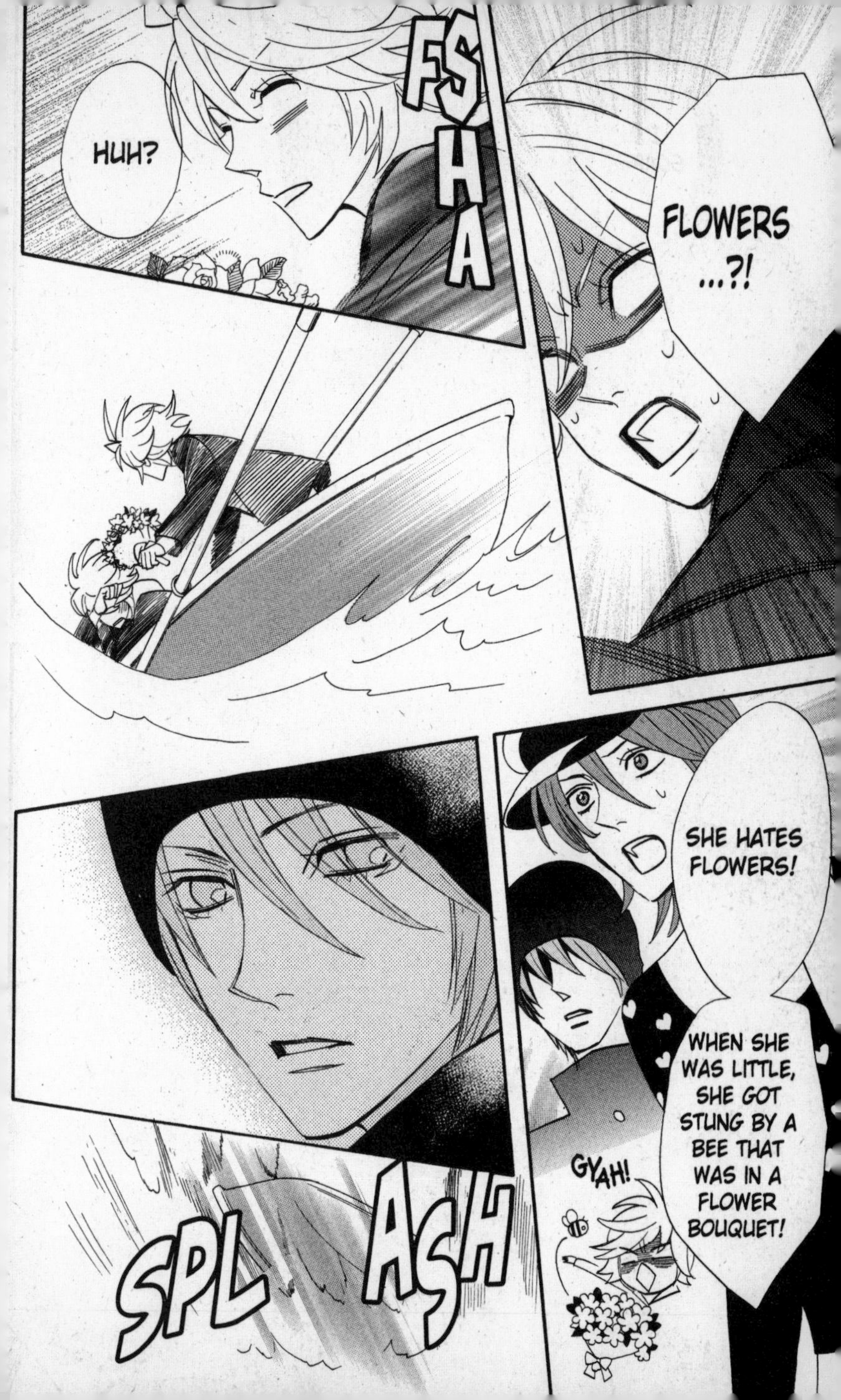
FLOWERS ...?!
HUH?
FSHA
SHE HATES FLOWERS!
WHEN SHE WAS LITTLE, SHE GOT STUNG BY A BEE THAT WAS IN A FLOWER BOUQUET!
GYAH!
SPLASH

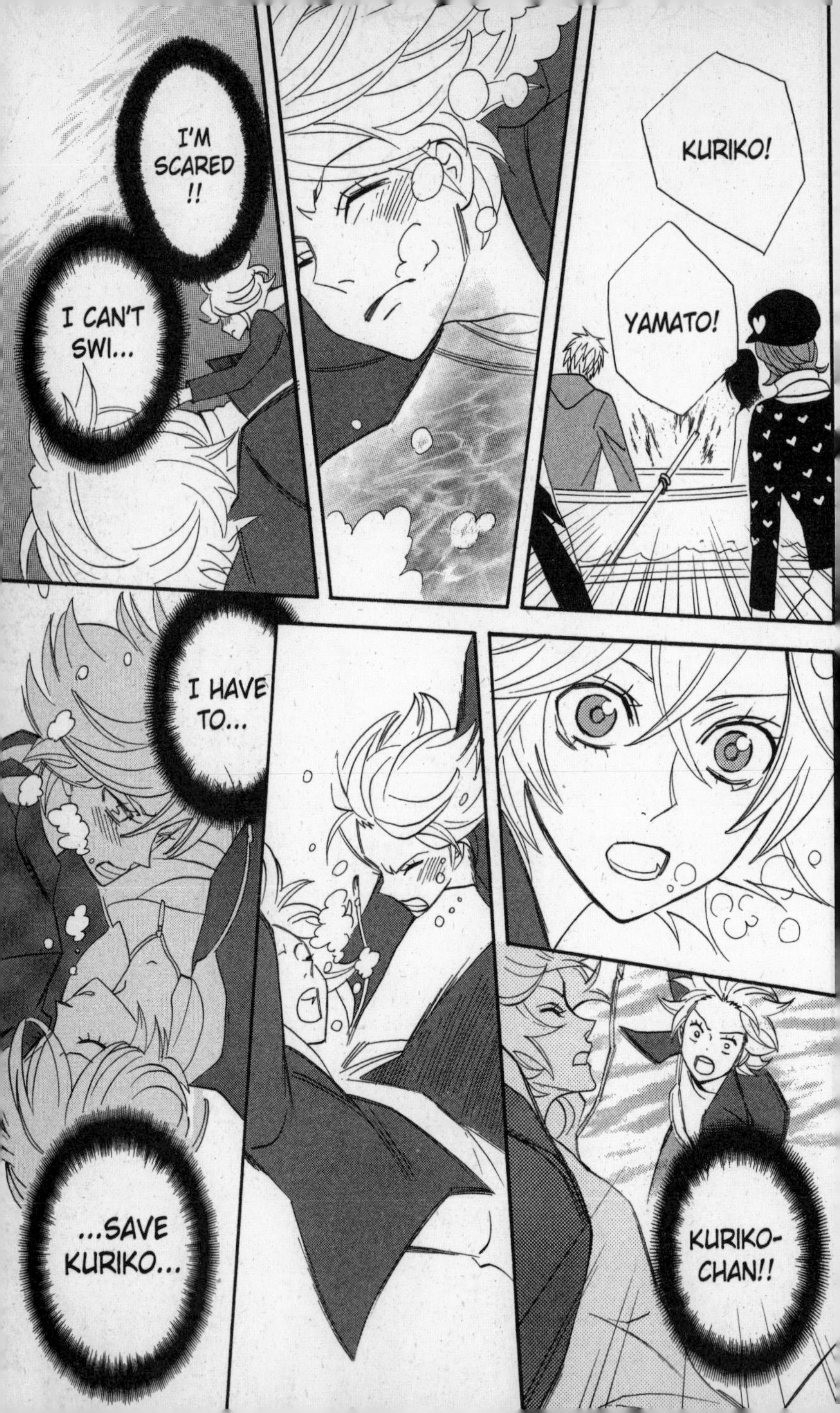
KURIKO!
YAMATO!
I'M SCARED!!
I CAN'T SWI...
KURIKO-CHAN!!
I HAVE TO...
...SAVE KURIKO...

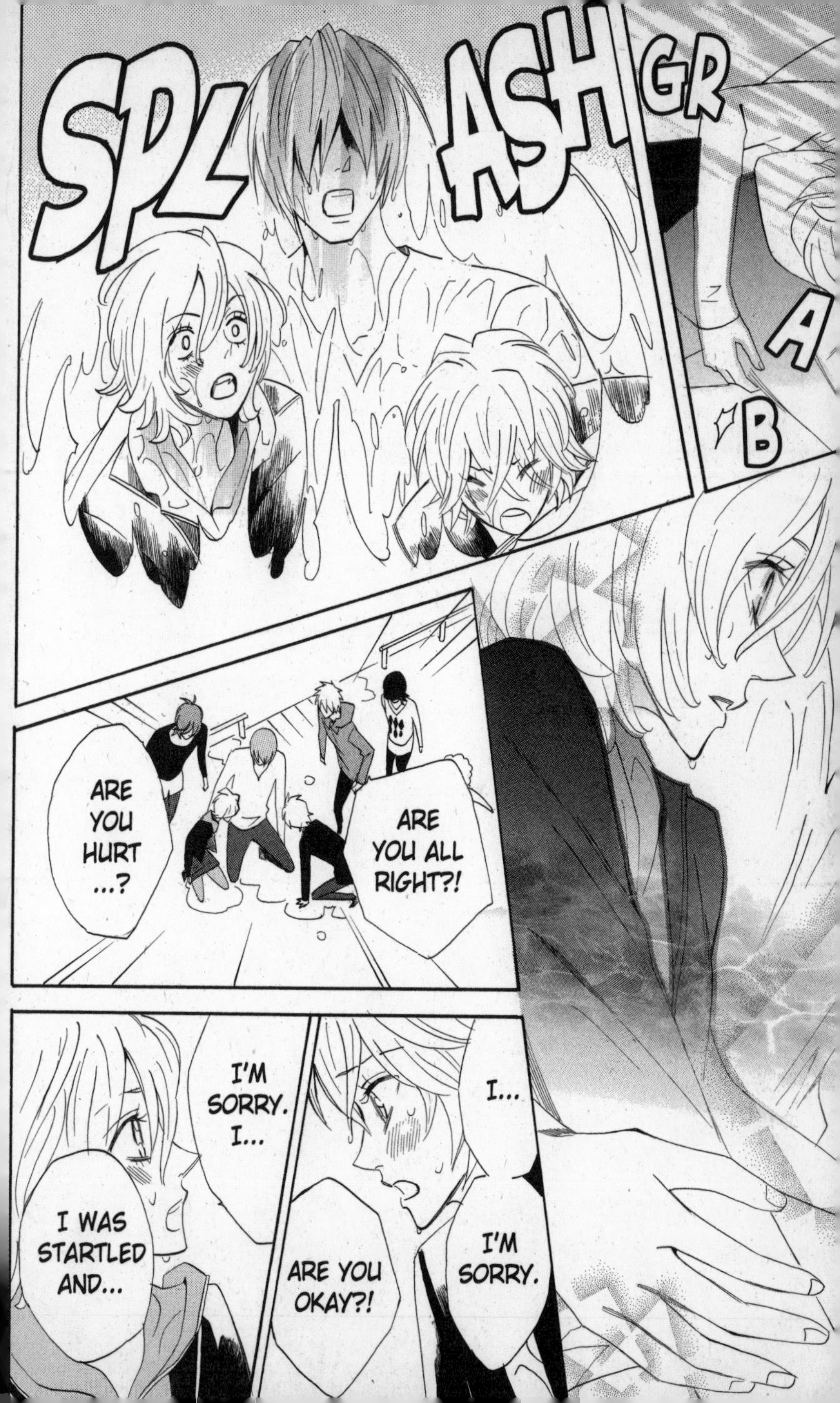
GRAB
SPLASH
ARE YOU ALL RIGHT?!
ARE YOU HURT ...?
I...
I'M SORRY.
ARE YOU OKAY?!
I'M SORRY. I...
I WAS STARTLED AND...

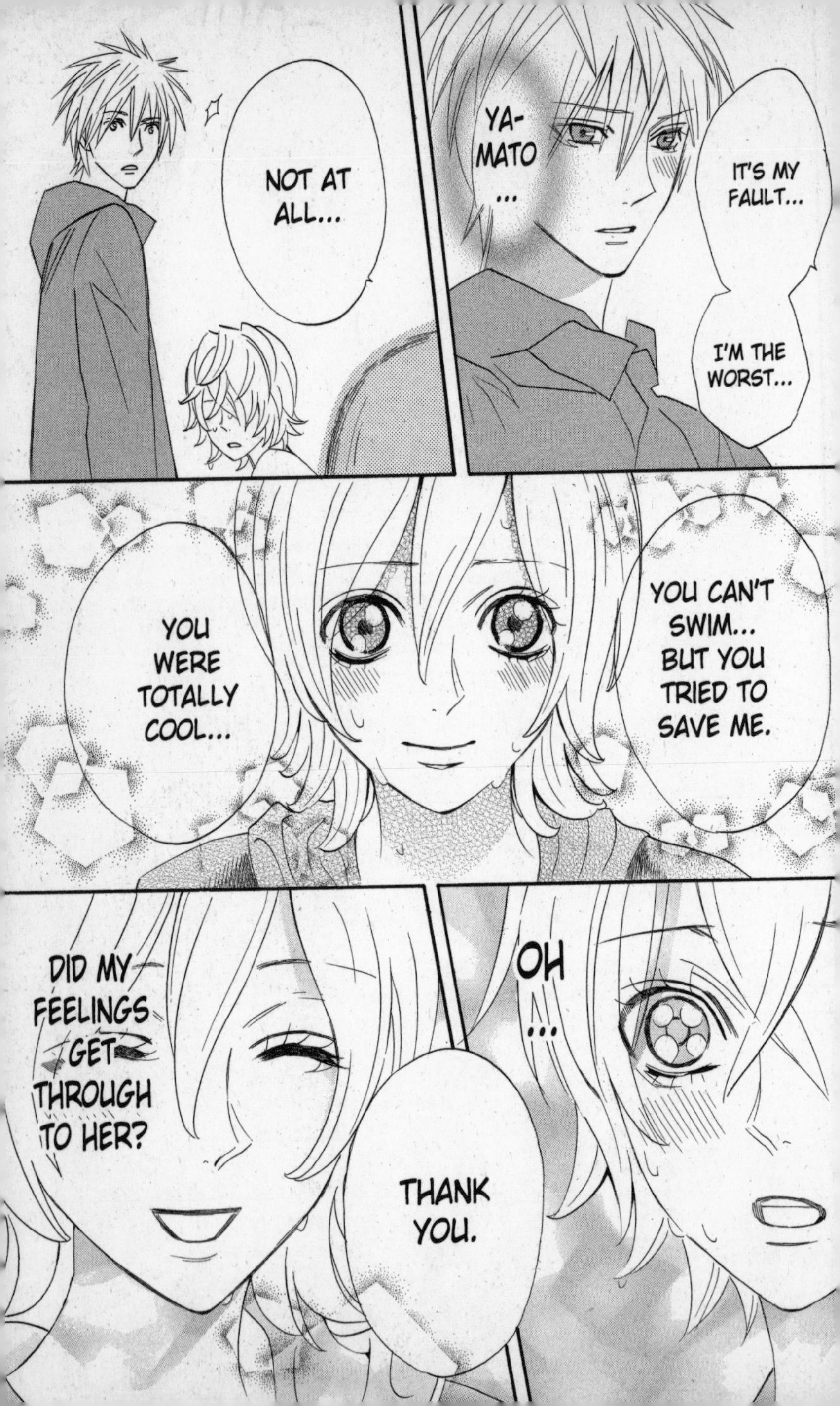
IT'S MY FAULT...
I'M THE WORST...
YA-MATO ...
NOT AT ALL...
YOU CAN'T SWIM... BUT YOU TRIED TO SAVE ME.
YOU WERE TOTALLY COOL...
OH ...
THANK YOU.
DID MY FEELINGS GET THROUGH TO HER?

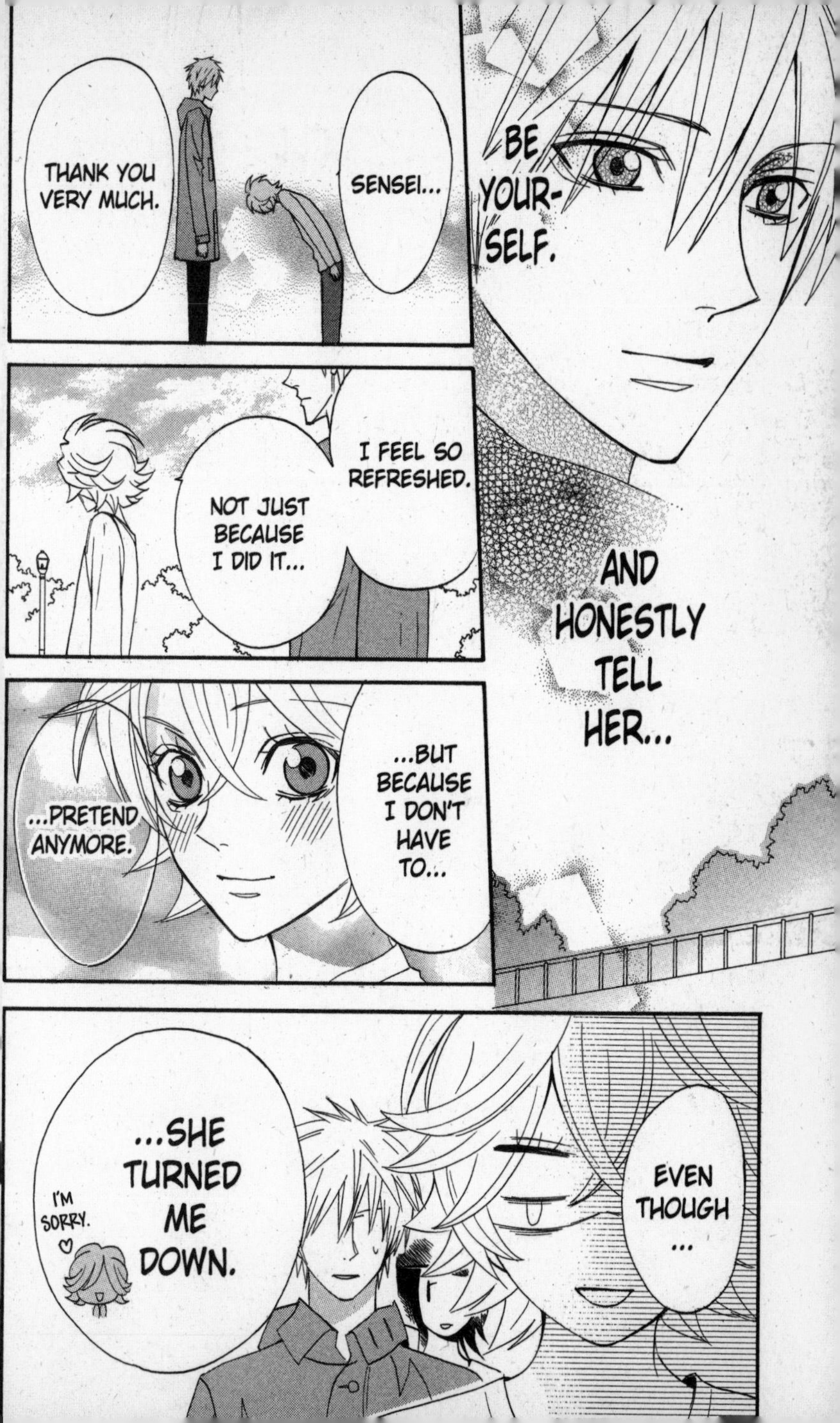
BE YOUR-SELF.
AND HONESTLY TELL HER...
SENSEI...
THANK YOU VERY MUCH.
I FEEL SO REFRESHED.
NOT JUST BECAUSE I DID IT...
...BUT BECAUSE I DON'T HAVE TO...
...PRETEND ANYMORE.
EVEN THOUGH...
...SHE TURNED ME DOWN.
I'M SORRY.

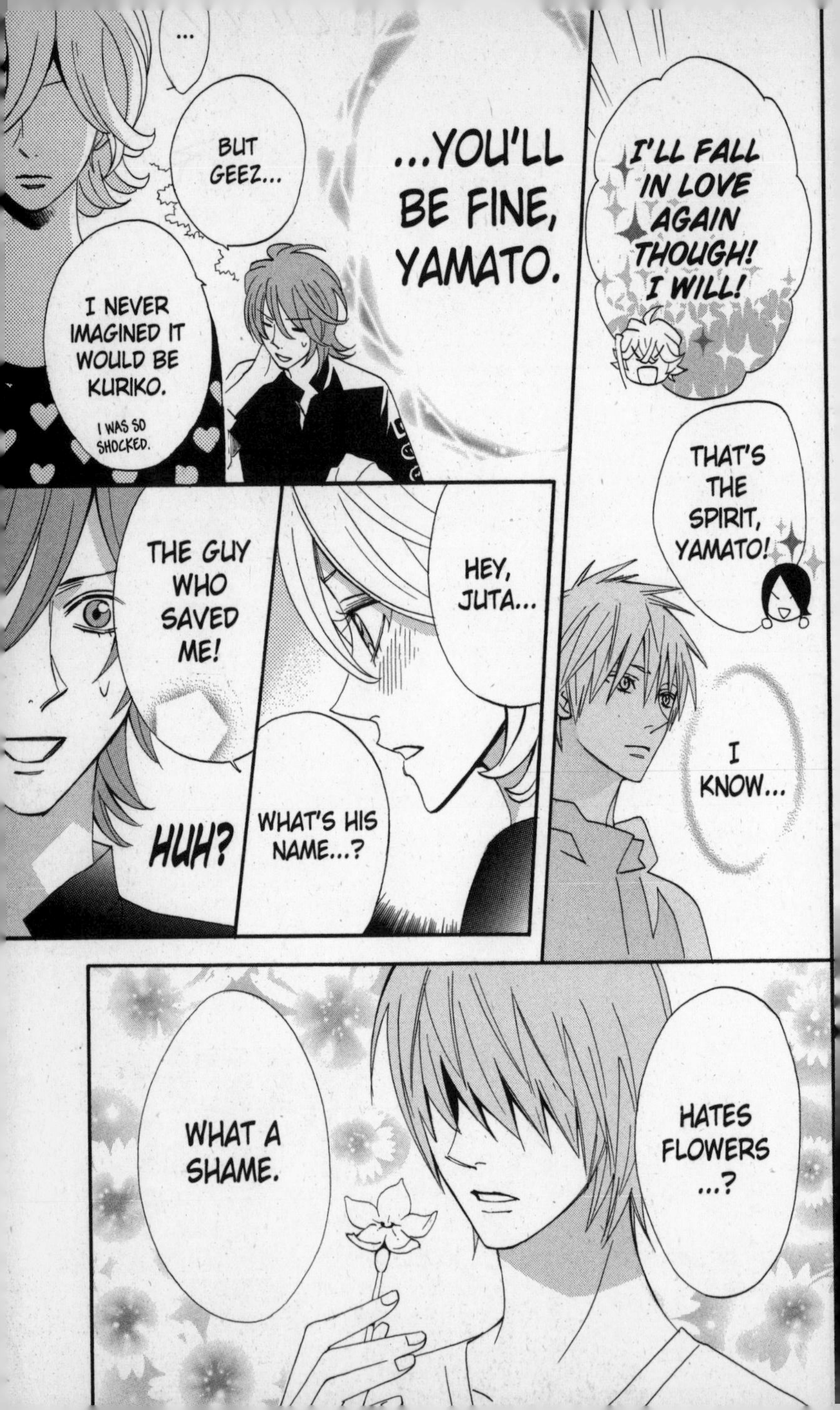
I'LL FALL IN LOVE AGAIN THOUGH! I WILL!
THAT'S THE SPIRIT, YAMATO!
I KNOW...
...YOU'LL BE FINE, YAMATO.
...
BUT GEEZ...
I NEVER IMAGINED IT WOULD BE KURIKO.
I WAS SO SHOCKED.
HEY, JUTA...
WHAT'S HIS NAME...?
THE GUY WHO SAVED ME!
HUH?
HATES FLOWERS ...?
WHAT A SHAME.

OTOMEN

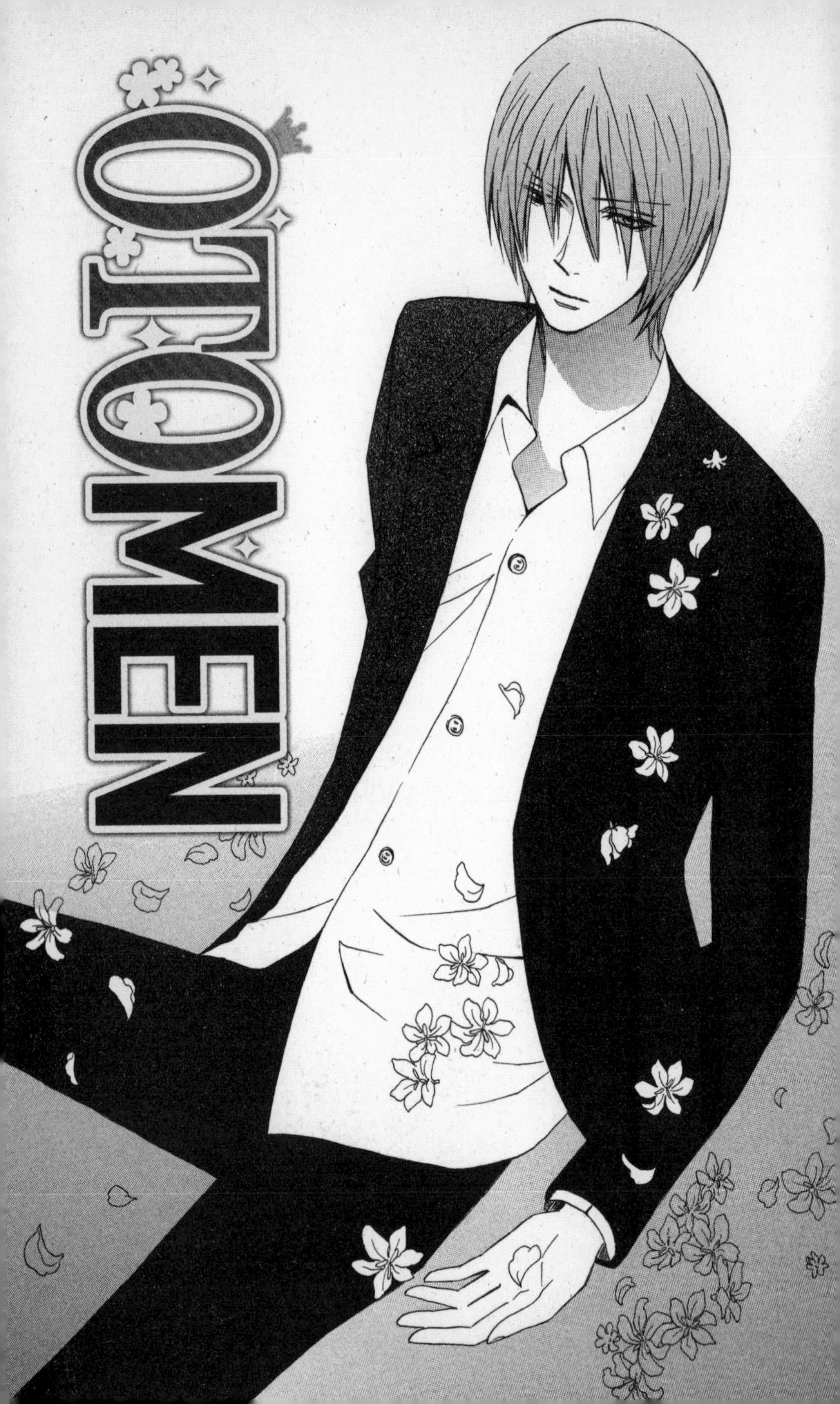
OTOMEN

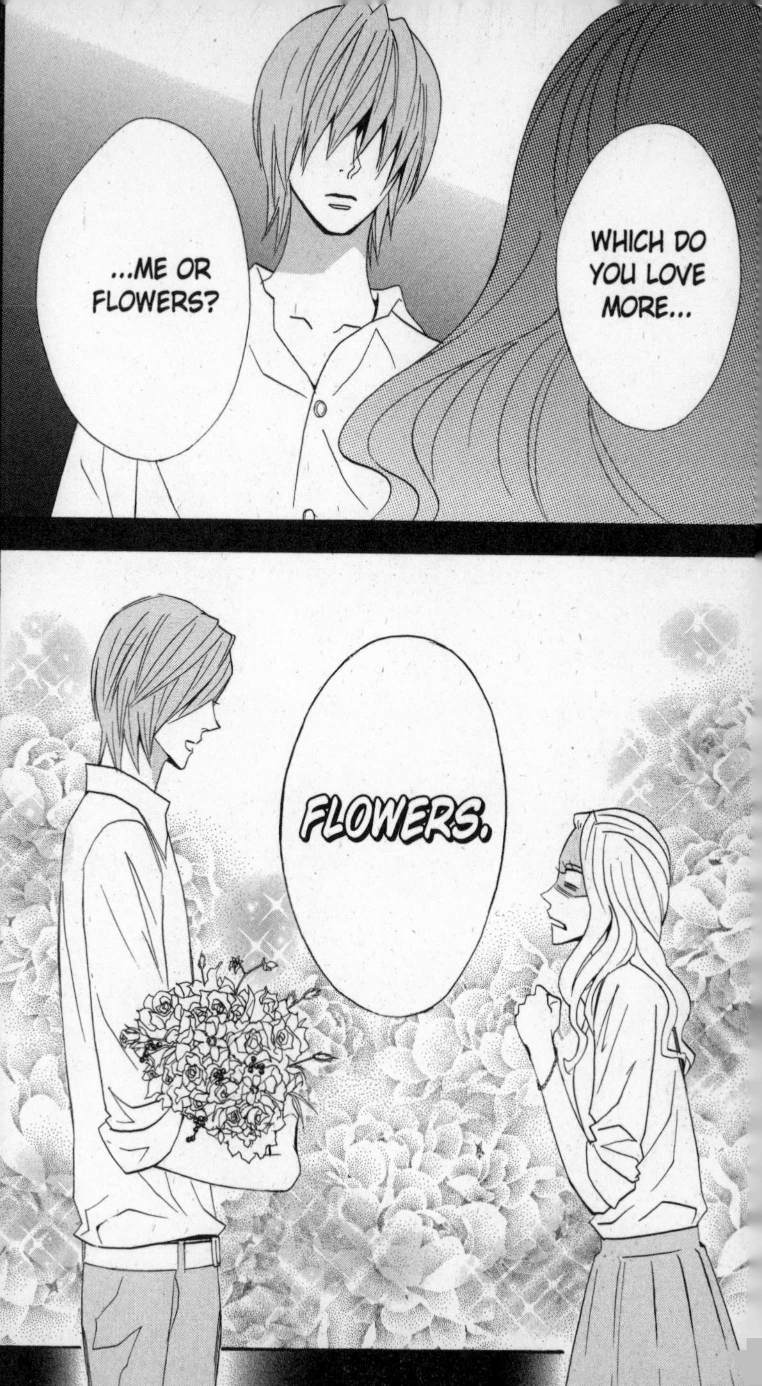
WHICH DO YOU LOVE MORE...
...ME OR FLOWERS?
FLOWERS.

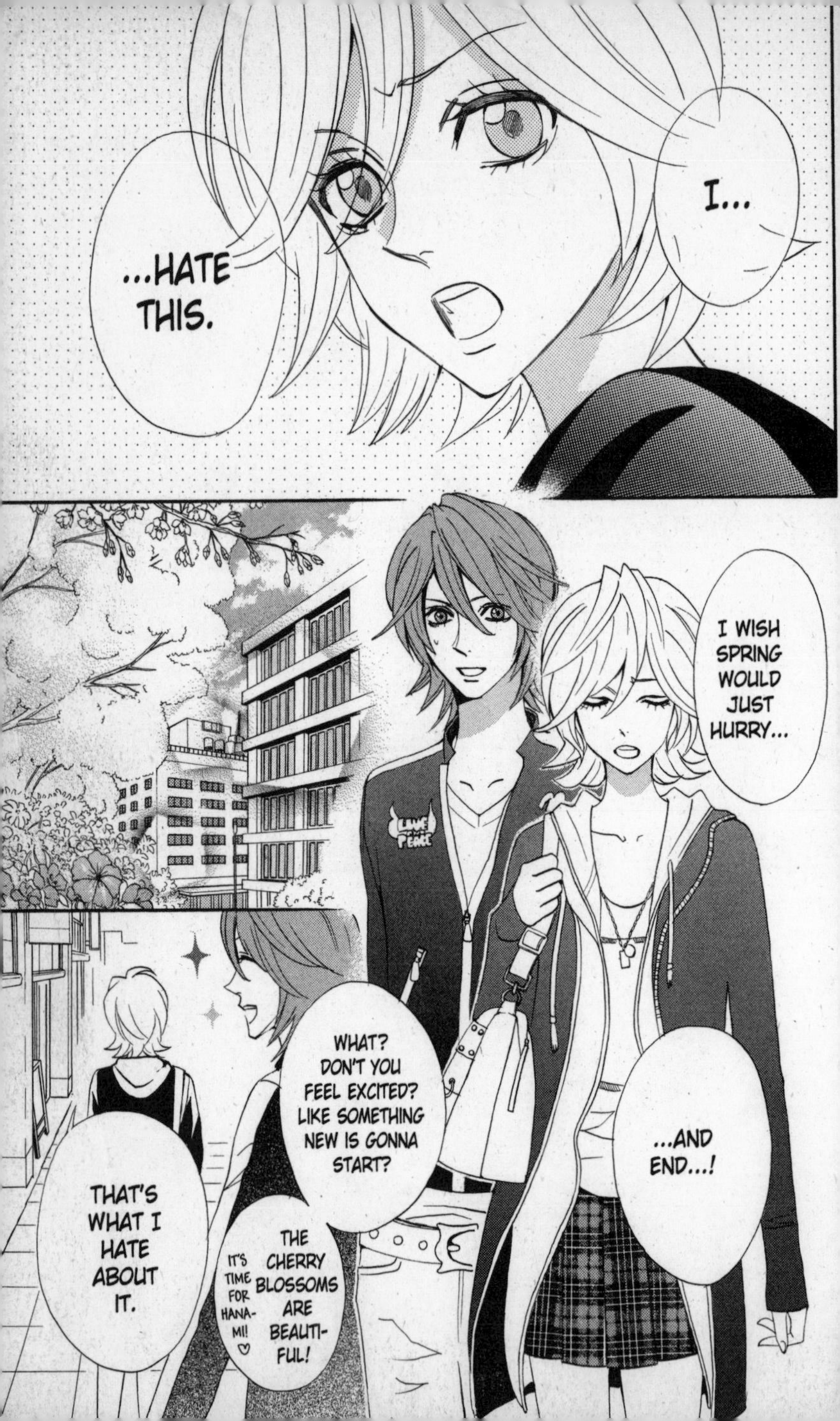
I...
...HATE THIS.
I WISH SPRING WOULD JUST HURRY...
...AND END...!
WHAT? DON'T YOU FEEL EXCITED? LIKE SOMETHING NEW IS GONNA START?
THE CHERRY BLOSSOMS ARE BEAUTIFUL!
IT'S TIME FOR HANAMI! ♡
THAT'S WHAT I HATE ABOUT IT.

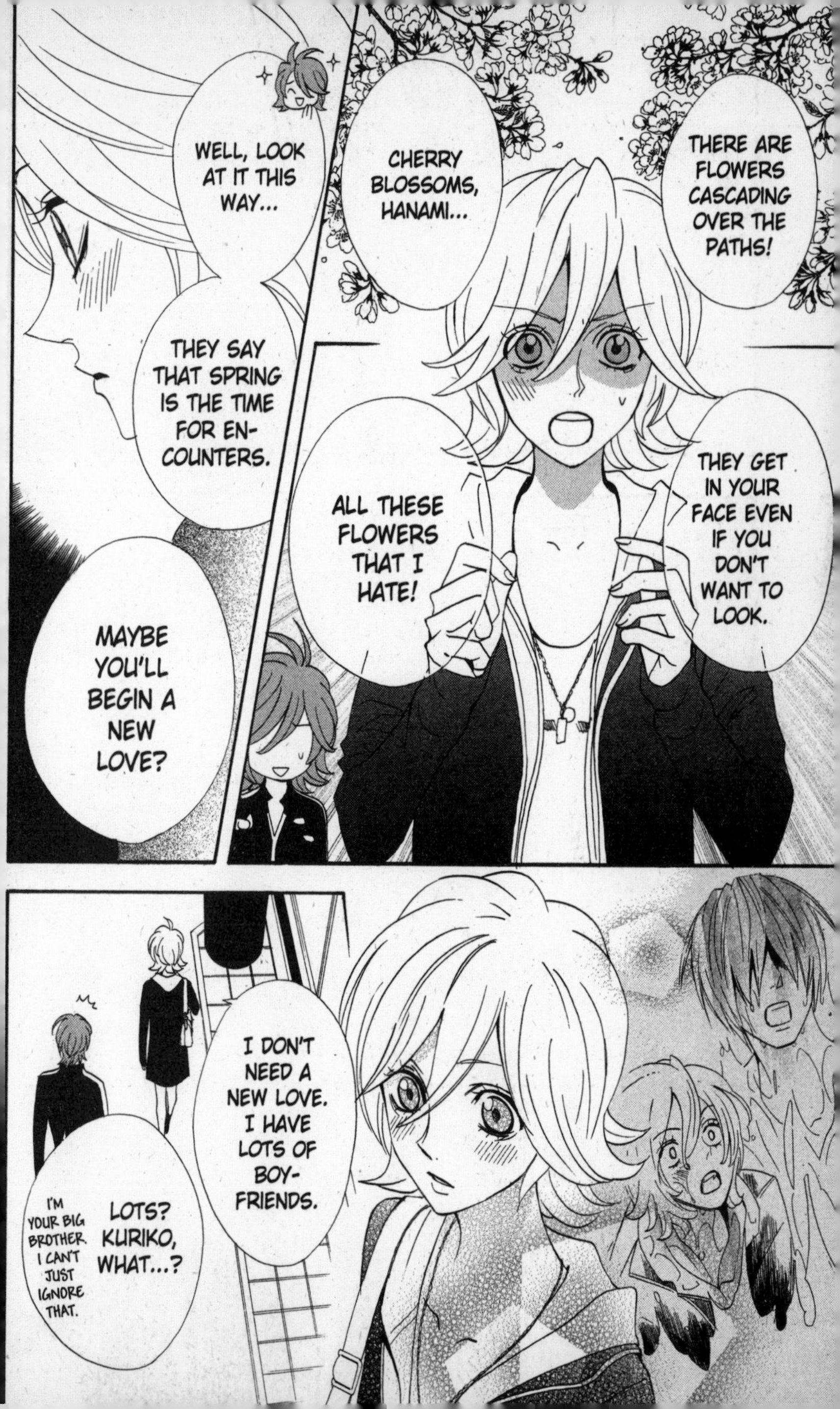
THERE ARE FLOWERS CASCADING OVER THE PATHS!
CHERRY BLOSSOMS, HANAMI...
THEY GET IN YOUR FACE EVEN IF YOU DON'T WANT TO LOOK.
ALL THESE FLOWERS THAT I HATE!
WELL, LOOK AT IT THIS WAY...
THEY SAY THAT SPRING IS THE TIME FOR EN-COUNTERS.
MAYBE YOU'LL BEGIN A NEW LOVE?
I DON'T NEED A NEW LOVE. I HAVE LOTS OF BOY-FRIENDS.
LOTS? KURIKO, WHAT...?
I'M YOUR BIG BROTHER. I CAN'T JUST IGNORE THAT.

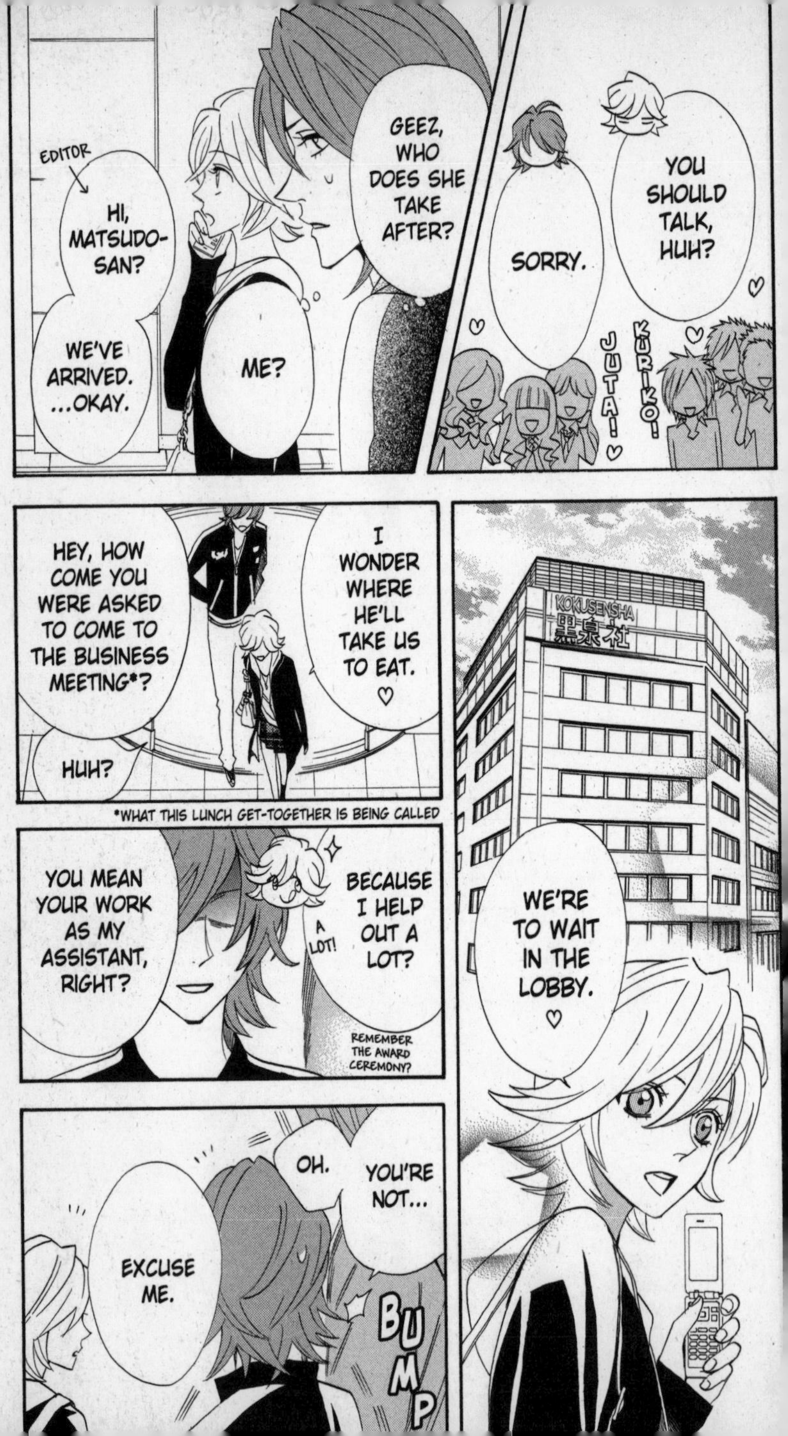
YOU SHOULD TALK, HUH?
KURIKO!
JUTA!
SORRY.
GEEZ, WHO DOES SHE TAKE AFTER?
ME?
EDITOR
HI, MATSUDO-SAN?
WE'VE ARRIVED. ...OKAY.
KOKUSENSHA
黒泉社
WE'RE TO WAIT IN THE LOBBY. ♡
I WONDER WHERE HE'LL TAKE US TO EAT. ♡
HEY, HOW COME YOU WERE ASKED TO COME TO THE BUSINESS MEETING*?
HUH?
*WHAT THIS LUNCH GET-TOGETHER IS BEING CALLED
BECAUSE I HELP OUT A LOT?
A LOT!
REMEMBER THE AWARD CEREMONY?
YOU MEAN YOUR WORK AS MY ASSISTANT, RIGHT?
YOU'RE NOT...
OH.
BUMP
EXCUSE ME.

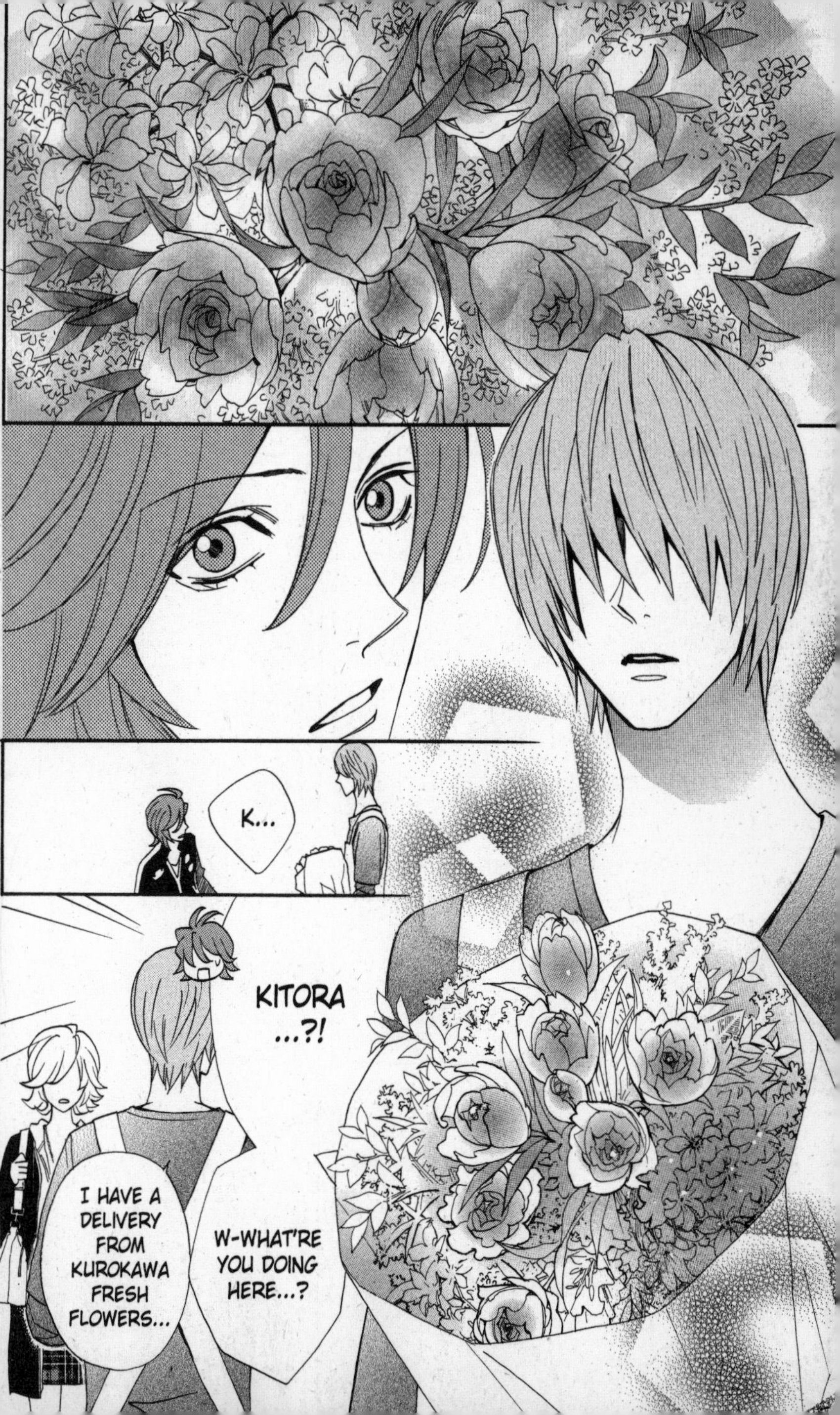
K...
KITORA ...?!
W-WHAT'RE YOU DOING HERE...?
I HAVE A DELIVERY FROM KUROKAWA FRESH FLOWERS...

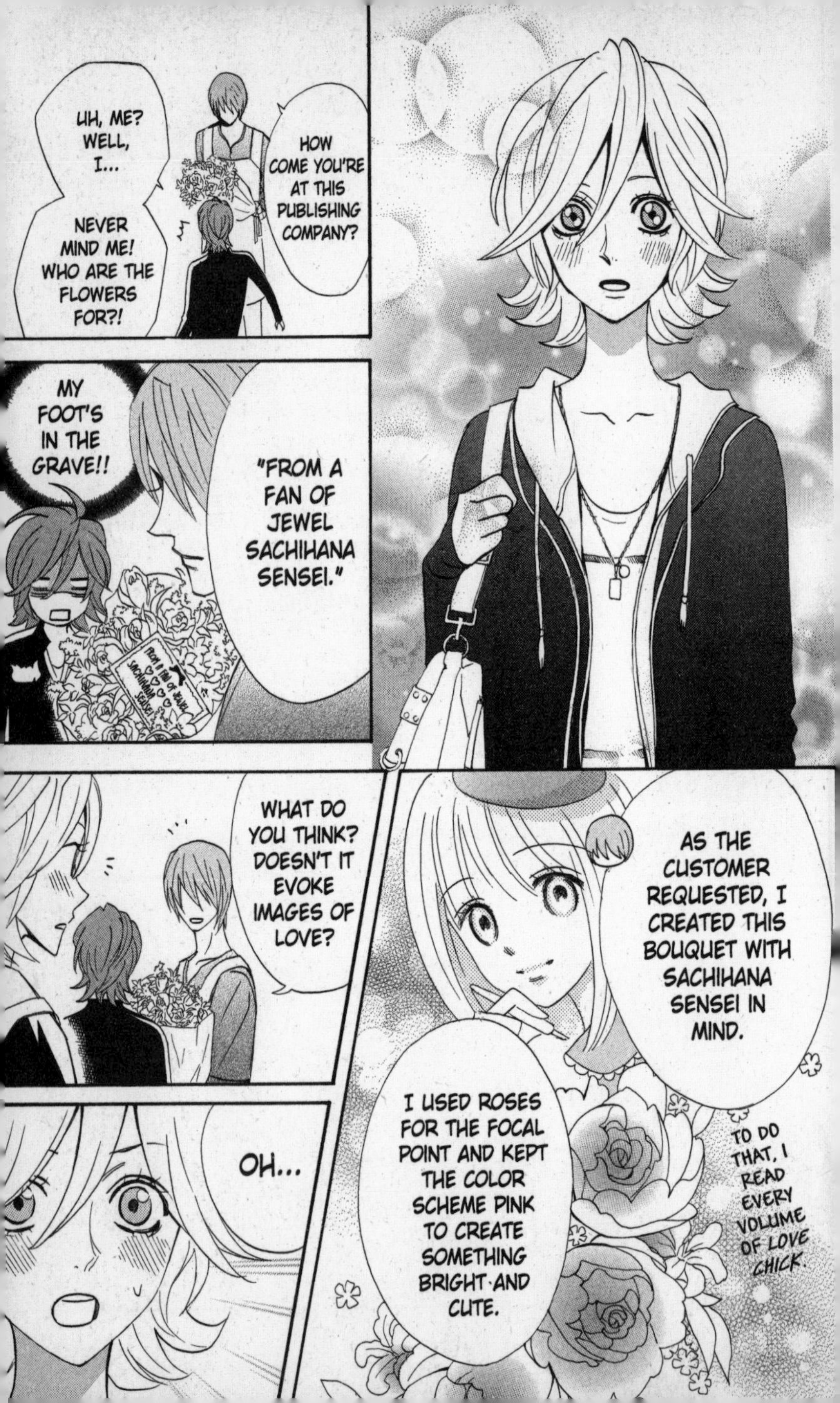
HOW COME YOU'RE AT THIS PUBLISHING COMPANY?
UH, ME? WELL, I...
NEVER MIND ME! WHO ARE THE FLOWERS FOR?!
"FROM A FAN OF JEWEL SACHIHANA SENSEI."
MY FOOT'S IN THE GRAVE!!
AS THE CUSTOMER REQUESTED, I CREATED THIS BOUQUET WITH SACHIHANA SENSEI IN MIND.
TO DO THAT, I READ EVERY VOLUME OF *LOVE CHICK*.
I USED ROSES FOR THE FOCAL POINT AND KEPT THE COLOR SCHEME PINK TO CREATE SOMETHING BRIGHT AND CUTE.
WHAT DO YOU THINK? DOESN'T IT EVOKE IMAGES OF LOVE?
OH...

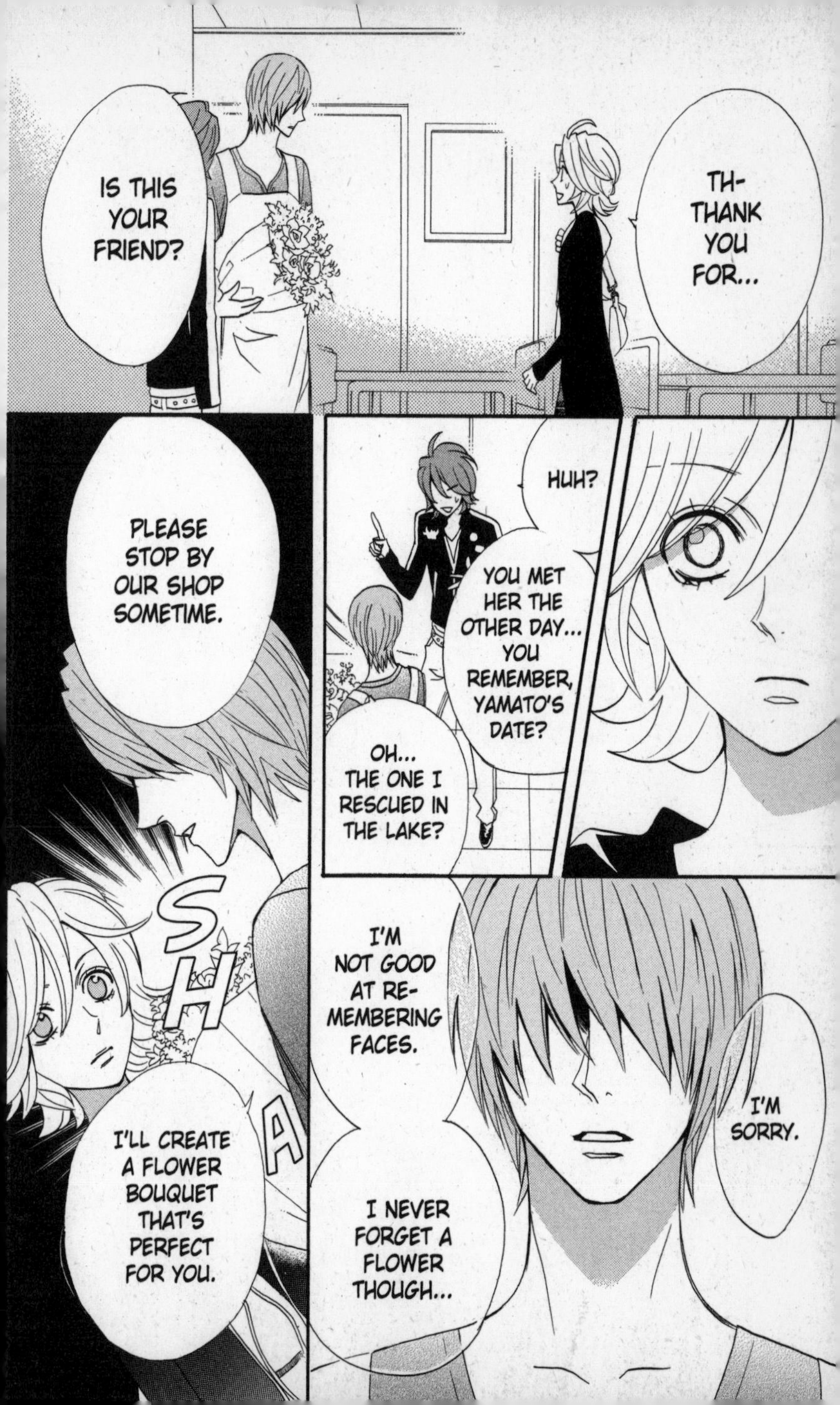
TH- THANK YOU FOR...
IS THIS YOUR FRIEND?
HUH?
YOU MET HER THE OTHER DAY... YOU REMEMBER, YAMATO'S DATE?
OH... THE ONE I RESCUED IN THE LAKE?
I'M SORRY.
I'M NOT GOOD AT RE-MEMBERING FACES.
I NEVER FORGET A FLOWER THOUGH...
PLEASE STOP BY OUR SHOP SOMETIME.
SHA
I'LL CREATE A FLOWER BOUQUET THAT'S PERFECT FOR YOU.

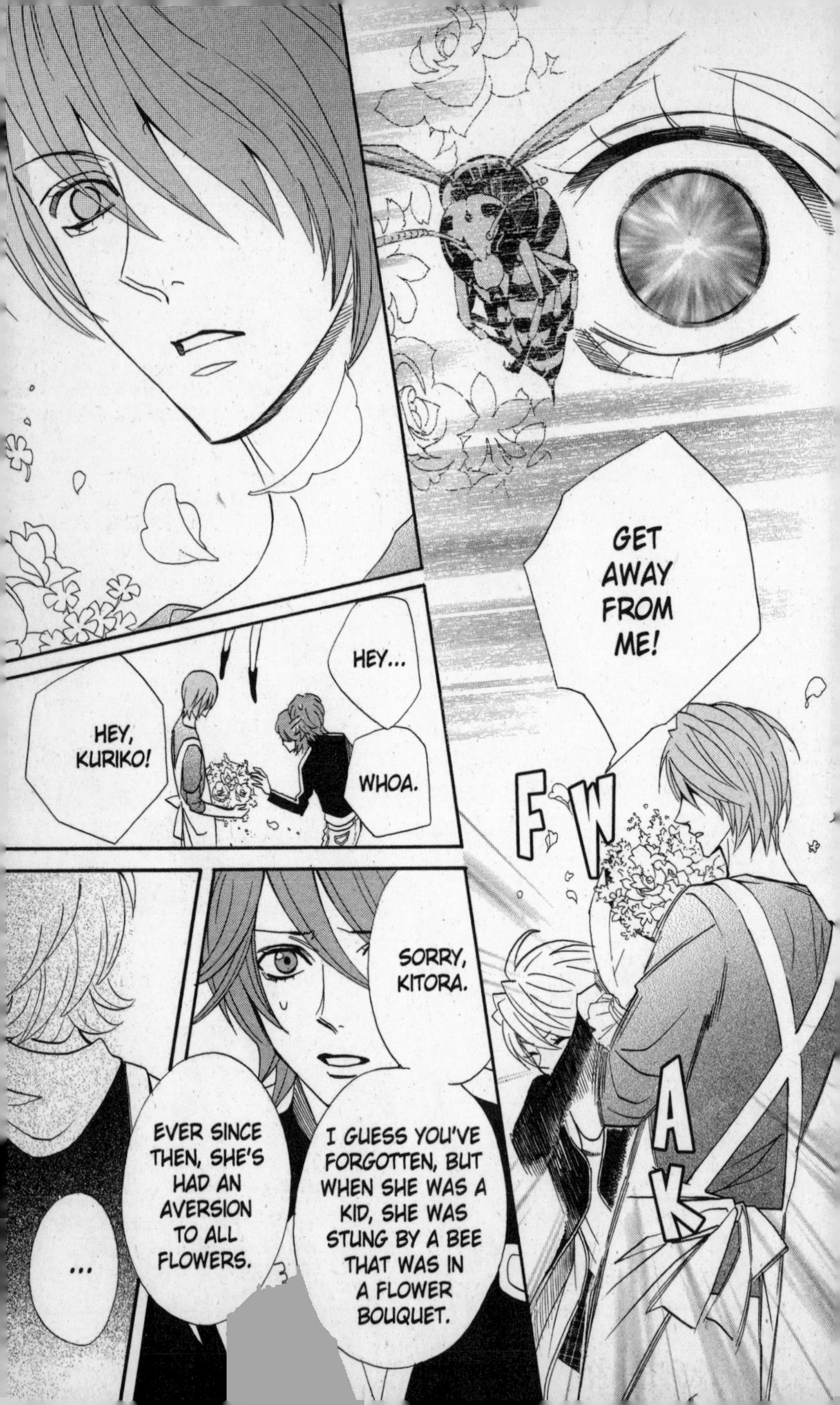
GET AWAY FROM ME!
FWAK
HEY...
HEY, KURIKO!
WHOA.
SORRY, KITORA.
I GUESS YOU'VE FORGOTTEN, BUT WHEN SHE WAS A KID, SHE WAS STUNG BY A BEE THAT WAS IN A FLOWER BOUQUET.
EVER SINCE THEN, SHE'S HAD AN AVERSION TO ALL FLOWERS.
...

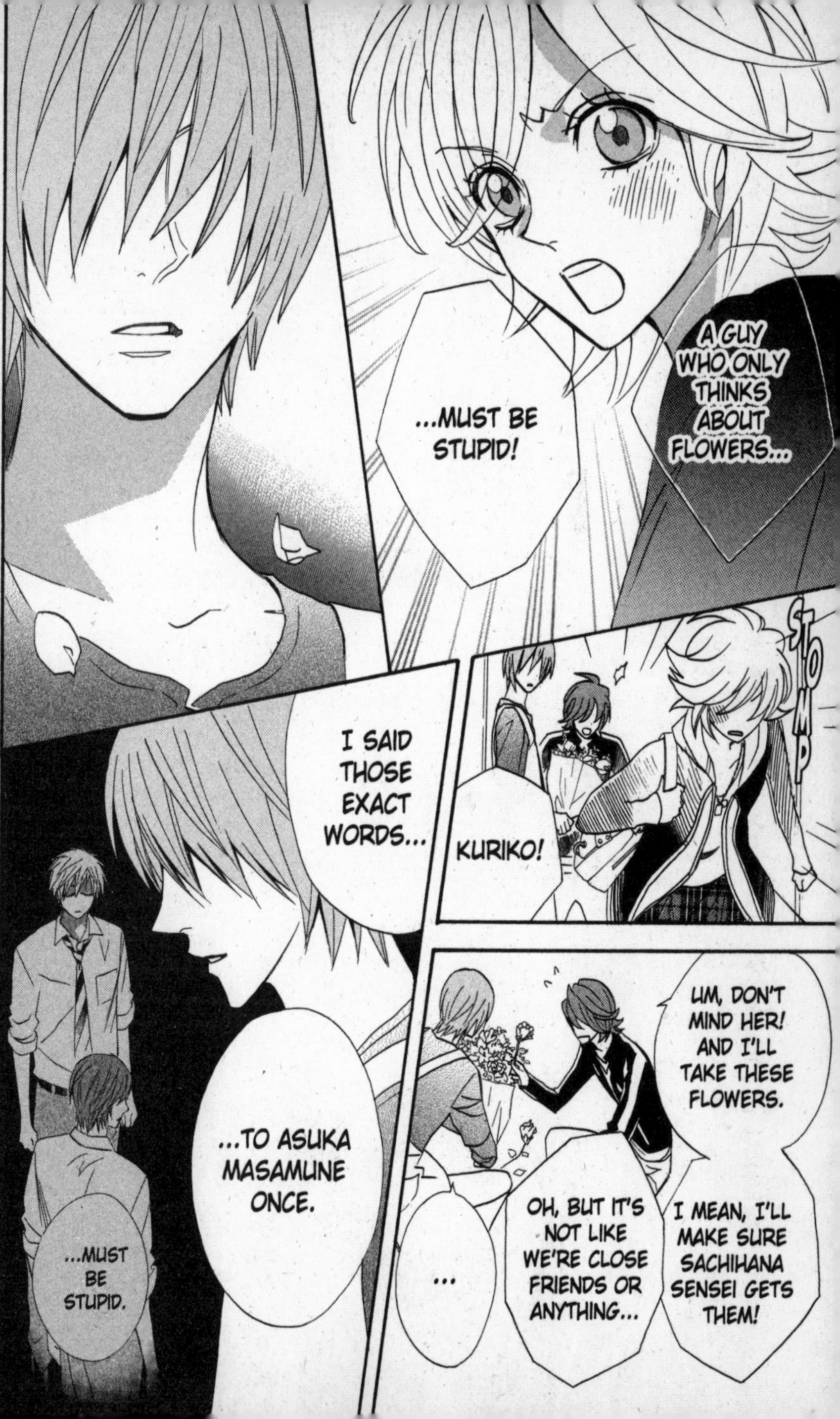
A GUY WHO ONLY THINKS ABOUT FLOWERS...
...MUST BE STUPID!
STOMP
KURIKO!
UM, DON'T MIND HER! AND I'LL TAKE THESE FLOWERS.
I MEAN, I'LL MAKE SURE SACHIHANA SENSEI GETS THEM!
OH, BUT IT'S NOT LIKE WE'RE CLOSE FRIENDS OR ANYTHING...
...
I SAID THOSE EXACT WORDS...
...TO ASUKA MASAMUNE ONCE.
...MUST BE STUPID.

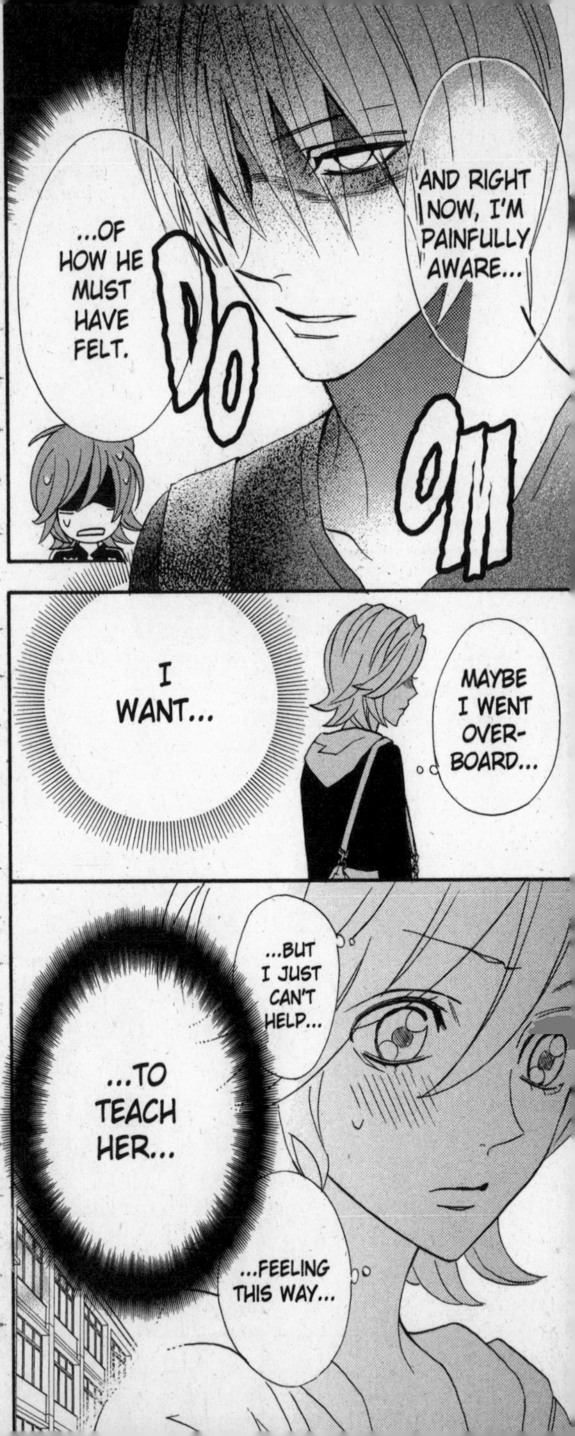
AND RIGHT NOW, I'M PAINFULLY AWARE...
...OF HOW HE MUST HAVE FELT.
MAYBE I WENT OVER-BOARD...
I WANT...
...BUT I JUST CAN'T HELP...
...TO TEACH HER...
...FEELING THIS WAY...

This story focuses on Kitora.
To go along with the last chapter, I wanted to write about someone else in love besides Asuka...
What do you think?

The next chapter is about bands and consequently love, but please don't misunderstand...
The lyrics are totally my own creation (naturally), but if it overlaps with something existing, please let me know.

By the way, the pompadour style falls into my top five favorite men's hairstyles. Guys should always keep their foreheads and ears exposed.

(Maybe I shouldn't be talking about this in Kitora's chapter...)

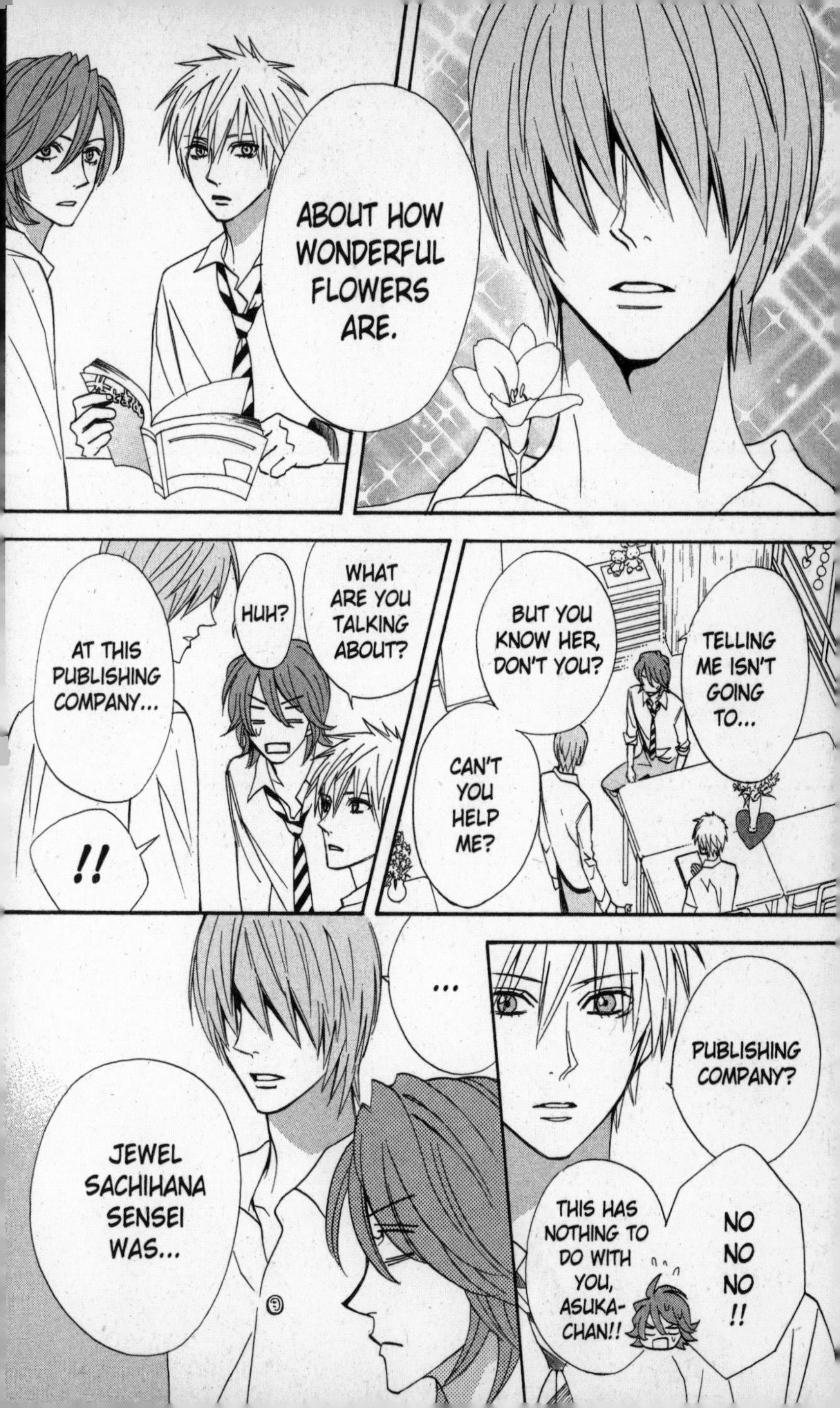
ABOUT HOW WONDERFUL FLOWERS ARE.
TELLING ME ISN'T GOING TO...
BUT YOU KNOW HER, DON'T YOU?
CAN'T YOU HELP ME?
WHAT ARE YOU TALKING ABOUT?
HUH?
AT THIS PUBLISHING COMPANY...
!!
PUBLISHING COMPANY?
NO NO NO !!
THIS HAS NOTHING TO DO WITH YOU, ASUKA-CHAN!!
...
JEWEL SACHIHANA SENSEI WAS...

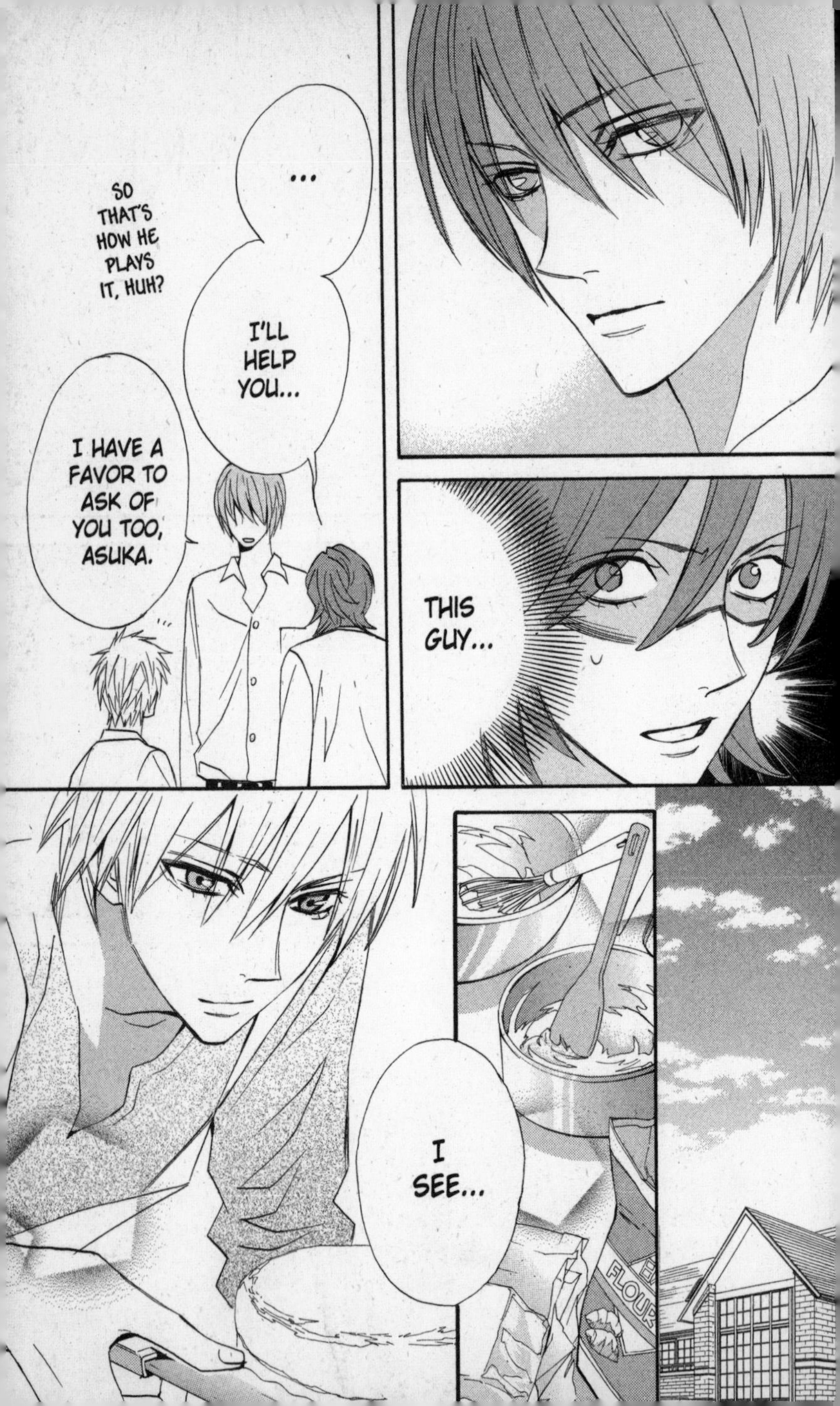
THIS GUY...
...
I'LL HELP YOU...
SO THAT'S HOW HE PLAYS IT, HUH?
I HAVE A FAVOR TO ASK OF YOU TOO, ASUKA.
FLOUR
I SEE...

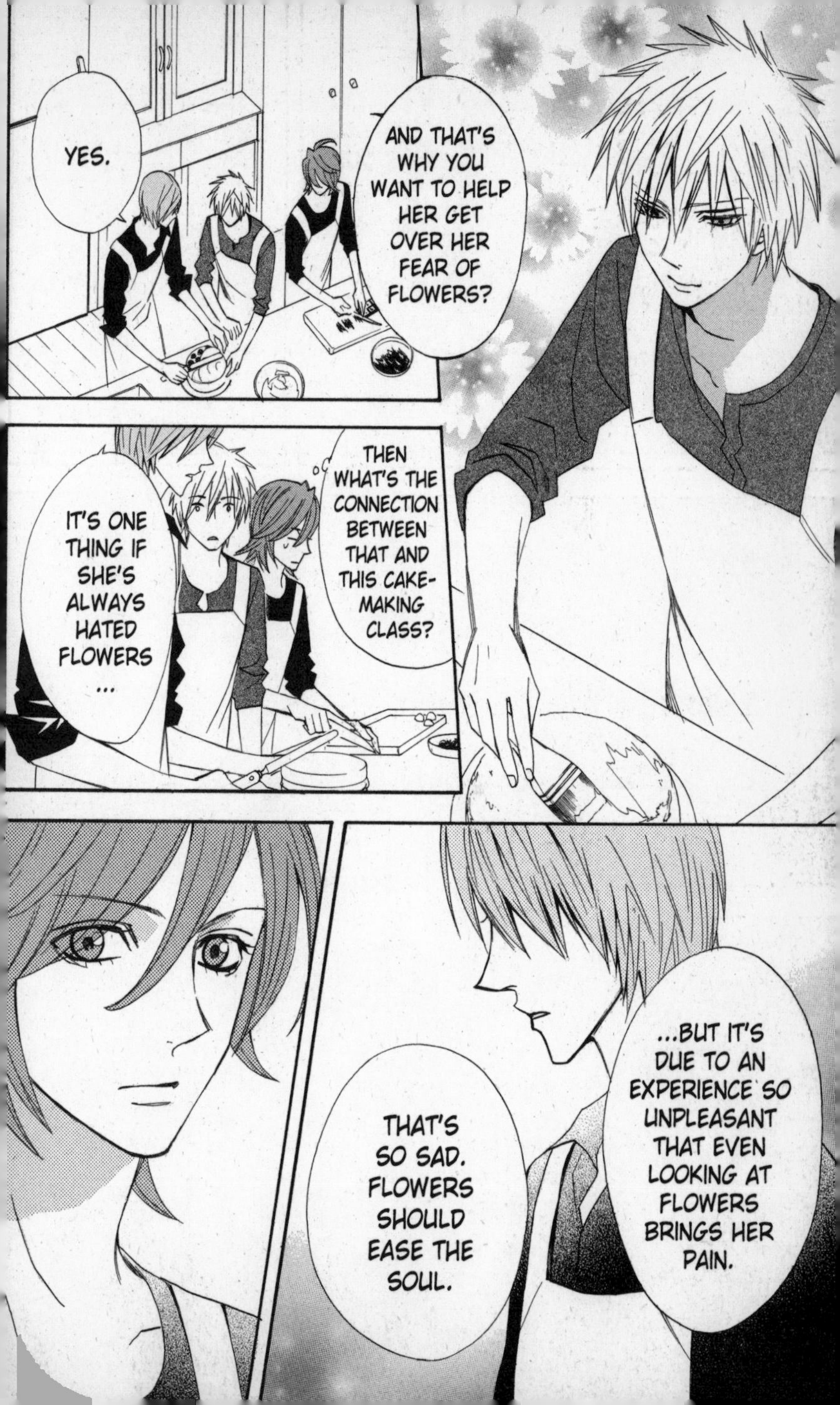
AND THAT'S WHY YOU WANT TO HELP HER GET OVER HER FEAR OF FLOWERS?
YES.
THEN WHAT'S THE CONNECTION BETWEEN THAT AND THIS CAKE-MAKING CLASS?
IT'S ONE THING IF SHE'S ALWAYS HATED FLOWERS ...
...BUT IT'S DUE TO AN EXPERIENCE SO UNPLEASANT THAT EVEN LOOKING AT FLOWERS BRINGS HER PAIN.
THAT'S SO SAD. FLOWERS SHOULD EASE THE SOUL.

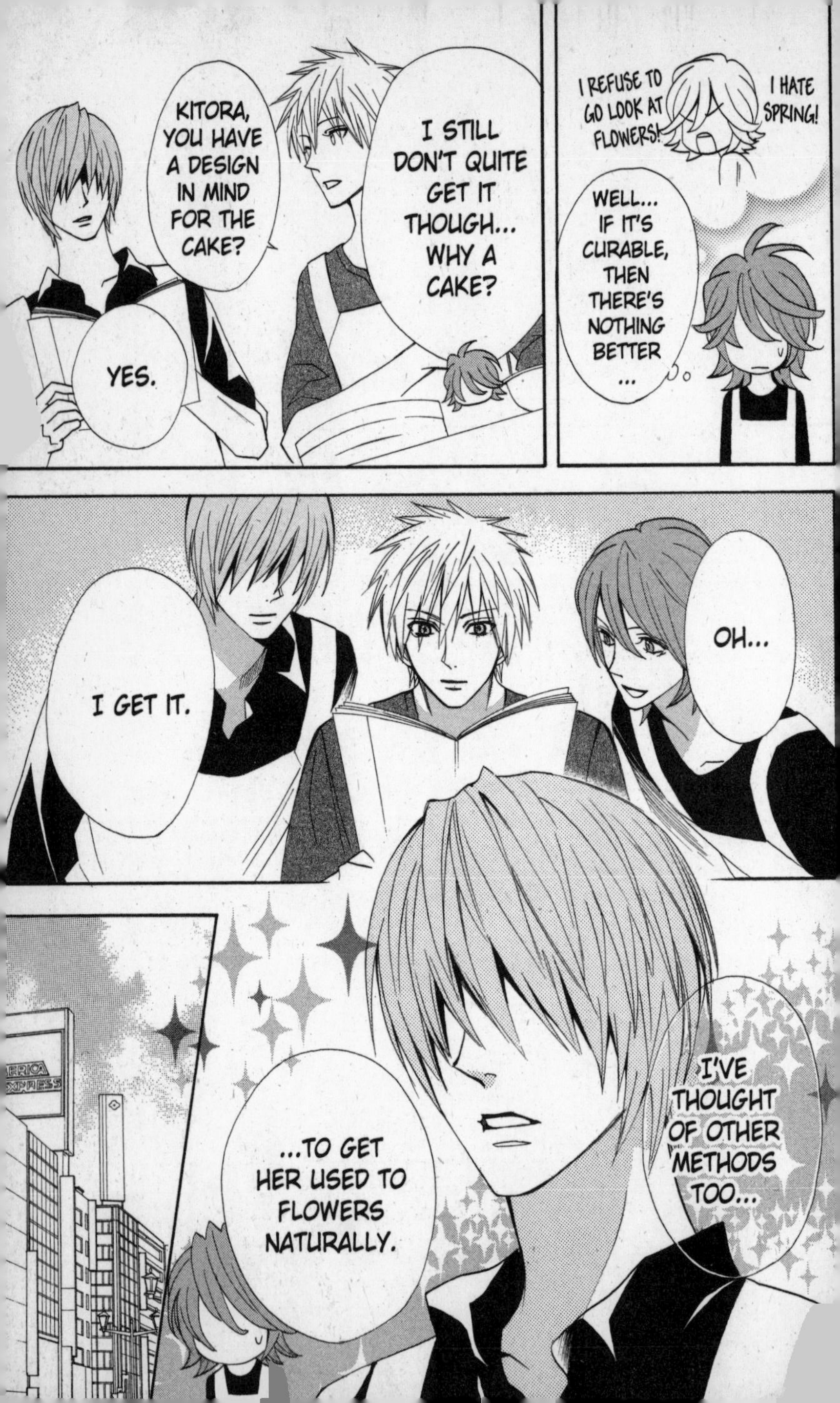
I HATE SPRING!
I REFUSE TO GO LOOK AT FLOWERS!
WELL... IF IT'S CURABLE, THEN THERE'S NOTHING BETTER...
I STILL DON'T QUITE GET IT THOUGH... WHY A CAKE?
KITORA, YOU HAVE A DESIGN IN MIND FOR THE CAKE?
YES.
OH...
I GET IT.
I'VE THOUGHT OF OTHER METHODS TOO...
...TO GET HER USED TO FLOWERS NATURALLY.

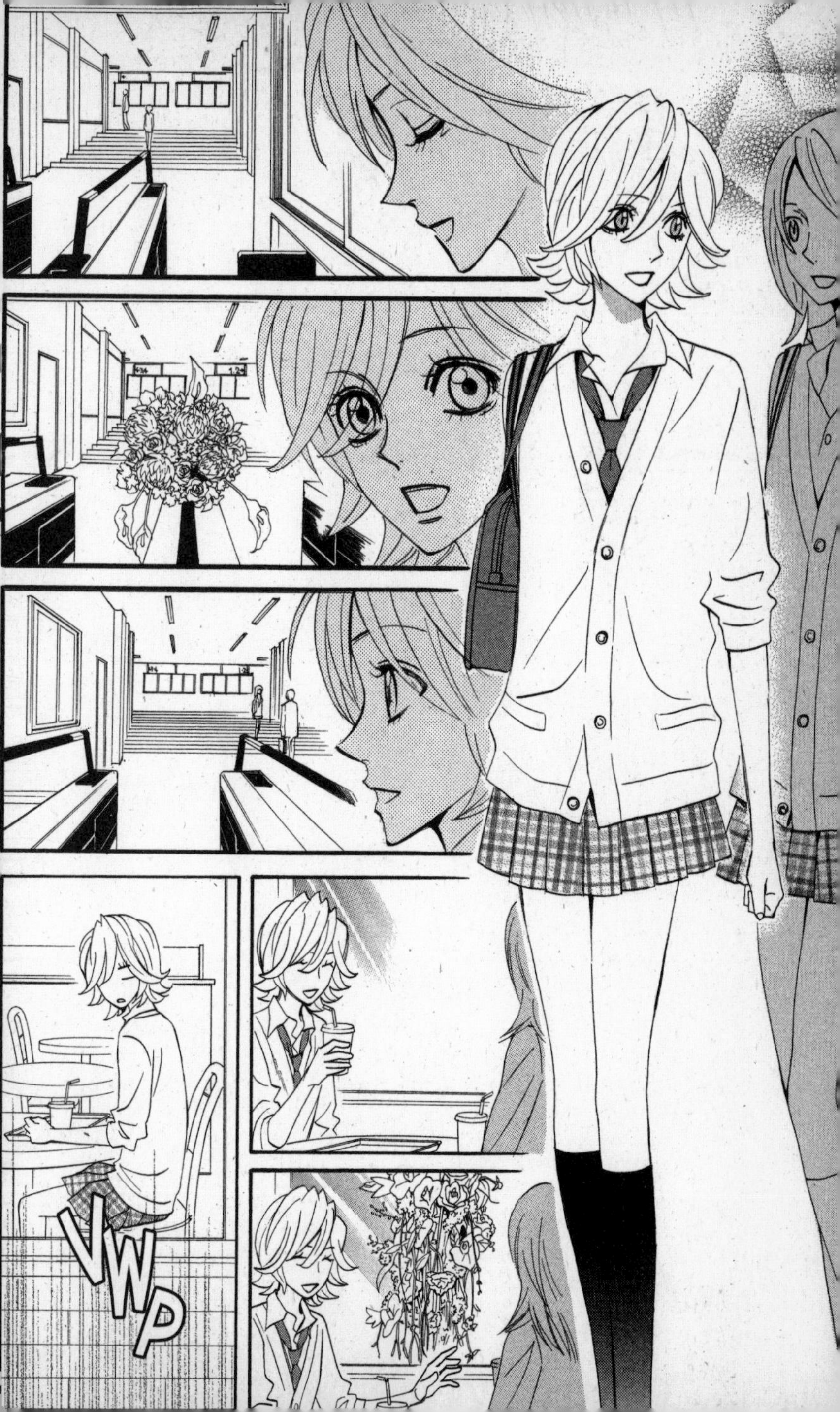
VWP

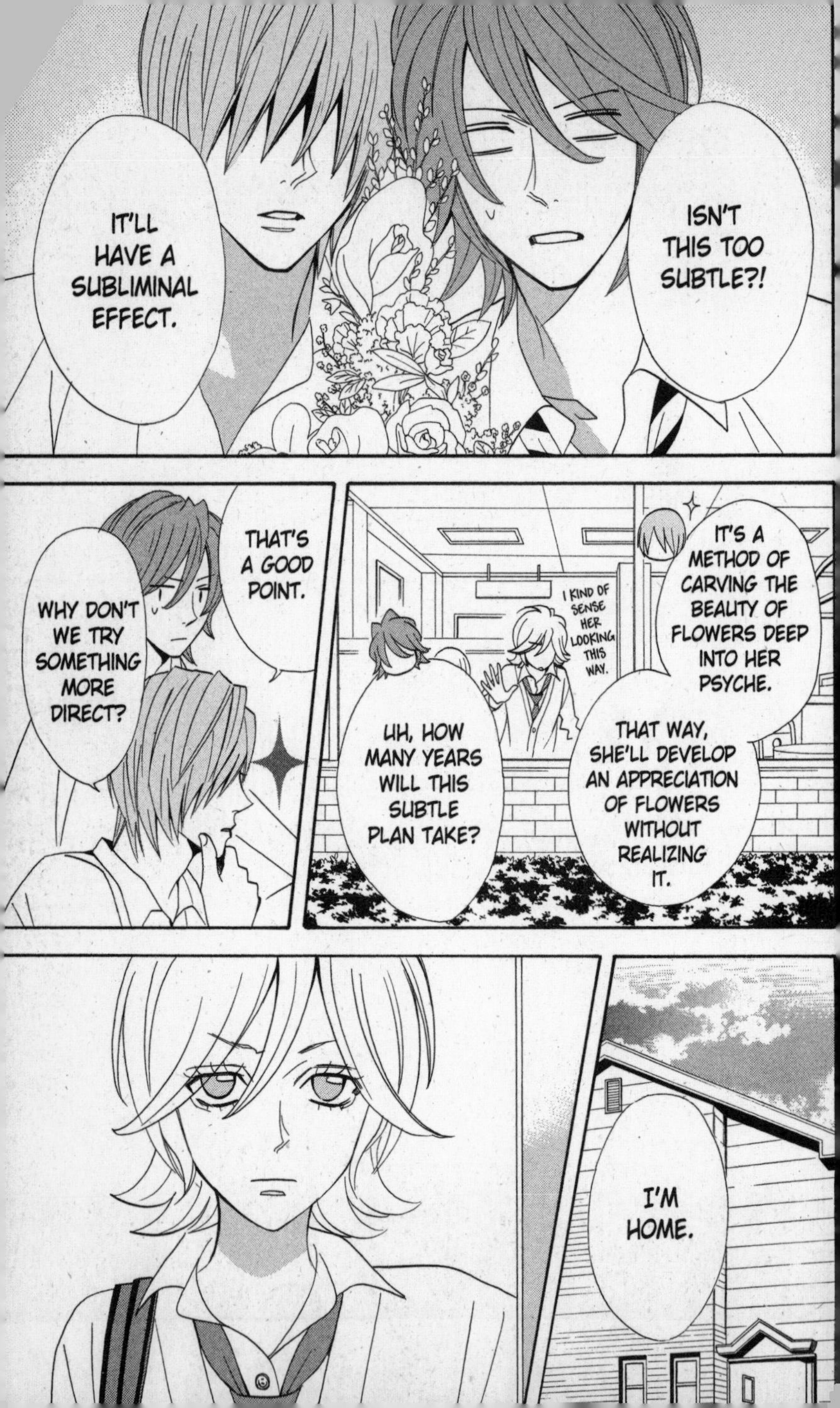
ISN'T THIS TOO SUBTLE?!
IT'LL HAVE A SUBLIMINAL EFFECT.
IT'S A METHOD OF CARVING THE BEAUTY OF FLOWERS DEEP INTO HER PSYCHE.
THAT WAY, SHE'LL DEVELOP AN APPRECIATION OF FLOWERS WITHOUT REALIZING IT.
I KIND OF SENSE HER LOOKING THIS WAY.
UH, HOW MANY YEARS WILL THIS SUBTLE PLAN TAKE?
THAT'S A GOOD POINT.
WHY DON'T WE TRY SOMETHING MORE DIRECT?
I'M HOME.

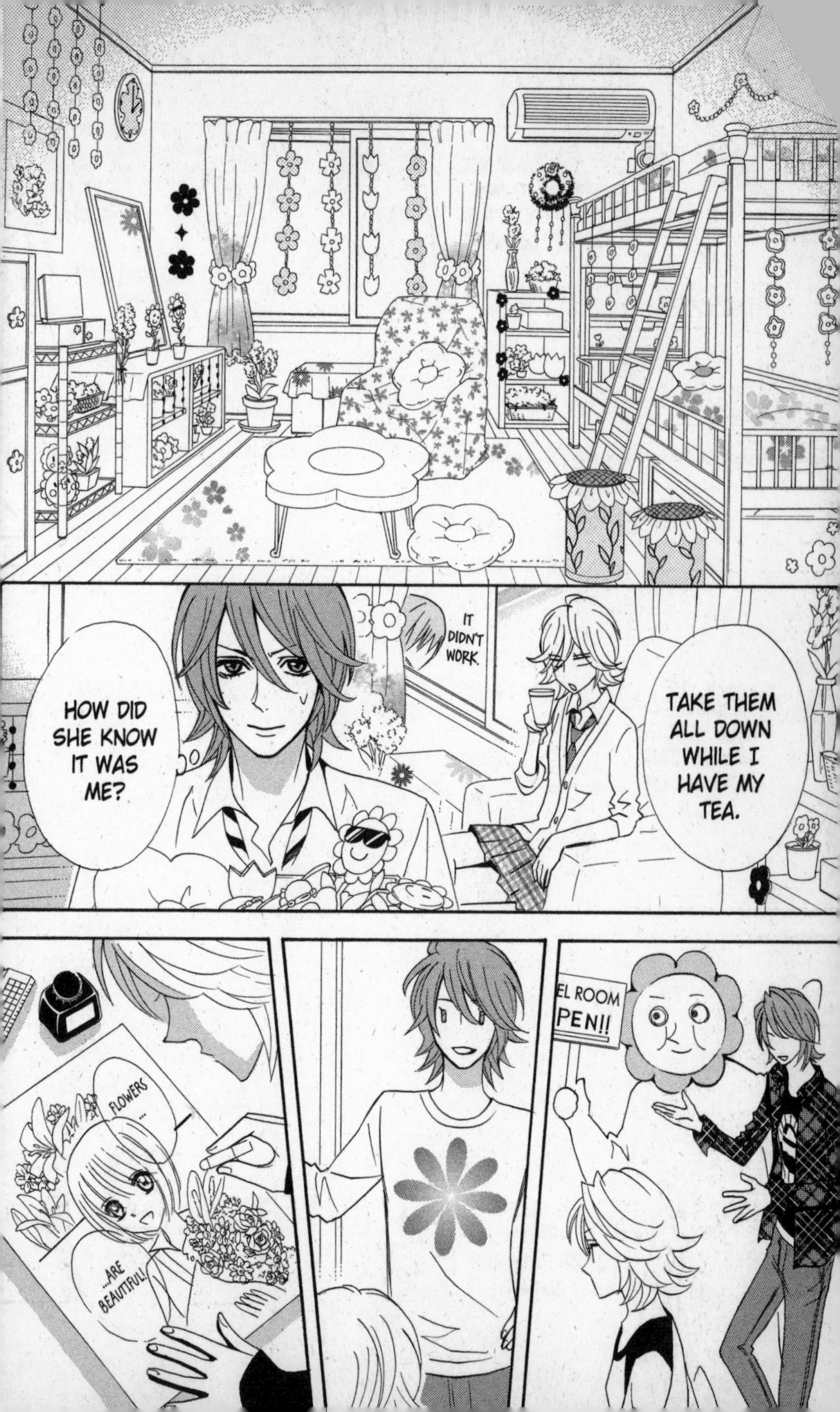
TAKE THEM ALL DOWN WHILE I HAVE MY TEA.
IT DIDN'T WORK.
HOW DID SHE KNOW IT WAS ME?
EL ROOM PEN!!
FLOWERS ...
...ARE BEAUTIFUL!

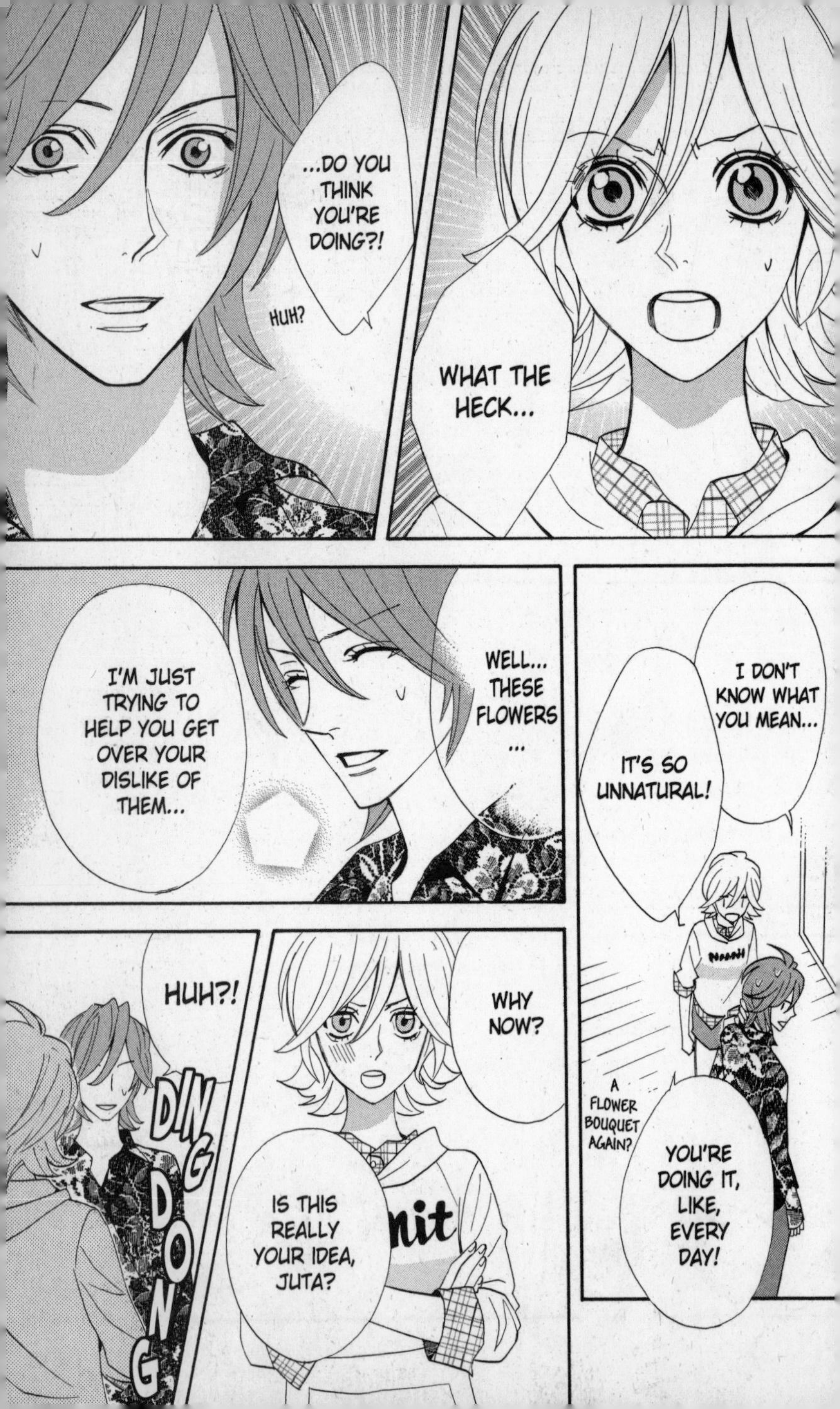
WHAT THE HECK...
...DO YOU THINK YOU'RE DOING?!
HUH?
I DON'T KNOW WHAT YOU MEAN...
IT'S SO UNNATURAL!
YOU'RE DOING IT, LIKE, EVERY DAY!
A FLOWER BOUQUET AGAIN?
WELL... THESE FLOWERS ...
I'M JUST TRYING TO HELP YOU GET OVER YOUR DISLIKE OF THEM...
WHY NOW?
IS THIS REALLY YOUR IDEA, JUTA?
HUH?!
DING DONG DING DONG

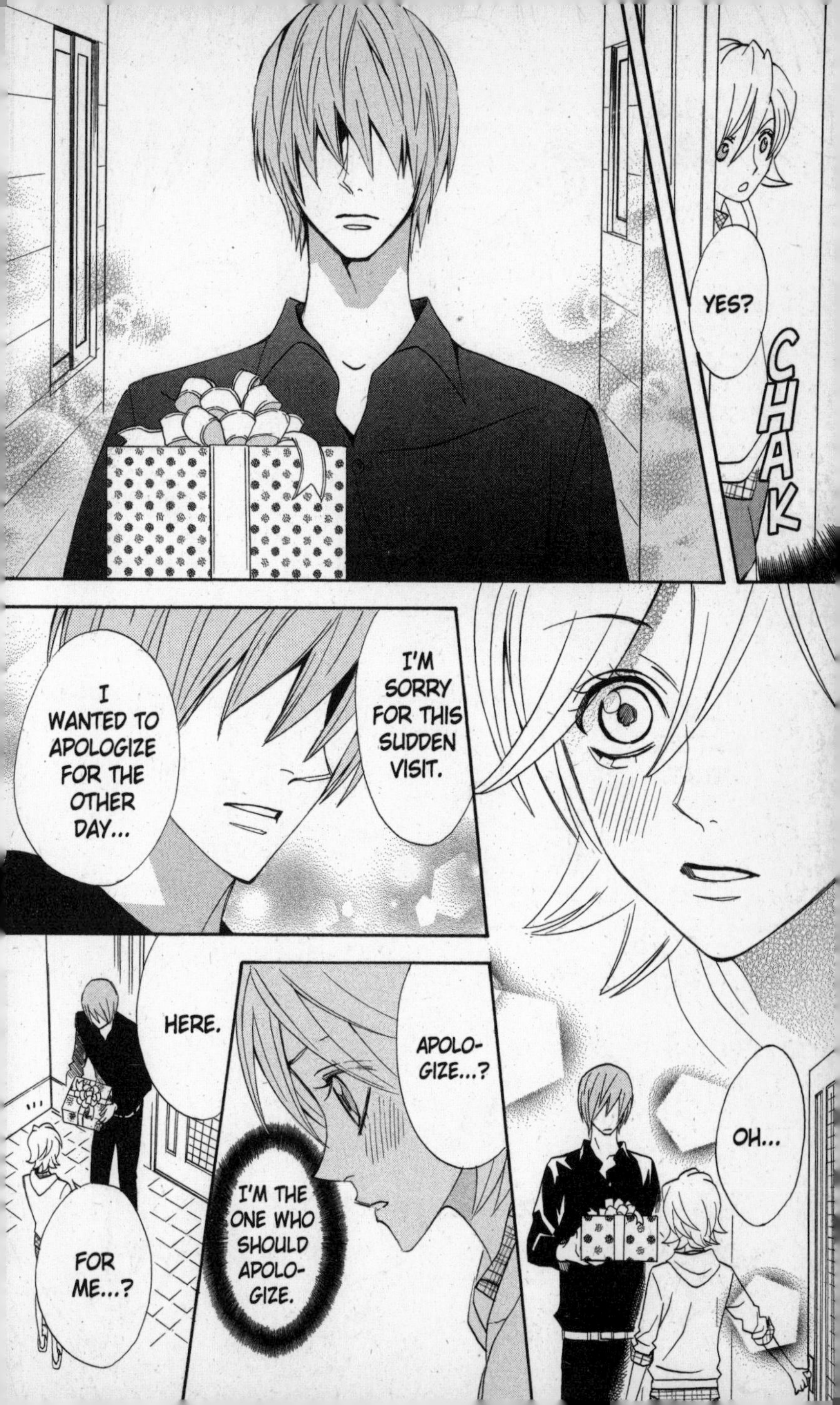
YES?
CHAK
I'M SORRY FOR THIS SUDDEN VISIT.
I WANTED TO APOLOGIZE FOR THE OTHER DAY...
OH...
APOLOGIZE...?
I'M THE ONE WHO SHOULD APOLOGIZE.
HERE.
...
FOR ME...?

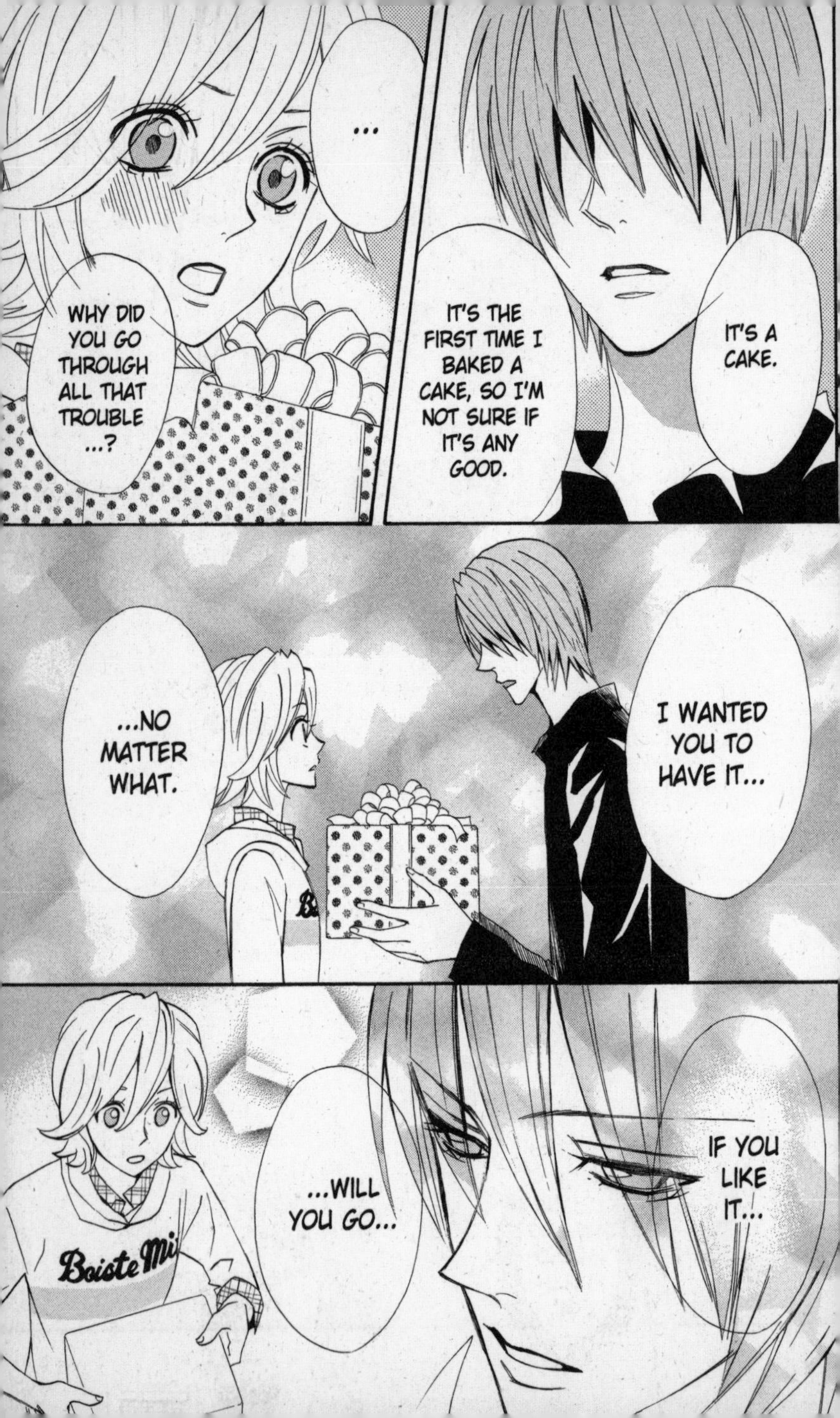
IT'S A CAKE.
IT'S THE FIRST TIME I BAKED A CAKE, SO I'M NOT SURE IF IT'S ANY GOOD.
...
WHY DID YOU GO THROUGH ALL THAT TROUBLE ...?
I WANTED YOU TO HAVE IT...
...NO MATTER WHAT.
IF YOU LIKE IT...
...WILL YOU GO...

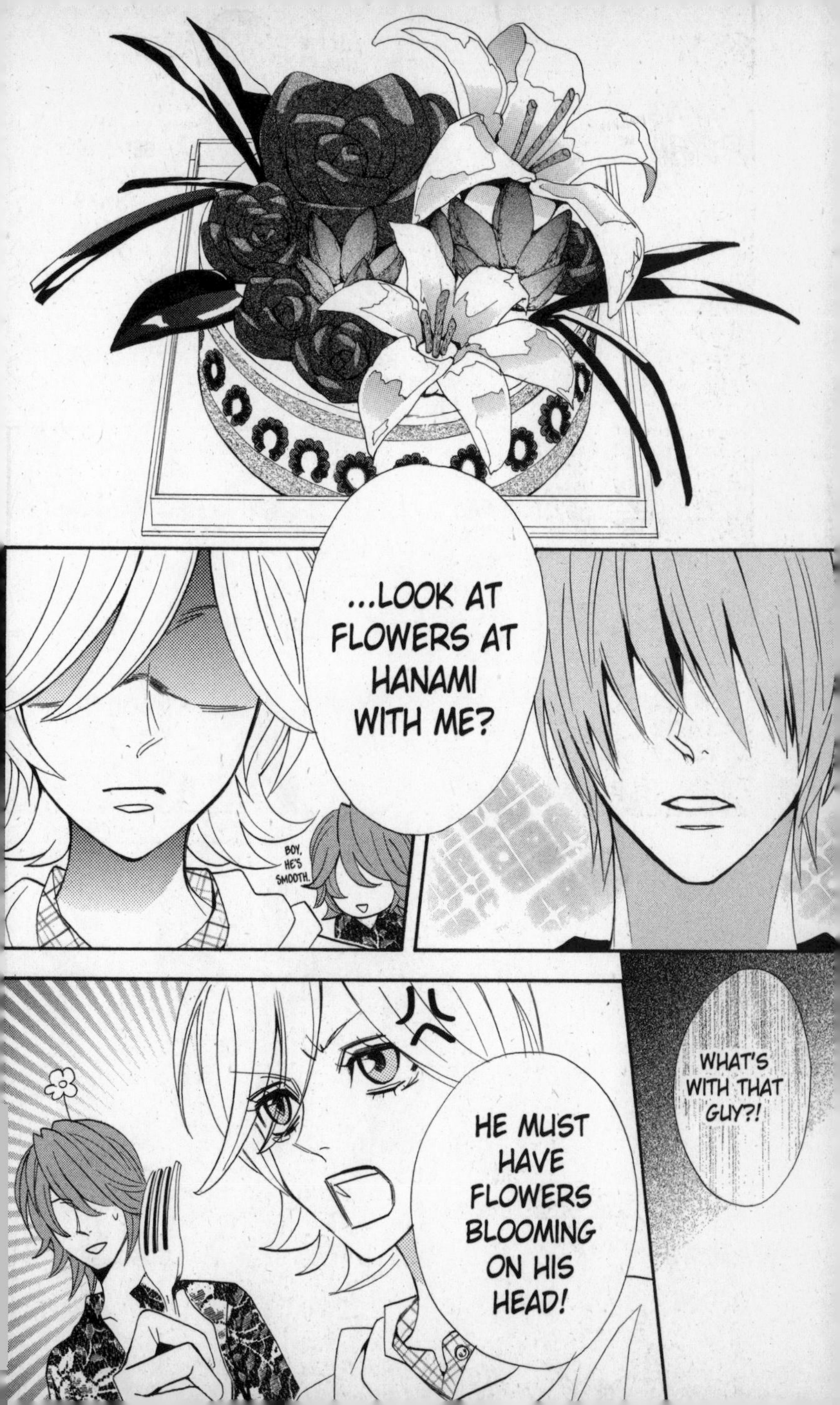
...LOOK AT FLOWERS AT HANAMI WITH ME?
BOY, HE'S SMOOTH.
WHAT'S WITH THAT GUY?!
HE MUST HAVE FLOWERS BLOOMING ON HIS HEAD!

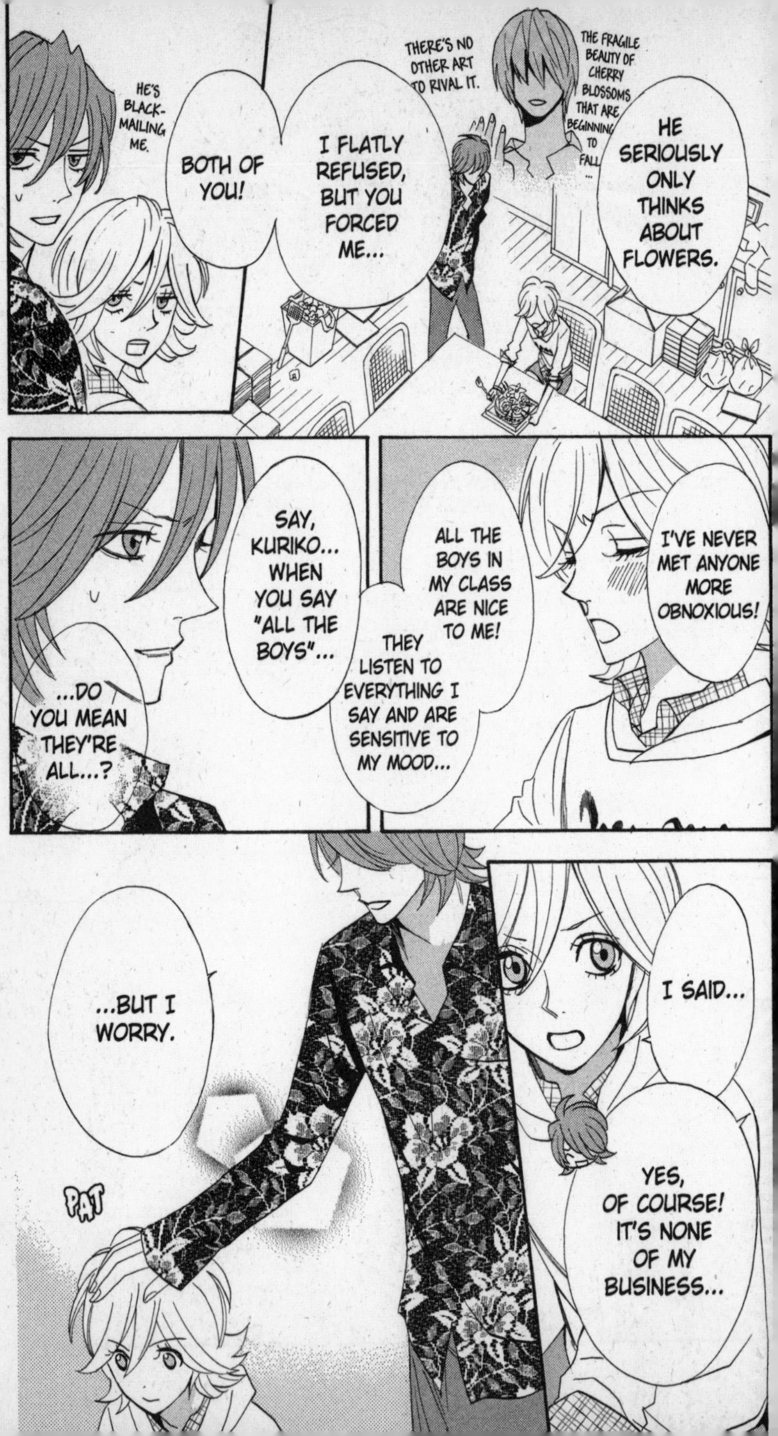
HE SERIOUSLY ONLY THINKS ABOUT FLOWERS.
THE FRAGILE BEAUTY OF CHERRY BLOSSOMS THAT ARE BEGINNING TO FALL...
THERE'S NO OTHER ART TO RIVAL IT.
I FLATLY REFUSED, BUT YOU FORCED ME...
BOTH OF YOU!
HE'S BLACK-MAILING ME.
I'VE NEVER MET ANYONE MORE OBNOXIOUS!
ALL THE BOYS IN MY CLASS ARE NICE TO ME!
THEY LISTEN TO EVERYTHING I SAY AND ARE SENSITIVE TO MY MOOD...
SAY, KURIKO... WHEN YOU SAY "ALL THE BOYS"...
...DO YOU MEAN THEY'RE ALL...?
I SAID...
YES, OF COURSE! IT'S NONE OF MY BUSINESS...
...BUT I WORRY.
PAT

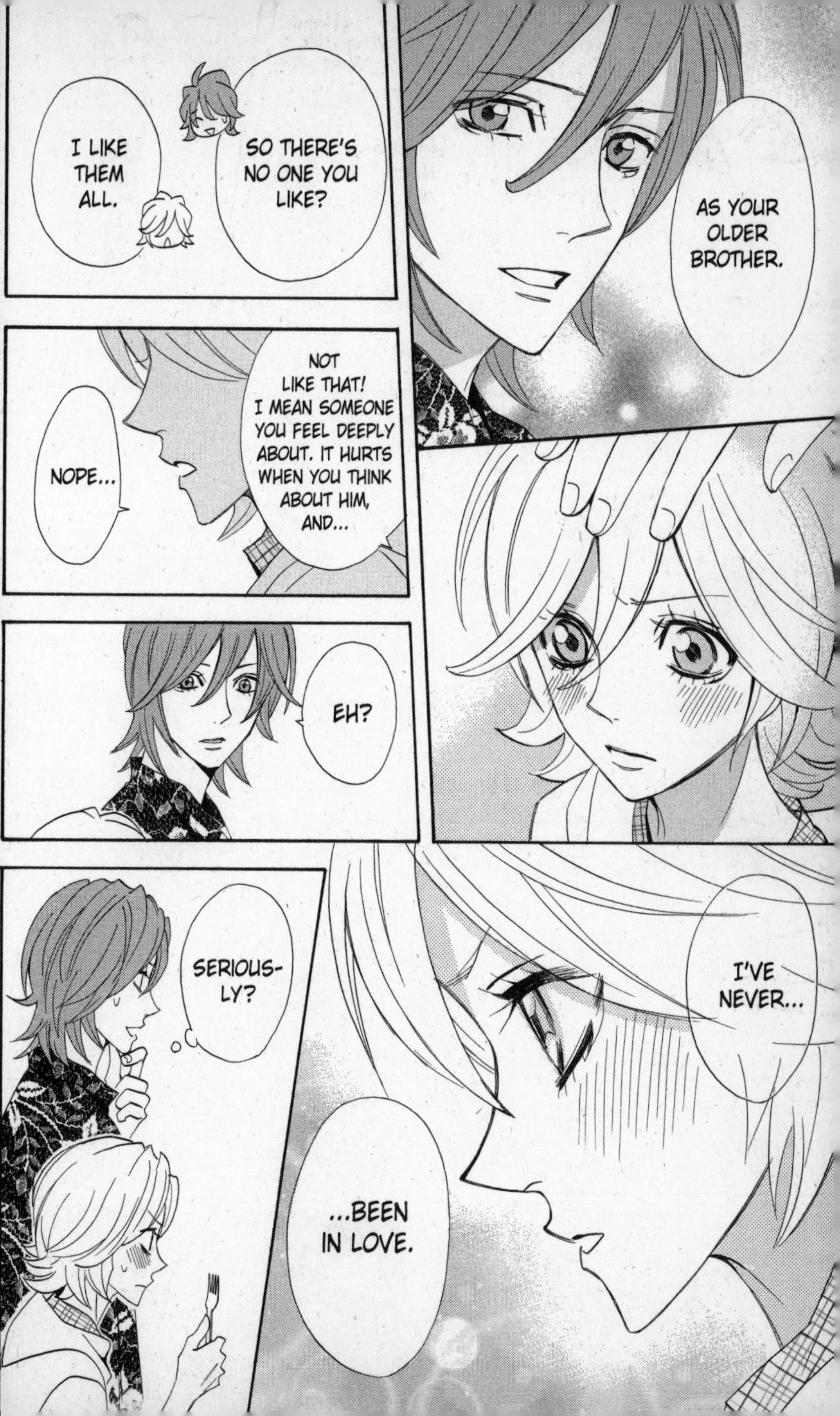
AS YOUR OLDER BROTHER.
SO THERE'S NO ONE YOU LIKE?
I LIKE THEM ALL.
NOT LIKE THAT! I MEAN SOMEONE YOU FEEL DEEPLY ABOUT. IT HURTS WHEN YOU THINK ABOUT HIM, AND...
NOPE...
EH?
I'VE NEVER...
...BEEN IN LOVE.
SERIOUS-LY?

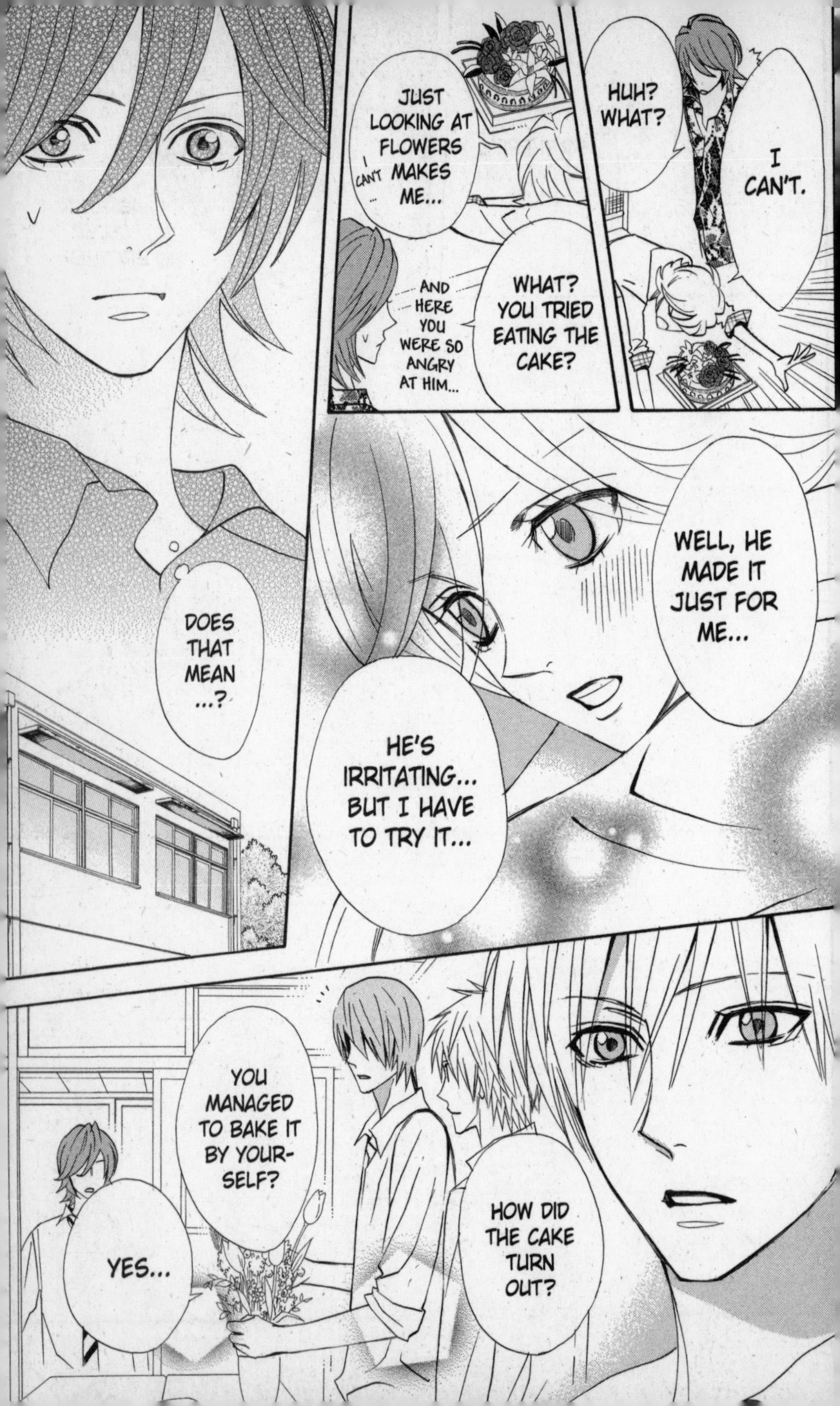
I CAN'T.
HUH? WHAT?
JUST LOOKING AT FLOWERS MAKES ME...
I CAN'T ...
WHAT? YOU TRIED EATING THE CAKE?
AND HERE YOU WERE SO ANGRY AT HIM...
WELL, HE MADE IT JUST FOR ME...
HE'S IRRITATING... BUT I HAVE TO TRY IT...
DOES THAT MEAN ...?
HOW DID THE CAKE TURN OUT?
YOU MANAGED TO BAKE IT BY YOUR-SELF?
YES...

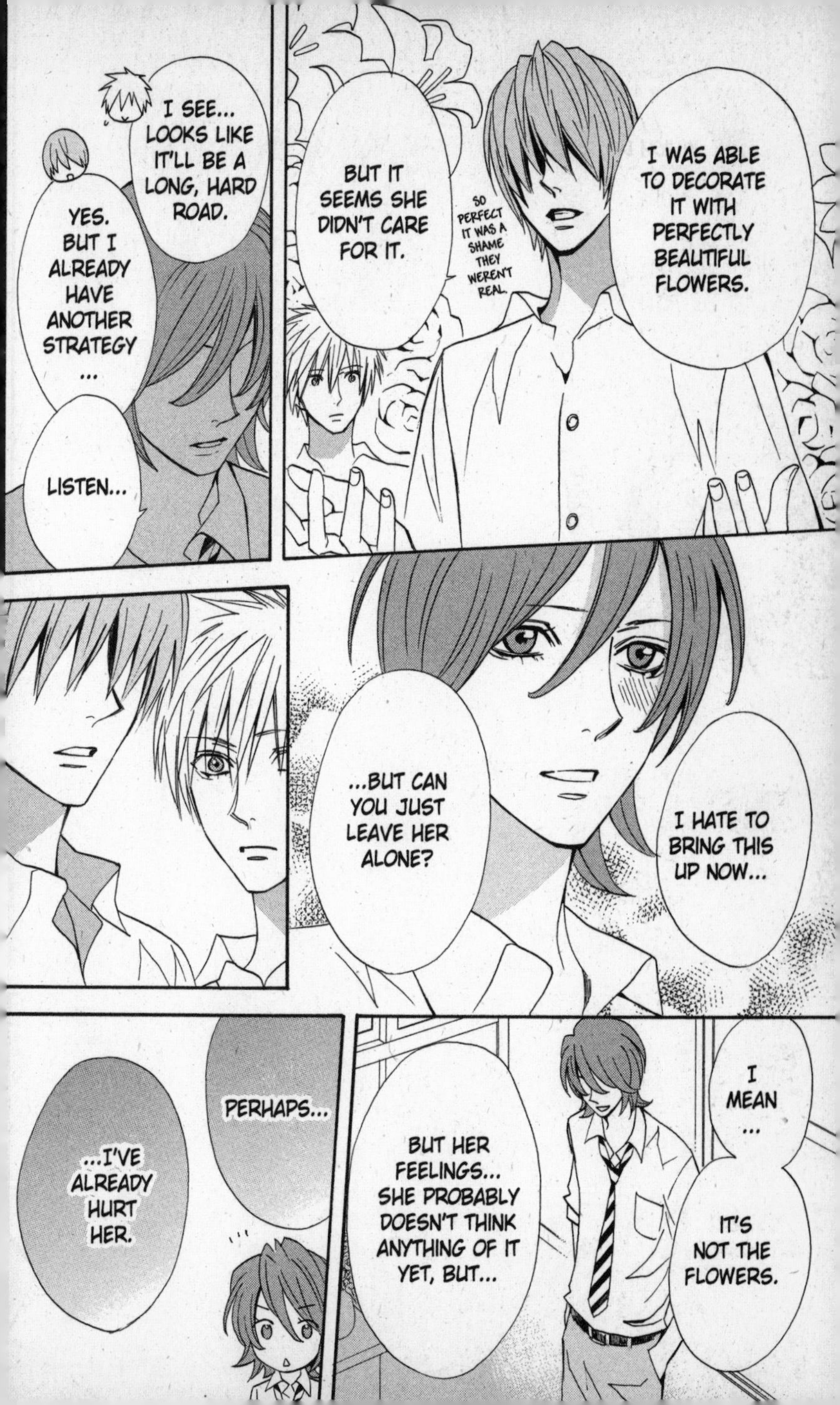
I WAS ABLE TO DECORATE IT WITH PERFECTLY BEAUTIFUL FLOWERS.
SO PERFECT IT WAS A SHAME THEY WEREN'T REAL.
BUT IT SEEMS SHE DIDN'T CARE FOR IT.
I SEE... LOOKS LIKE IT'LL BE A LONG, HARD ROAD.
YES. BUT I ALREADY HAVE ANOTHER STRATEGY...
LISTEN...
I HATE TO BRING THIS UP NOW...
...BUT CAN YOU JUST LEAVE HER ALONE?
I MEAN...
IT'S NOT THE FLOWERS.
BUT HER FEELINGS... SHE PROBABLY DOESN'T THINK ANYTHING OF IT YET, BUT...
PERHAPS...
...I'VE ALREADY HURT HER.

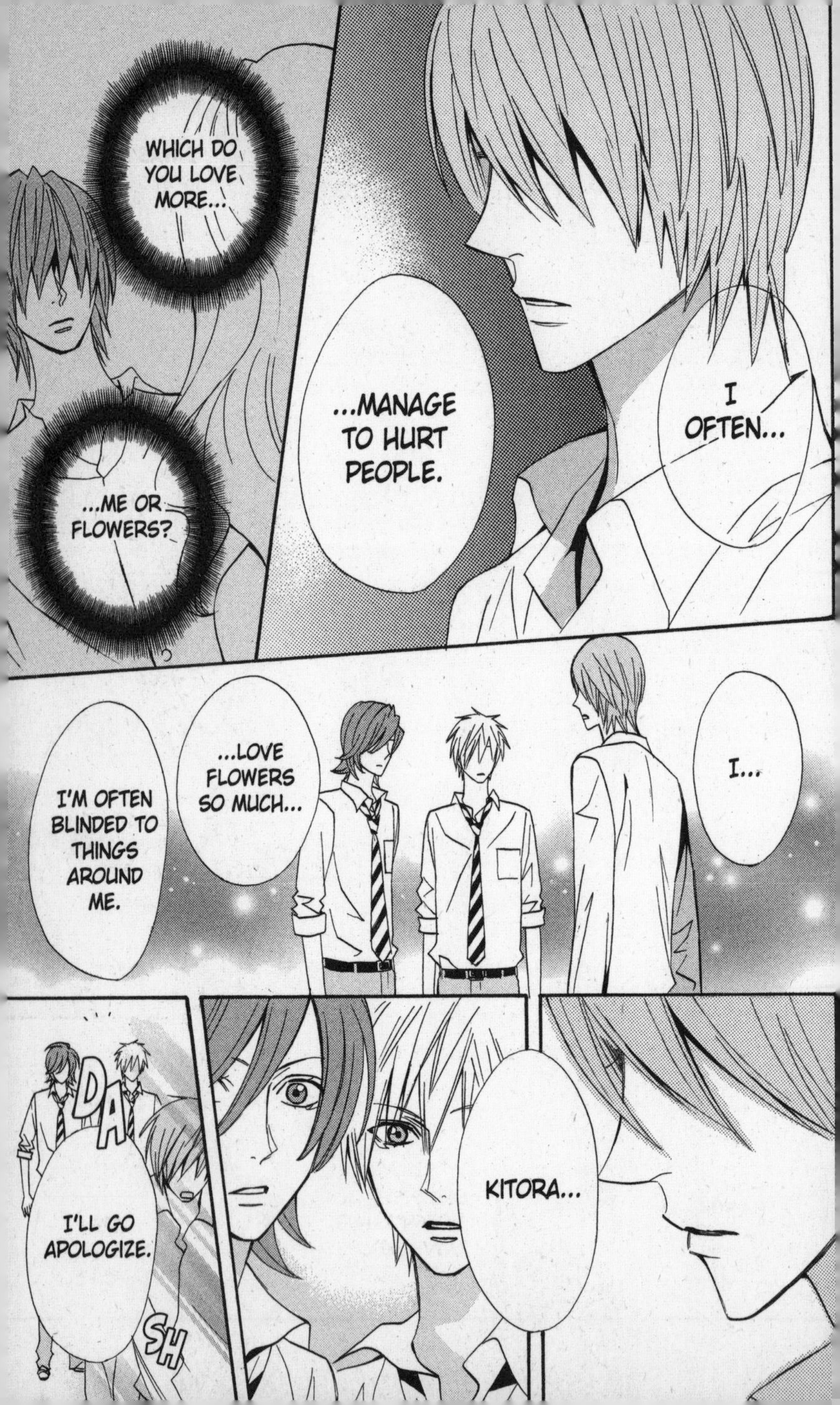
I OFTEN...
...MANAGE TO HURT PEOPLE.
WHICH DO YOU LOVE MORE...
...ME OR FLOWERS?
I...
...LOVE FLOWERS SO MUCH...
I'M OFTEN BLINDED TO THINGS AROUND ME.
KITORA...
DA
I'LL GO APOLOGIZE.
SH

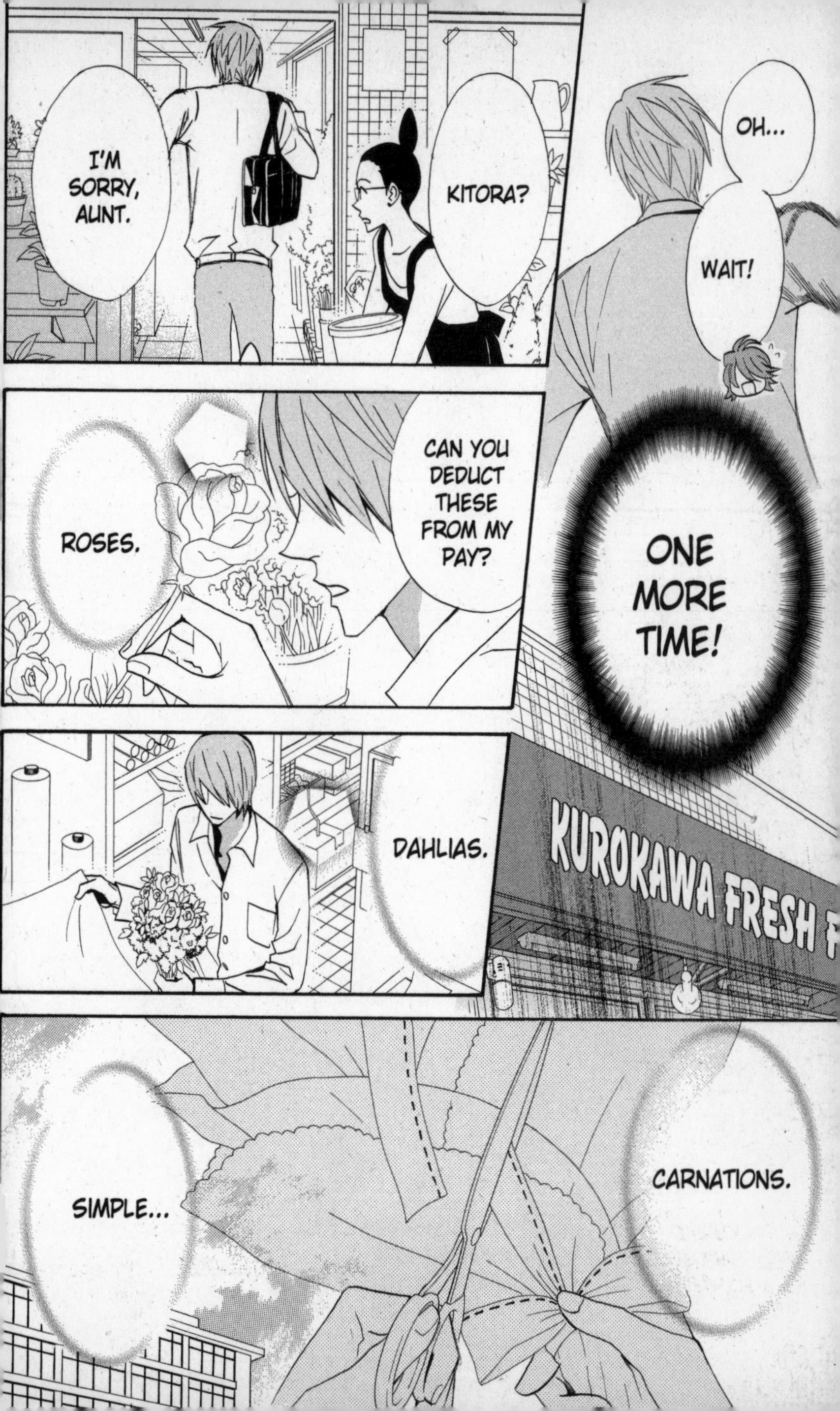
OH...
WAIT!
ONE MORE TIME!
KUROKAWA FRESH F
KITORA?
I'M SORRY, AUNT.
CAN YOU DEDUCT THESE FROM MY PAY?
ROSES.
DAHLIAS.
CARNATIONS.
SIMPLE...

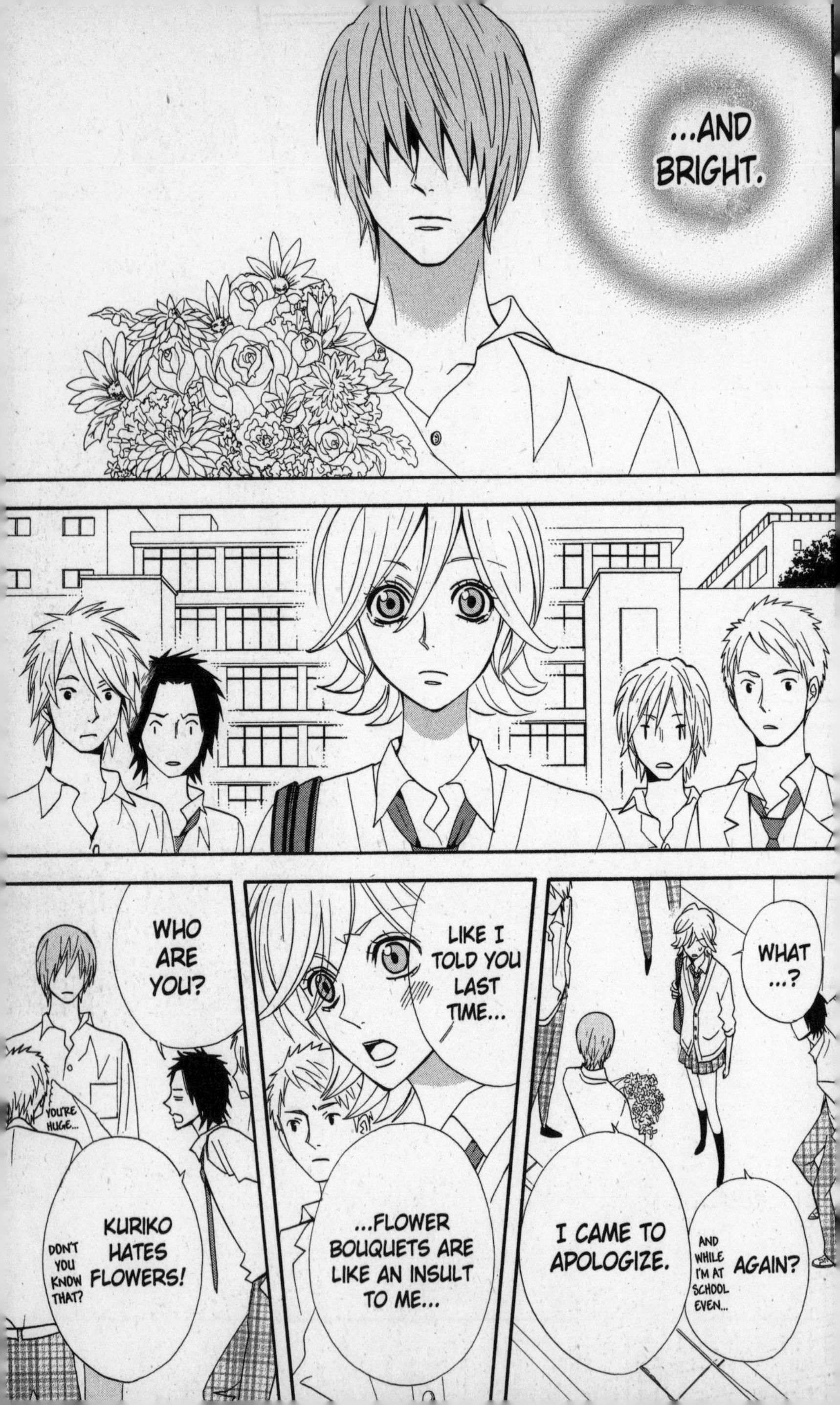
...AND BRIGHT.
WHAT ...?
AGAIN?
AND WHILE I'M AT SCHOOL EVEN...
I CAME TO APOLOGIZE.
LIKE I TOLD YOU LAST TIME...
...FLOWER BOUQUETS ARE LIKE AN INSULT TO ME...
WHO ARE YOU?
YOU'RE HUGE...
KURIKO HATES FLOWERS!
DON'T YOU KNOW THAT?

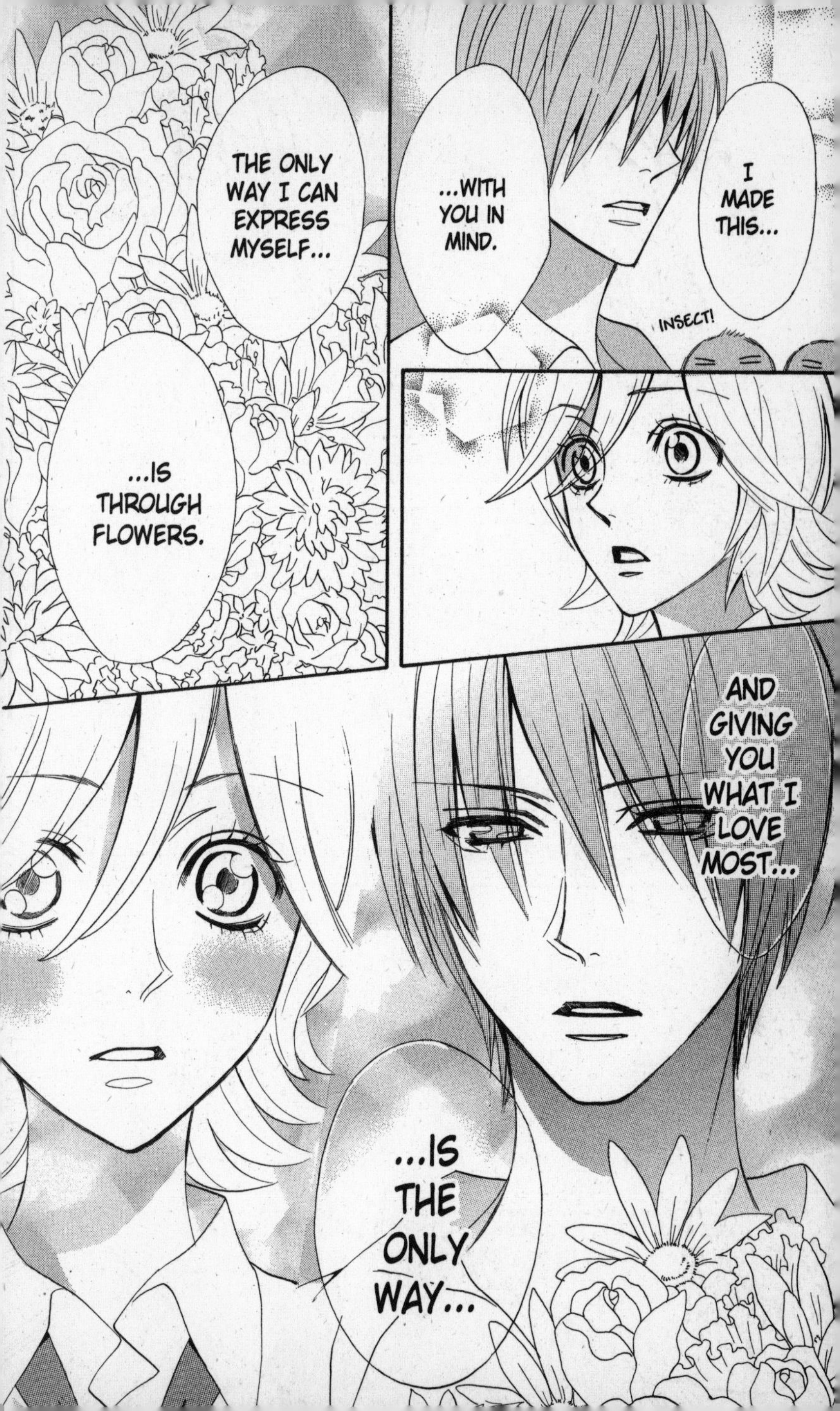
I MADE THIS...
...WITH YOU IN MIND.
INSECT!
THE ONLY WAY I CAN EXPRESS MYSELF...
...IS THROUGH FLOWERS.
AND GIVING YOU WHAT I LOVE MOST...
...IS THE ONLY WAY...

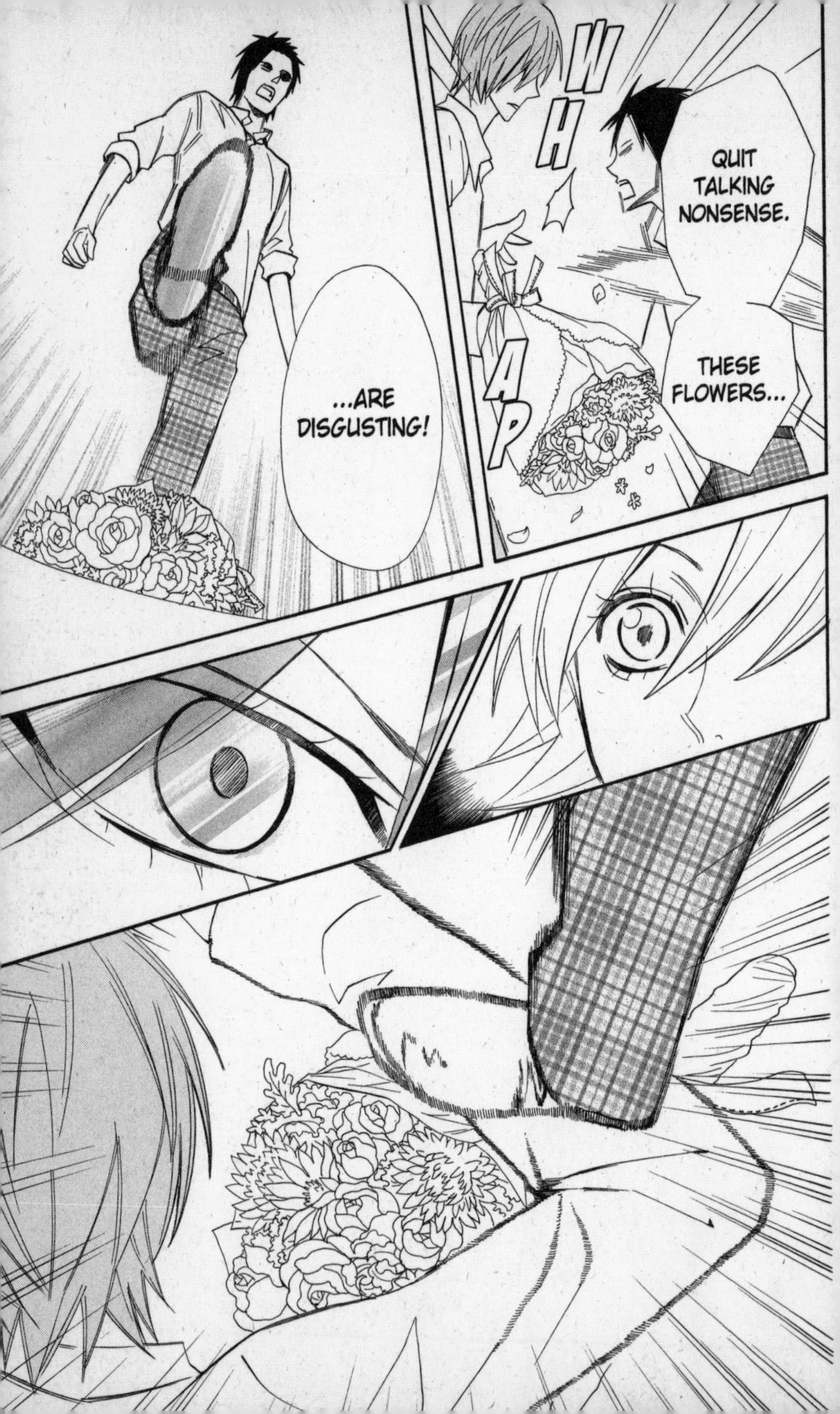
QUIT TALKING NONSENSE.
THESE FLOWERS...
WHAP
...ARE DISGUSTING!

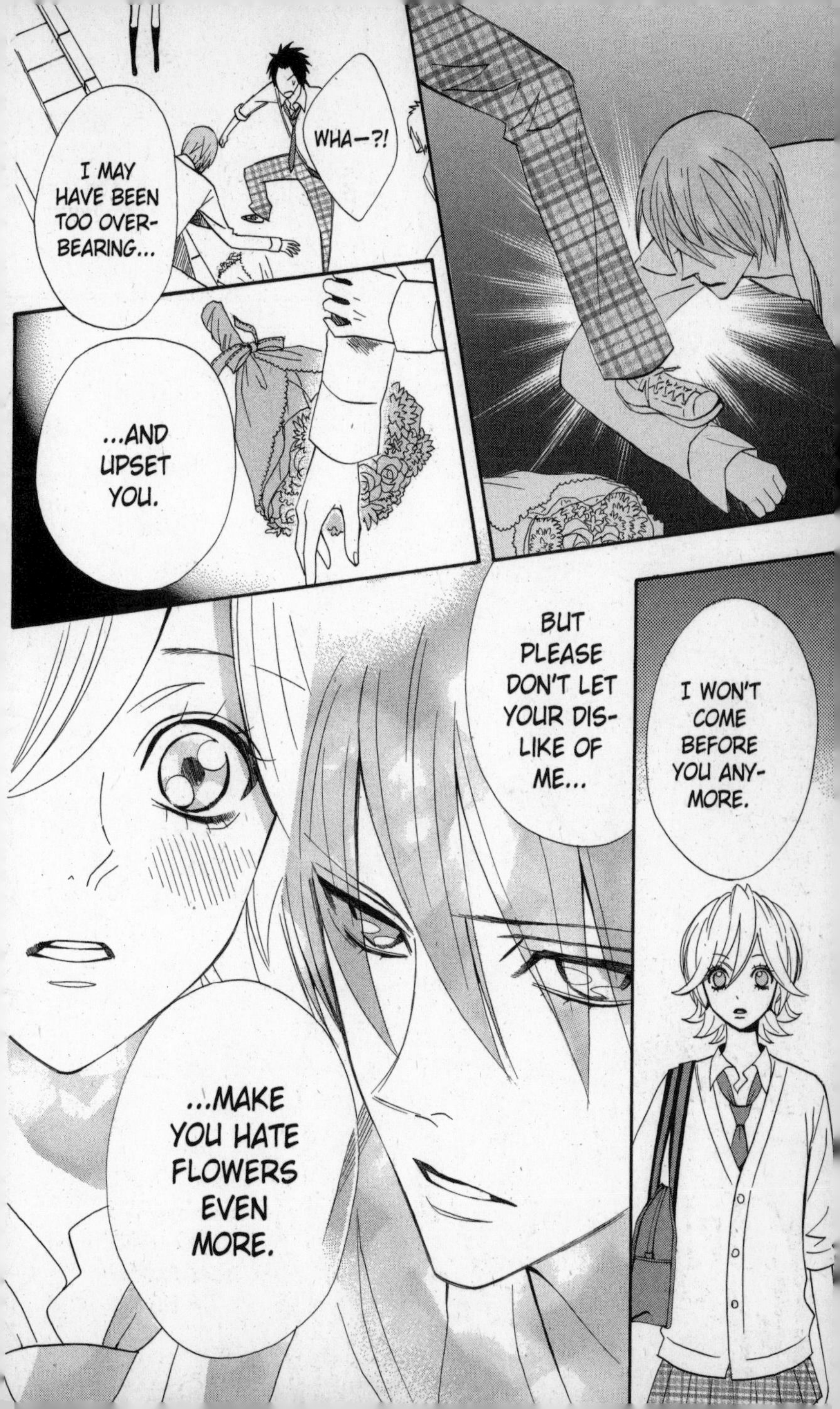
WHA—?!
I MAY HAVE BEEN TOO OVER-BEARING...
...AND UPSET YOU.
I WON'T COME BEFORE YOU ANY-MORE.
BUT PLEASE DON'T LET YOUR DIS-LIKE OF ME...
...MAKE YOU HATE FLOWERS EVEN MORE.

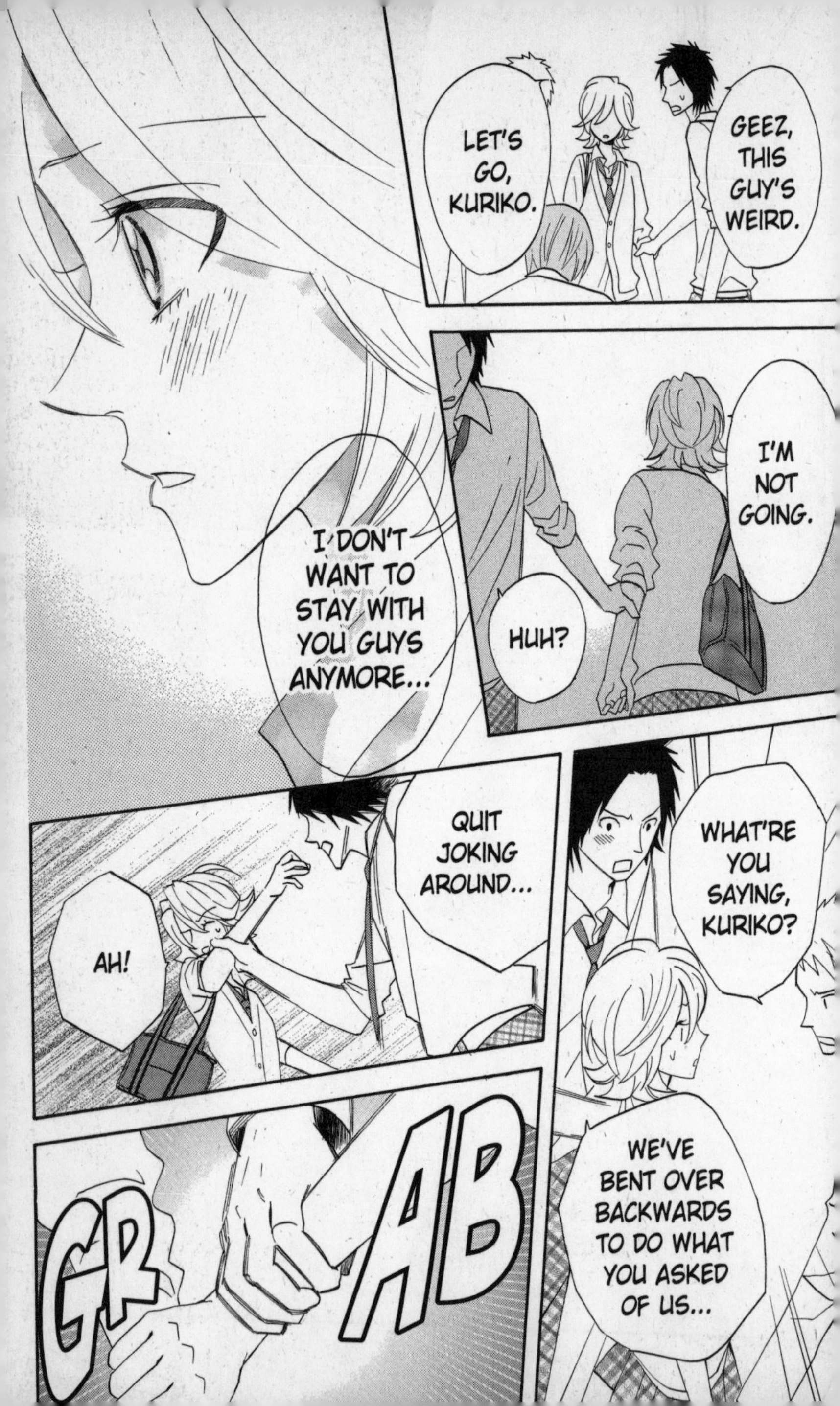
GEEZ, THIS GUY'S WEIRD.
LET'S GO, KURIKO.
I'M NOT GOING.
HUH?
I DON'T WANT TO STAY WITH YOU GUYS ANYMORE...
WHAT'RE YOU SAYING, KURIKO?
WE'VE BENT OVER BACKWARDS TO DO WHAT YOU ASKED OF US...
QUIT JOKING AROUND...
AH!
GRAB

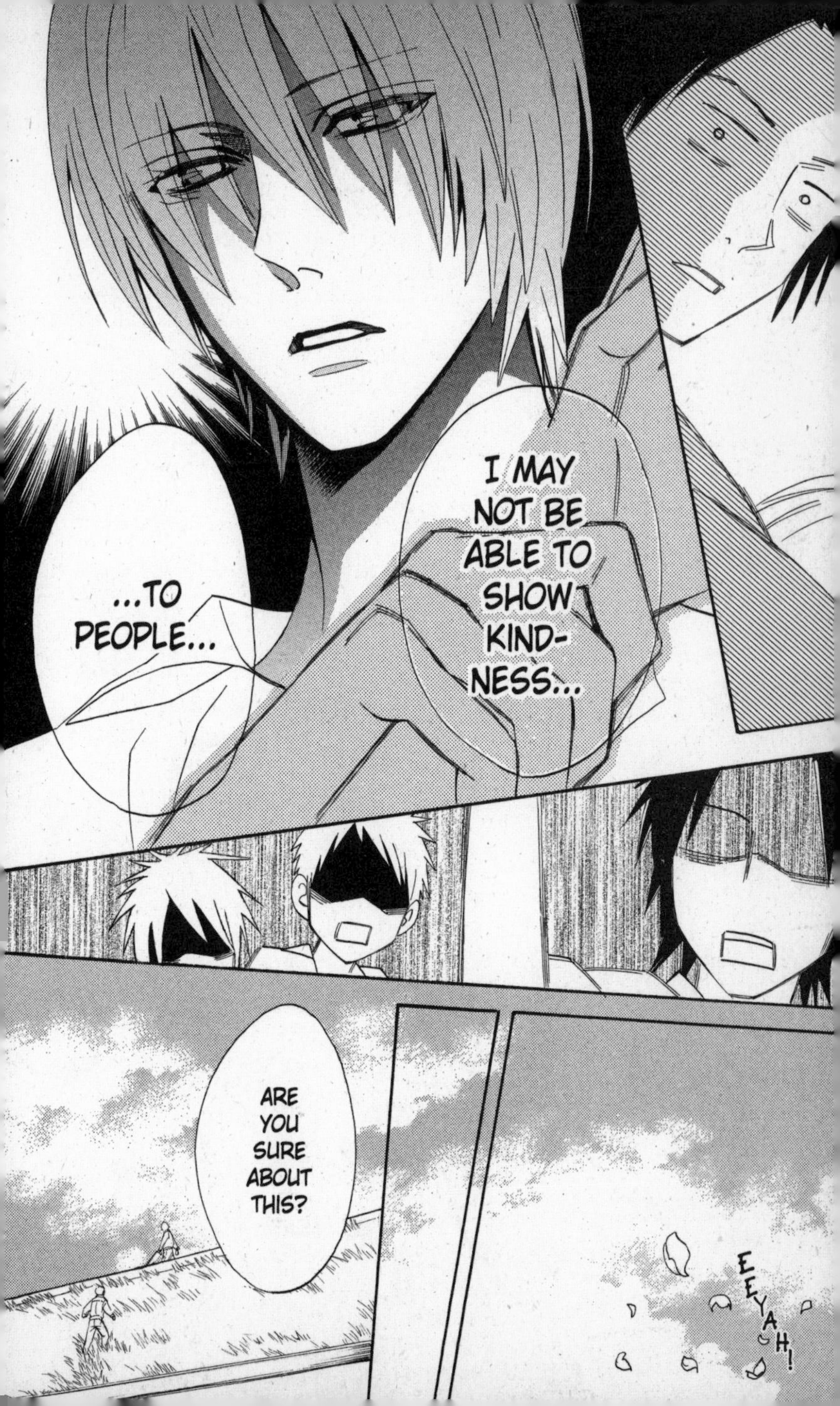
I MAY NOT BE ABLE TO SHOW KINDNESS...
...TO PEOPLE...
EEYAH!
ARE YOU SURE ABOUT THIS?

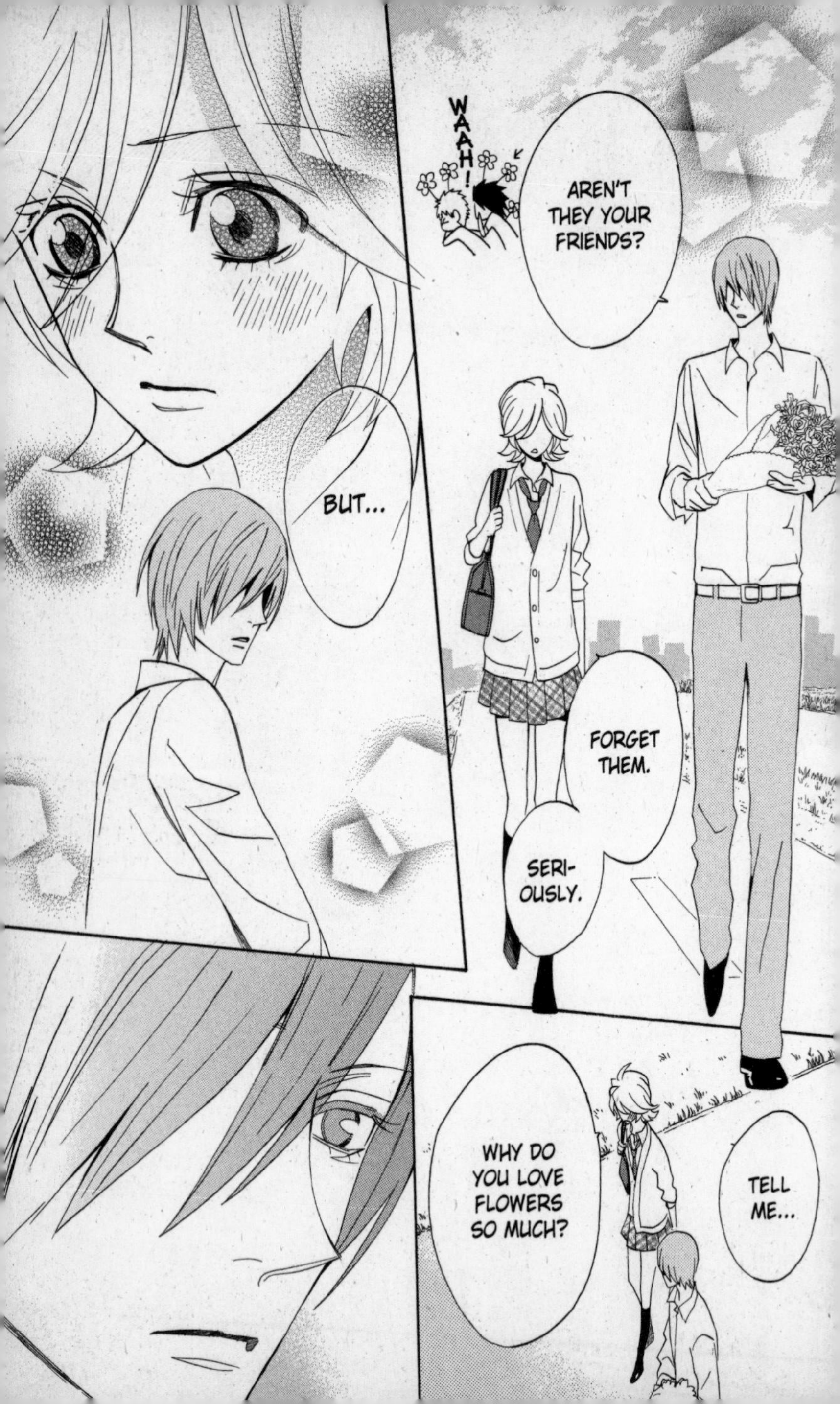
AREN'T THEY YOUR FRIENDS?
WAAH!
FORGET THEM.
SERI-OUSLY.
BUT...
TELL ME...
WHY DO YOU LOVE FLOWERS SO MUCH?

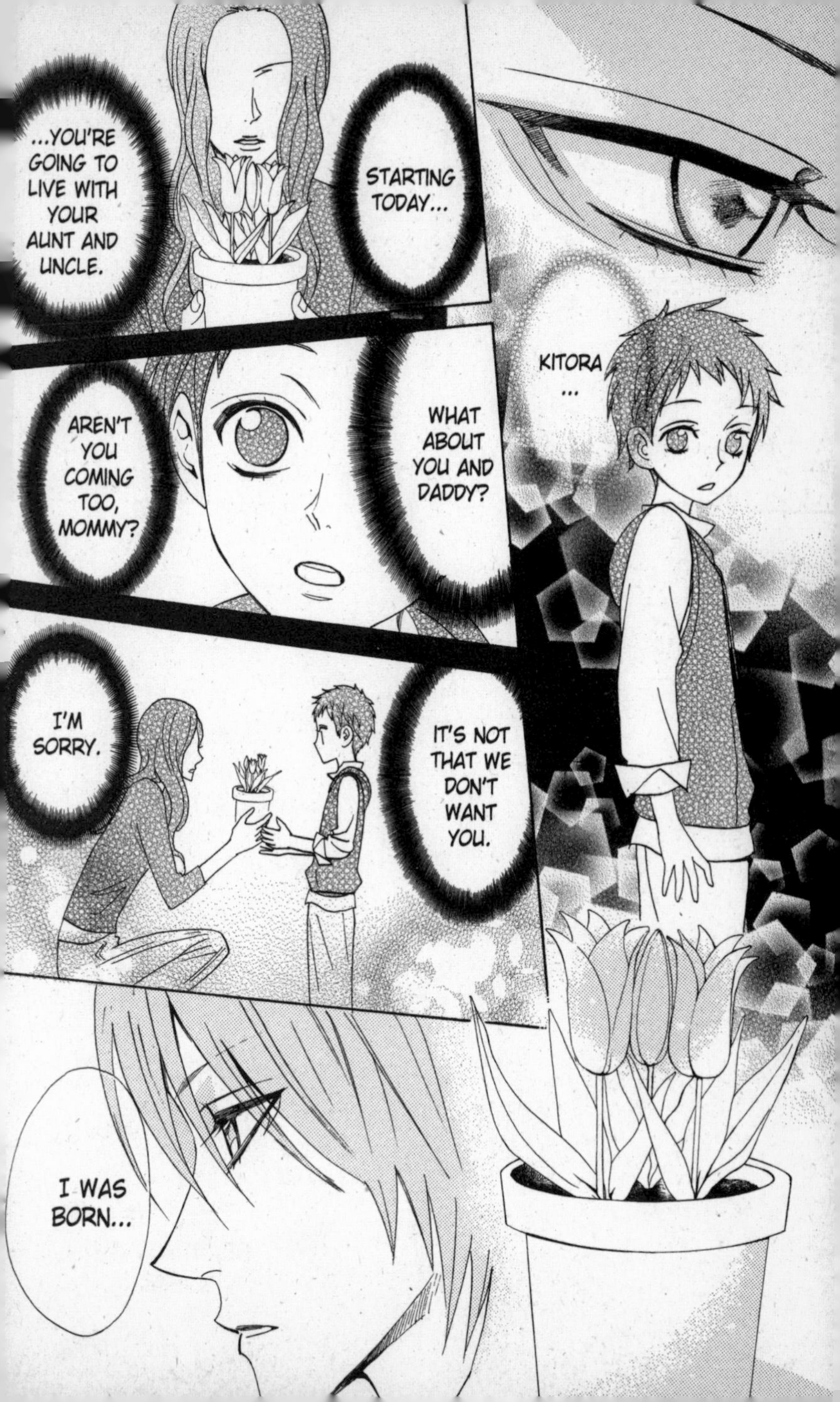
KITORA ...
STARTING TODAY...
...YOU'RE GOING TO LIVE WITH YOUR AUNT AND UNCLE.
WHAT ABOUT YOU AND DADDY?
AREN'T YOU COMING TOO, MOMMY?
IT'S NOT THAT WE DON'T WANT YOU.
I'M SORRY.
I WAS BORN...

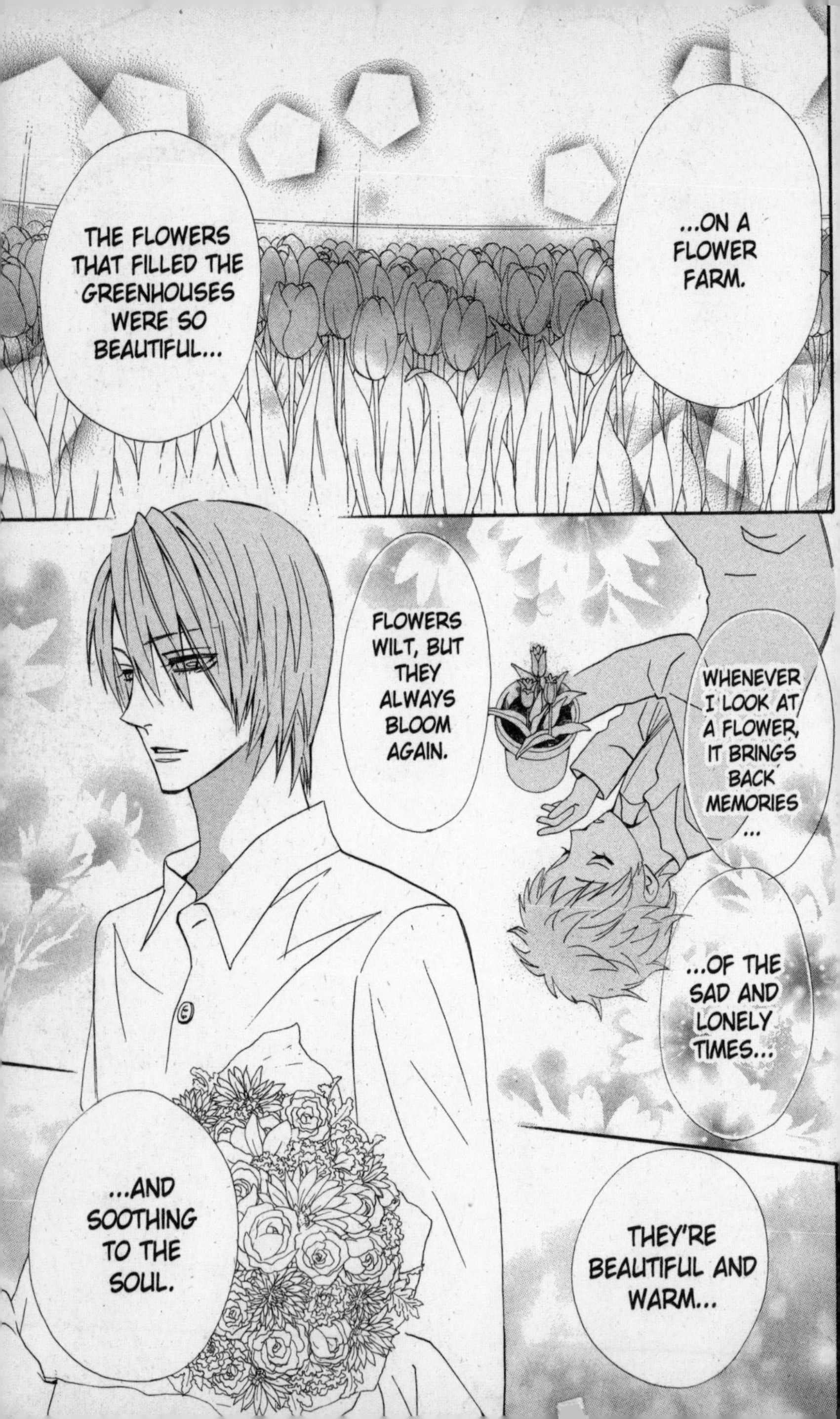
...ON A FLOWER FARM.
THE FLOWERS THAT FILLED THE GREENHOUSES WERE SO BEAUTIFUL...
WHENEVER I LOOK AT A FLOWER, IT BRINGS BACK MEMORIES...
...OF THE SAD AND LONELY TIMES...
FLOWERS WILT, BUT THEY ALWAYS BLOOM AGAIN.
THEY'RE BEAUTIFUL AND WARM...
...AND SOOTHING TO THE SOUL.

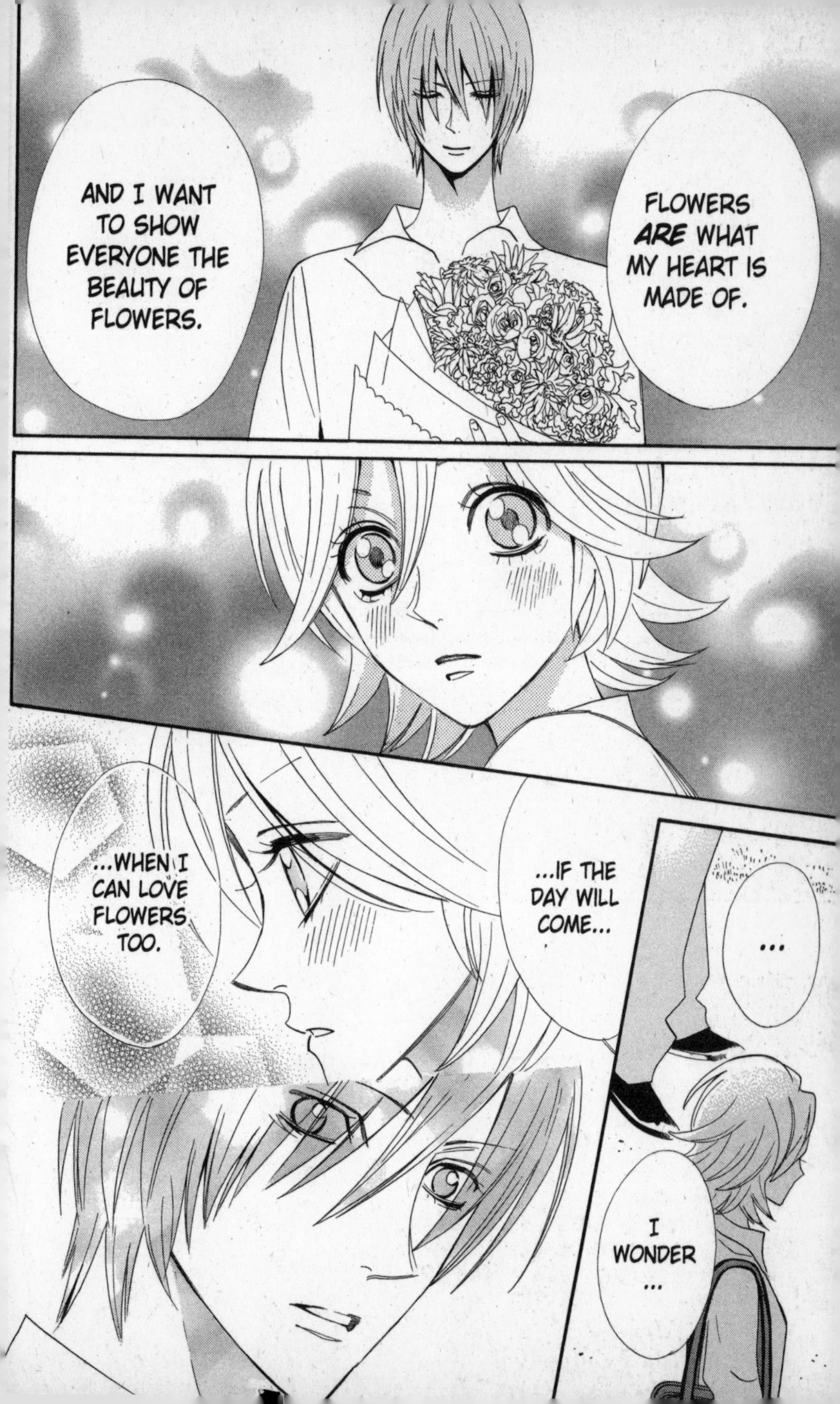
FLOWERS ARE WHAT MY HEART IS MADE OF.
AND I WANT TO SHOW EVERYONE THE BEAUTY OF FLOWERS.
...
I WONDER ...
...IF THE DAY WILL COME...
...WHEN I CAN LOVE FLOWERS TOO.

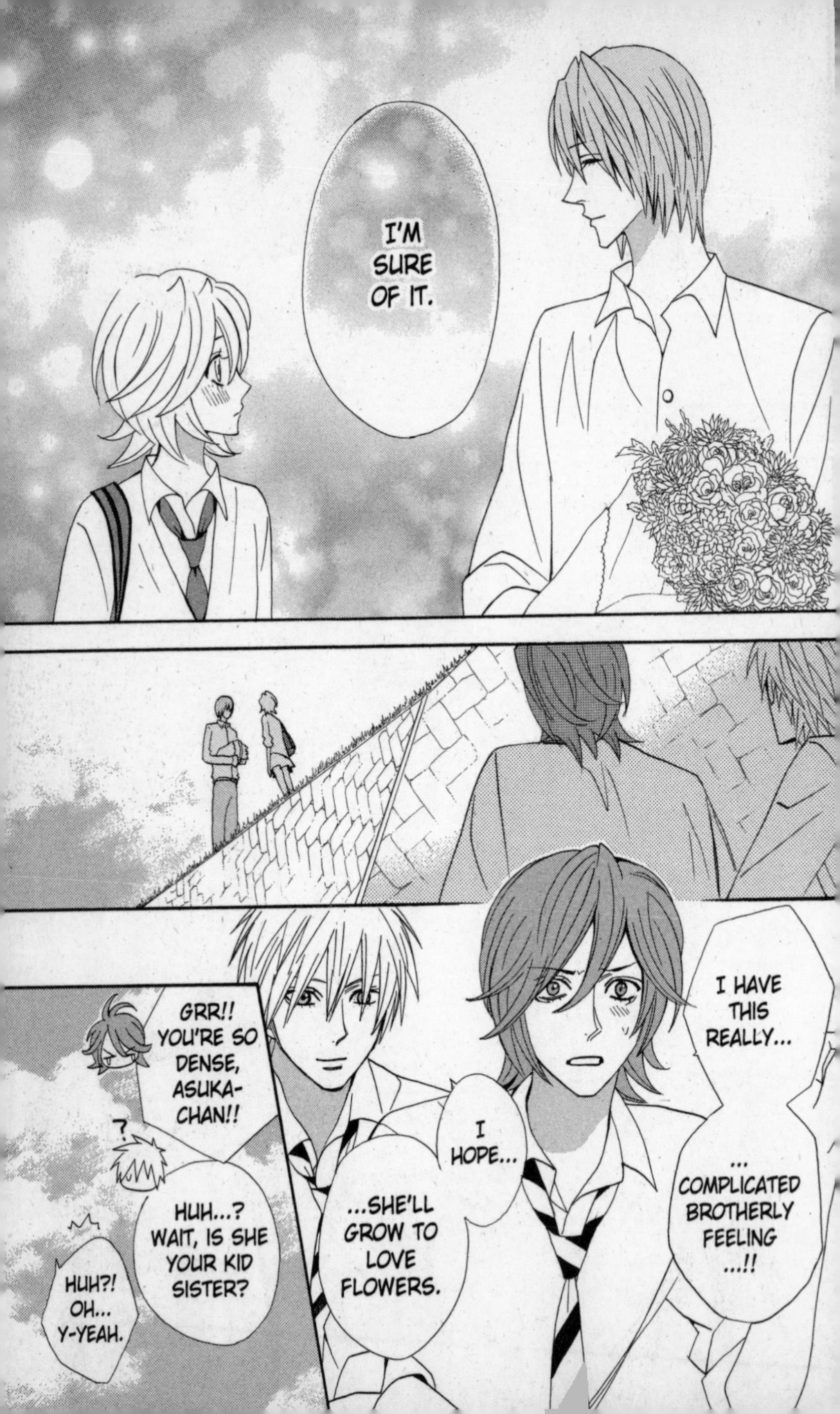
I'M SURE OF IT.
I HAVE THIS REALLY...
...COMPLICATED BROTHERLY FEELING ...!!
I HOPE...
...SHE'LL GROW TO LOVE FLOWERS.
GRR!! YOU'RE SO DENSE, ASUKA-CHAN!!
?
HUH...? WAIT, IS SHE YOUR KID SISTER?
HUH?! OH... Y-YEAH.

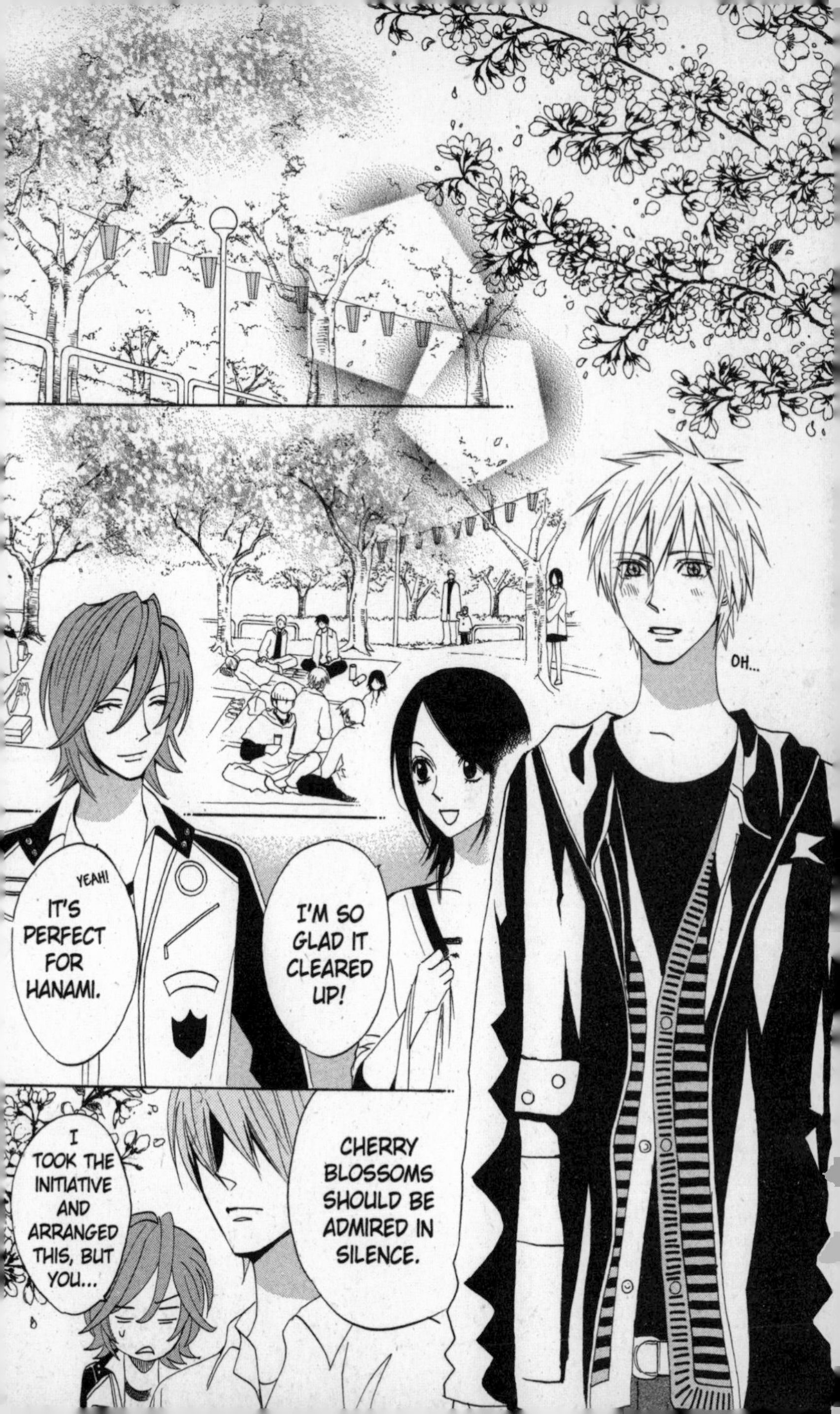
OH...
I'M SO GLAD IT CLEARED UP!
YEAH!
IT'S PERFECT FOR HANAMI.
CHERRY BLOSSOMS SHOULD BE ADMIRED IN SILENCE.
I TOOK THE INITIATIVE AND ARRANGED THIS, BUT YOU...

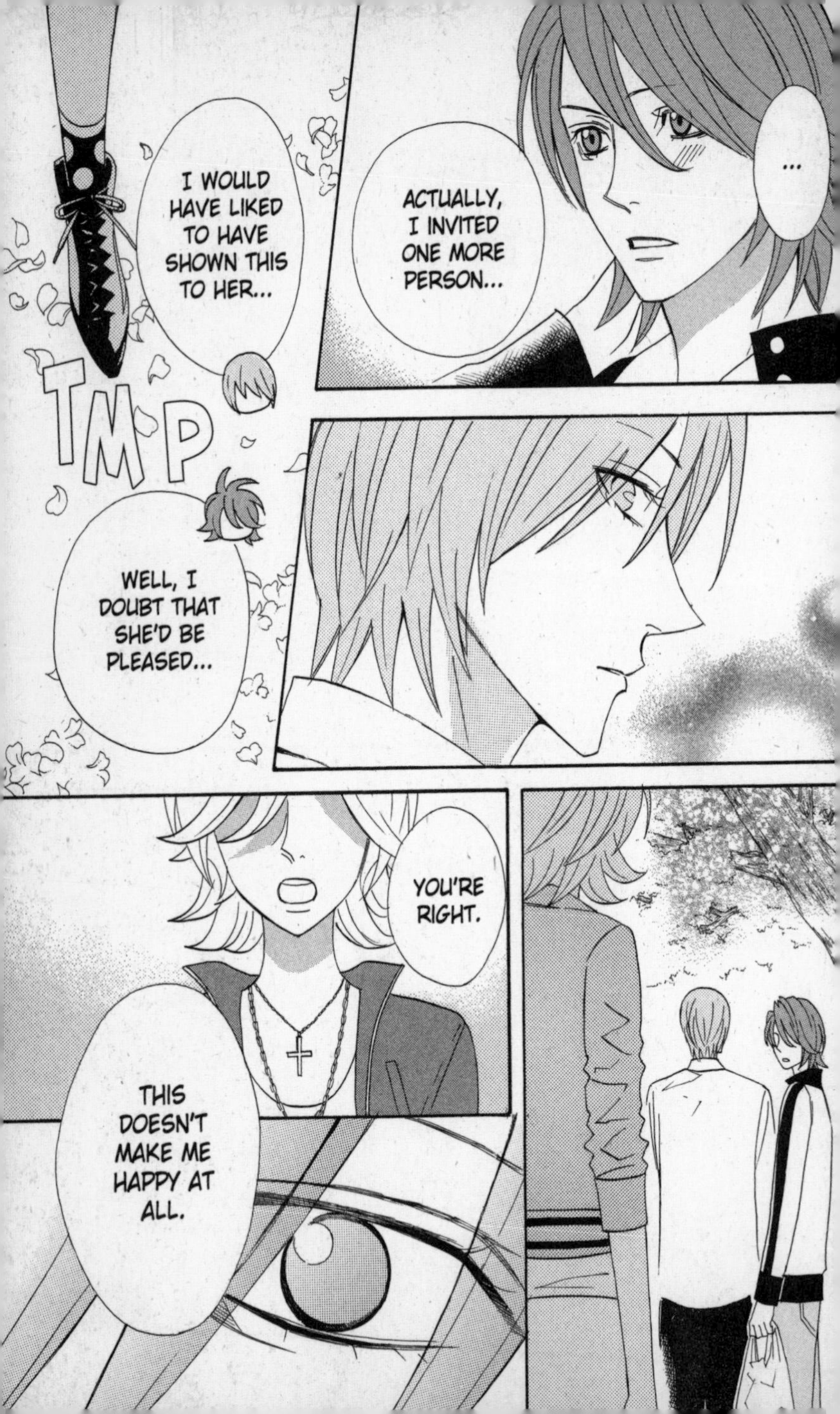
...
ACTUALLY, I INVITED ONE MORE PERSON...
I WOULD HAVE LIKED TO HAVE SHOWN THIS TO HER...
TMP
WELL, I DOUBT THAT SHE'D BE PLEASED...
YOU'RE RIGHT.
THIS DOESN'T MAKE ME HAPPY AT ALL.

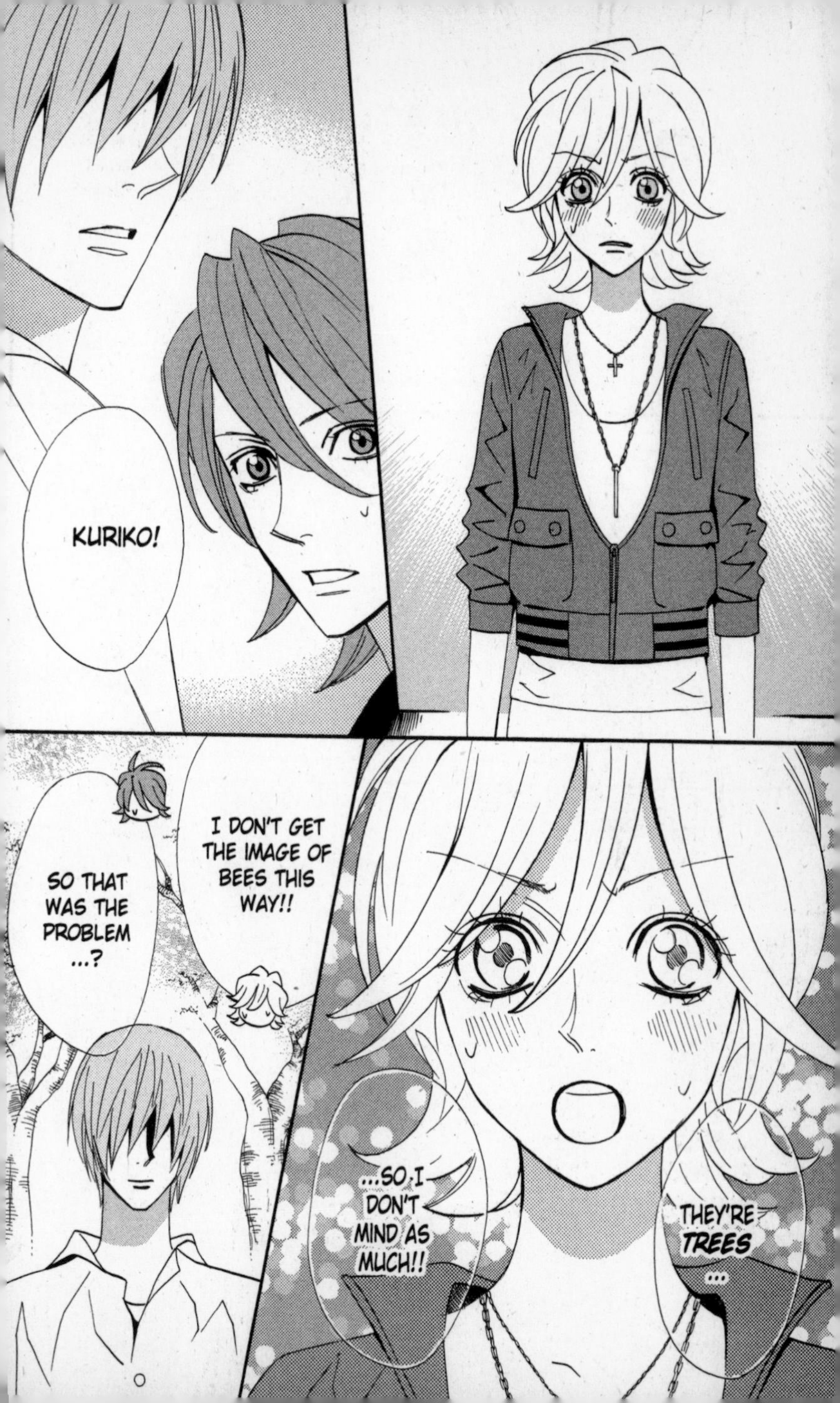
KURIKO!
THEY'RE TREES ...
...SO I DON'T MIND AS MUCH!!
I DON'T GET THE IMAGE OF BEES THIS WAY!!
SO THAT WAS THE PROBLEM ...?

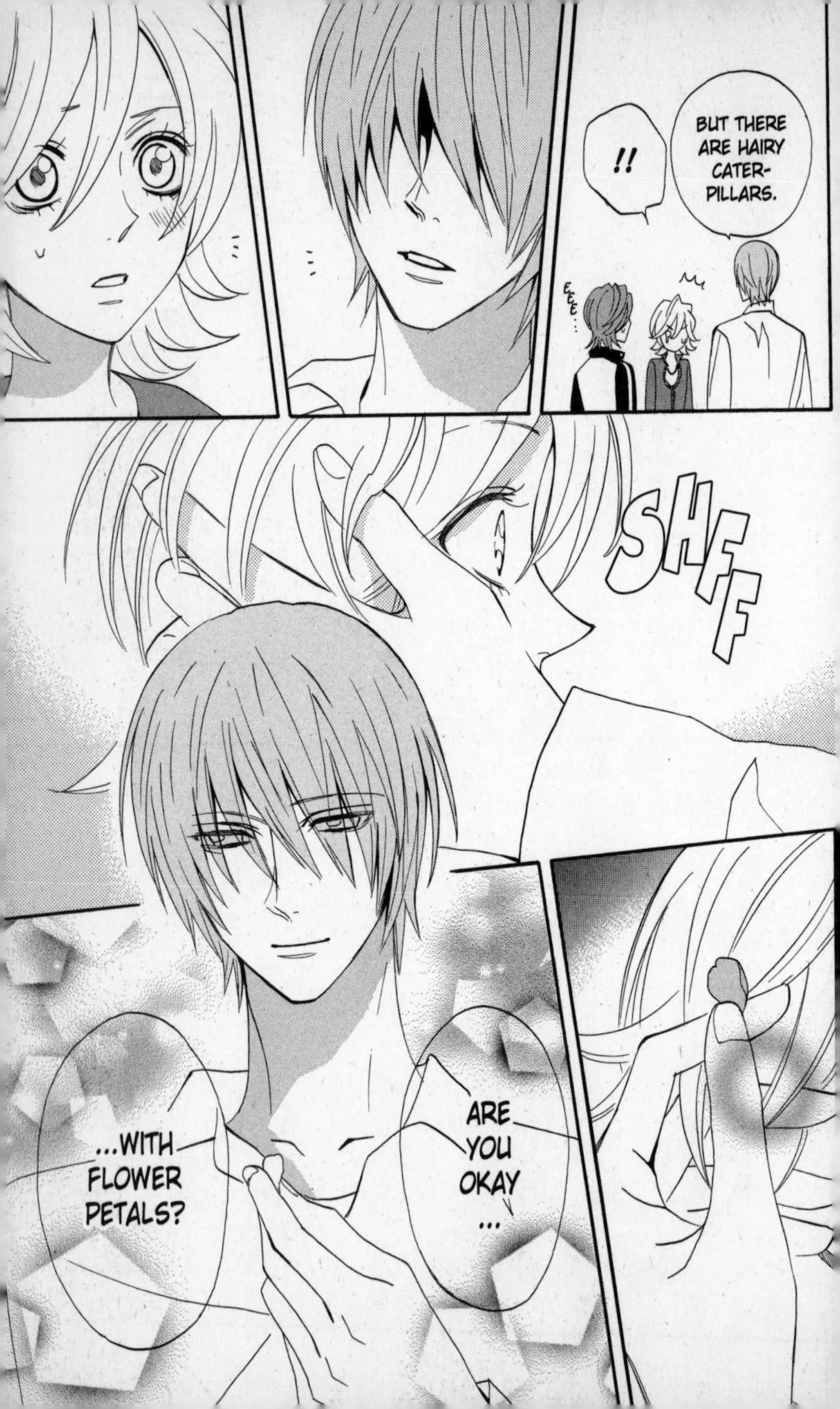
BUT THERE ARE HAIRY CATER-PILLARS.
!!
EEE...
SHFF
ARE YOU OKAY ...
...WITH FLOWER PETALS?

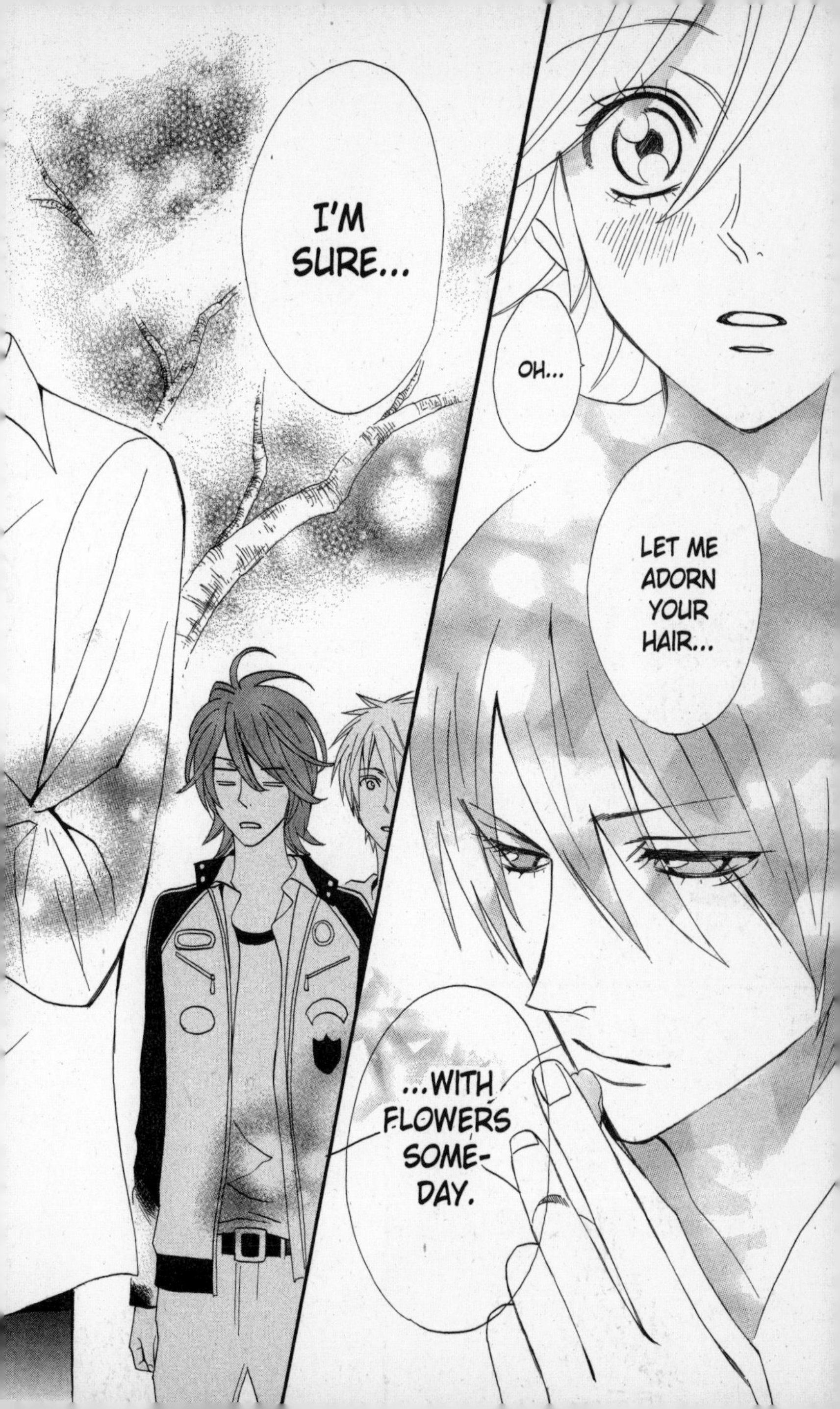
OH...
LET ME ADORN YOUR HAIR...
...WITH FLOWERS SOME-DAY.
I'M SURE...

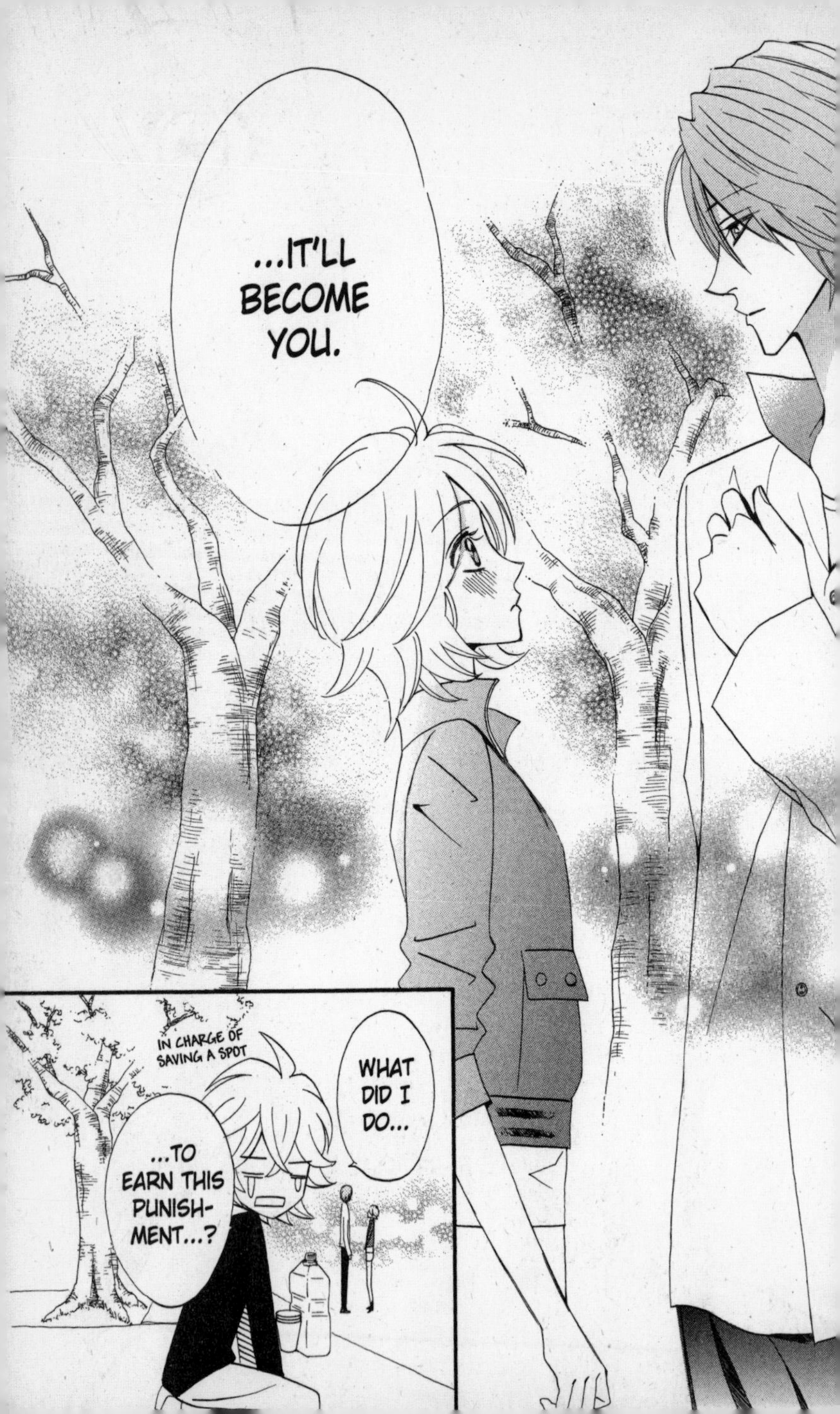
...IT'LL BECOME YOU.
WHAT DID I DO...
IN CHARGE OF SAVING A SPOT
...TO EARN THIS PUNISH-MENT...?

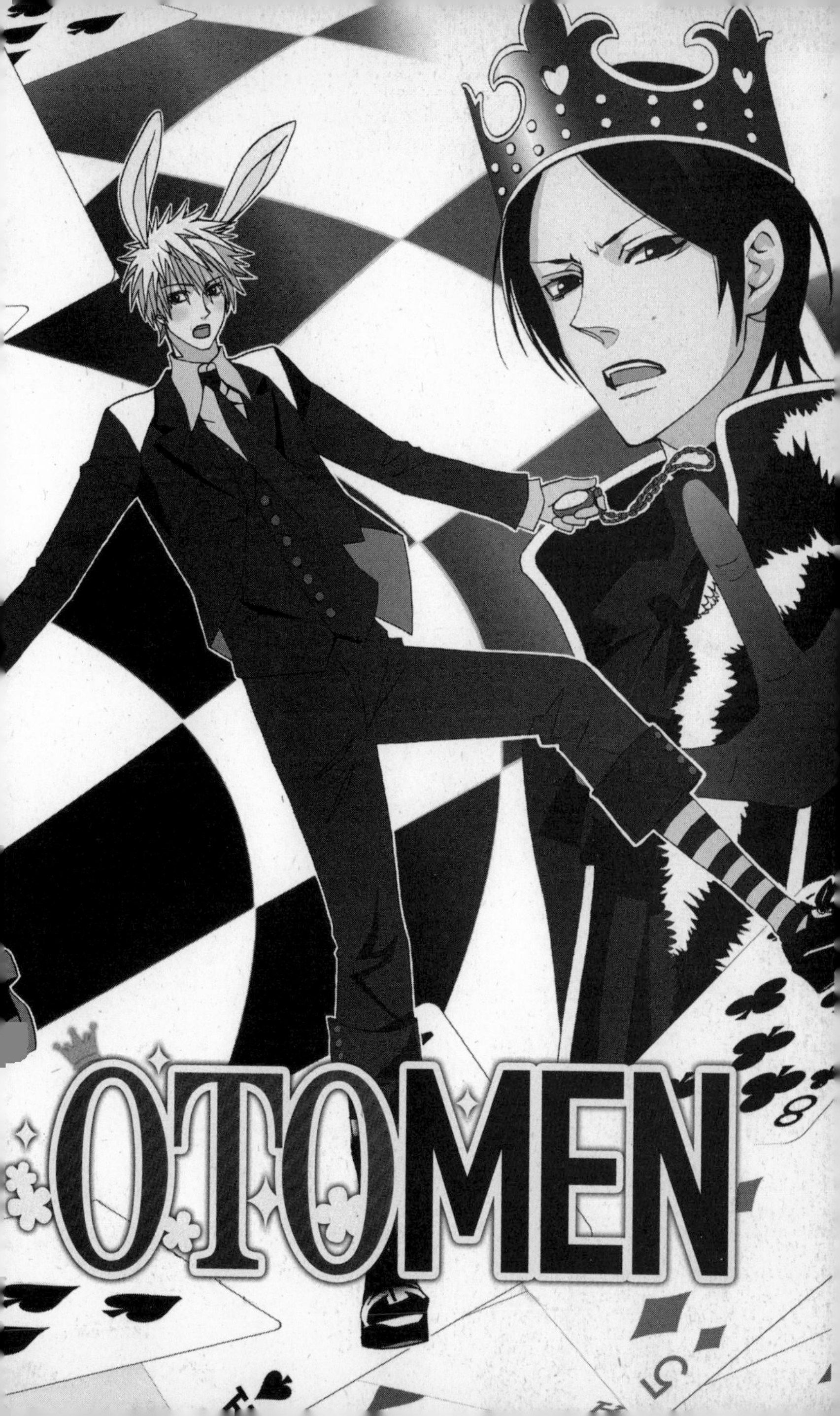
OTOMEN

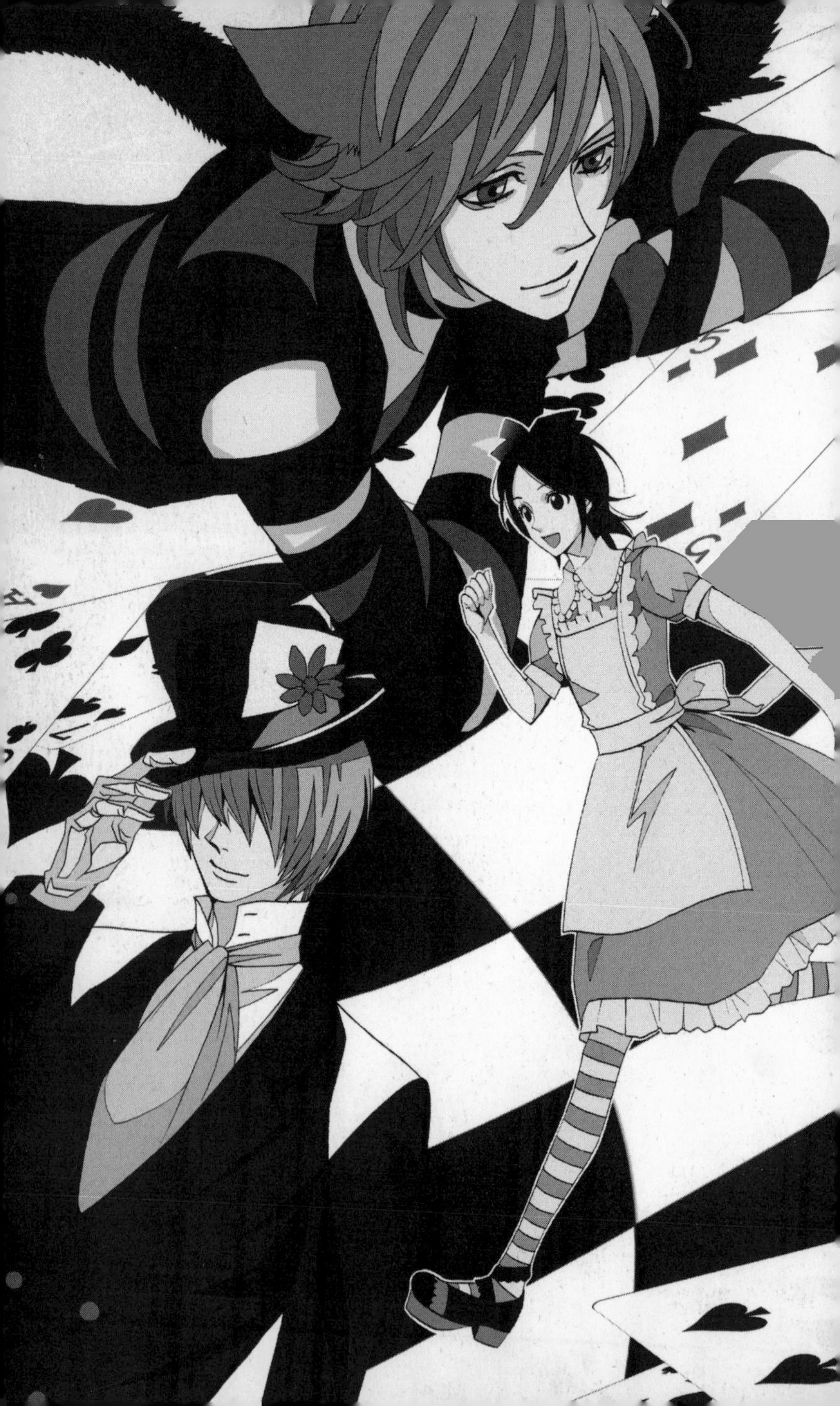

OTOMEN

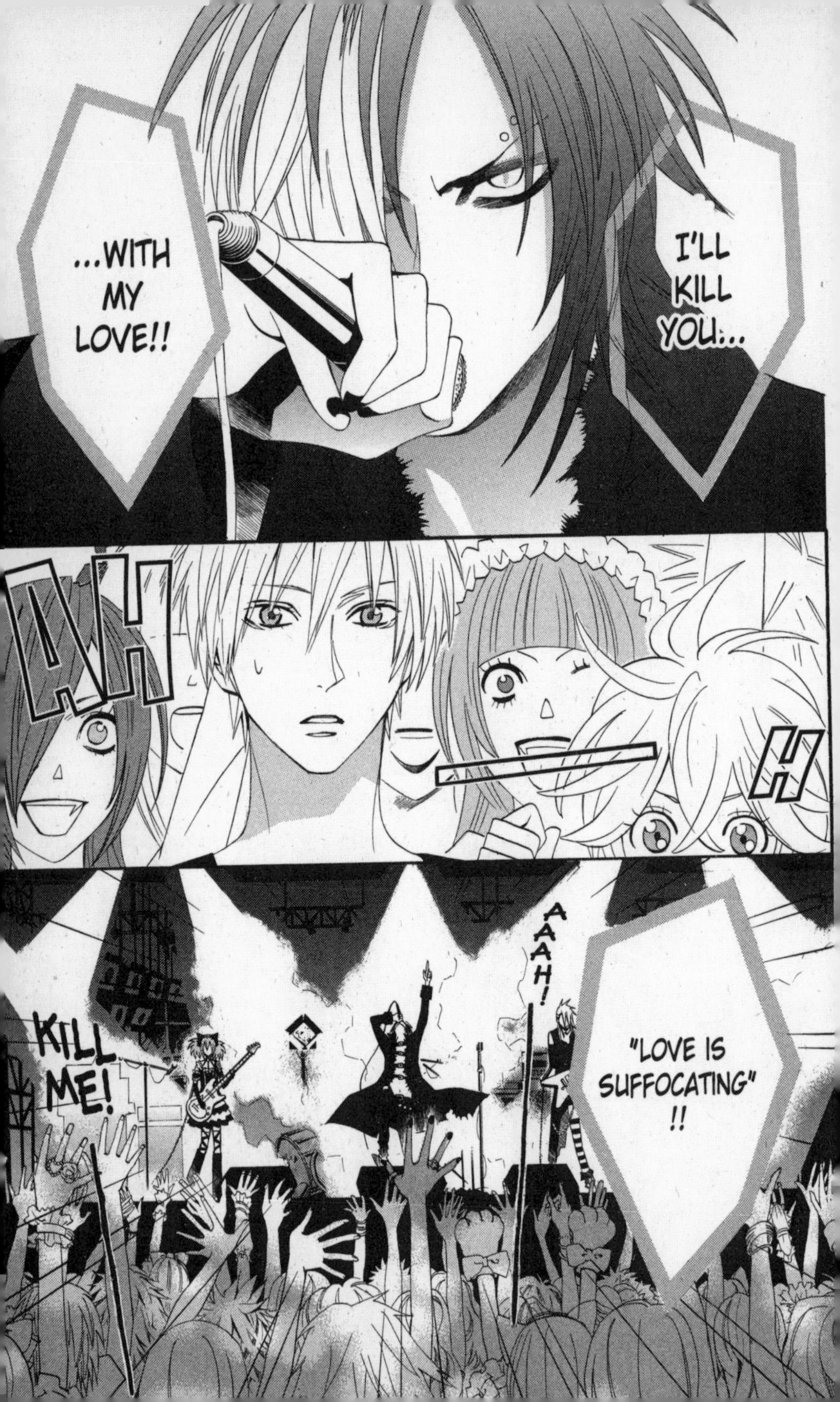
I'LL KILL YOU...
...WITH MY LOVE!!
H
AH
"LOVE IS SUFFOCATING" !!
AAAH!
KILL ME!

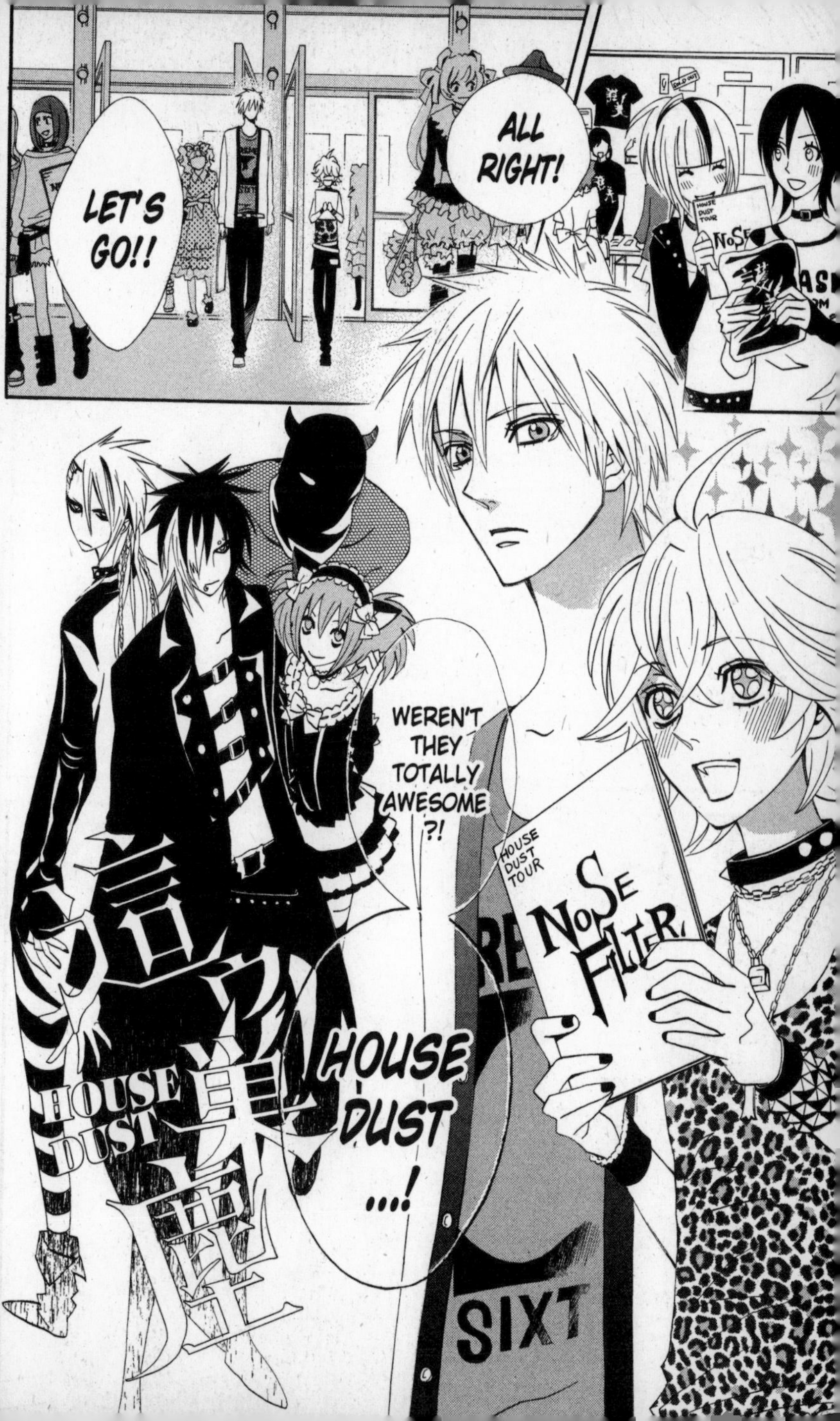
ALL RIGHT!
LET'S GO!!
HOUSE DUST TOUR
NOSE FILTER
WEREN'T THEY TOTALLY AWESOME ?!
HOUSE DUST ...!
SIXT
HOUSE DUST

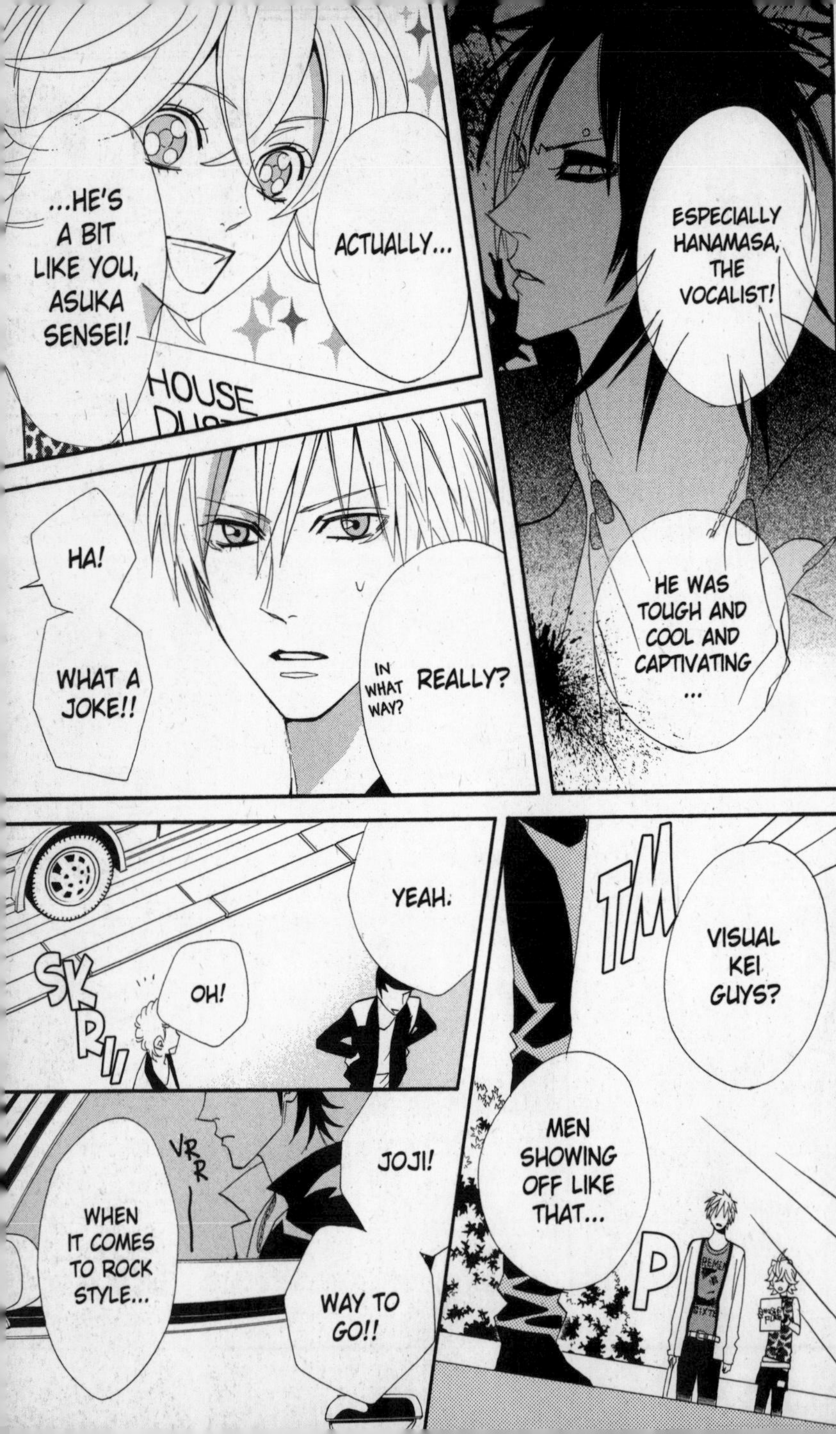
ESPECIALLY HANAMASA, THE VOCALIST!
HE WAS TOUGH AND COOL AND CAPTIVATING ...
ACTUALLY...
...HE'S A BIT LIKE YOU, ASUKA SENSEI!
HOUSE
REALLY?
IN WHAT WAY?
HA!
WHAT A JOKE!!
TM
VISUAL KEI GUYS?
MEN SHOWING OFF LIKE THAT...
P
YEAH.
OH!
SKRII
JOJI!
WAY TO GO!!
VRR
WHEN IT COMES TO ROCK STYLE...

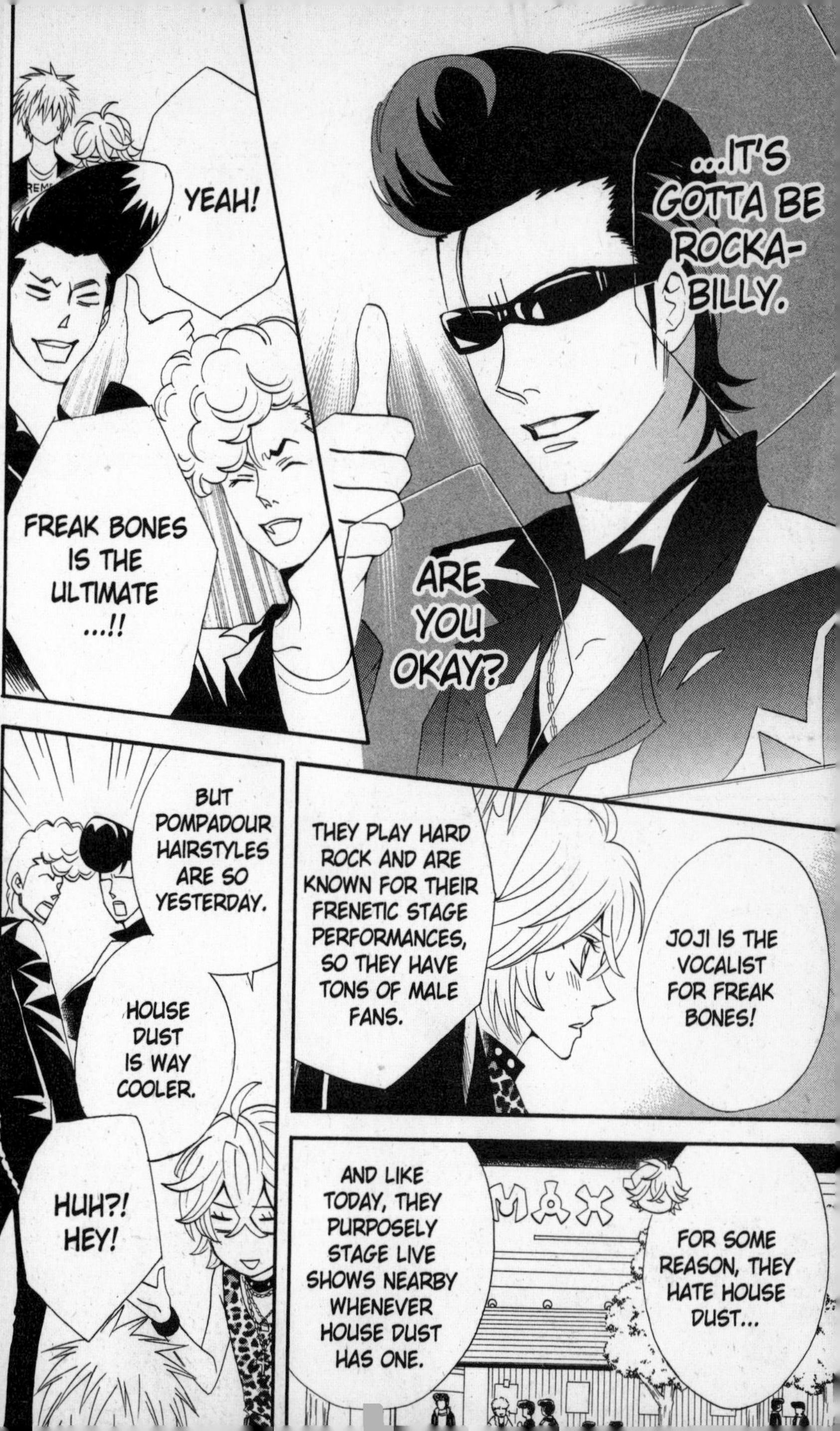
...IT'S GOTTA BE ROCKA-BILLY.
ARE YOU OKAY?
YEAH!
FREAK BONES IS THE ULTIMATE ...!!
JOJI IS THE VOCALIST FOR FREAK BONES!
THEY PLAY HARD ROCK AND ARE KNOWN FOR THEIR FRENETIC STAGE PERFORMANCES, SO THEY HAVE TONS OF MALE FANS.
FOR SOME REASON, THEY HATE HOUSE DUST...
MAX
AND LIKE TODAY, THEY PURPOSELY STAGE LIVE SHOWS NEARBY WHENEVER HOUSE DUST HAS ONE.
BUT POMPADOUR HAIRSTYLES ARE SO YESTERDAY.
HOUSE DUST IS WAY COOLER.
HUH?! HEY!

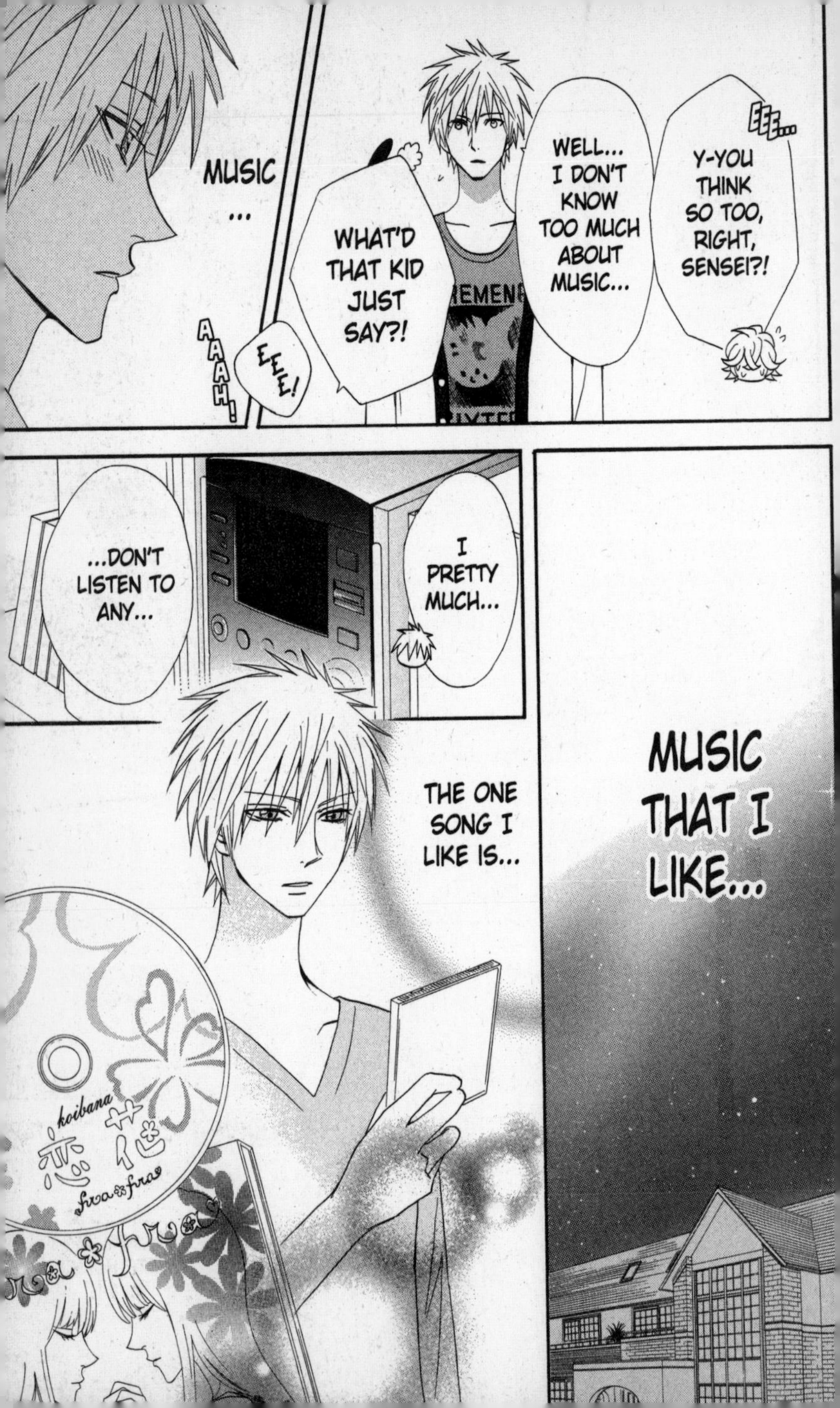
EEE...
Y-YOU THINK SO TOO, RIGHT, SENSEI?!
WELL... I DON'T KNOW TOO MUCH ABOUT MUSIC...
WHAT'D THAT KID JUST SAY?!
EEE!
MUSIC...
AAAAH!
MUSIC THAT I LIKE...
I PRETTY MUCH...
...DON'T LISTEN TO ANY...
THE ONE SONG I LIKE IS...
koibana
恋花
fra*fra

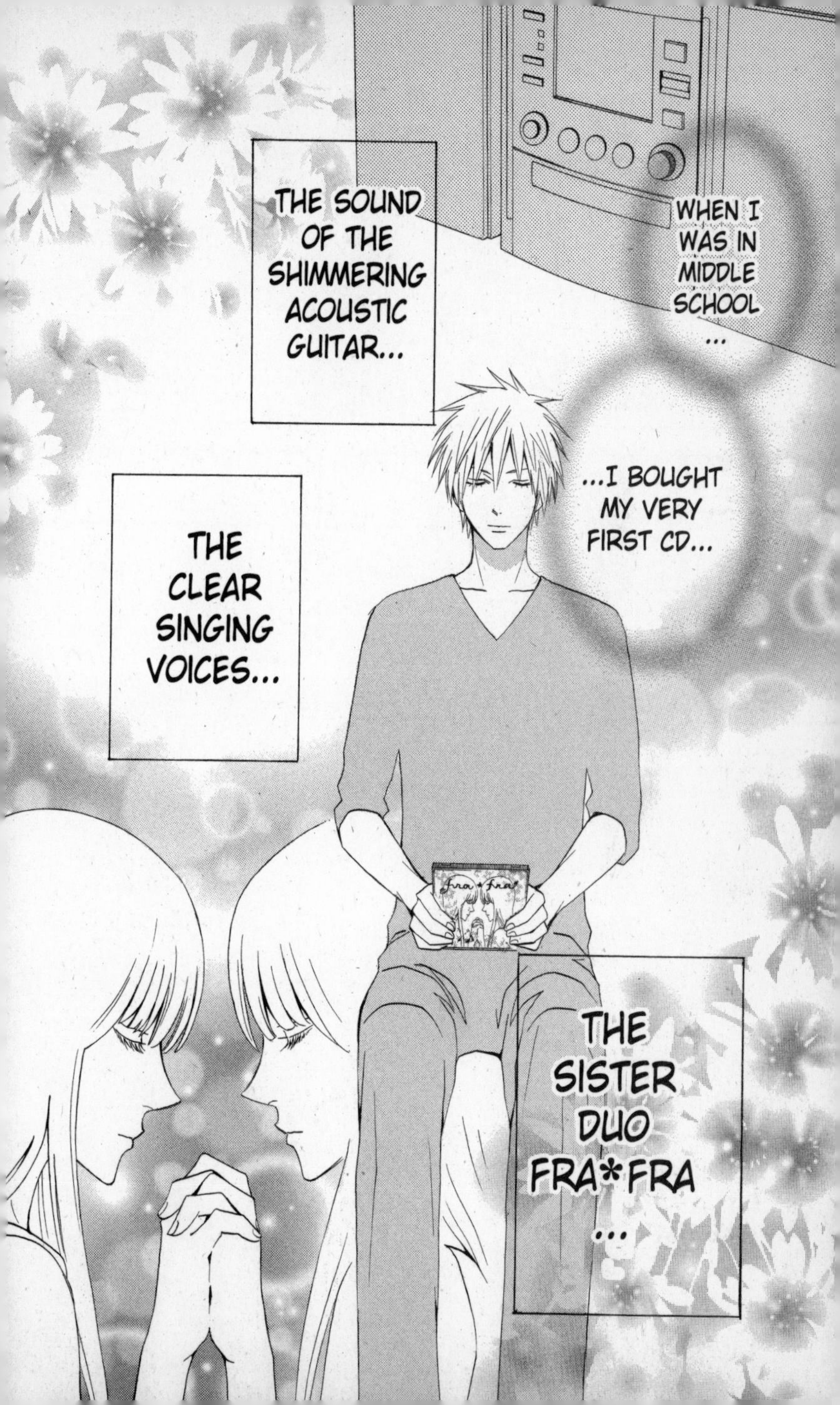
WHEN I WAS IN MIDDLE SCHOOL...
THE SOUND OF THE SHIMMERING ACOUSTIC GUITAR...
...I BOUGHT MY VERY FIRST CD...
THE CLEAR SINGING VOICES...
THE SISTER DUO FRA*FRA...

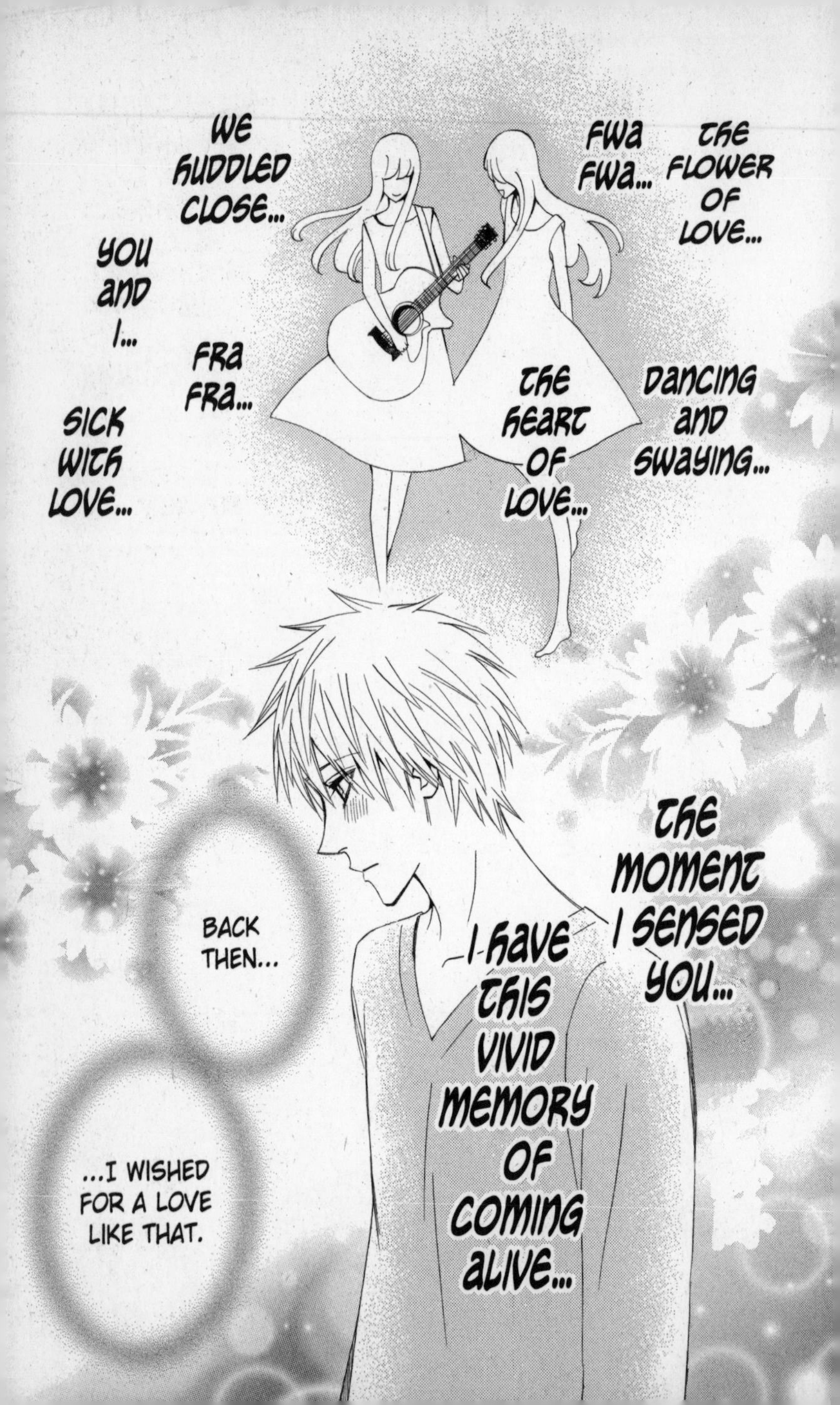
THE FLOWER OF LOVE...
FWA FWA...
WE HUDDLED CLOSE...
YOU AND I...
DANCING AND SWAYING...
THE HEART OF LOVE...
FRA FRA...
SICK WITH LOVE...
THE MOMENT I SENSED YOU...
I HAVE THIS VIVID MEMORY OF COMING ALIVE...
BACK THEN...
...I WISHED FOR A LOVE LIKE THAT.

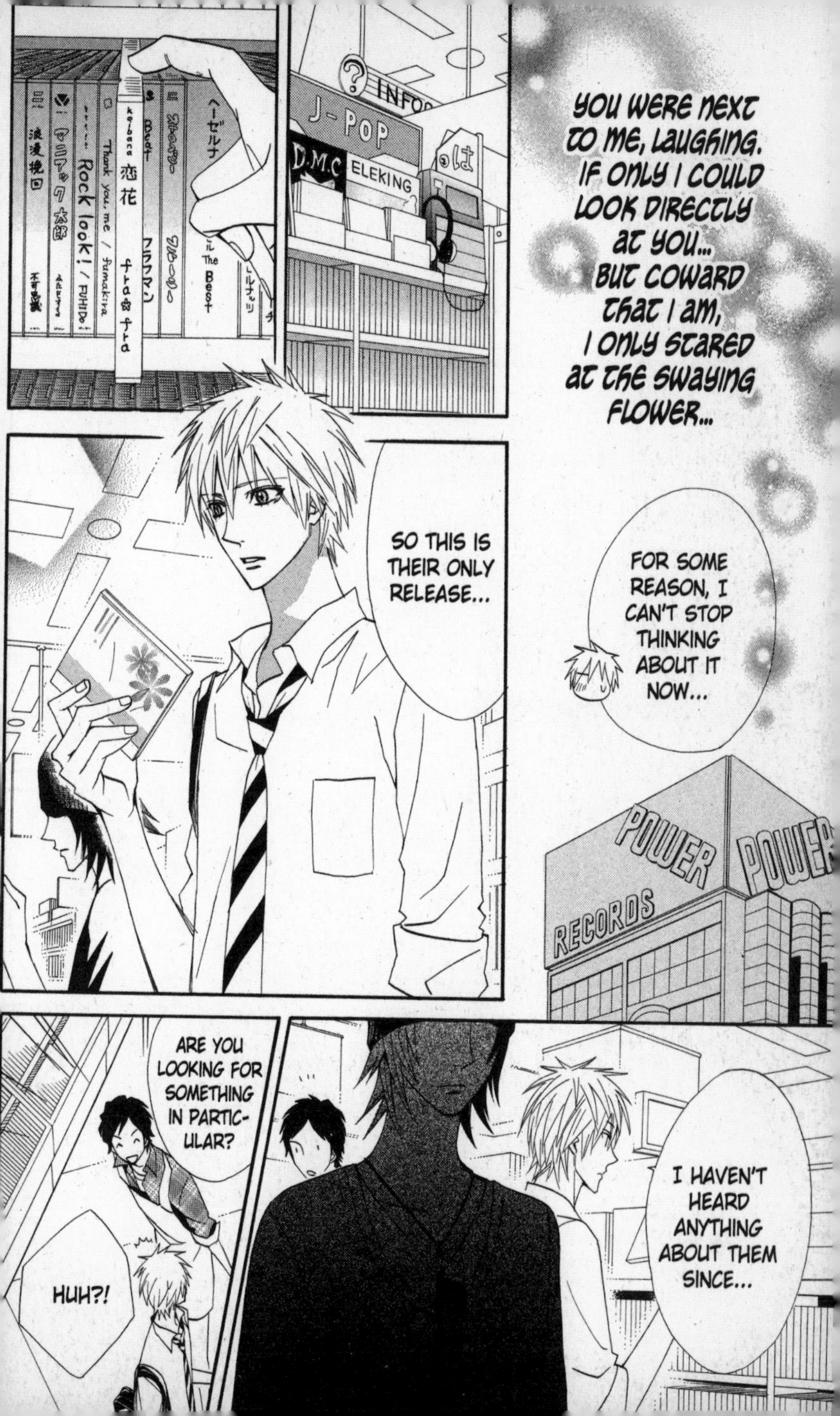
YOU WERE NEXT TO ME, LAUGHING. IF ONLY I COULD LOOK DIRECTLY AT YOU... BUT COWARD THAT I AM, I ONLY STARED AT THE SWAYING FLOWER...
FOR SOME REASON, I CAN'T STOP THINKING ABOUT IT NOW...
POWER
POWER
RECORDS
INFO
J-POP
D.M.C
ELEKING
は
ヘーゼルナ
The Best
koibana 恋花
Thank you, me / fumakira
fra fra
フラフマン
Rock look!
マニアック太郎
浪漫挽回
SO THIS IS THEIR ONLY RELEASE...
I HAVEN'T HEARD ANYTHING ABOUT THEM SINCE...
ARE YOU LOOKING FOR SOMETHING IN PARTIC-ULAR?
HUH?!

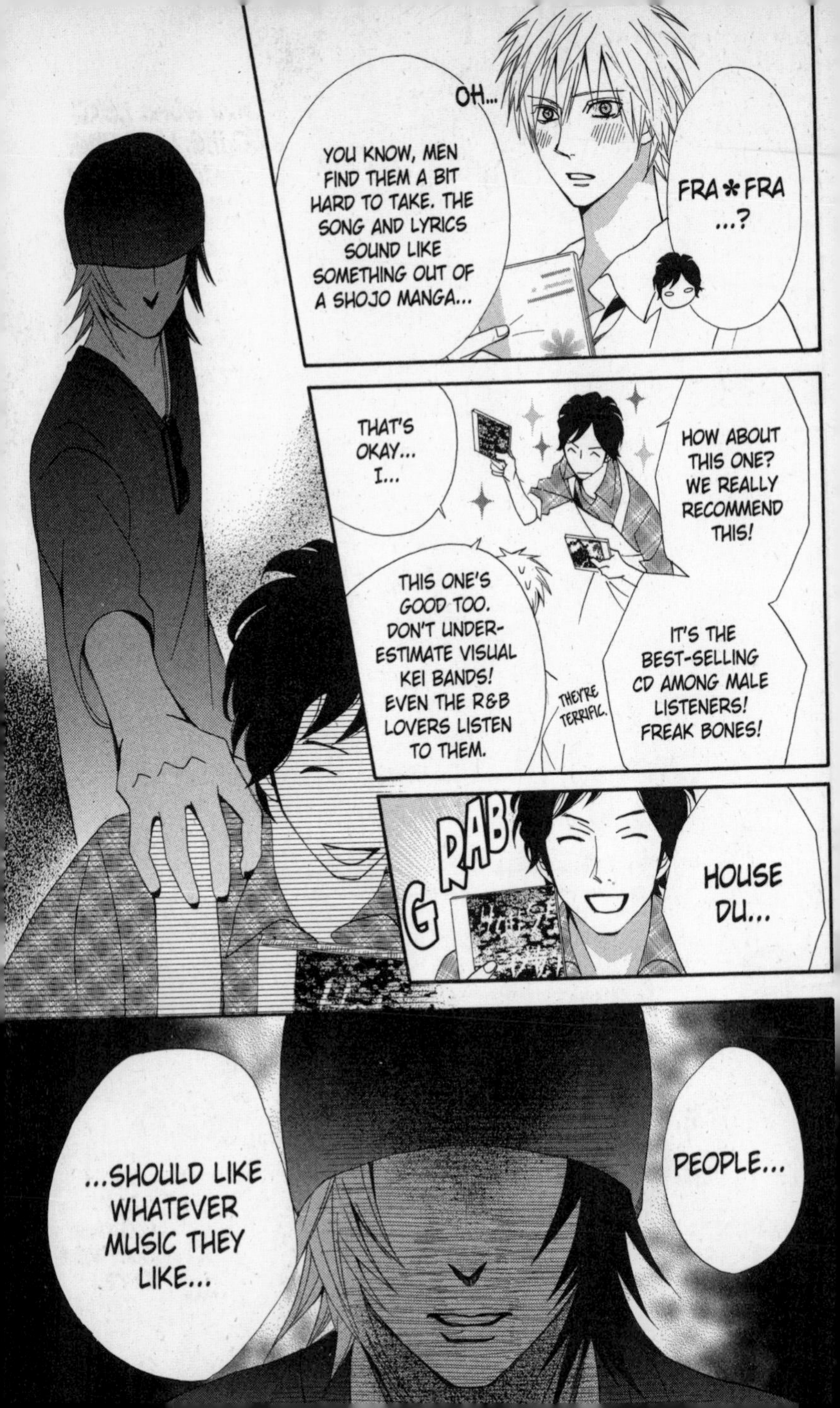
FRA*FRA ...?
OH...
YOU KNOW, MEN FIND THEM A BIT HARD TO TAKE. THE SONG AND LYRICS SOUND LIKE SOMETHING OUT OF A SHOJO MANGA...
HOW ABOUT THIS ONE? WE REALLY RECOMMEND THIS!
THAT'S OKAY... I...
IT'S THE BEST-SELLING CD AMONG MALE LISTENERS! FREAK BONES!
THEY'RE TERRIFIC.
THIS ONE'S GOOD TOO. DON'T UNDER-ESTIMATE VISUAL KEI BANDS! EVEN THE R&B LOVERS LISTEN TO THEM.
HOUSE DU...
GRAB
PEOPLE...
...SHOULD LIKE WHATEVER MUSIC THEY LIKE...

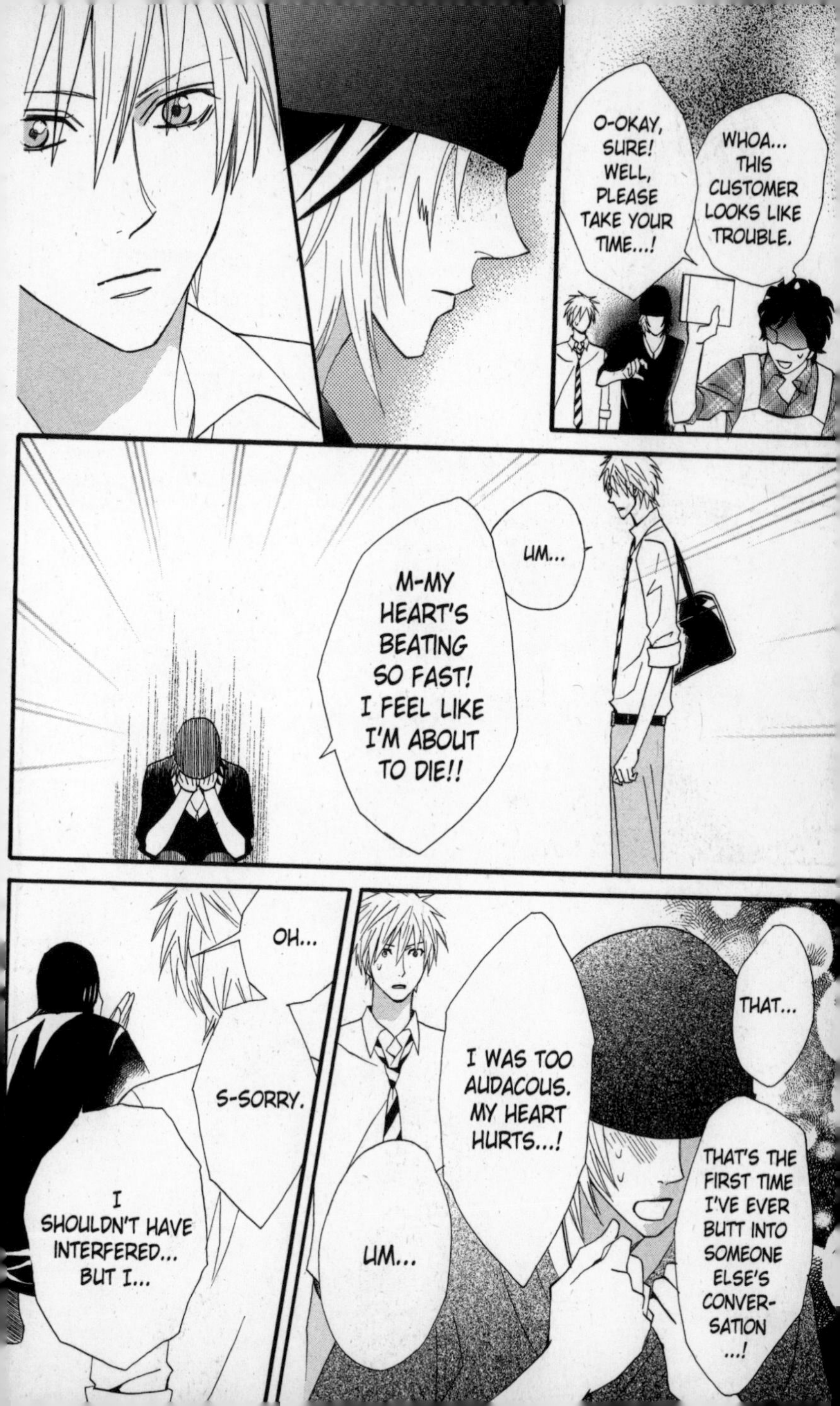
WHOA... THIS CUSTOMER LOOKS LIKE TROUBLE.
O-OKAY, SURE! WELL, PLEASE TAKE YOUR TIME...!
UM...
M-MY HEART'S BEATING SO FAST! I FEEL LIKE I'M ABOUT TO DIE!!
THAT...
THAT'S THE FIRST TIME I'VE EVER BUTT INTO SOMEONE ELSE'S CONVER-SATION ...!
I WAS TOO AUDACOUS. MY HEART HURTS...!
UM...
OH...
S-SORRY.
I SHOULDN'T HAVE INTERFERED... BUT I...

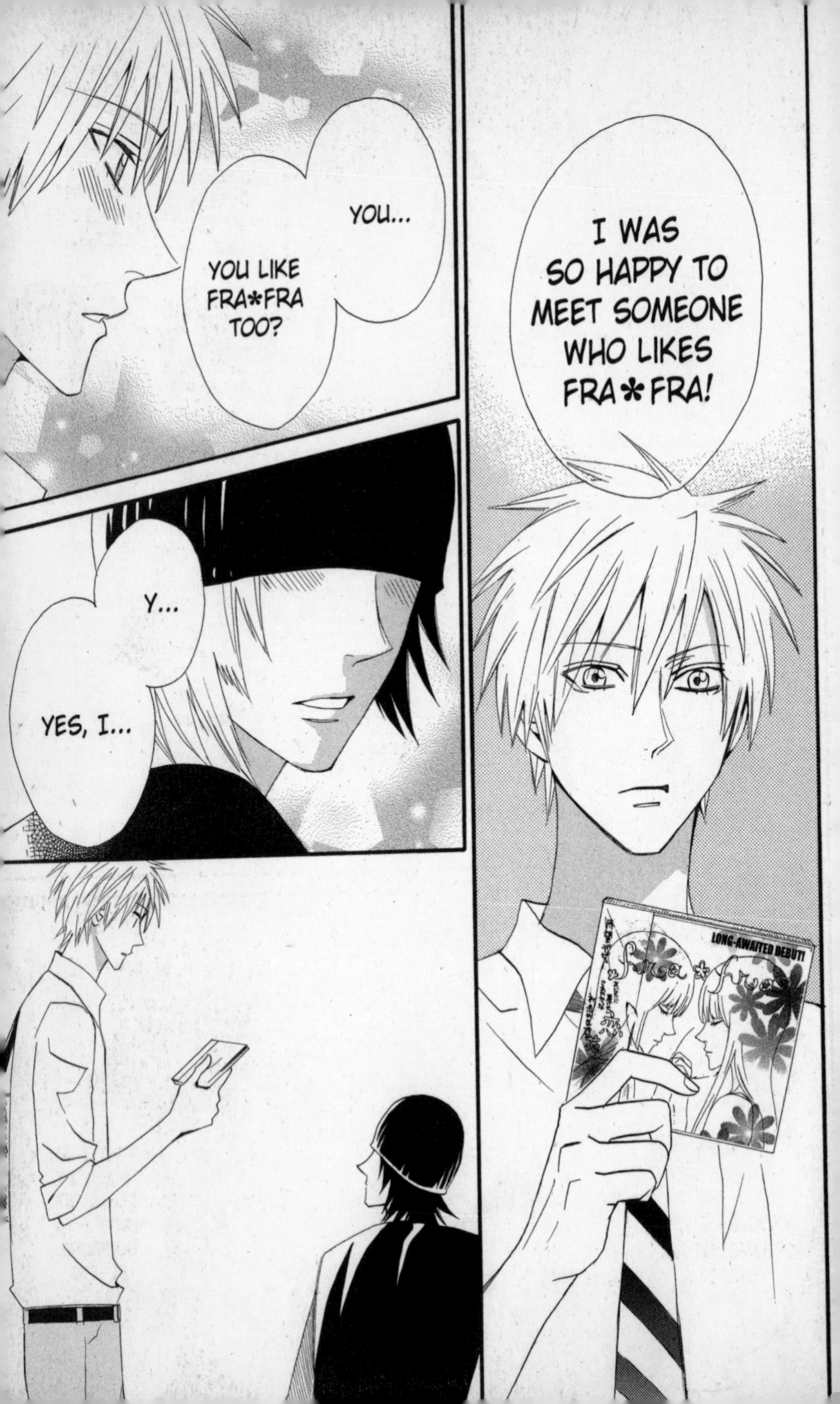
I WAS SO HAPPY TO MEET SOMEONE WHO LIKES FRA*FRA!
LONG-AWAITED DEBUT!
YOU...
YOU LIKE FRA*FRA TOO?
Y...
YES, I...

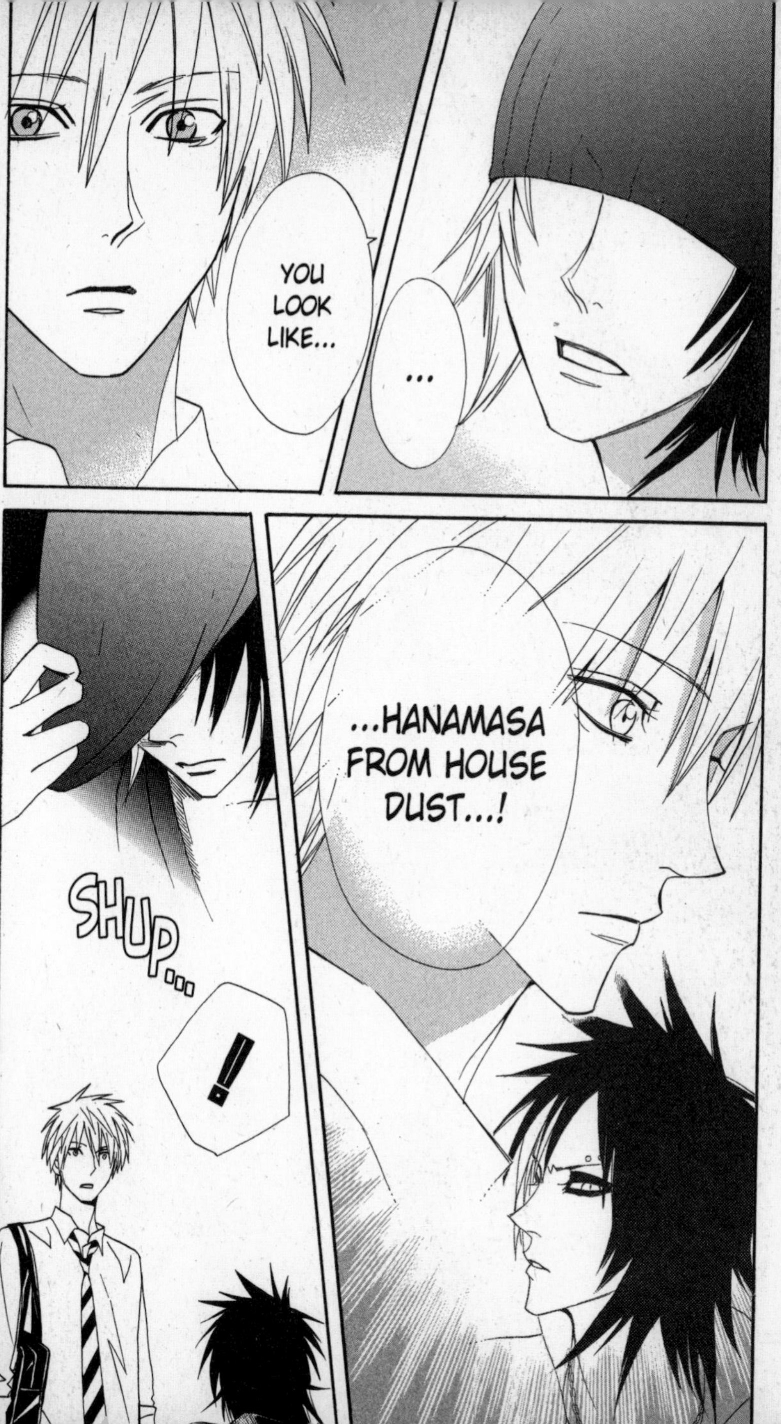
...
YOU LOOK LIKE...
...HANAMASA FROM HOUSE DUST...!
SHUP...
!

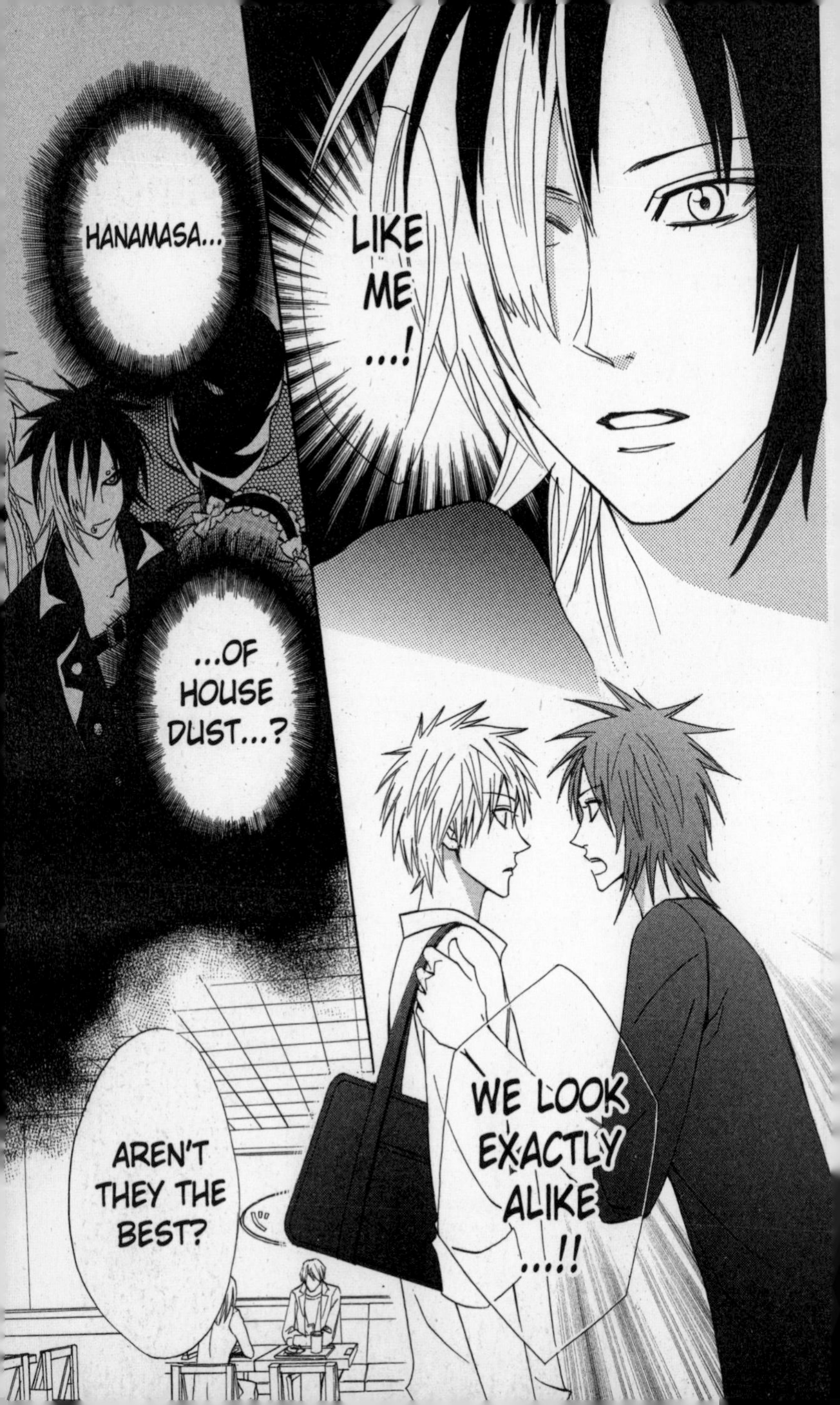
LIKE ME ...!
WE LOOK EXACTLY ALIKE ...!!
HANAMASA...
...OF HOUSE DUST...?
AREN'T THEY THE BEST?

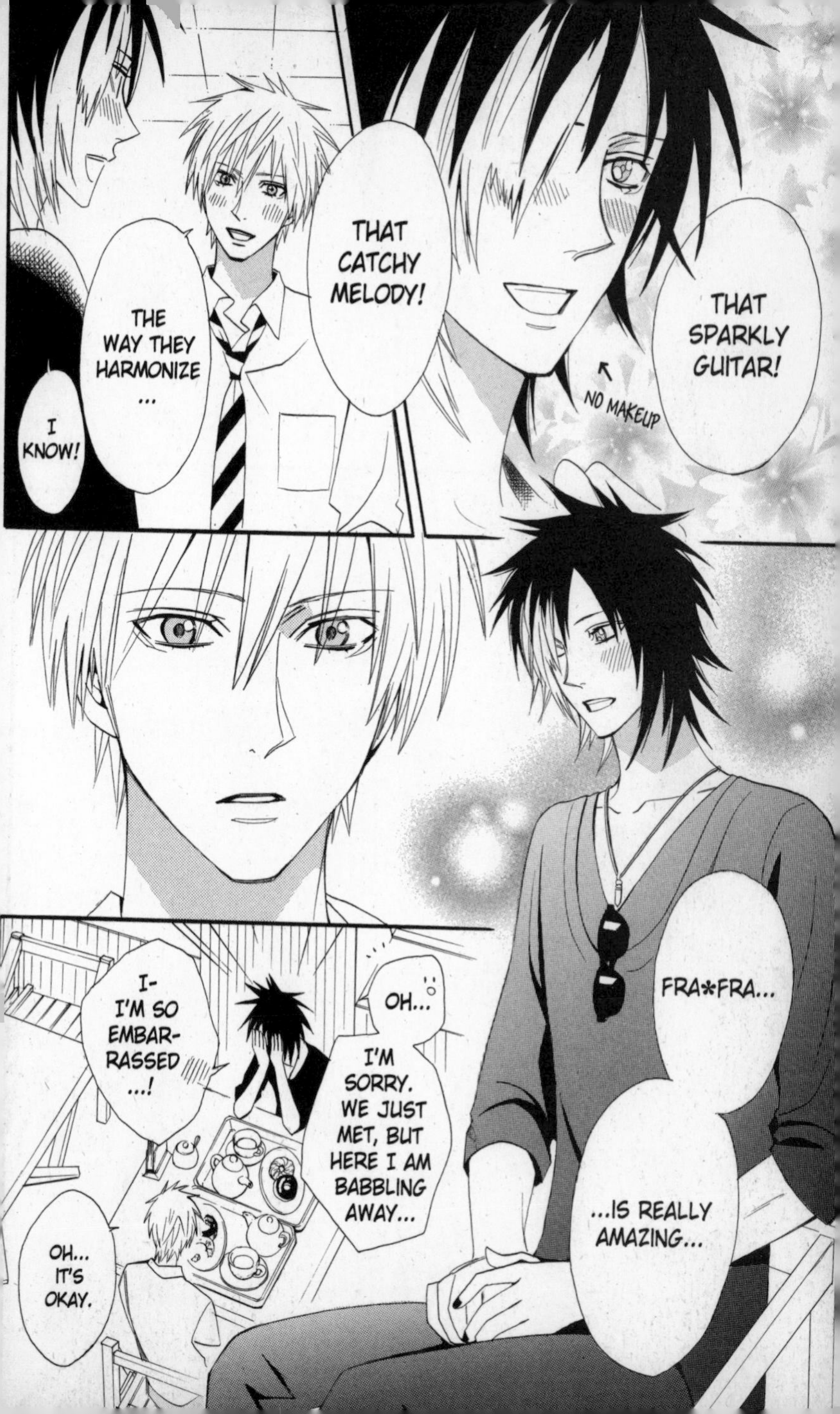
THAT SPARKLY GUITAR!
NO MAKEUP
THAT CATCHY MELODY!
THE WAY THEY HARMONIZE...
I KNOW!
FRA*FRA...
...IS REALLY AMAZING...
...
OH...
I'M SORRY. WE JUST MET, BUT HERE I AM BABBLING AWAY...
I- I'M SO EMBARRASSED...!
OH... IT'S OKAY.

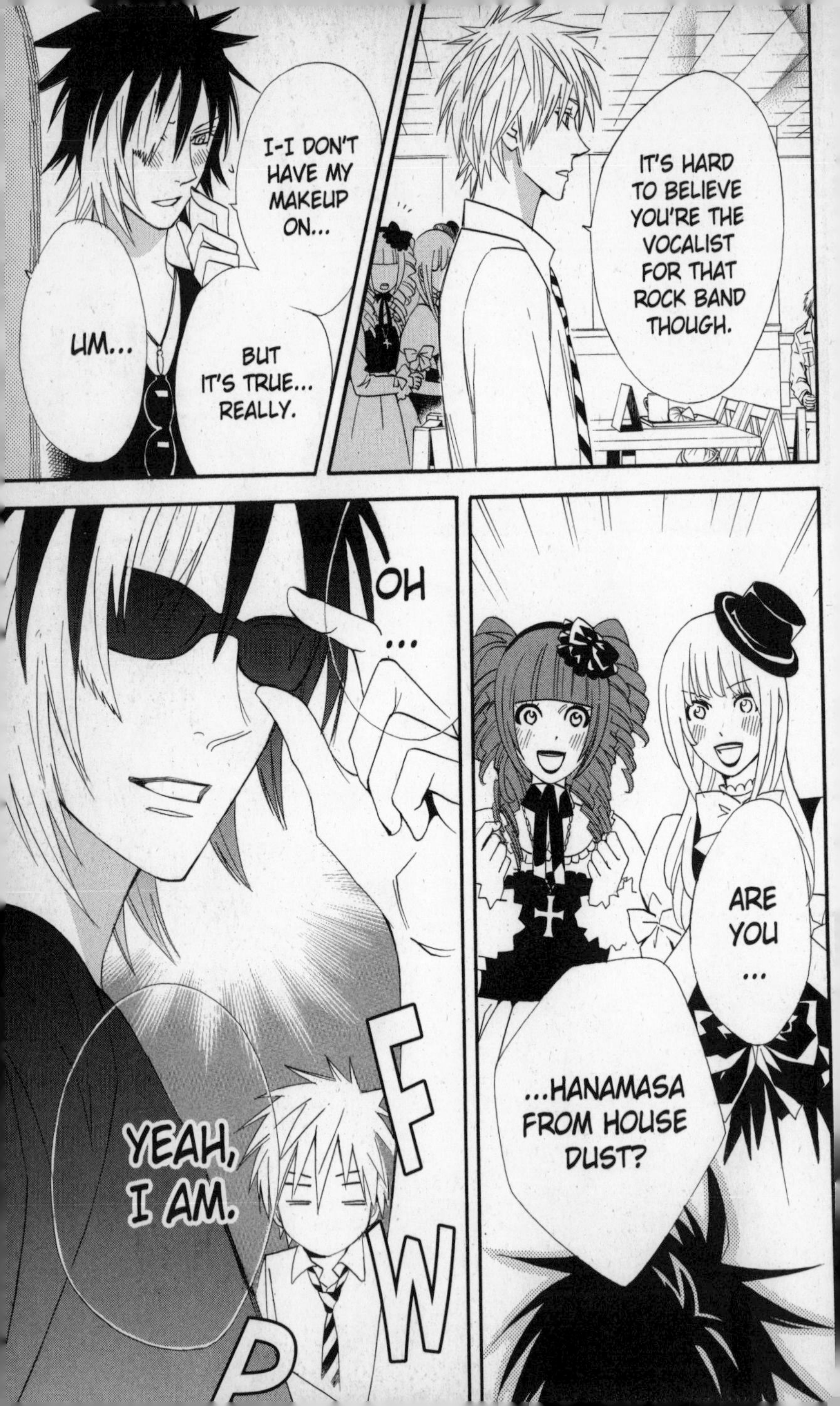
IT'S HARD TO BELIEVE YOU'RE THE VOCALIST FOR THAT ROCK BAND THOUGH.
I-I DON'T HAVE MY MAKEUP ON...
BUT IT'S TRUE... REALLY.
UM...
ARE YOU ...
...HANAMASA FROM HOUSE DUST?
OH ...
YEAH, I AM.
FWP

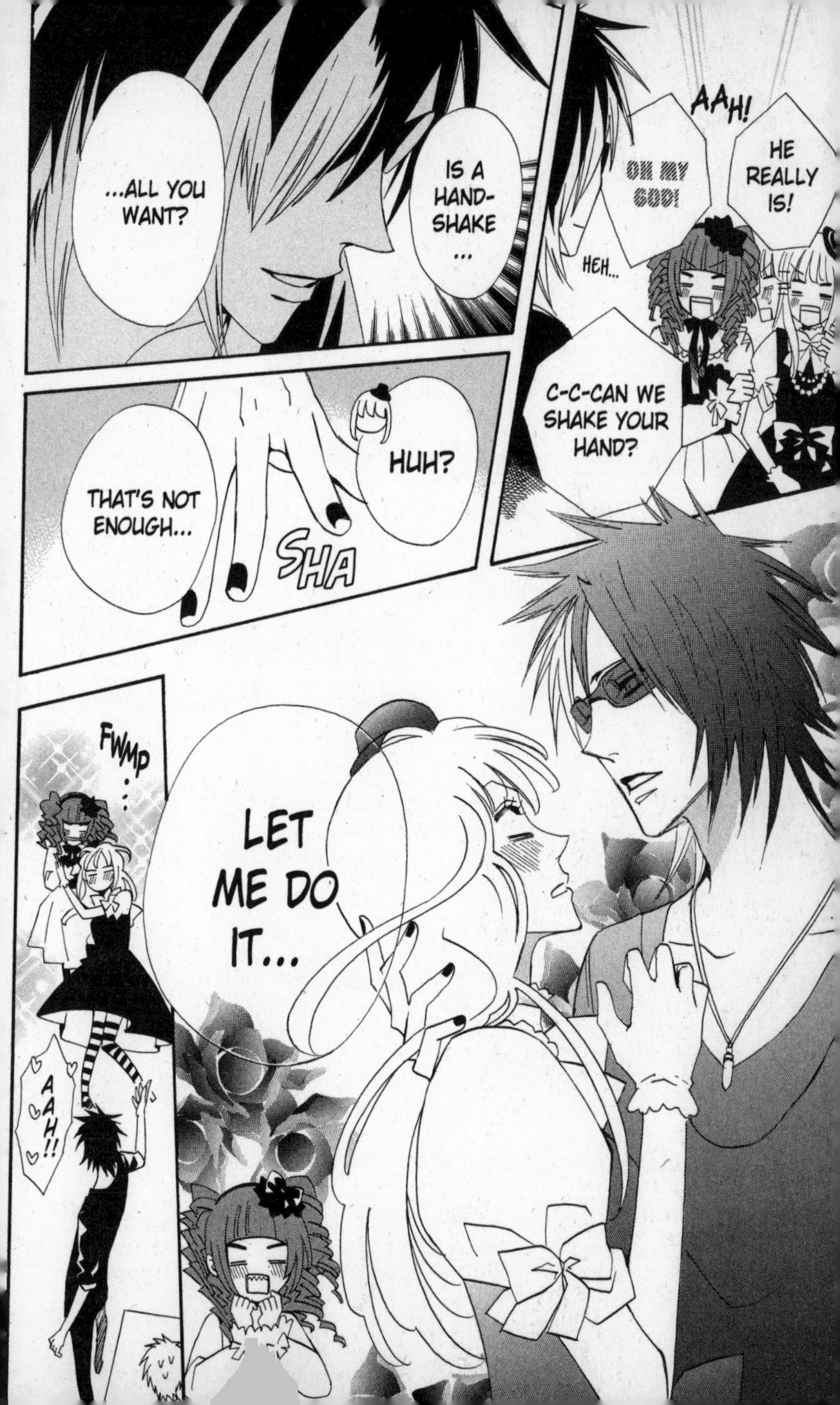
AAH!
HE REALLY IS!
OH MY GOD!
HEH...
C-C-CAN WE SHAKE YOUR HAND?
IS A HAND-SHAKE ...
...ALL YOU WANT?
HUH?
SHA
THAT'S NOT ENOUGH...
LET ME DO IT...
FWMP
AAH!!

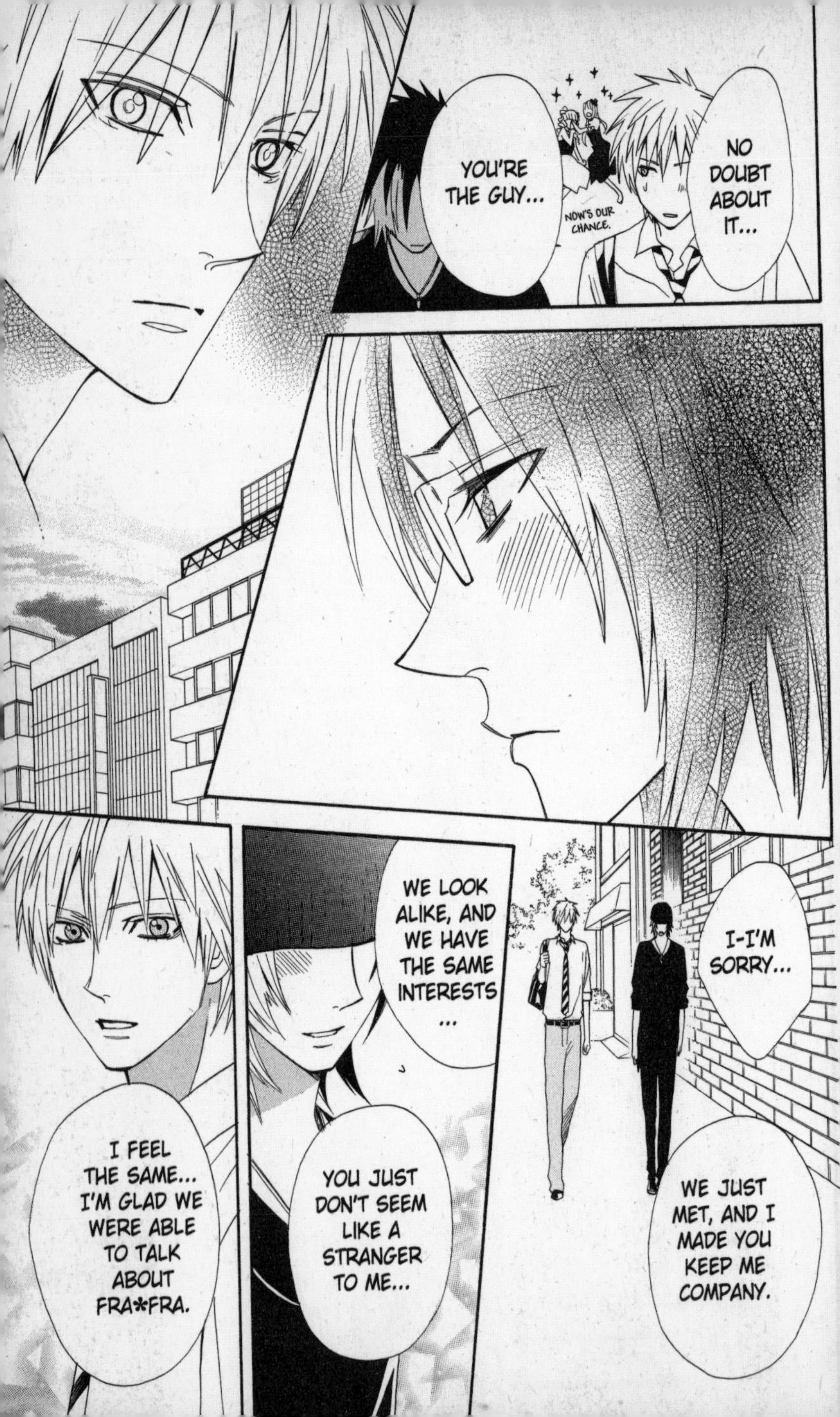
NO DOUBT ABOUT IT...
YOU'RE THE GUY...
NOW'S OUR CHANCE.
I-I'M SORRY...
WE JUST MET, AND I MADE YOU KEEP ME COMPANY.
WE LOOK ALIKE, AND WE HAVE THE SAME INTERESTS ...
YOU JUST DON'T SEEM LIKE A STRANGER TO ME...
I FEEL THE SAME... I'M GLAD WE WERE ABLE TO TALK ABOUT FRA*FRA.

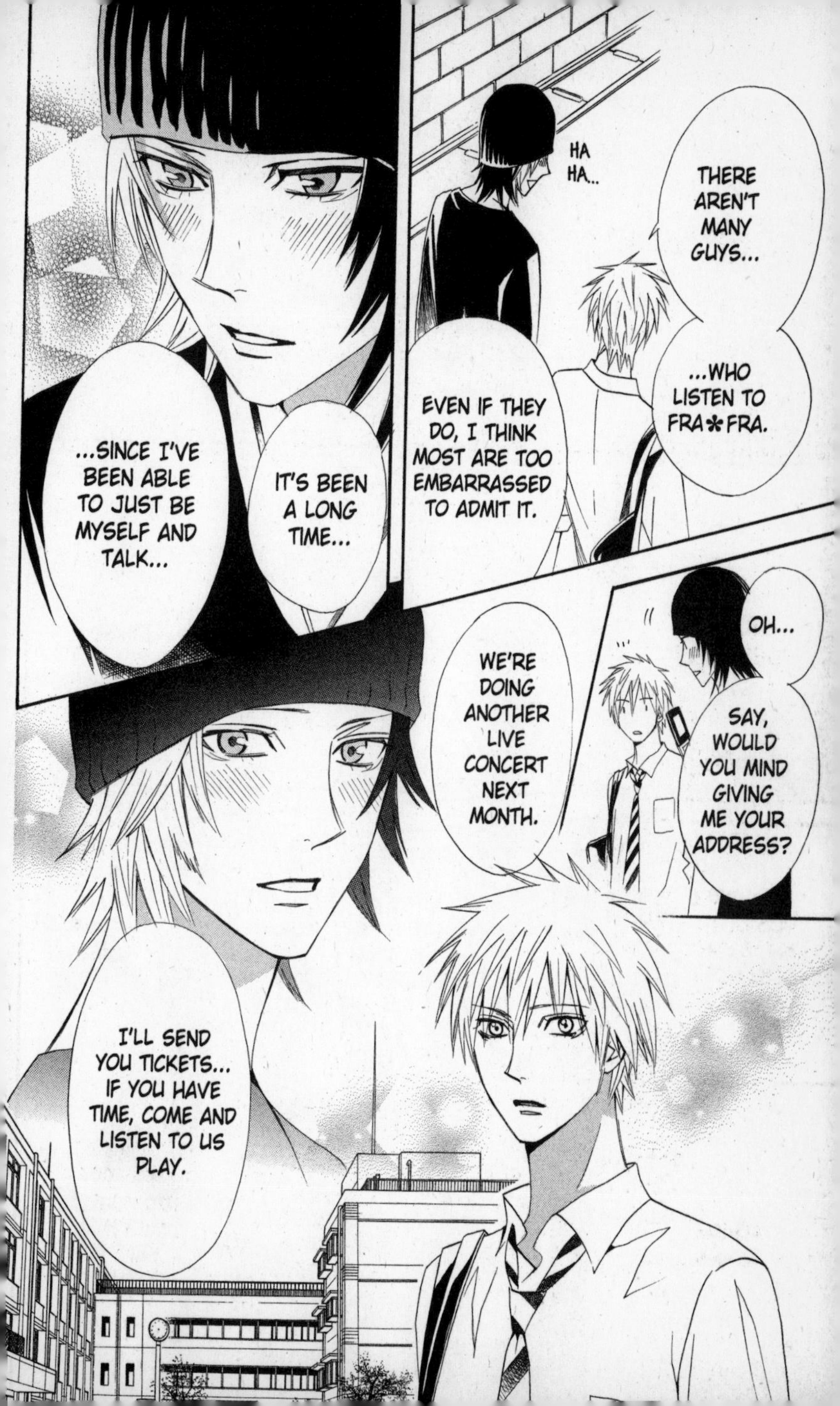
THERE AREN'T MANY GUYS...
...WHO LISTEN TO FRA✻FRA.
HA HA...
EVEN IF THEY DO, I THINK MOST ARE TOO EMBARRASSED TO ADMIT IT.
IT'S BEEN A LONG TIME...
...SINCE I'VE BEEN ABLE TO JUST BE MYSELF AND TALK...
OH...
SAY, WOULD YOU MIND GIVING ME YOUR ADDRESS?
WE'RE DOING ANOTHER LIVE CONCERT NEXT MONTH.
I'LL SEND YOU TICKETS... IF YOU HAVE TIME, COME AND LISTEN TO US PLAY.

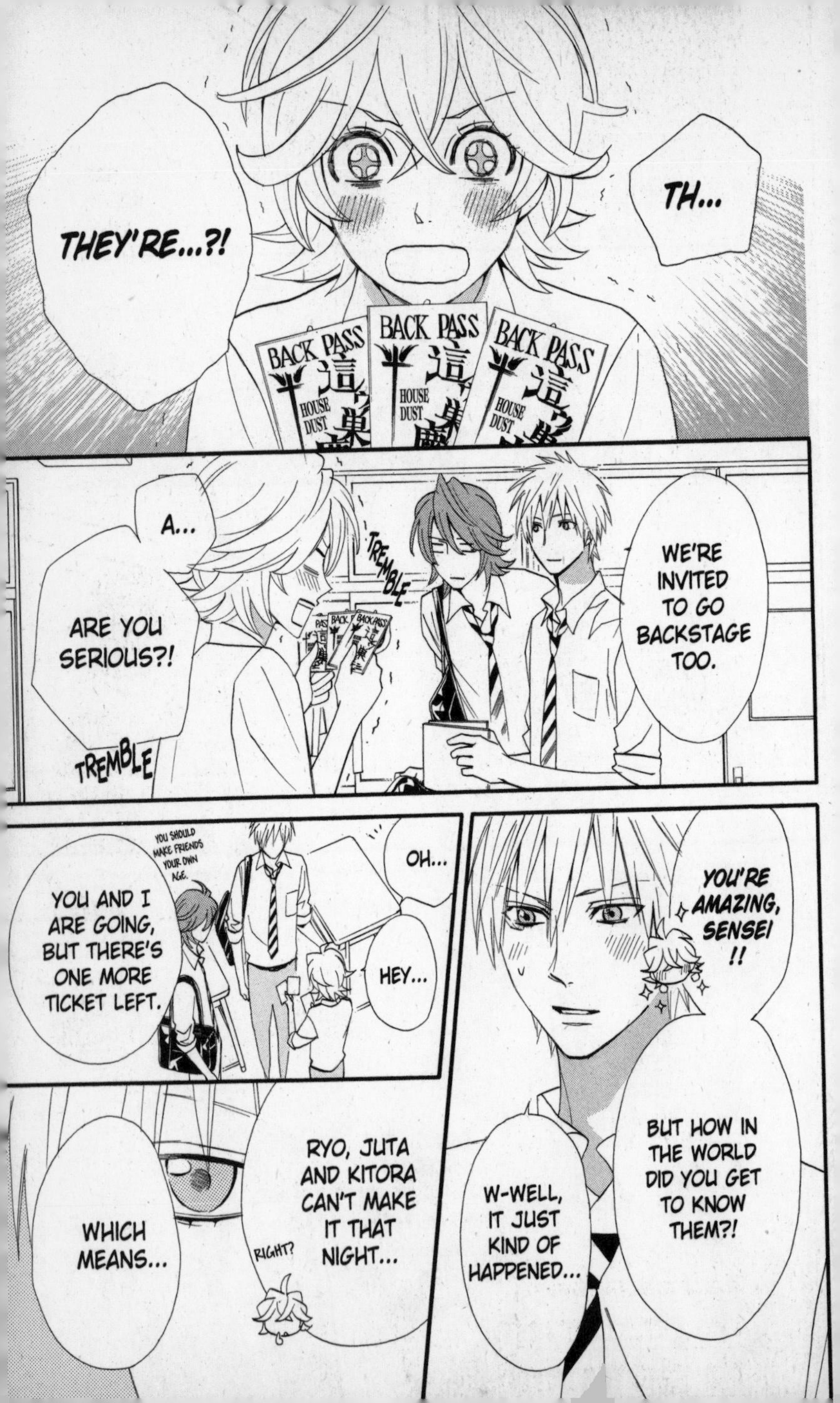
TH...
THEY'RE...?!
BACK PASS
HOUSE DUST
WE'RE INVITED TO GO BACKSTAGE TOO.
A...
TREMBLE
ARE YOU SERIOUS?!
TREMBLE
YOU'RE AMAZING, SENSEI !!
BUT HOW IN THE WORLD DID YOU GET TO KNOW THEM?!
W-WELL, IT JUST KIND OF HAPPENED...
OH...
HEY...
YOU AND I ARE GOING, BUT THERE'S ONE MORE TICKET LEFT.
YOU SHOULD MAKE FRIENDS YOUR OWN AGE.
RYO, JUTA AND KITORA CAN'T MAKE IT THAT NIGHT...
RIGHT?
WHICH MEANS...

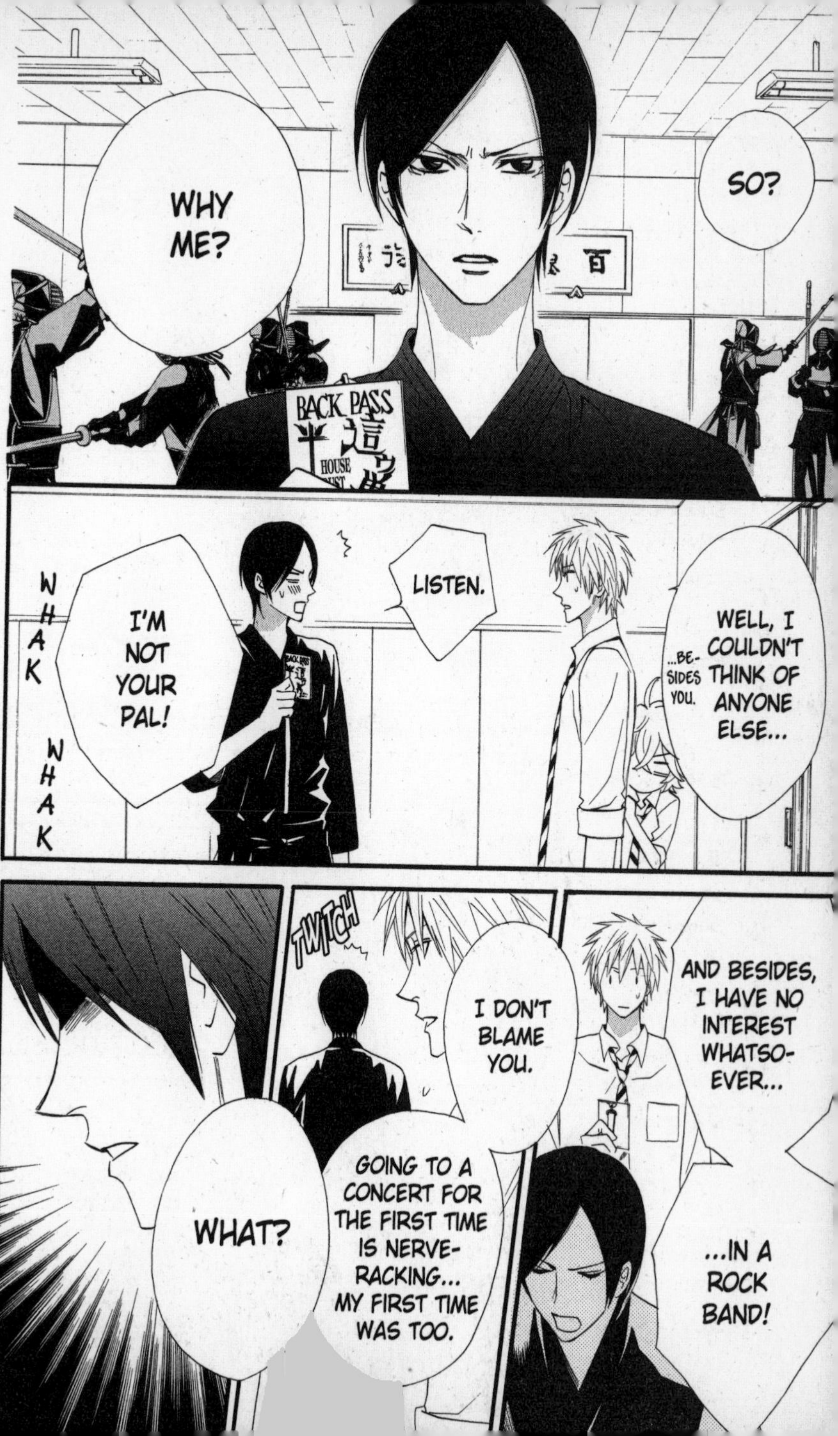

SO?
WHY ME?
BACK PASS
WELL, I COULDN'T THINK OF ANYONE ELSE...
...BE-SIDES YOU.
LISTEN.
I'M NOT YOUR PAL!
WHAK
WHAK
AND BESIDES, I HAVE NO INTEREST WHATSO-EVER...
...IN A ROCK BAND!
TWITCH
I DON'T BLAME YOU.
GOING TO A CONCERT FOR THE FIRST TIME IS NERVE-RACKING... MY FIRST TIME WAS TOO.
WHAT?

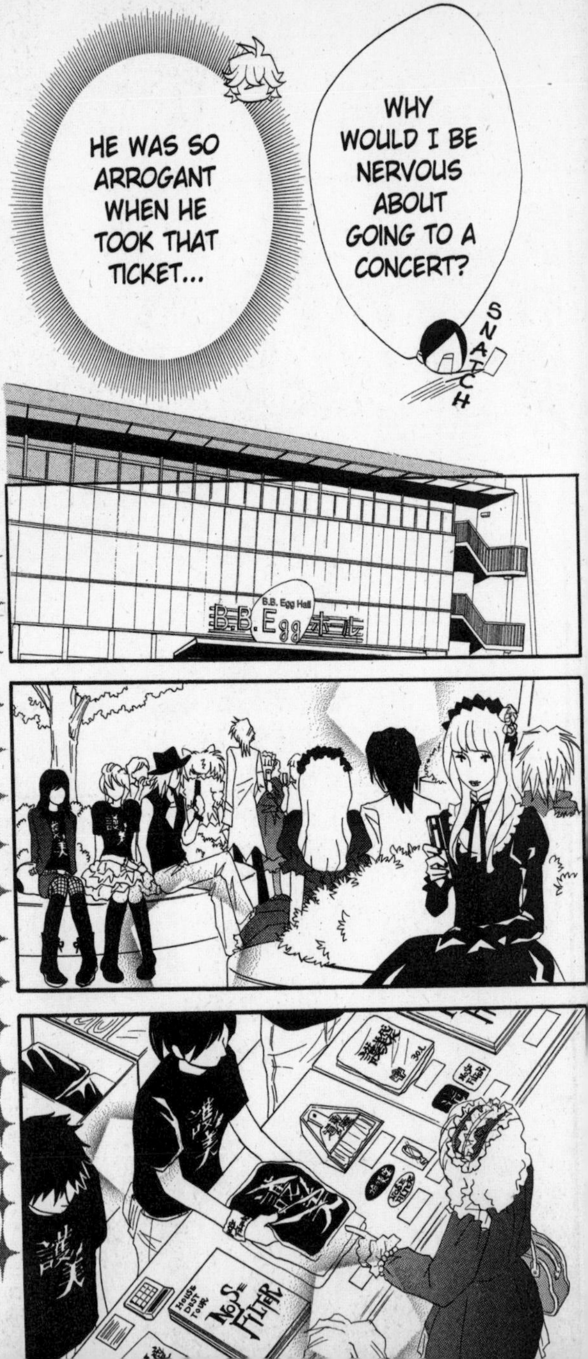
WHY WOULD I BE NERVOUS ABOUT GOING TO A CONCERT?
SNATCH
HE WAS SO ARROGANT WHEN HE TOOK THAT TICKET...
B.B. Egg Hall
HOUSE DIST TOUR
NoSe FILTER

Production Assistance:

Shimada-san
Takowa-san
Kawasaki-san
Sayaka-san
Kuwana-san
Tanaka-san
Nakasu-san
Sakurai-san
Yoneyan
Kaneko-san

Special Thanks:

Abe-san
Abewo
All My Readers

If you have any comments or suggestions, please write to:
Aya Kanno
c/o Otomen Editor
Viz Media
P.O. Box 77010
San Francisco, CA
94107

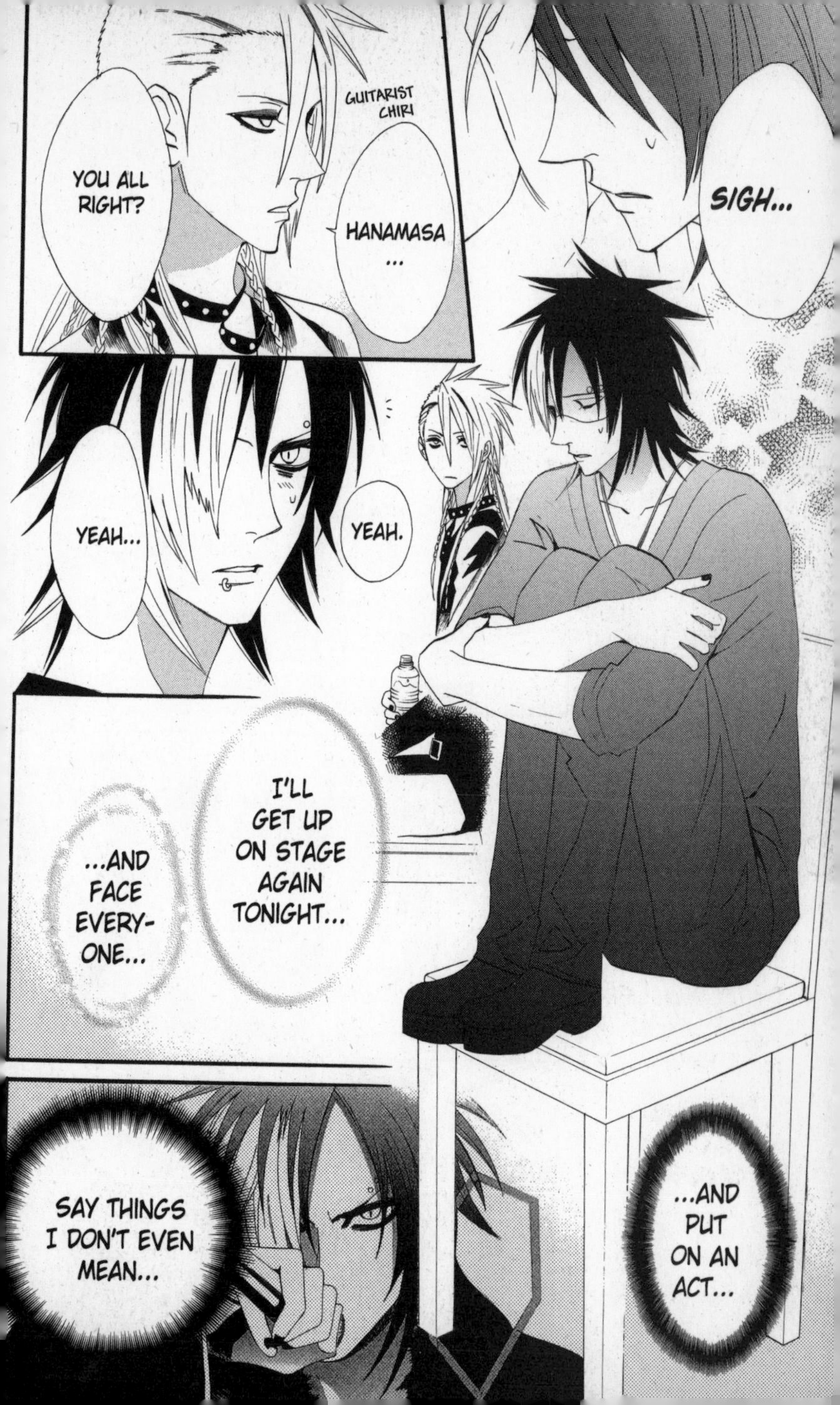
SIGH...
GUITARIST CHIRI
HANAMASA ...
YOU ALL RIGHT?
YEAH.
YEAH...
I'LL GET UP ON STAGE AGAIN TONIGHT...
...AND FACE EVERY-ONE...
SAY THINGS I DON'T EVEN MEAN...
...AND PUT ON AN ACT...

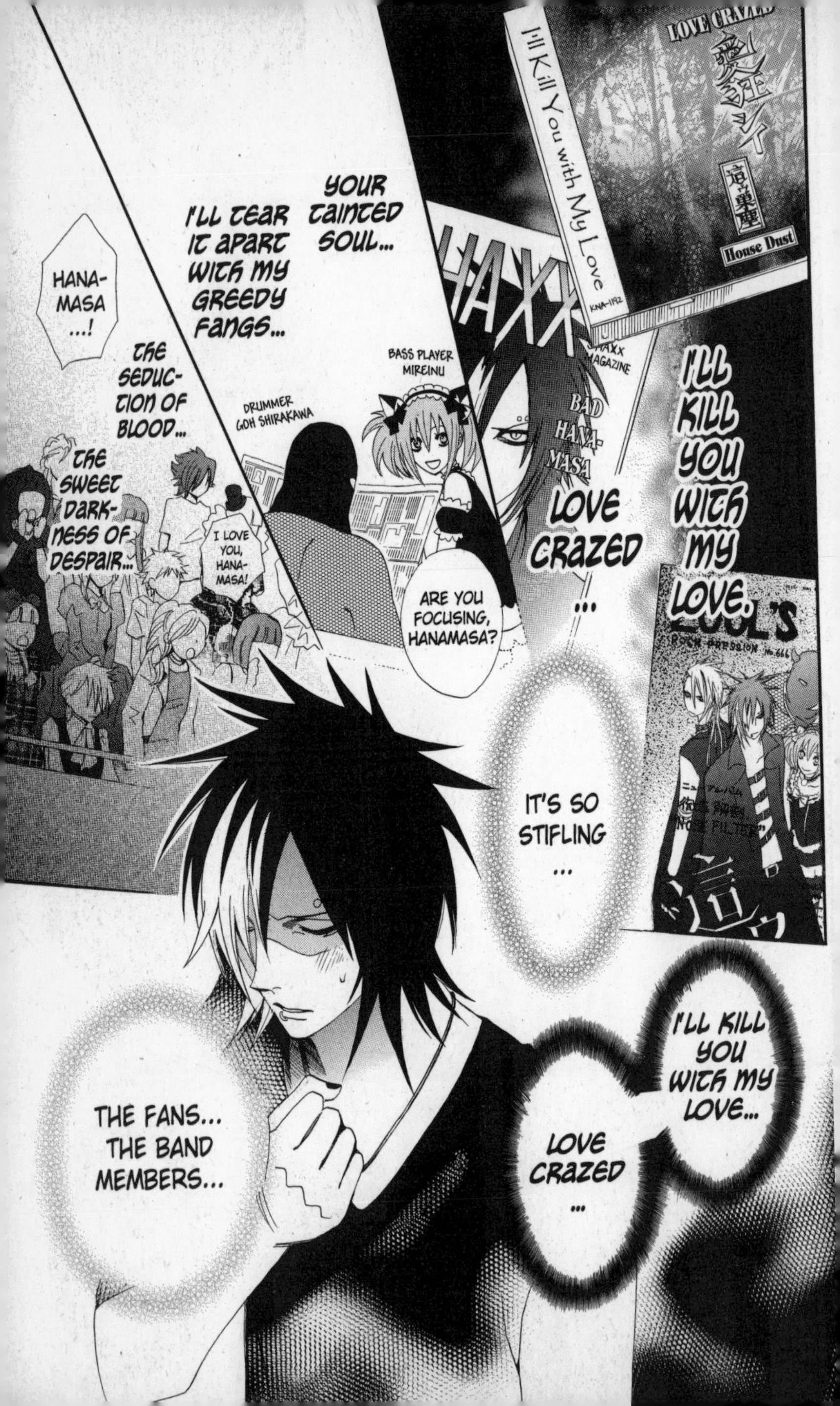

House Dust
I'll Kill You with My Love
KNA-1192
SHAXX MAGAZINE
BAD HANA-MASA
I'LL KILL YOU WITH MY LOVE.
LOVE CRAZED...
ROCK PRESSION No.666
YOUR TAINTED SOUL...
I'LL TEAR IT APART WITH MY GREEDY FANGS...
BASS PLAYER MIREINU
DRUMMER GOH SHIRAKAWA
ARE YOU FOCUSING, HANAMASA?
HANA-MASA ...!
THE SEDUCTION OF BLOOD...
THE SWEET DARKNESS OF DESPAIR...
I LOVE YOU, HANAMASA!
IT'S SO STIFLING ...
I'LL KILL YOU WITH MY LOVE...
LOVE CRAZED ...
THE FANS... THE BAND MEMBERS...

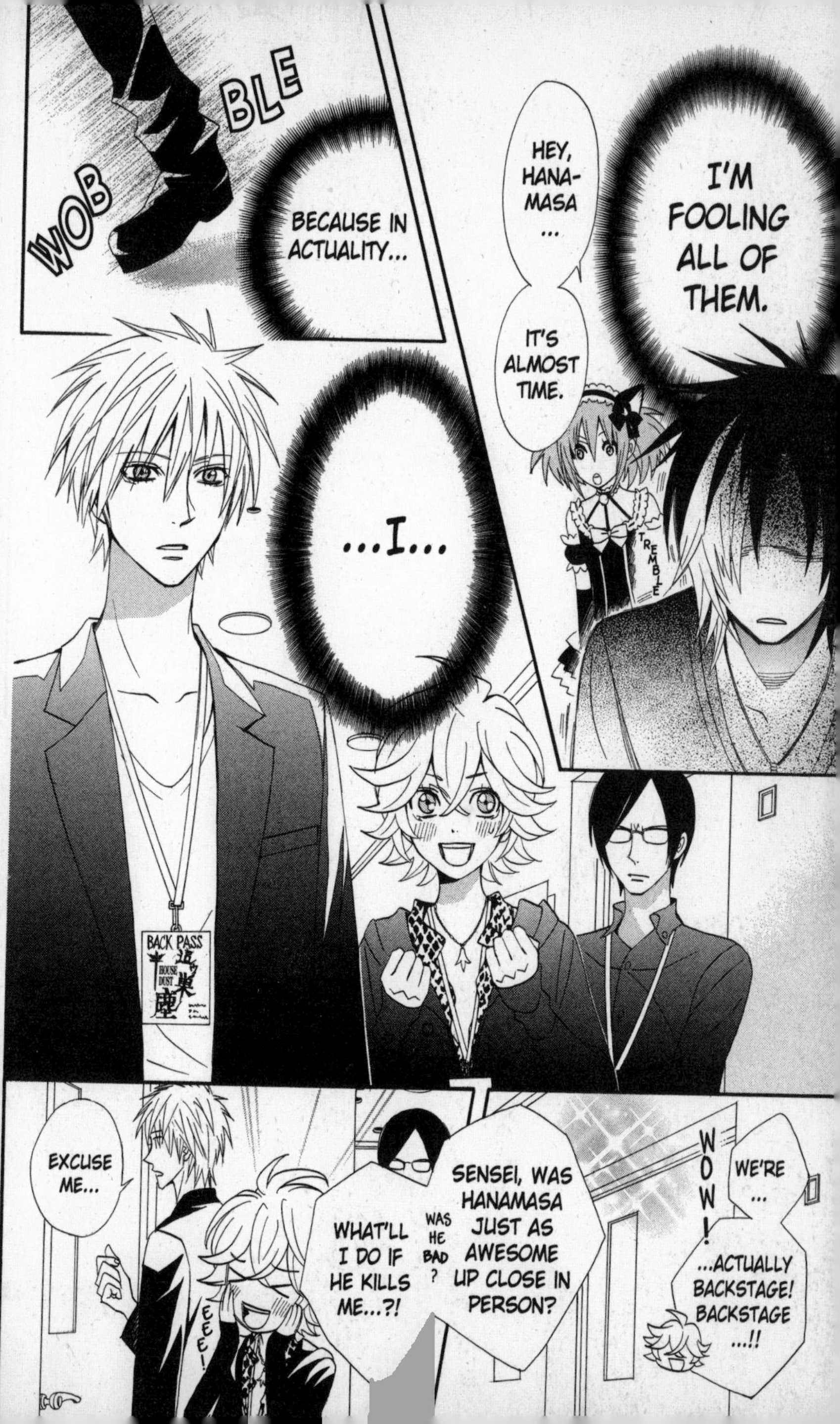
I'M FOOLING ALL OF THEM.
HEY, HANA-MASA ...
IT'S ALMOST TIME.
TREMBLE
WOBBLE
BECAUSE IN ACTUALITY...
...I...
BACK PASS
HOUSE DUST
WOW!
WE'RE ...
...ACTUALLY BACKSTAGE! BACKSTAGE ...!!
SENSEI, WAS HANAMASA JUST AS AWESOME UP CLOSE IN PERSON?
WAS HE BAD?
WHAT'LL I DO IF HE KILLS ME...?!
EEE!
EXCUSE ME...

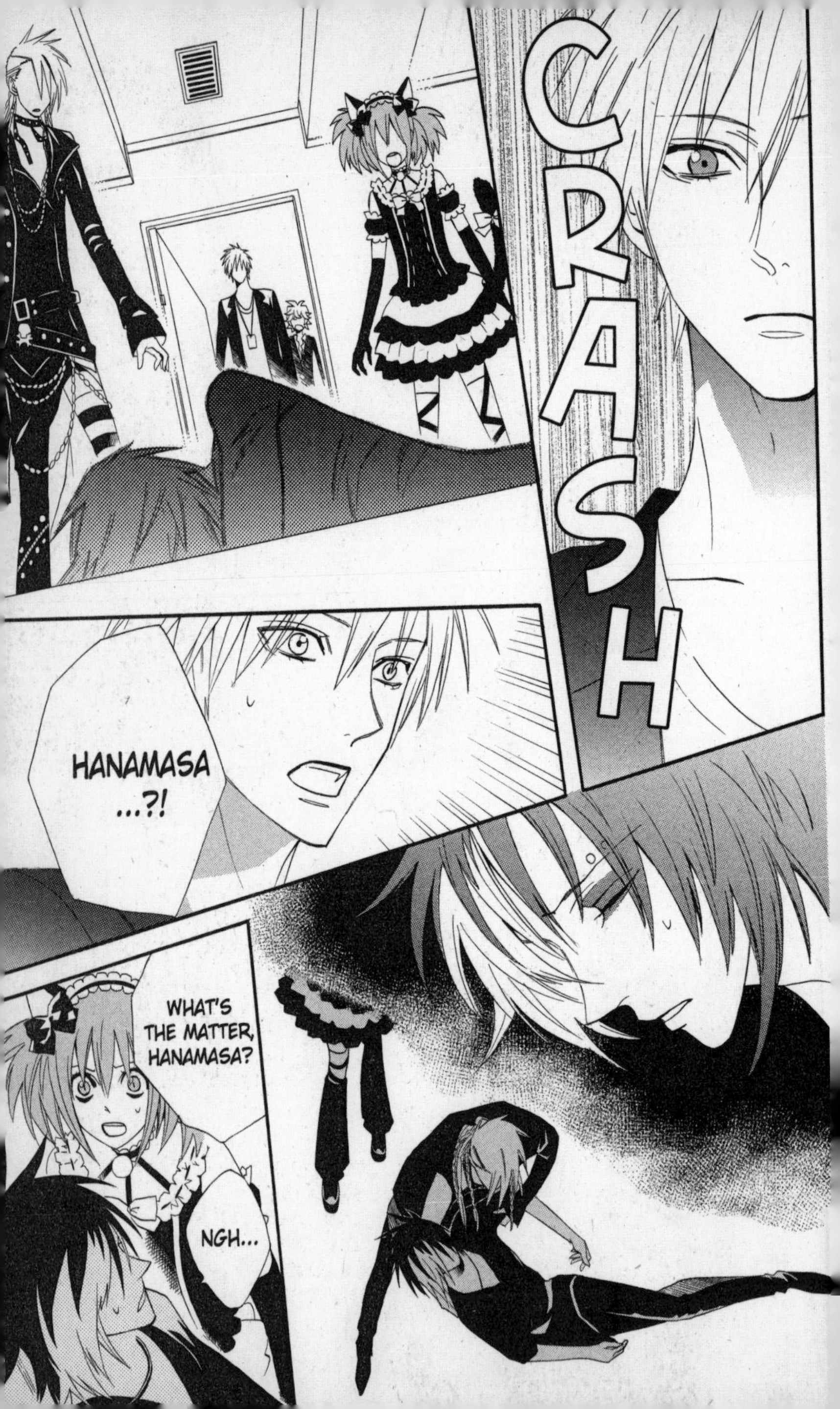
CRASH
HANAMASA ...?!
WHAT'S THE MATTER, HANAMASA?
NGH...

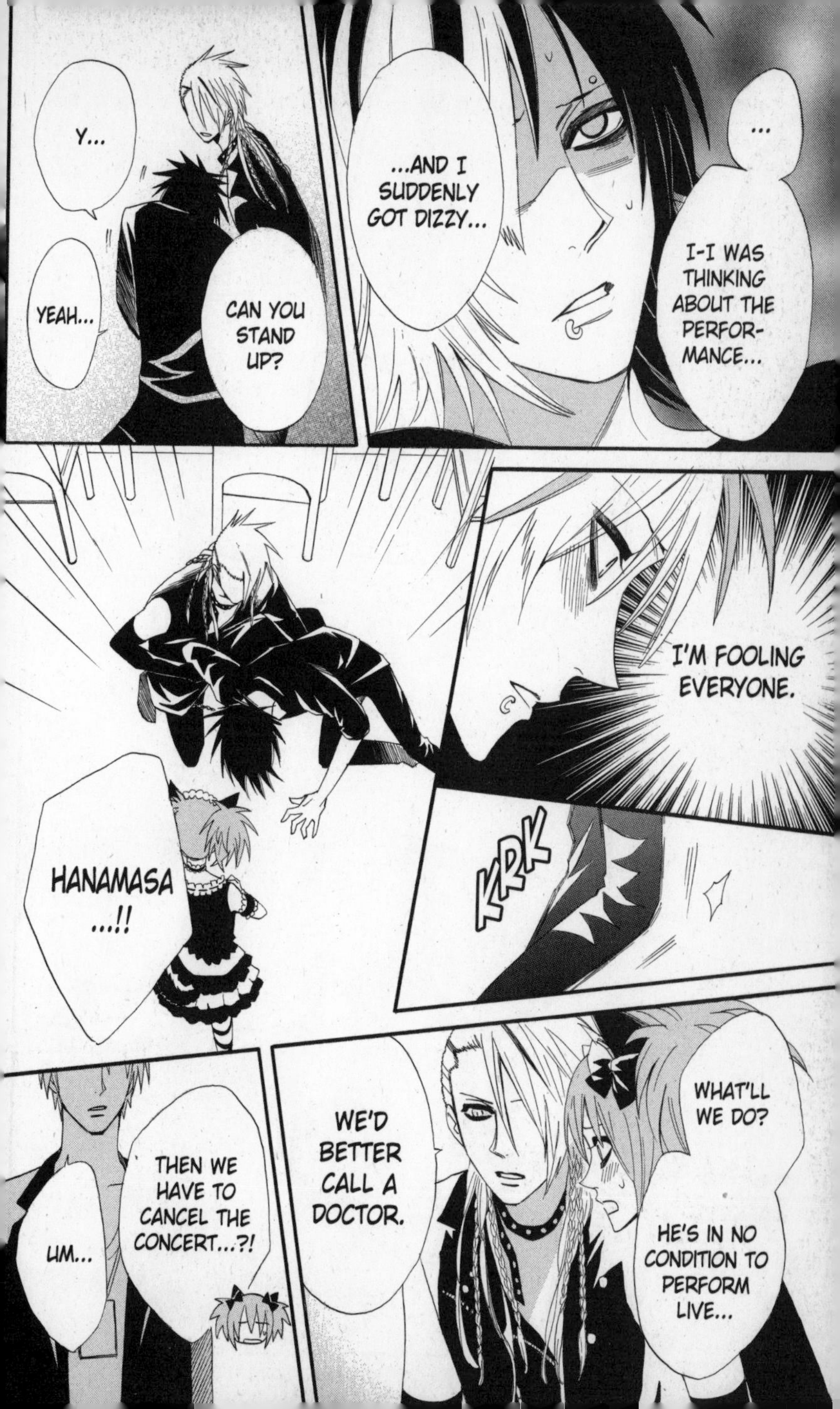
...
I-I WAS THINKING ABOUT THE PERFORMANCE...
...AND I SUDDENLY GOT DIZZY...
Y...
CAN YOU STAND UP?
YEAH...
I'M FOOLING EVERYONE.
KRK
HANAMASA ...!!
WHAT'LL WE DO?
HE'S IN NO CONDITION TO PERFORM LIVE...
WE'D BETTER CALL A DOCTOR.
THEN WE HAVE TO CANCEL THE CONCERT...?!
UM...

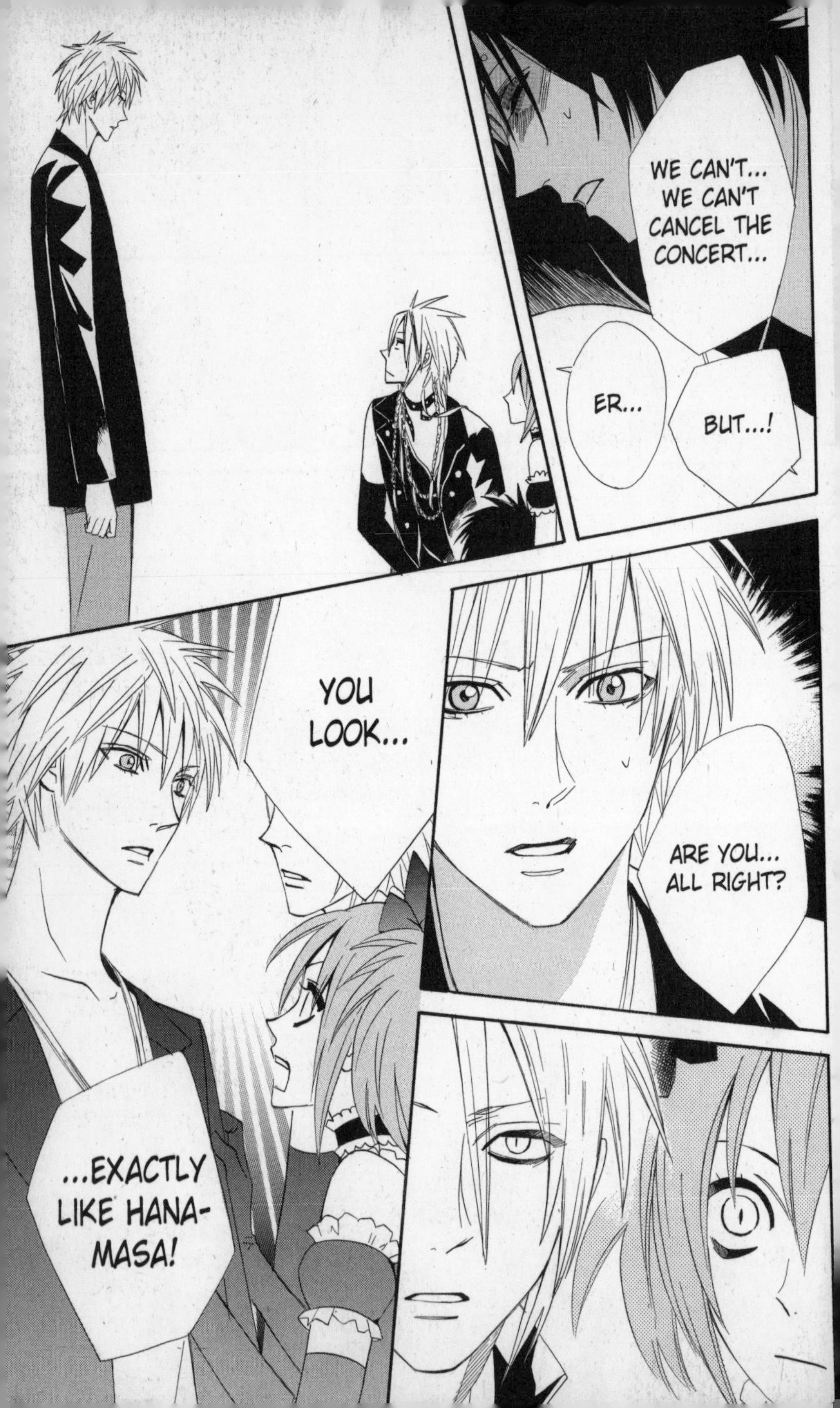
WE CAN'T... WE CAN'T CANCEL THE CONCERT...
BUT...!
ER...
ARE YOU... ALL RIGHT?
YOU LOOK...
...EXACTLY LIKE HANA-MASA!

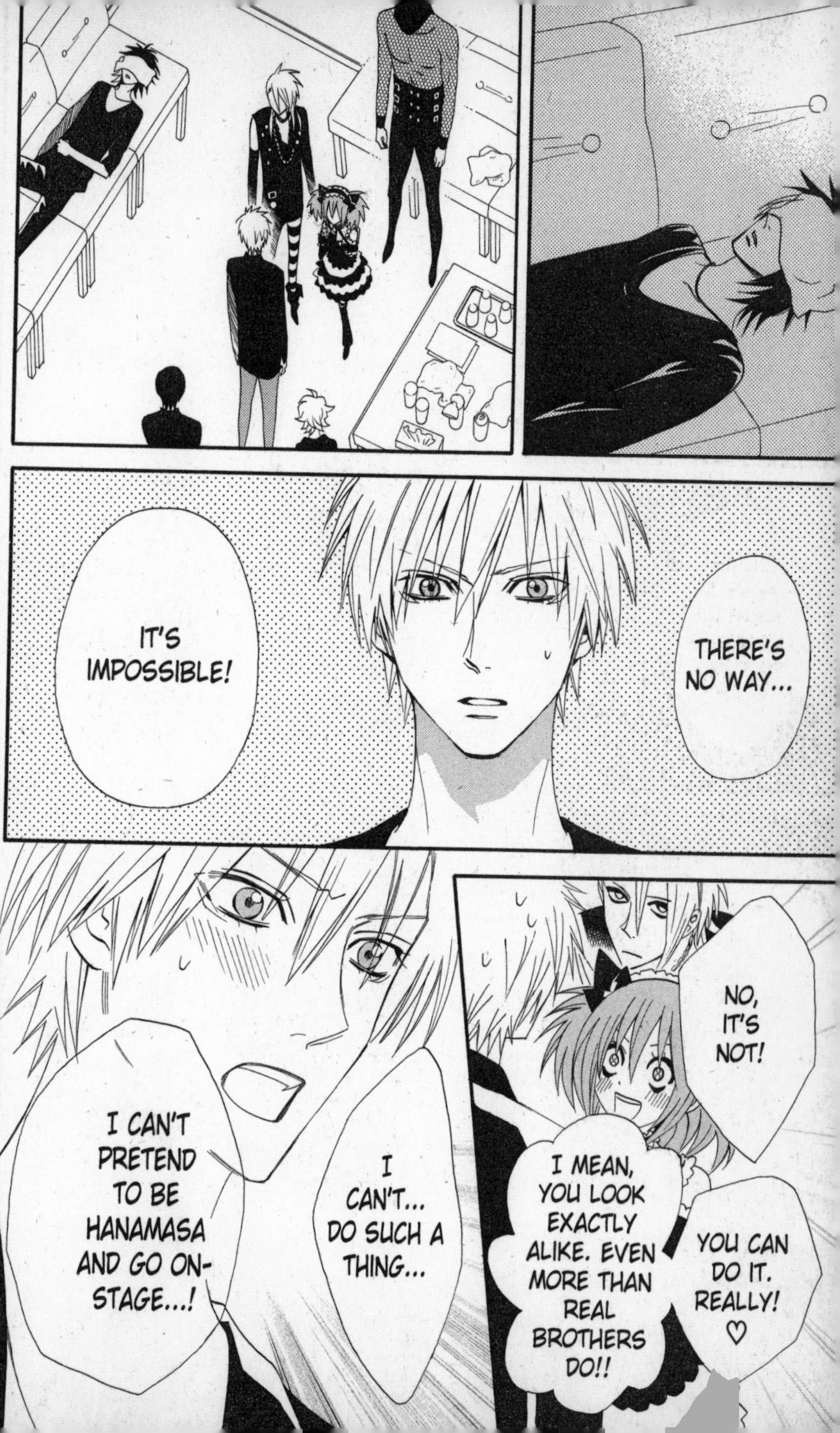
THERE'S NO WAY...
IT'S IMPOSSIBLE!
NO, IT'S NOT!
I MEAN, YOU LOOK EXACTLY ALIKE. EVEN MORE THAN REAL BROTHERS DO!!
YOU CAN DO IT. REALLY! ♡
I CAN'T... DO SUCH A THING...
I CAN'T PRETEND TO BE HANAMASA AND GO ON-STAGE...!

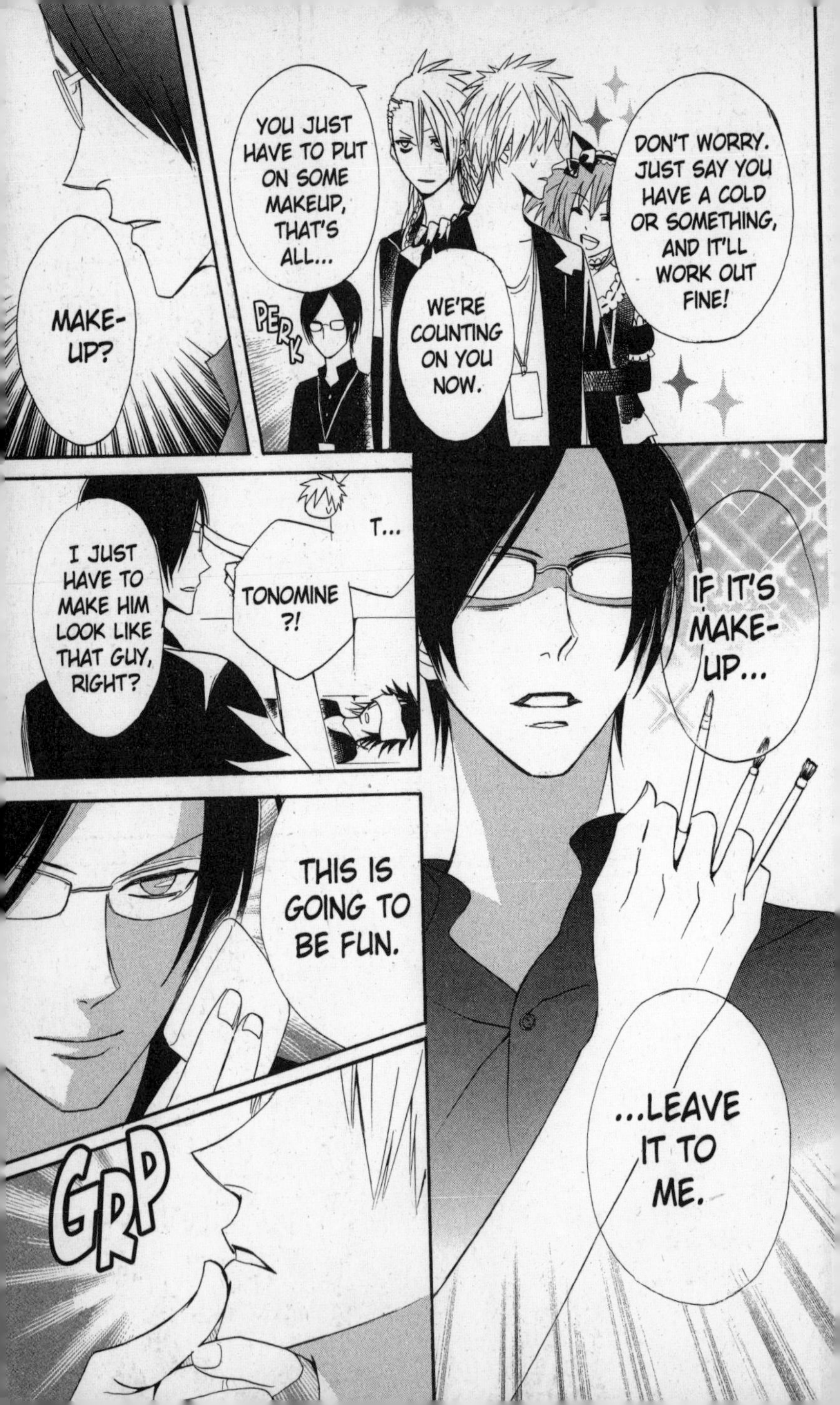

DON'T WORRY. JUST SAY YOU HAVE A COLD OR SOMETHING, AND IT'LL WORK OUT FINE!
YOU JUST HAVE TO PUT ON SOME MAKEUP, THAT'S ALL...
WE'RE COUNTING ON YOU NOW.
PERK
MAKE-UP?
IF IT'S MAKE-UP...
...LEAVE IT TO ME.
T...
TONOMINE ?!
I JUST HAVE TO MAKE HIM LOOK LIKE THAT GUY, RIGHT?
THIS IS GOING TO BE FUN.
GRP

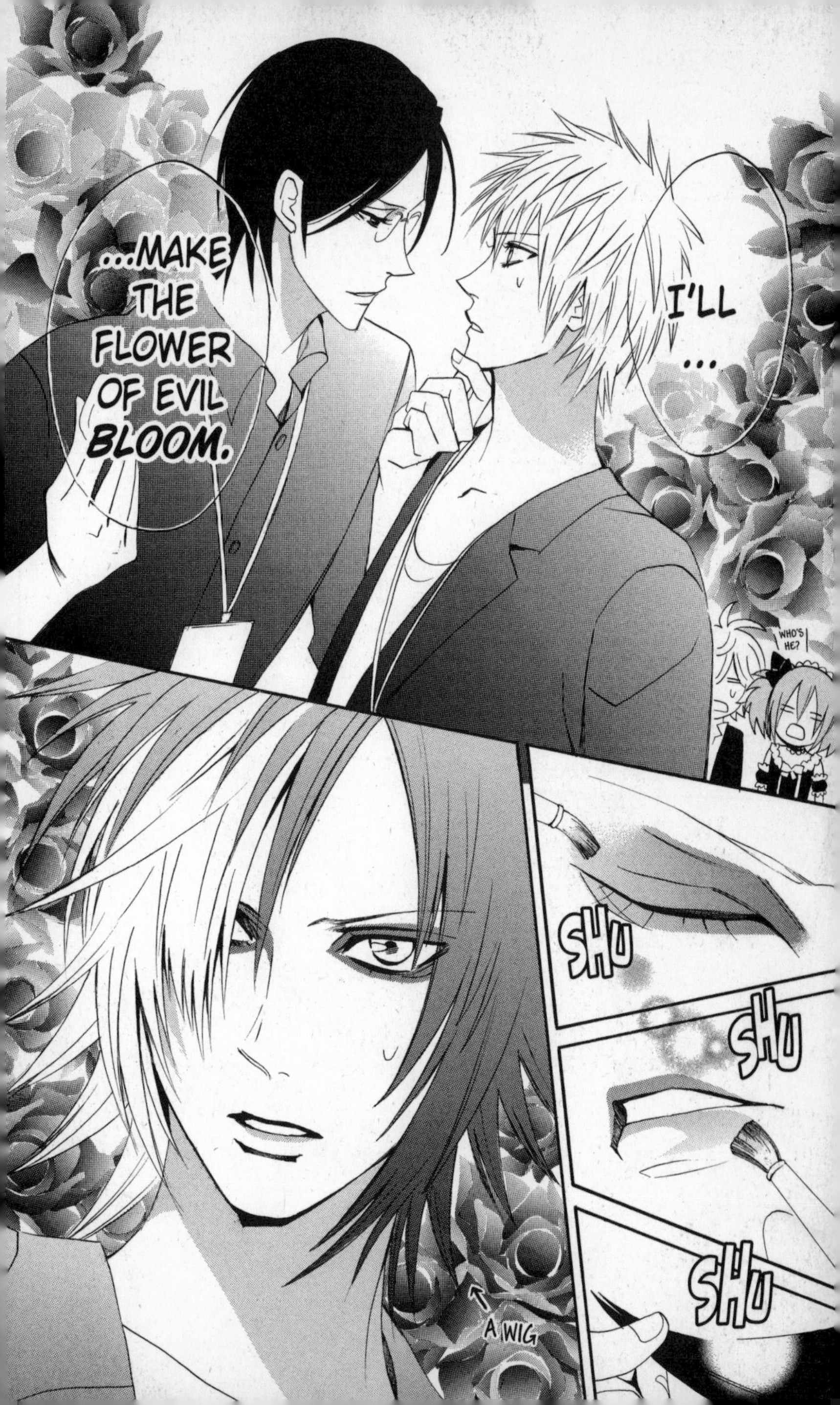
I'LL
...
...MAKE THE FLOWER OF EVIL BLOOM.
WHO'S HE?
SHU
SHU
SHU
A WIG

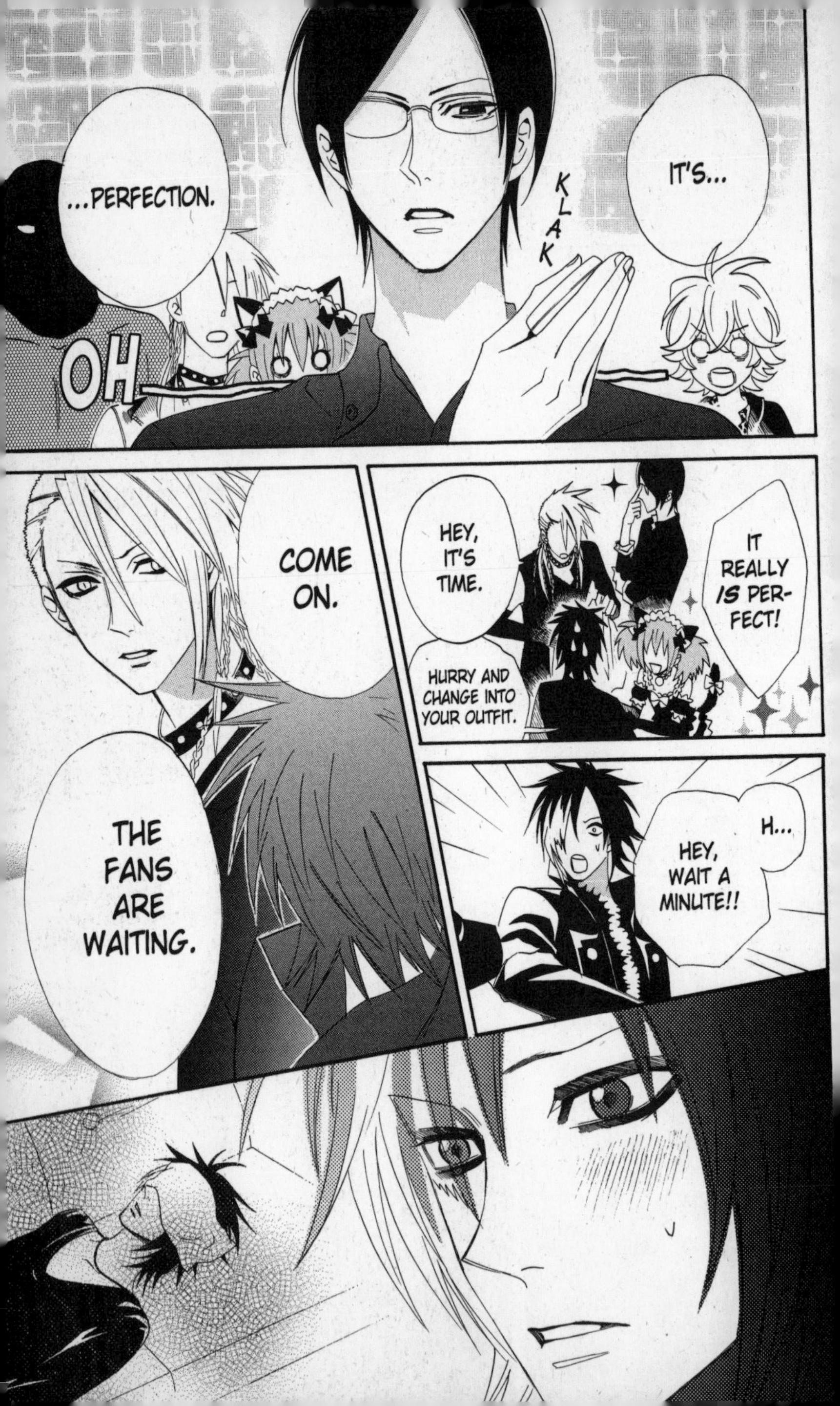
IT'S...
KLAK
...PERFECTION.
OH—
IT REALLY *IS* PERFECT!
HEY, IT'S TIME.
HURRY AND CHANGE INTO YOUR OUTFIT.
H...
HEY, WAIT A MINUTE!!
COME ON.
THE FANS ARE WAITING.

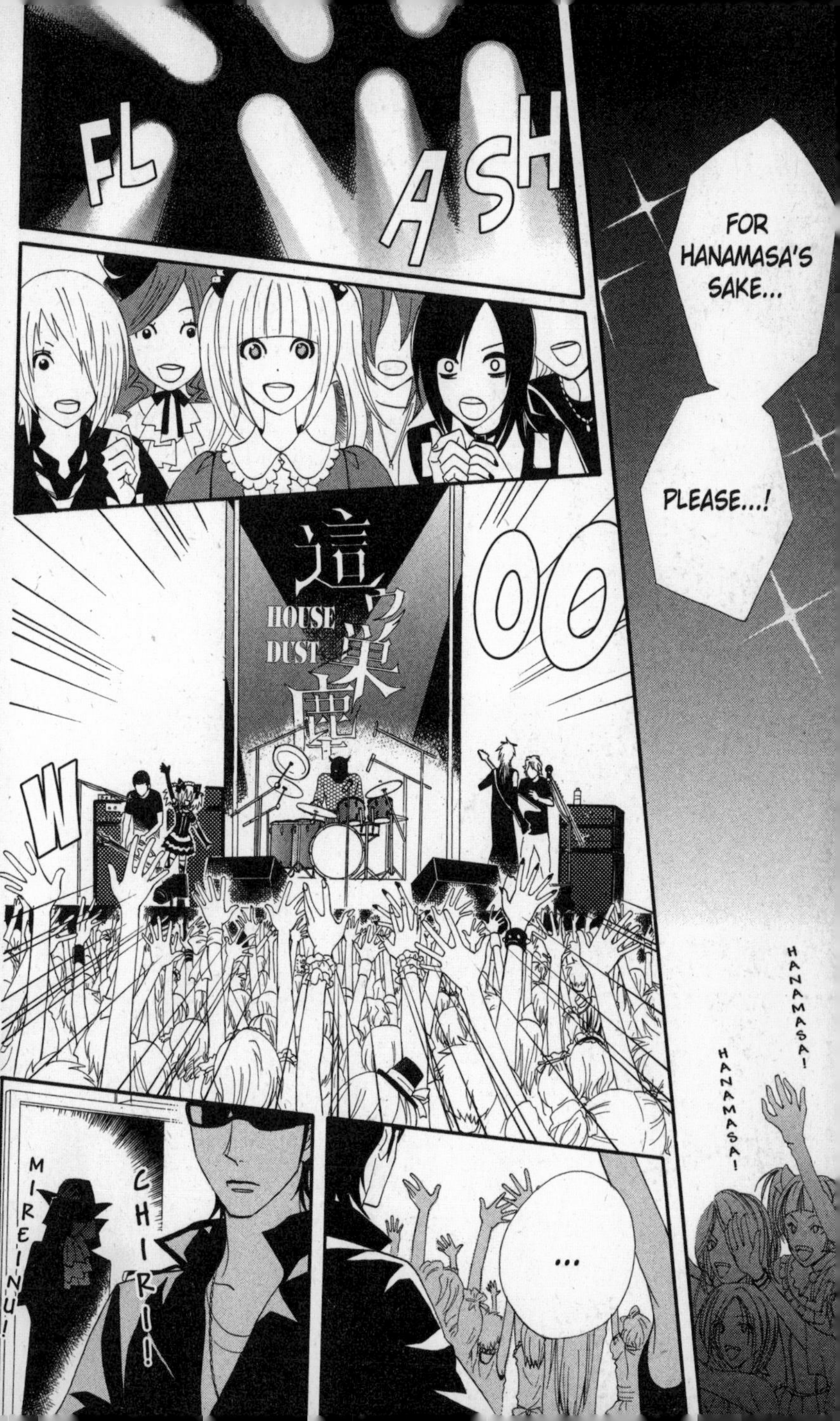
FOR HANAMASA'S SAKE...
PLEASE...!
HANAMASA!
HANAMASA!
FLASH
WOO
這ウ巣塵
HOUSE DUST
...
CHIRI!
MIREINU!

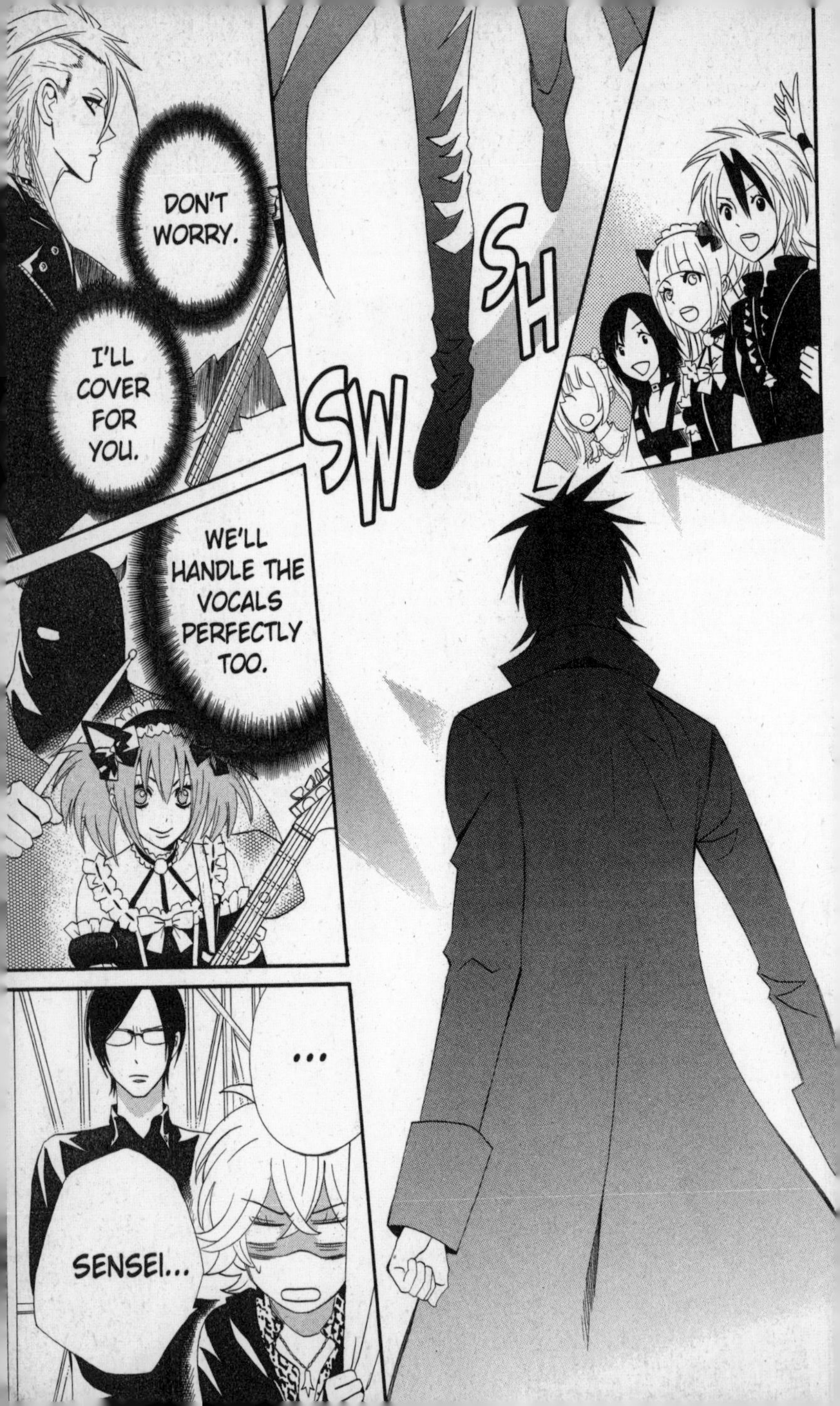
SWSH
DON'T WORRY.
I'LL COVER FOR YOU.
WE'LL HANDLE THE VOCALS PERFECTLY TOO.
...
SENSEI...

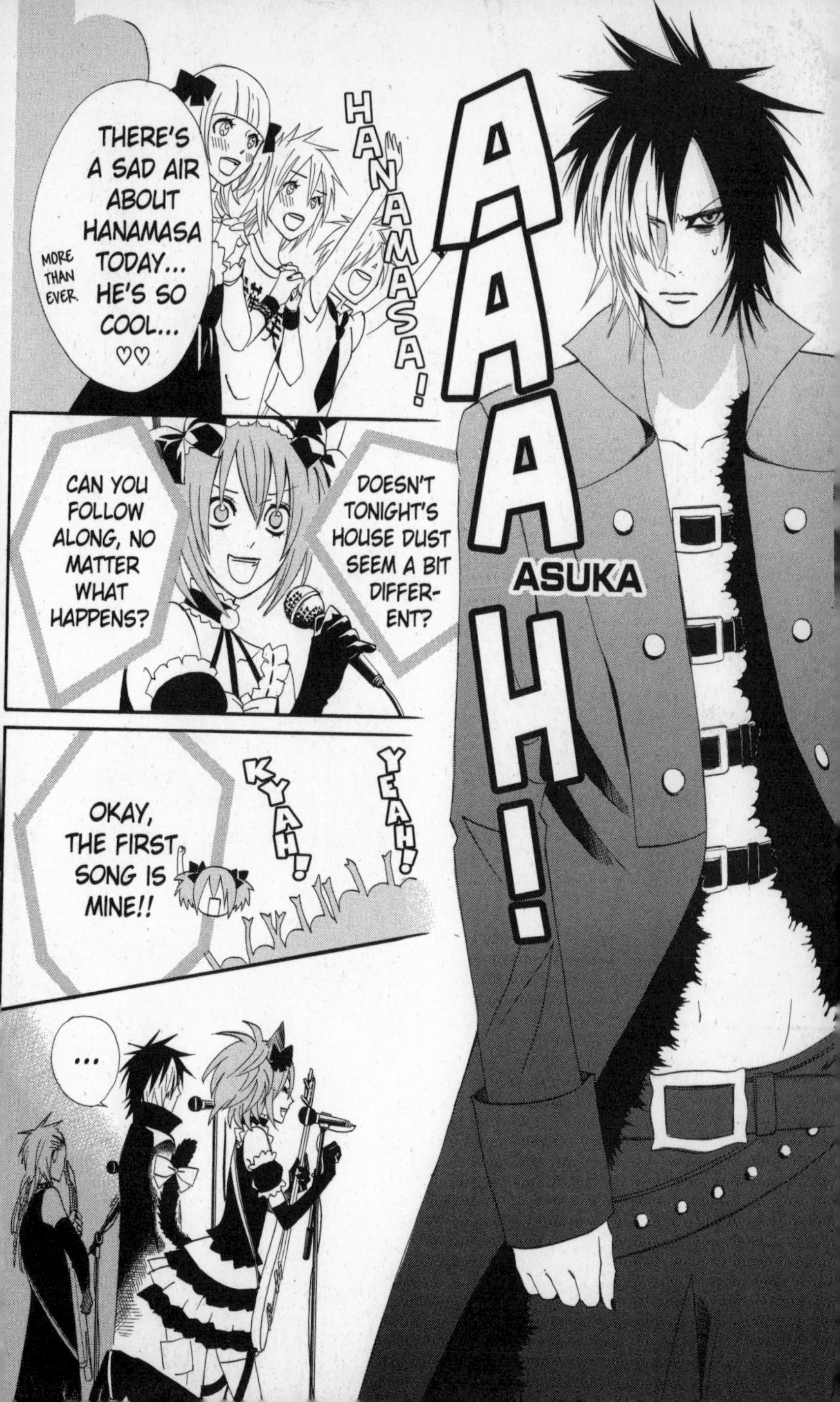
AAAAAH!!
ASUKA
HANAMASA!
THERE'S A SAD AIR ABOUT HANAMASA TODAY... HE'S SO COOL... ♡♡
MORE THAN EVER.
DOESN'T TONIGHT'S HOUSE DUST SEEM A BIT DIFFER-ENT?
CAN YOU FOLLOW ALONG, NO MATTER WHAT HAPPENS?
YEAH!
KYAH!
OKAY, THE FIRST SONG IS MINE!!
...

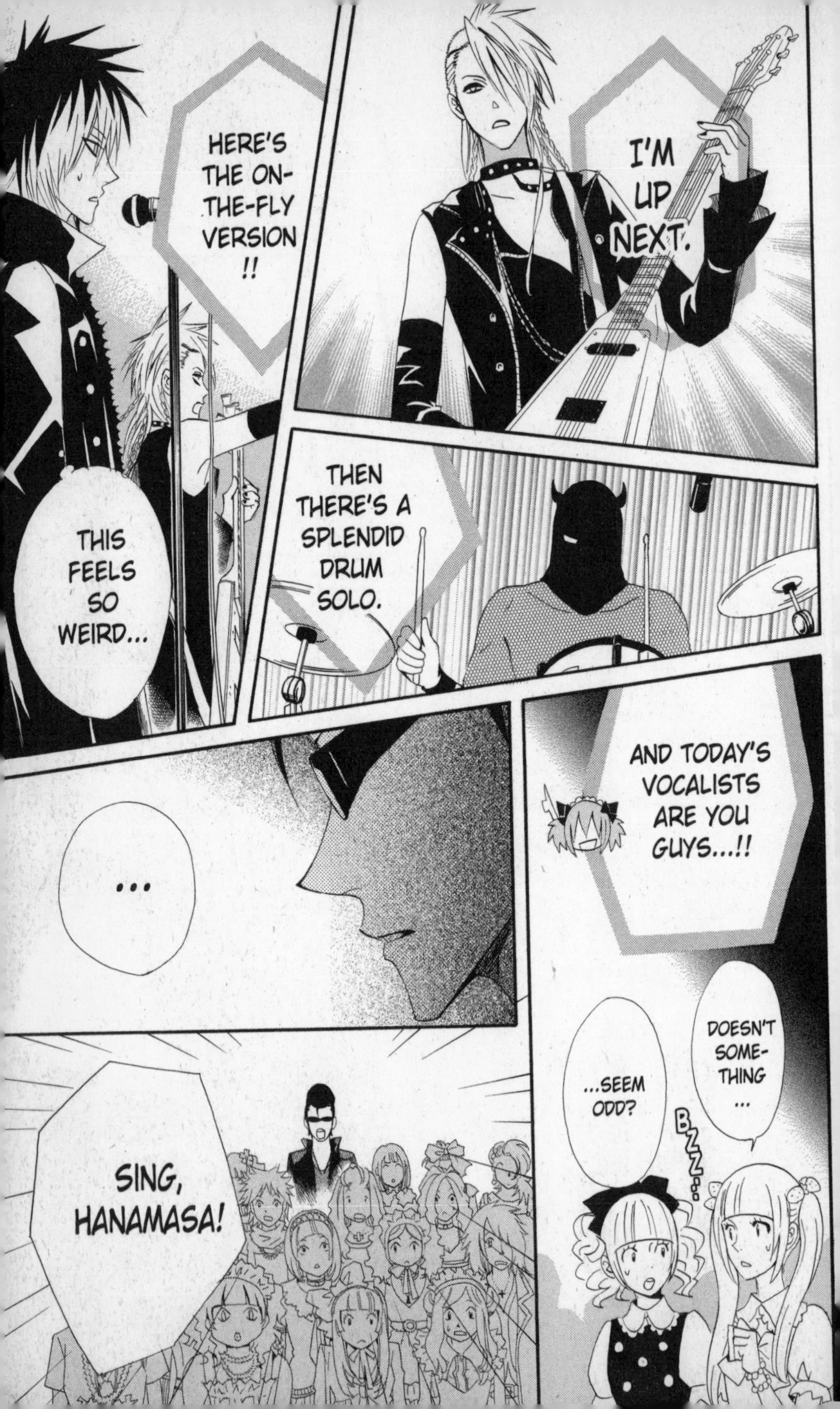

I'M UP NEXT.
THEN THERE'S A SPLENDID DRUM SOLO.
HERE'S THE ON-THE-FLY VERSION!!
THIS FEELS SO WEIRD...
AND TODAY'S VOCALISTS ARE YOU GUYS...!!
...
DOESN'T SOMETHING...
BZZ...
...SEEM ODD?
SING, HANAMASA!

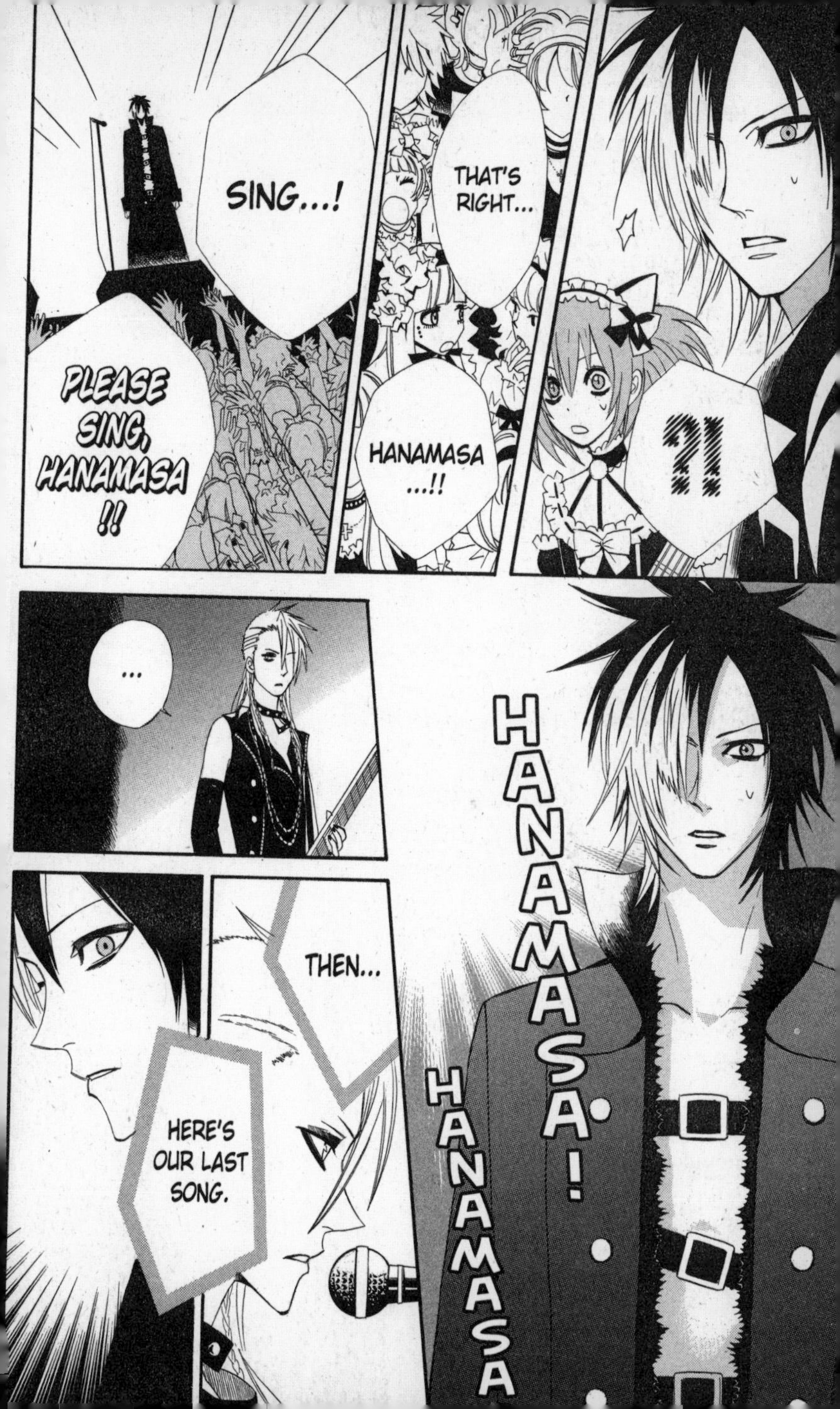
?!
THAT'S RIGHT...
HANAMASA ...!!
SING...!
PLEASE SING, HANAMASA !!
HANAMASA!
HANAMASA
...
THEN...
HERE'S OUR LAST SONG.

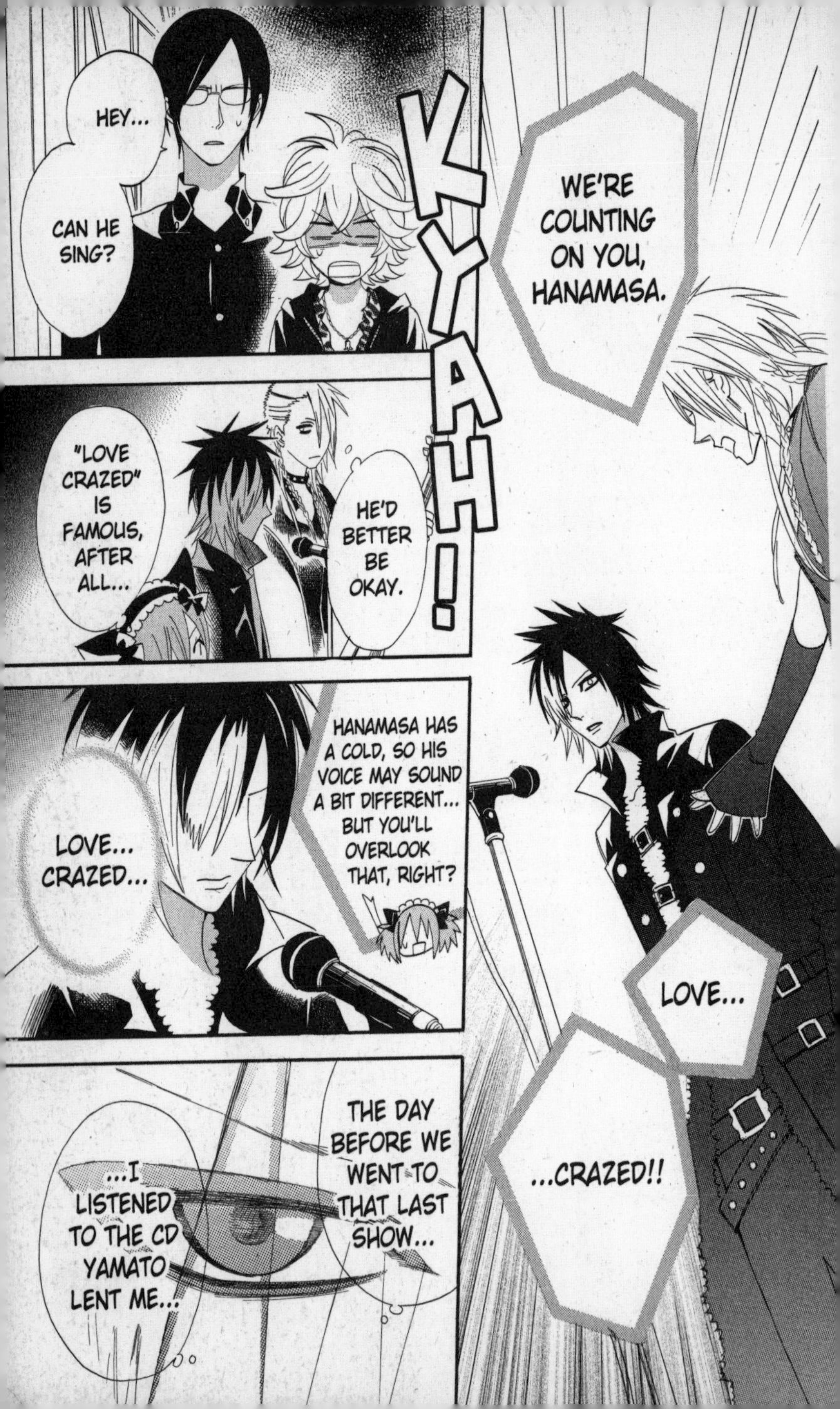
WE'RE COUNTING ON YOU, HANAMASA.
LOVE...
...CRAZED!!
KYAH!
HEY...
CAN HE SING?
HE'D BETTER BE OKAY.
"LOVE CRAZED" IS FAMOUS, AFTER ALL...
HANAMASA HAS A COLD, SO HIS VOICE MAY SOUND A BIT DIFFERENT... BUT YOU'LL OVERLOOK THAT, RIGHT?
LOVE... CRAZED...
THE DAY BEFORE WE WENT TO THAT LAST SHOW...
...I LISTENED TO THE CD YAMATO LENT ME...

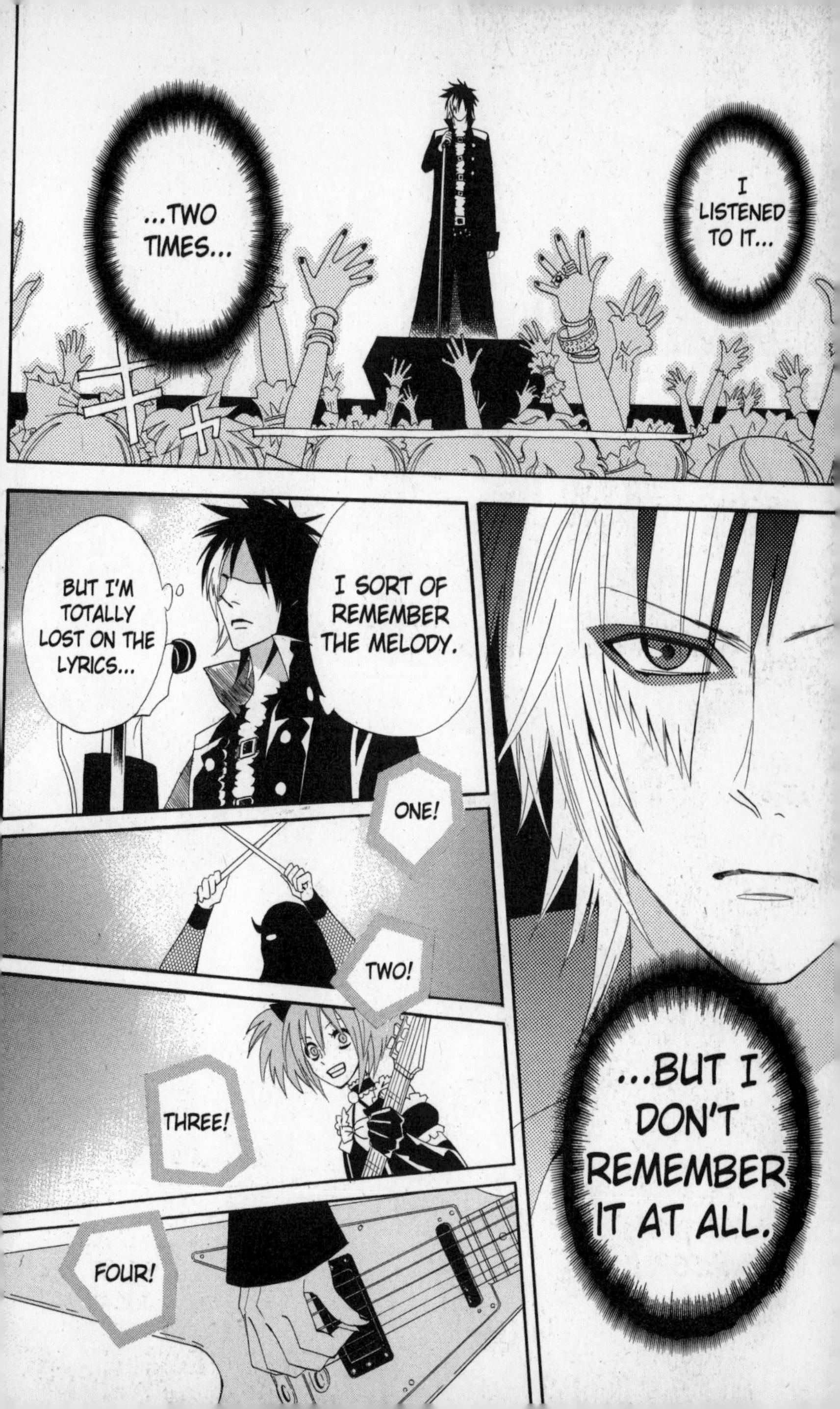
I LISTENED TO IT...
...TWO TIMES...
...BUT I DON'T REMEMBER IT AT ALL.
I SORT OF REMEMBER THE MELODY.
BUT I'M TOTALLY LOST ON THE LYRICS...
ONE!
TWO!
THREE!
FOUR!

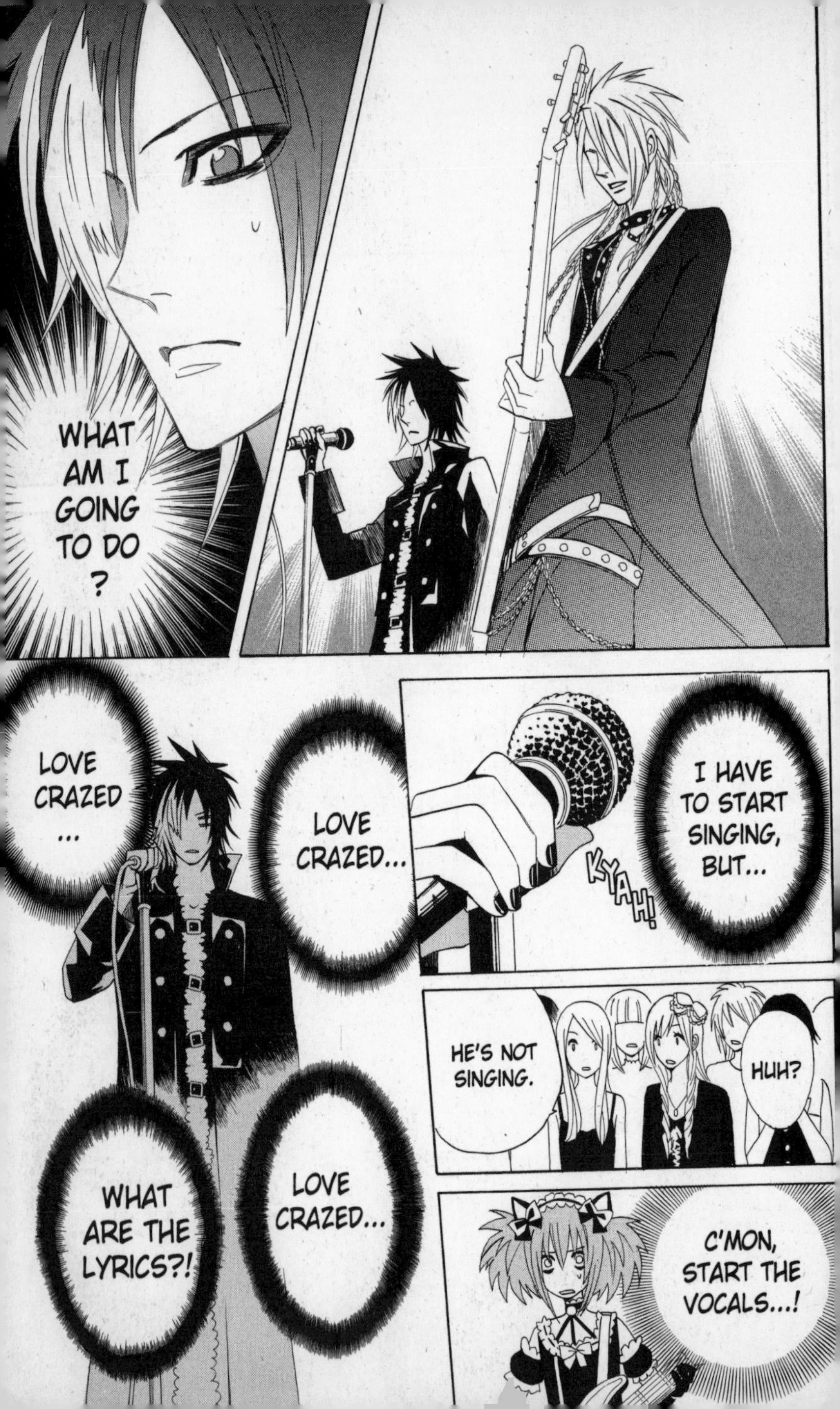
WHAT AM I GOING TO DO ?
I HAVE TO START SINGING, BUT...
KYAH!
HUH?
HE'S NOT SINGING.
C'MON, START THE VOCALS...!
LOVE CRAZED...
LOVE CRAZED ...
LOVE CRAZED...
WHAT ARE THE LYRICS?!

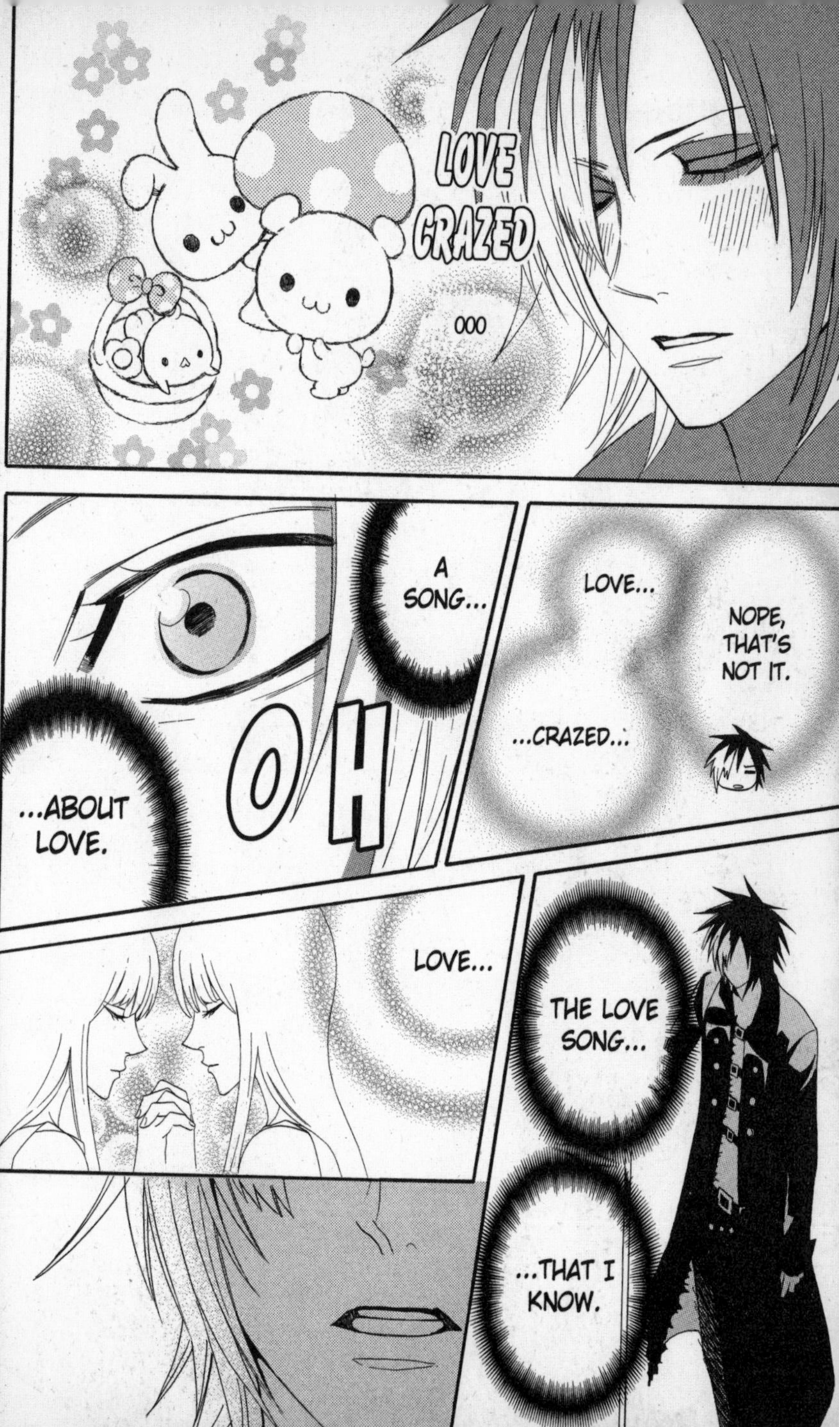
LOVE CRAZED
ooo
LOVE...
...CRAZED...
NOPE, THAT'S NOT IT.
A SONG...
OH
...ABOUT LOVE.
THE LOVE SONG...
...THAT I KNOW.
LOVE...

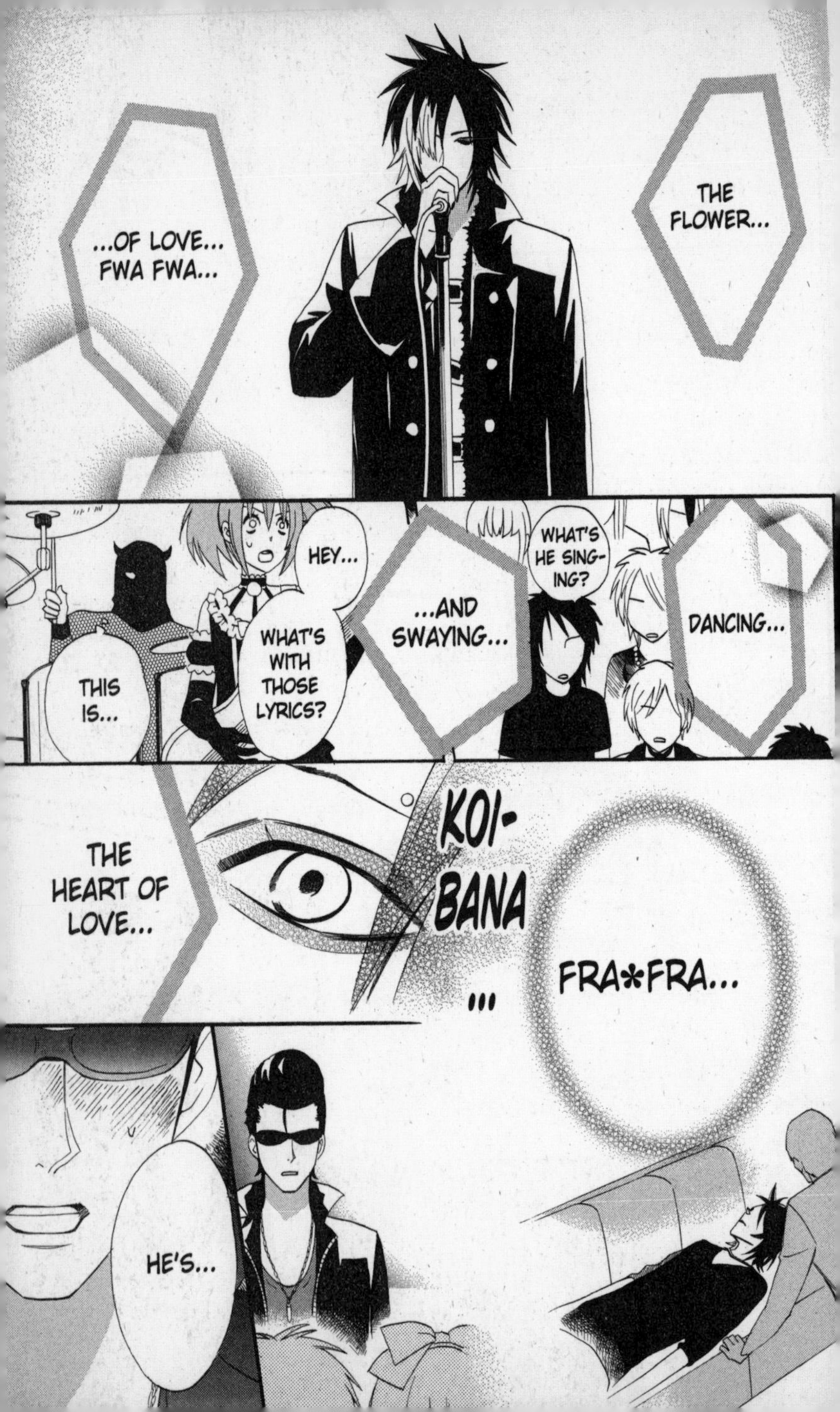
THE FLOWER...
...OF LOVE... FWA FWA...
DANCING...
WHAT'S HE SING-ING?
...AND SWAYING...
HEY...
WHAT'S WITH THOSE LYRICS?
THIS IS...
FRA*FRA...
KOI-BANA ...
THE HEART OF LOVE...
HE'S...

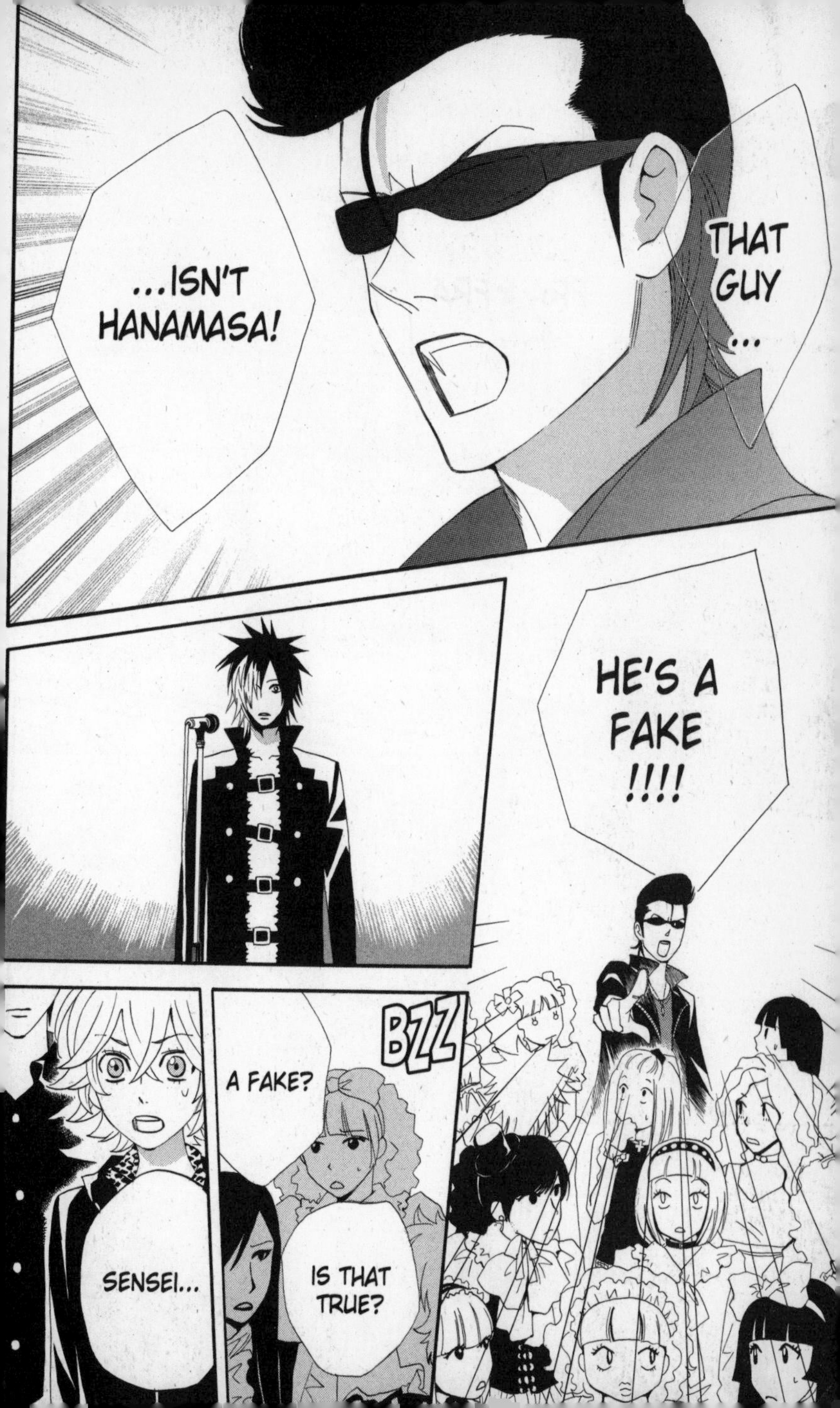
THAT GUY ...
...ISN'T HANAMASA!
HE'S A FAKE !!!!
BZZ
A FAKE?
IS THAT TRUE?
SENSEI...

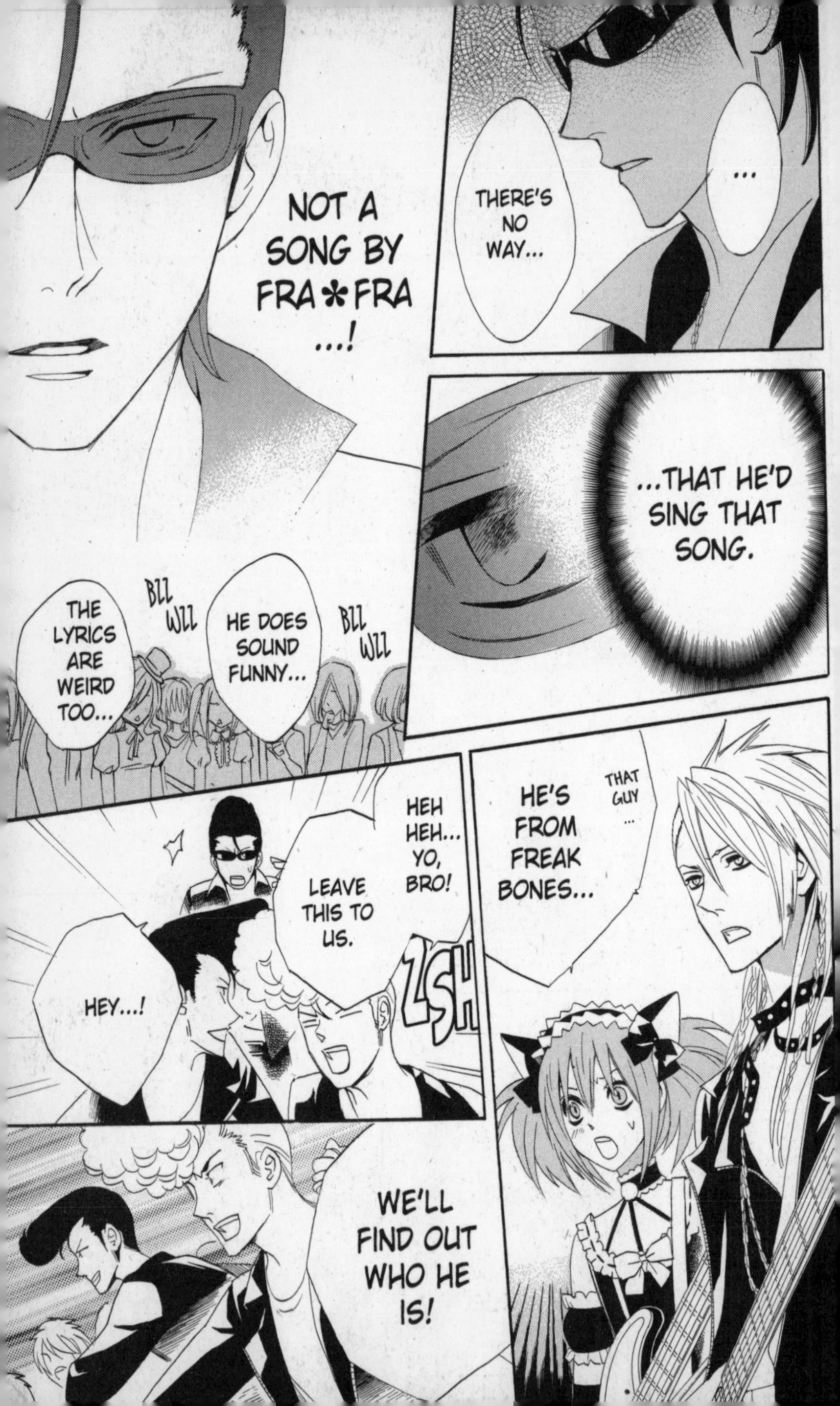
...
THERE'S NO WAY...
...THAT HE'D SING THAT SONG.
NOT A SONG BY FRA✻FRA ...!
BZZ WZZ
HE DOES SOUND FUNNY...
BZZ WZZ
THE LYRICS ARE WEIRD TOO...
THAT GUY ...
HE'S FROM FREAK BONES...
HEH HEH... YO, BRO!
LEAVE THIS TO US.
ZSH
HEY...!
WE'LL FIND OUT WHO HE IS!

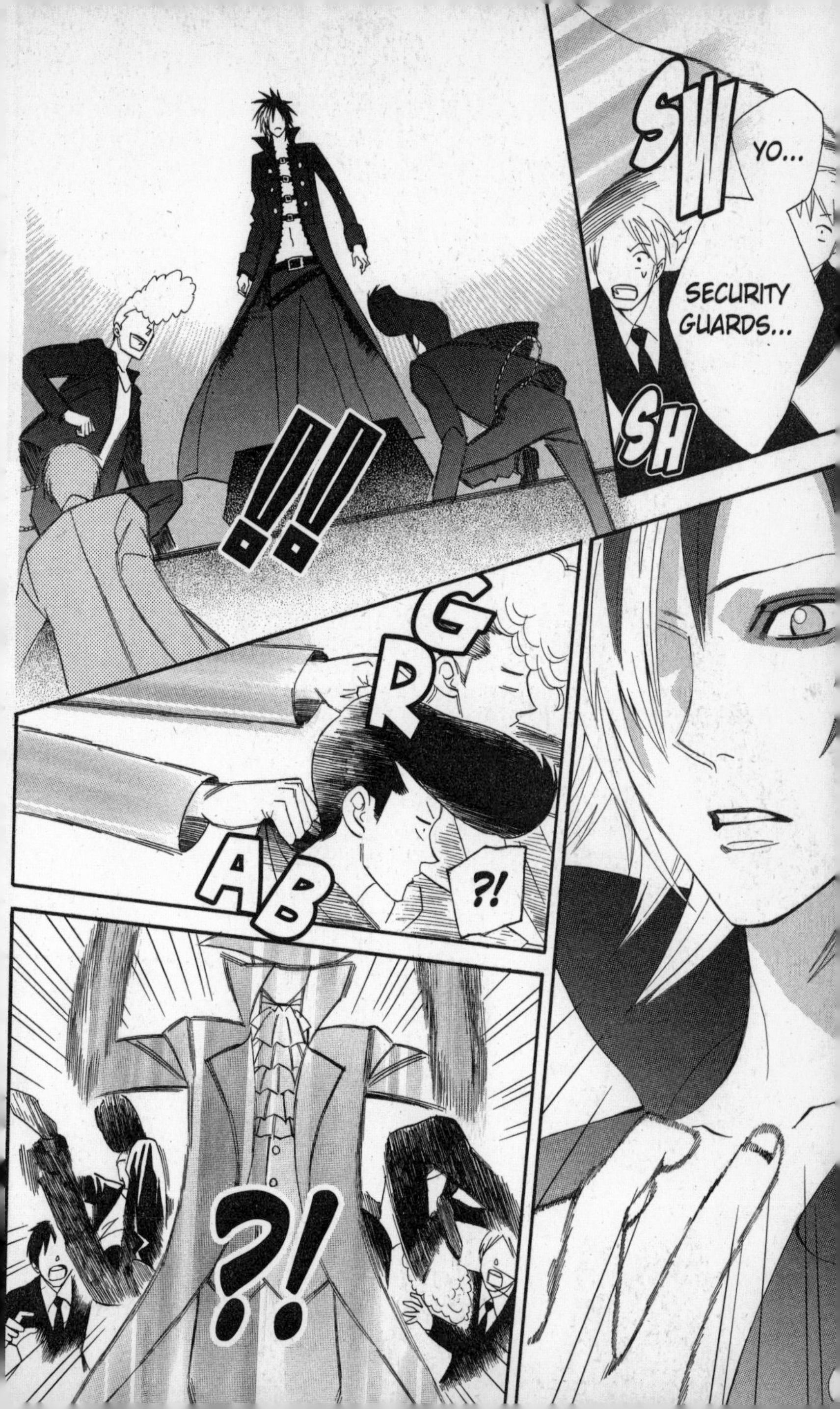
SW
YO...
SECURITY GUARDS...
SH
!!
GRAB
?!
?!

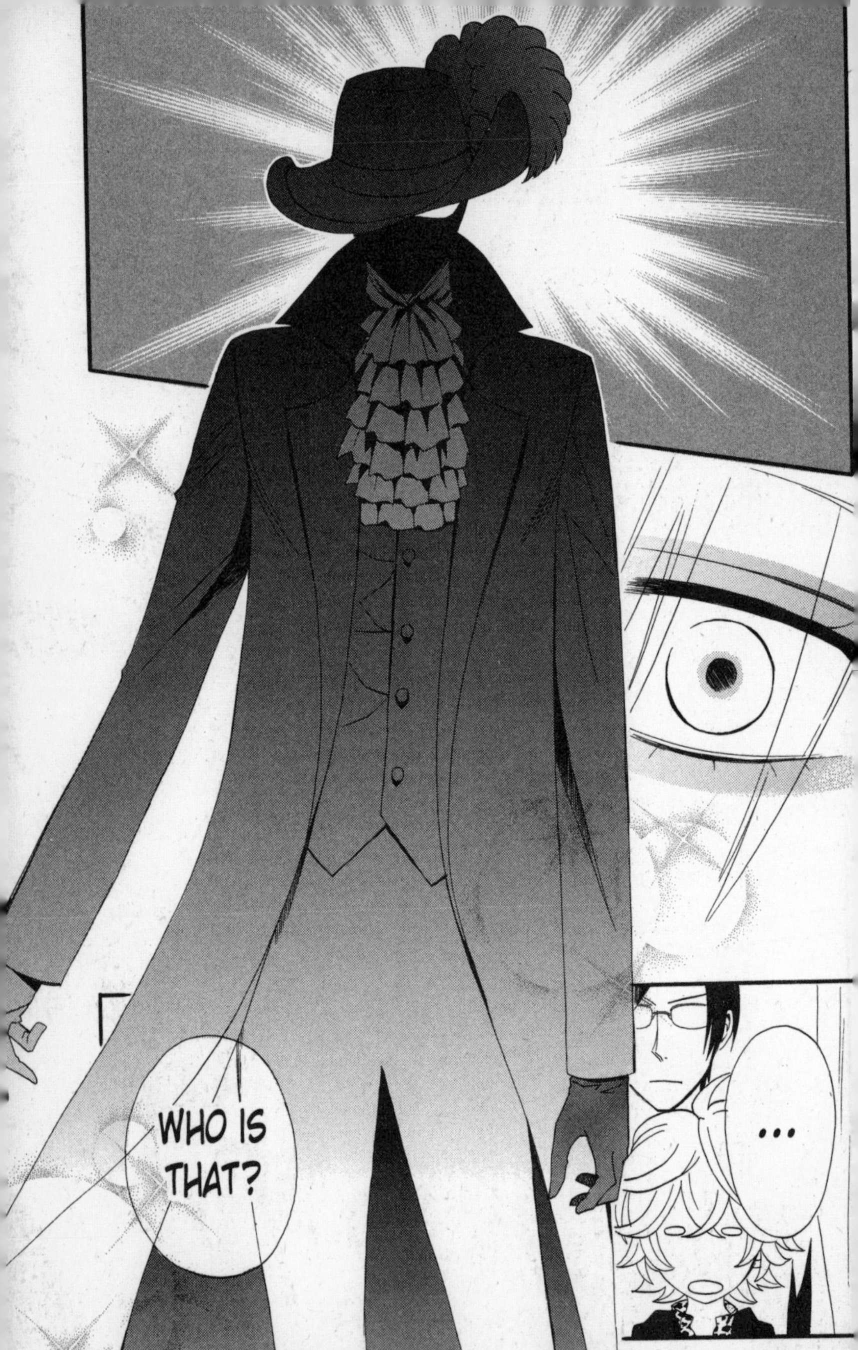
...
WHO IS THAT?

OTOMEN 6 / THE END

OTOMEN

Confused by some of the terms, but too MANLY to ask for help?

Here are some **cultural notes** to assist you!

honorifics

Chan – an informal honorific used to address children and females. *Chan* can also be used toward animals, lovers, intimate friends and people whom one has known since childhood.

San – the most common honorific title. It is used to address people outside one's immediate family and close circle of friends.

Sensei – honorific title used to address teachers as well as professionals such as doctors, lawyers and artists.

Sama – honorific used to address persons much higher in rank than oneself.

NOTES

Page 1 | Asuka's Coat
Asuka is wearing a *tokkofuku*, a long coat covered in kanji characters that is often worn by delinquents known as *yanki* or *bosozoku*. The various kanji on Asuka's *tokkofuku* break down as follows: 1) right pocket – "Six"; 2) left pocket – "Otomen"; 3) left sleeve – "Male Fight Male" (with the phonetic sound of "otomen"); 4) left side – "Ginyuri Conquest," "Lovely" and "First-Class Heartthrob"; 5) right side – "Cute and Sweet," "Beauty Samurai" and "Best Regards."

Page 3 | Hana to Mame
The name *Hana to Mame* (Flowers and Beans) is a play on the real shojo manga magazine *Hana to Yume* (Flowers and Dreams) published by Hakusensha.

Page 3 | Tsun-sama
Juta makes this word up by combining *tsundere* and *ore-sama*. *Tsundere* describes a character who is *tsuntsun* (cold or irritable) and later becomes *deredere* (affectionate or sentimental). *Ore-sama* describes a pompous and arrogant person, as it combines *ore* (me) with the honorific *sama*.

Page 55, panel 2 | Hanami
Hanami literally means "flower viewing," and it traditionally refers to having a picnic party underneath cherry blossoms.

Page 59, panel 3 | M*n's Kn*ck*e
The author is referring to a men's magazine in Japan that describes itself as a "new outlaw fashion and lifestyle magazine."

Page 60, panel 3 | Pachiko
A wordplay on Hachiko, the name of an Akita dog famous for his loyalty to his owner. There is a statue of Hachiko outside Shibuya Station in Tokyo.

Page 61, panel 4 | Datewaru
A type of "bad boy" fashion and lifestyle promoted in *M*n's Kn*ck*e* magazine.

Page 147, panel 4 | Visual Kei
Similar to glam rock, visual kei is a branch of Japanese rock where the musicians' hairstyles, makeup and costumes convey an outrageous and sometimes androgynous look.

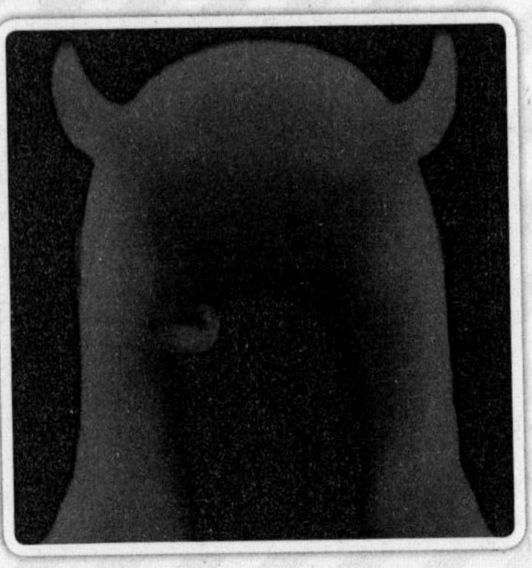

Aya Kanno was born in Tokyo, Japan.
She is the creator of *Soul Rescue* and *Blank Slate*
(originally published as *Akusaga* in Japan's
BetsuHana magazine). Her latest work, *Otomen*,
is currently being serialized in *BetsuHana*.

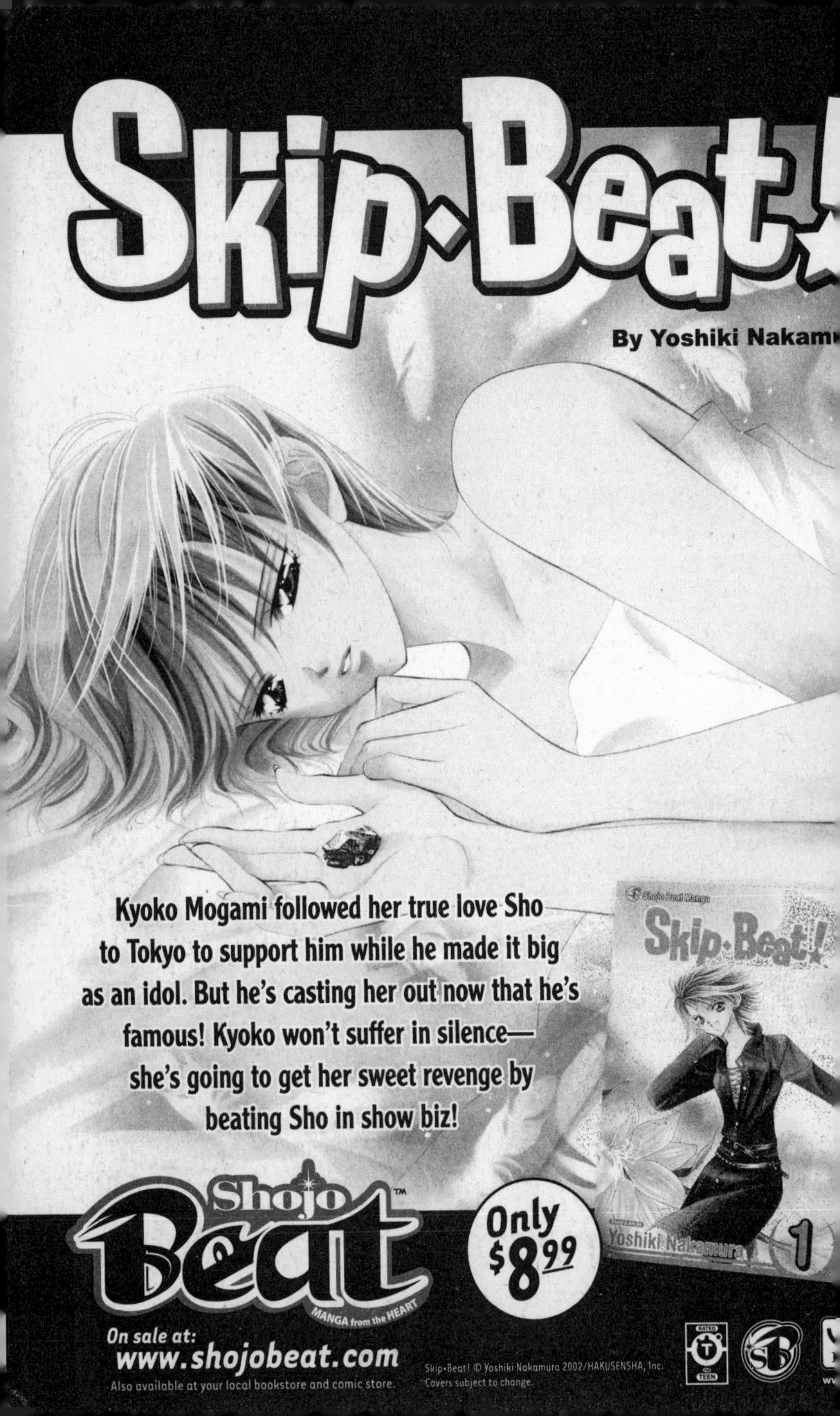
Skip·Beat!
By Yoshiki Nakam
Kyoko Mogami followed her true love Sho to Tokyo to support him while he made it big as an idol. But he's casting her out now that he's famous! Kyoko won't suffer in silence—she's going to get her sweet revenge by beating Sho in show biz!
Shojo Beat Manga
Skip·Beat!
Yoshiki Nakamura
1
Shojo Beat™
MANGA from the HEART
Only $8.99
On sale at:
www.shojobeat.com
Also available at your local bookstore and comic store.
Skip·Beat! © Yoshiki Nakamura 2002/HAKUSENSHA, Inc.
Covers subject to change.
RATED T TEEN

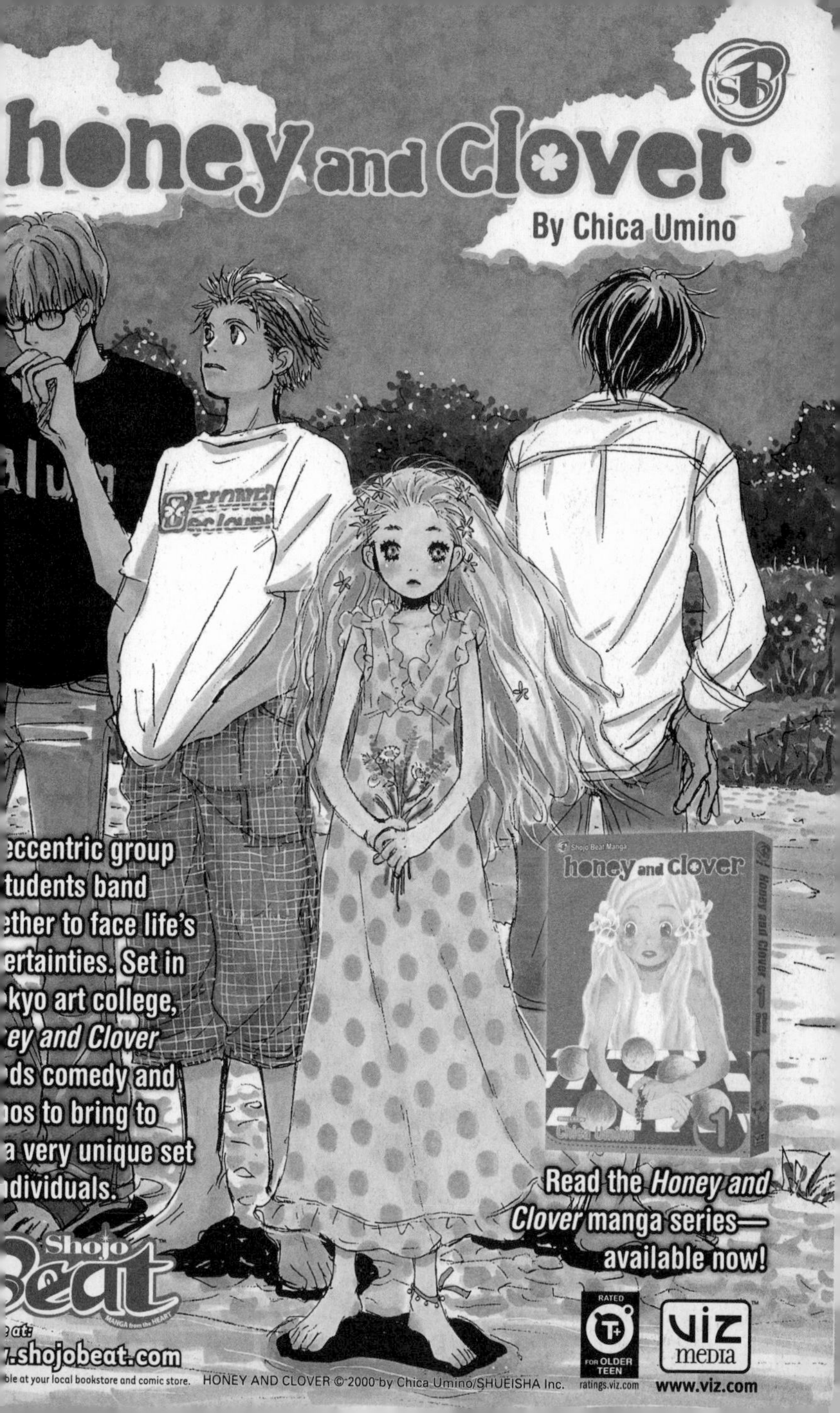
honey and clover
By Chica Umino
eccentric group
tudents band
ether to face life's
ertainties. Set in
kyo art college,
ey and Clover
ds comedy and
os to bring to
a very unique set
dividuals.
Shojo Beat
MANGA from the HEART
e at:
.shojobeat.com
ble at your local bookstore and comic store.
HONEY AND CLOVER © 2000 by Chica Umino/SHUEISHA Inc.
Shojo Beat Manga
honey and clover
Chica Umino
1
Read the Honey and Clover manga series—available now!
RATED
T+
FOR OLDER TEEN
ratings.viz.com
VIZ media
www.viz.com

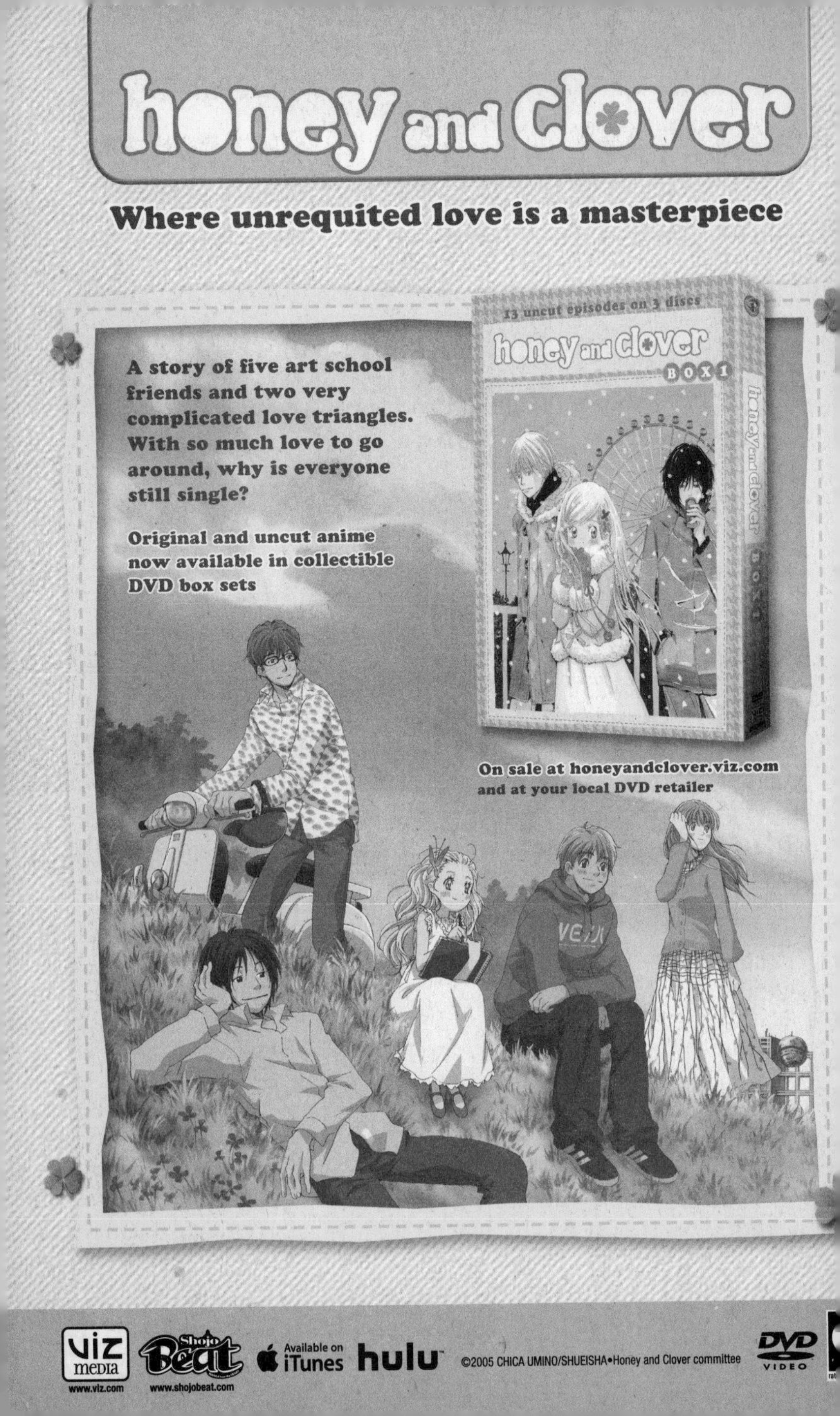
honey and clover
Where unrequited love is a masterpiece
A story of five art school friends and two very complicated love triangles. With so much love to go around, why is everyone still single?
Original and uncut anime now available in collectible DVD box sets
13 uncut episodes on 3 discs
honey and clover
BOX 1
On sale at honeyandclover.viz.com and at your local DVD retailer
viz media
www.viz.com
Shojo Beat
www.shojobeat.com
Available on iTunes
hulu
©2005 CHICA UMINO/SHUEISHA•Honey and Clover committee
DVD VIDEO